Contents

100 Essays from Time

Edited by
Don Knefel
Loras College

ALLYN AND BACON

Boston   London   Toronto   Sydney   Tokyo   Singapore

Copyright © 1992 by Allyn and Bacon
A Division of Simon & Schuster, Inc.
160 Gould Street
Needham Heights, MA 02194

Library of Congress Cataloging-in-Publication Data

100 Essays from Time/[compiled by] Don Knefel.
    p.   cm.
    Includes index.
    ISBN 0–205–13594–3
    I. Knefel, Don. II. Time, the weekly news-magazine.
AC5.E6485 1992
081—DC20   91–41786
                                                       CIP

Printed in the United States of America

10 9 8 7 6 5 4 3 2 1 95 94 93 92 91

13 *Challenges of Democracy*   **171**

Do we really value our own way of life, or, too often, do we take it for granted? This chapter considers the nature of democratic society.

14 *Youth & Family Life*   **186**

Is the family dead? Here, the authors examine some difficulties and disturbing trends in the American family.

15 *The American Character*   **200**

Is there such a thing as the national character? Three pieces by a single author ask what it means to be an American.

PART III: **Global Issues**   **215**

16 *War*   **215**

Will war always be with us, or is there a way to end it? The pieces in this chapter consider war and the human condition.

25 *Honesty*   354

How far are you willing to go to get what you want? This chapter looks at the question of daily moral conduct.

26 *Wealth, Status and Snobbery*   369

What do class and material things mean to you? Here, three writers take a sharp view of our hunger for money and status.

27 *The Work Ethic*   384

Do you believe that work is, or should be, valuable and meaningful, or is it just an obstacle to leisure? Some views of an old American idea.

28 *Mortality*   401

What do we think about our own human limits, about the death of ourselves and others? The authors in this chatper consider aspects of mortality.

PART VI: For Further Reading   417

Preface

When Briton Hadden and Henry R. Luce founded *Time, The Weekly News-Magazine,* and published their first issue on March 3, 1923, World War I had been over for only a few years, Congress had just granted women the right to vote, the "return to normalcy" administration of Warren G. Harding was nearing its embarrassing end, and the decade that would come to be known as the Roaring Twenties was off and running.

A lot has changed since those days. But *Time Magazine* is still with us, having spawned a number of imitators, and has grown to become a world-wide institution in journalism and publishing.

When Hadden and Luce put out that first issue, the magazine was only a few pages long and contained hardly any advertising, but it already had the highly defined editorial shape that has come down to us today. Original departments such as National Affairs, Foreign News, Books, Art, Cinema, Education, The Press (some names altered over the years), still form the core of the *Time* approach. Now in its eighth decade, the magazine has continued to evolve, using ever more color and photography, expanding coverage for cover stories, special sections, and entire issues devoted to single subjects. But it remains a weekly habit in millions of households, libraries, businesses, and college dorms throughout the world.

One of the most interesting changes in *Time's* editorial mix occurred on April 2, 1965. A new department, the Essay, was launched.

In his "letter from the publisher" page in that issue, Bernhard M. Auer wrote: "Like the other sections of the magazine, Essay will treat topics in the news, but ... in greater detail and length. ... The new department will not treat a story or an issue when it is making the biggest headlines ... [but] later, when the problem is still far from settled but when second thoughts and greater reflection can be of particular benefit." *Time* Essays joined the great tradition of essay-writing, giving authors occasion to reflect, interpret, persuade, speculate. For the first few years, Essays were published without by-lines, like the other material in the magazine, but in mid-1970 Essays began carrying their authors' names.

In the years since 1965, hundreds of pieces have been published—ranging across the spectrum of world, national, and individual interest. The essays have been, and continue to be, highly informed, carefully reflective and analytical, written with persuasive intelligence and wit.

And today, more than ever, *Time* essays remain a vital part of the magazine's weekly news.

100 Essays From Time, an anthology of *Time* essays for college students, is designed to accent what *Time Magazine* does best: to hold a mirror up to the moment and to record it for history. *Time* writers have addressed virtually every subject of contemporary interest, and have recorded changing attitudes toward those subjects. *100 Essays From Time* provides a glimpse of such subjects and attitudes—a reflection of recorded moments the magazine has given us over the past quarter-century.

As a college text, and because a merely chronological arrangement of several dozen essays would not give teachers and students sufficient focus for writing and discussion, the book is structured according to a number of popular and recurring themes that *Time* essayists continue to address. *100 Essays From Time* classifies pieces according to general categories, and to specific themes within each.

The book contains units under six major headings:

1. Arts and Humanities

2. Domestic Politics and Social Life

3. Global Issues

4. Science and Technology

5. Values and Beliefs

6. For Further Reading

Parts 1–5 contain 28 thematic chapters, each with three essays, a topic introduction, discussion and writing suggestions after each reading, as well as end-of-the-unit ideas. With the thematic blocks and two additional, expanded units (Assorted Issues and Ideas, and Language and Its Uses), the book contains 30 chapters—100 essays—and is meant to provide attractive and abundant choices for writing assignments, enough for a two-semester course. The book also includes alternate rhetorical and chronological contents.

100 Essays From Time takes a thematic approach—but it is designed as well for cross-curricular courses, and especially for composition courses emphasizing argumentative writing or contemporary issues. The book is aimed at a wide audience of teachers and students who enjoy reading and writing thoughtful essays on current as well as historical subjects. Many in that audience are already among those who regularly read and appreciate *Time* essays for their diversity, quality, and depth.

PART ONE: Arts and Humanities

1

Censorship and Freedom of Expression

One of the most persistent and pressing issues in a free society is the limits of such freedom. In the United States, perhaps our most central freedom, set forth in the First Amendment, is the right of free speech and expression. But throughout American history, that freedom has been tested, and it continues to be today, as more potentially offensive works of art, music, and literature find their way into the public arena.

How are we to decide whether free expression should have limits, what those limits should be, and, if so, who should enforce them? It's much more than just a question of banning obscene junk—though even that issue is far from clearcut. When is free expression "harmful"? Who should impose censorship—the communities, the states, the Federal Courts?

Time writers have addressed questions of censorship and freedom frequently over the years, as the following essays illustrate. In "The Growing Battle of the Books," from January 1981, Frank Trippett reports on an increasing tendency toward censorship of literature. In "Pornography Through the Looking Glass," from March 1984, Charles Krauthammer uses the case of a Minneapolis city council ordinance to consider a larger issue in the censorship wars. And in "An Age of Organized Touchiness," from April 1984, John Leo takes a somewhat lighter look at an early manifestation of political correctness—a phenomenon that has clearly come into its own in the 1990s.

The Growing Battle of the Books

FRANK TRIPPETT

Written words running loose have always presented a challenge   1
to people bent on ruling others. In times past, religious zealots burned
heretical ideas and heretics with impartiality. Modern tyrannies promote the contentment and obedience of their subjects by ruthlessly
keeping troubling ideas out of their books and minds. Censorship can
place people in bondage more efficiently than chains.

Thanks to the First Amendment, the U.S. has been remarkably, if   2
not entirely, free of such official monitoring. Still, the nation has always
had more than it needs of voluntary censors, vigilantes eager to protect
everybody from hazards like ugly words, sedition, blasphemy, unwelcome ideas and, perhaps worst of all, reality. Lately, however, it has been
easy to assume that when the everything-goes New Permissiveness
gusted forth in the 1960s, it blew the old book-banning spirit out of
action for good.

Quite the contrary. In fact, censorship has been on the rise in the   3
U.S. for the past ten years. Every region of the country and almost every
state has felt the flaring of the censorial spirit. Efforts to ban or squelch
books in public libraries and schools doubled in number, to 116 a year,
in the first five years of the 1970s over the last five of the 1960s—as
Author L.B. Woods documents in *A Decade of Censorship in America—The
Threat to Classrooms and Libraries, 1966-1975*. The upsurge in book banning has not since let up, one reason being that some 200 local, state and
national organizations now take part in skirmishes over the contents of
books circulating under public auspices. The American Library Association, which has been reporting an almost yearly increase in censorial
pressures on public libraries, has just totted up the score for 1980. It
found, without surprise, yet another upsurge: from three to five episodes a week to just as many in a day. Says Judith Krug, director of the
A.L.A.'s Office for Intellectual Freedom: "This sort of thing has a
chilling effect."

That, of course, is precisely the effect that censorship always   4
intends. And the chill, whether intellectual, political, moral or artistic,
is invariably hazardous to the open traffic in ideas that not only nour-
ishes a free society but defines its essence. The resurgence of a populist

2

censorial spirit has, in a sense, sneaked up on the nation. National attention has focused on a few notorious censorship cases, such as the book-banning crusade that exploded into life-threatening violence in Kanawha County, W. Va., in 1974. But most kindred episodes that have been cropping up all over have remained localized and obscure. The Idaho Falls, Idaho, school book review committee did not make a big splash when it voted, 21 to 1, to ban *One Flew Over the Cuckoo's Nest*—in response to one parent's objection to some of the language. It was not much bigger news when Anaheim, Calif., school officials authorized a list of approved books that effectively banned many previously studied books, including Richard Wright's classic *Black Boy*. And who recalls the Kanawha, Iowa, school board's banning *The Grapes of Wrath* because some scenes involved prostitutes?

Such cases, numbering in the hundreds, have now been thoroughly tracked down and sorted out by English Education Professor Edward B. Jenkinson of Indiana University in a study, *Censors in the Classroom—The Mind Benders*. He began digging into the subject after he became chairman of the Committee Against Censorship of the National Council of Teachers of English. His 184-page report reviews hundreds of cases (notorious and obscure), suggests the scope of censorship activity (it is ubiquitous), discusses the main censorial tactics (usually pure power politics) and points to some of the subtler ill effects. Popular censorship, for one thing, induces fearful teachers and librarians to practice what Jenkinson calls "closet censorship." The targets of the book banners? Jenkinson answers the question tersely: "Nothing is safe."

Case histories make that easy to believe. The books that are most often attacked would make a nice library for anybody with broad-gauged taste. Among them: *Catcher in the Rye, Brave New World, Grapes of Wrath, Of Mice and Men, Catch-22, Soul on Ice,* and *To Kill a Mockingbird. Little Black Sambo* and *Merchant of Venice* run into recurring protests based on suspicions that the former is anti-black, the latter anti-Semitic. One school board banned *Making It with Mademoiselle,* but reversed the decision after finding out it was a how-to pattern book for youngsters hoping to learn dressmaking. Authorities in several school districts have banned the *American Heritage Dictionary* not only because it contains unacceptable words but because some organizations, the Texas Daughters of the American Revolution among them, have objected to the sexual intimations of the definition of the word bed as a transitive verb.

Censorship can, and often does, lead into absurdity, though not often slapstick absurdity like the New Jersey legislature achieved in the 1960s when it enacted a subsequently vetoed antiobscenity bill so

5

6

7

explicit that it was deemed too dirty to be read in the legislative chambers without clearing out the public first. The mother in White-ville, N.C., who demanded that the Columbus County library keep adult books out of the hands of children later discovered that her own daughter had thereby been made ineligible to check out the Bible. One group, a Florida organization called Save Our Children, has simplified its censorship goals by proposing to purge from libraries all books by such reputed homosexuals as Emily Dickinson, Willa Cather, Virginia Woolf, Tennessee Williams, Walt Whitman and John Milton.

Most often, censors wind up at the ridiculous only by going a very   8 dangerous route. The board of the Island Trees Union Free School District on Long Island, N.Y., in a case still being contested by former students in court, banned eleven books as "anti-American, anti-Chris-tian, anti-Semitic and just plain filthy." Later they discovered that the banished included two Pulitzer prizewinners: Bernard Malamud's *The Fixer* and Oliver La Farge's *Laughing Boy*. For censors to ban books they have never read is commonplace. For them to deny that they are censoring is even more so. Said Attorney George W. Lipp Jr., announc-ing plans to continue the legal fight for the Island Trees board: "This is not book burning or book banning but a rational effort to transmit community values."

Few censors, if any, tend to see that censorship itself runs counter   9 to certain basic American values. But why have so many people with such an outlook begun lurching forth so aggressively in recent years? They quite likely have always suffered the censorial impulse. But they have been recently emboldened by the same resurgent moralistic mood that has enspirited evangelical fundamentalists and given form to the increasingly outspoken constituency of the Moral Majority. At another level, they probably hunger for some power over something, just as everybody supposedly does these days. Thus they are moved, as Amer-ican Library Association President Peggy Sullivan says, "by a despera-tion to feel some control over what is close to their lives."

Americans are in no danger of being pushed back to the prudery   10 of the 19th century. The typical U.S. newsstand, with its sappy pornutopian reek, is proof enough of that, without even considering prime-time TV. But the latter-day inflamed censor is no laughing matter. One unsettling feature of the current censorial vigilantism is its signs of ugly inflammation. There is, for instance, the cheerily incendiary atti-tude expressed by the Rev. George A. Zarris, chairman of the Moral Majority in Illinois. Says Zarris: "I would think moral-minded people might object to books that are philosophically alien to what they be-lieve. If they have the books and feel like burning them, fine." The notion of book burning is unthinkable to many and appalling to others, if only because it brings to mind the rise of Adolf Hitler's Germany—an event marked by widespread bonfires fed by the works of scores of writers including Marcel Proust, Thomas Mann, H.G. Wells and Jack London.

Unthinkable? In fact, the current wave of censorship has precipi-   11
tated two of the most outrageous episodes of book burning in the U.S. since 1927, when Chicago Mayor William ("Big Bill") Thompson, an anglophobe miffed by a view sympathetic to the British, had a flunky put the torch on the city hall steps to one of Historian Arthur Schlesinger Sr.'s books. In Drake, N. Dak., the five-member school board in 1973 ordered the confiscation and burning of three books that, according to Professor Jenkinson, none of the members had read: Kurt Vonnegut's *Slaughterhouse Five*, James Dickey's *Deliverance* and an anthology of short stories by writers like Joseph Conrad, John Steinbeck and William Faulkner. Said the school superintendent later: "I don't regret it one bit, and we'd do it again. I'm just sorry about all the publicity that we got." In Warsaw, Ind., a gaggle of citizens in 1977 publicly burned 40 copies of *Values Clarifications*, a textbook, as a show of support for a school board that decided to ban both written matter and independent-minded teachers from its system. Said William I. Chapel, a member of that board: "The bottom line is: Who will control the minds of the students?"

An interesting question. It baldly reveals the ultimate purpose of   12
all censorship—mind control—just as surely as the burning of books dramatizes a yearning latent in every consecrated censor. The time could not be better for recalling something Henry Seidel Canby wrote after Big Bill Thompson put Arthur Schlesinger to the flame. Said Canby: "There will always be a mob with a torch ready when someone cries, 'Burn those books!'" The real bottom line is: How many more times is he going to be proved right?

For Discussion and Writing

1. The first paragraph of Trippett's essay acts as a set of assumptions, givens, in which he'll ground his argument. To what extent do you agree with these ideas? Are there any you would question or dispute?
2. In paragraph nine, Trippett speculates about why censorship is on the rise. What does he think? What reasons would you offer to explain the increase?
3. Beyond its limits to free speech, Trippett sees censorship as an aspect of something perhaps even more threatening to American democracy. What is it?
4. Write an argumentative essay for or against censorship in one of the arts (visual arts, music, literature). Base your case on clear assumptions, and apply those premises to specific examples of works you think should or should not be protected.

Pornography Through the Looking Glass

CHARLES KRAUTHAMMER

Television ushered in the new year by cracking what it breath- 1
lessly billed as "the last taboo": incest. Liberal Minneapolis celebrated
by backtracking a couple of taboos and considering a ban on pornography. One would have thought that that particular hang-up had been
overcome. But even though the ban voted by the Minneapolis city
council was eventually vetoed by Mayor Donald Fraser, pornography
is evidently a hang-up of considerable tenacity. And according to the
proposed law it is more than that: it is a violation of civil rights.

Now that seems like a peculiar notion, but one has to read the 2
proposed ordinance to see just how peculiar it is. The city council
proposed banning "discrimination . . . based on race, color, creed, religion, ancestry, national origin, sex, including . . . pornography." What
can that possibly mean? How can one discriminate based on pornography?

Anticipating such questions, the bill helpfully provides "special 3
findings on pornography." If it ever passes (immediately after the
mayor's veto proponents vowed to bring it up again), the findings are
destined to be the most famous gifts from social science to law since
footnote eleven of *Brown* vs. *Board of Education*.* The *Brown* findings,
however, were based on real empirical data. The Minneapolis findings
are of a more metaphysical nature. They begin: "The council finds that
pornography is central in creating and maintaining the civil inequality
of the sexes." If that were true, then it would follow that where pornography is banned—as in the U.S. of 50 years ago or the Tehran of
today—one should not expect to find civil inequality of the sexes. Next
finding. "Pornography is a systematic practice of exploitation and
subordination based on sex which differentially harms women." While
it is true that some pornography subordinates women, some does not,
and none is "systematic" or a "practice." Outside the Minneapolis city
council chambers, pornography means the traffic in obscenity. Inside,
as in Alice's Wonderland, words will mean what the council wants them
to mean.

The liberal mayor of Minneapolis was sympathetic with the   4
proposal's aims, but vetoed it nonetheless. He found it too vague and
ambiguous, a classic complaint against obscenity laws, old and new. In
simpler times Justice Potter Stewart answered the question what is
pornography with a succinct "I know it when I see it." But would even
he know "subordination based on sex which differentially harms
women" when he saw it? After all, the new dispensation seems to
exclude homosexual pornography. And only embarrassment, not logic,
would prevent including those weddings at which the bride is old-fashioned enough to vow "to love, honor and *obey*."

The head of the Minneapolis Civil Liberties Union says, unkindly,   5
that the ordinance "has no redeeming social value." That seems a bit
harsh. Set aside for a moment the pseudo findings, the creative definitions, the ambiguities. The intent of the bill is to do away with the blight
of pornography. What can be wrong with that?

A good question, and an important one. Over the decades it has   6
spawned a fierce debate between a certain kind of conservative (usually
called cultural conservative) on the one hand and civil libertarians on
the other. The argument went like this. The conservative gave the
intuitive case against pornography based on an overriding concern for,
it now sounds almost too quaint to say, public morality. Pornography
is an affront to decency; it coarsens society. As Susan Sontag, not a
conservative, writing in defense of pornography says, it serves to "drive
a wedge between one's existence as a full human being and one's
existence as a sexual being." The ordinary person, of course, does not
need a philosopher, conservative or otherwise, to tell him why he wants
to run pornography out of his neighborhood. It cheapens and demeans.
Even though he may occasionally be tempted by it, that temptation is
almost invariably accompanied by a feeling of shame and a desire to
shield his children from the fleshy come-ons of the magazine rack.

That may be so, say the civil libertarians, but it is irrelevant.   7
Government has no business regulating morality. The First Amendment guarantees freedom of expression, and though you may prefer not
to express yourself by dancing naked on a runway in a bar, some people
do, and you have no business stopping them. Nor do you have any
business trying to stop those who like to sit by the runway and imbibe
this form of expression. It may not be *Swan Lake*, but the First Amendment does not hinge on judgments of artistic merit or even redeeming
value.

---

*The Supreme Court's 1954 ruling cited seven scholars to prove that separate-but-equal
schooling harmed black children, and led one critic to complain that it thus needlessly gave
ammunition to those who wished to see the *Brown* decision not as an expression of civilized
truth but as a brand of sociology.

Now this traditional debate over pornography is clear and com-   8
prehensible. It involves the clash of two important values: public morality *vs.* individual liberty. The conservative is prepared to admit that
his restrictions curtail liberty, though a kind of liberty he does not think
is particularly worth having. The civil libertarian admits that a price of
liberty is that it stands to be misused, and that pornography may be one
of those misuses; public morality may suffer, but freedom is more
precious. Both sides agree, however, that one cannot have everything
and may sometimes have to trade one political good for another.

Not the Minneapolis bill, and that is what made it so audacious—   9
and perverse. It manages the amazing feat of restoring censorship,
which after all is a form of coercion, while at the same time claiming
not to restrict rights but expand them. The logic is a bit tortuous. It finds
that pornography promotes bigotry and fosters acts of aggression
against women, both of which, in turn, "harm women's opportunities
for equality of rights in employment, education, property rights, . . .
contribute significantly to restricting women from full exercise of citizenship . . . and undermine women's equal exercise of rights to speech
and action."

Apart from the questionable logical leaps required at every step   10
of the syllogism, the more immediate question is: Why take this remote
and improbable route to arrive at a point—banning pornography—that
one can reach directly by citing the venerable argument that porngra-
phy damages the moral fiber of society? Why go from St. Paul to
Minneapolis by way of Peking?

The answer is simple. As a rallying cry, public morality has no sex   11
appeal; civil rights has. Use words like moral fiber and people think of
Jerry Falwell. Use words like rights and they think of Thomas Jefferson.
Use civil rights and they think of Martin Luther King Jr. Because civil
rights is justly considered among the most sacred of political values,
appropriating it for partisan advantage can be very useful. (The fiercest
battle in the fight over affirmative action, for example, is over which
side has rightful claim to the mantle of civil rights.) Convince people
that censorship is really a right, and you can win them over. It won over
the Minneapolis city council. And if to do so, you have to pretend that
fewer rights are more, so be it.

Civil rights will not be the first political value to have its meaning   12
reversed. The use of the term freedom to describe unfreedom goes back
at least as far as Rousseau, who wrote, without irony, of an ideal
republic in which men would be "forced to be free." In our day, the
word democracy is so beloved of tyrants that some have named their
countries after it, as in the German Democratic Republic (a.k.a. East
Germany). And from Beirut to San Salvador, every gang of political
thugs makes sure to kneel at least five times a day in the direction of
"peace." So why not abuse civil rights?

The virtue of calling a spade a spade is that when it is traded in,   13
accountants can still make sense of the books. The virtue of calling
political values by their real names is that when social policy is to be
made, citizens can make sense of the choices. That used to be the case
in the debate about pornography. If Minneapolis is any indication of
where that debate is heading, it will not be the case for long.

That is a pity, because while it is easy to quarrel with the method   14
of the Minneapolis ban, it is hard to quarrel with the motive. After a
decade's experience with permissiveness, many Americans have become acutely aware that there is a worm in the apple of sexual liberation. That a community with a reputation for liberalism should decide
that things have gone too far is not really news. The call for a pause in
the frantic assault on the limits of decency (beyond which lies the terra
cognita of what used to be taboos) is the quite natural expression of a
profound disappointment with the reality, as opposed to the promise,
of unrestricted freedom. There are pushes and pulls in the life of the
national superego, and now there is a pulling—back. Many are prepared to make expression a bit less free in order to make their community a bit more whole, or, as skeptics might say, wholesome.

That is nothing to be ashamed of. So why disguise it as a campaign   15
for civil rights? (True, liberals may be somewhat embarrassed to be
found in bed with bluenoses, but the Minneapolis case is easily explained away as a one-issue marriage of convenience.) In an age when
the most private of human activities is everywhere called by its most
common name, why be so coy about giving censorship its proper name
too?

For Discussion and Writing

1. If pornography is, as Krauthammer admits, "an affront to decency" (6),
   on what grounds does he dispute the Minneapolis effort to ban it?
2. Krauthammer summarizes what he calls the traditional debate over this
   issue. Which two values clash in this debate, and what common ground,
   if any, lies between opposing sides?
3. Why does Krauthammer say the argument has shifted from public
   morality to civil rights in the Minneapolis case? Why does he say civil
   rights is a more powerful (if less logical) appeal?
4. In an essay of your own, logically defend or attack the notion that
   pornography is "central in creating and maintaining the civil inequality
   of the sexes." How will you support your case?

An Age of Organized Touchiness

JOHN LEO

Wendy's first "Where's the beef?" television commercial is a   1
small masterpiece of lunacy and perfect timing. But the Michigan
Commission on Services to the Aging was not amused. The hamburger
drama, said Commission Chairman Joseph Rightley, gave the impression that "elderly people, in particular women, are senile, deaf and have
difficulty seeing." The point of the ad, of course, is that non-Wendy's
hamburgers are so small that anyone would have difficulty seeing
them, regardless of race, creed, sex, age or membership in an organized
pressure group.

To their credit, the Gray Panthers issued a statement declaring   2
Wendy's innocent of ageism and announcing themselves pleased that
the three women were not shown as quiet victims in the face of hamburger abuse. The Panthers, as it happens, have their own problems
with overreaction, attacking the immortal Christmas song *Grandma Got
Run Over by a Reindeer* (Grandma had too much eggnog and forgot her
pills) and letting scriptwriters know that old people should not be
shown with wheelchairs, canes or hearing aids. In supporting Wendy's,
the Panthers took the opportunity to fire a warning shot, disguised as
a compliment: ". . . it is especially accurate to portray the elderly as the
critical and discriminating consumers they are, from hamburgers to
health care." One may wonder why it is "especially accurate" to portray
oldsters as all-round shrewd consumers when the rest of us are bilked
regularly enough and will presumably remain just as bilkable in old
age.

The choice of language by the Panthers and Mr. Rightley gives the   3
game away. In an age of organized touchiness, the goal of many lobbying groups is not so much to erase stereotypes but to reverse them so
that there is never an image of any group that falls very far short of
idealization. Infirm oldsters and ethnic criminals exist in the real world,
but they are not to exist on screen.

John Blamphin, director of public affairs for the American Psychi-   4
atric Association, thinks many of his fellow media watchdogs are overly
sensitive. He hated the "terrible stereotype" of cruel psychiatry in *One
Flew over the Cuckoo's Nest* and loved the kindly, concerned therapists of

Ordinary People and *M *A * S * H*. But he does not expect every fictional psychiatrist to be unremittingly wonderful. The Dudley Moore character in *Lovesick* left him properly ambivalent. "The good news is that he tells her, 'I can't be your doctor any more,' " Blamphin says. "The bad news is he's standing in her shower when he says it."

Those who monitor entertainment and advertising for various   5 lobbying groups could use a dollop of Mr. Blamphin's balance and humor. Stage and screen these days are littered with the gored oxen of one outraged group or another. Puerto Ricans and blacks sued to block the filming of *Fort Apache, The Bronx*, declaring it racist. Homosexuals tried to disrupt production of *Cruising*. Oriental activists protested a recent *Charlie Chan* movie, forcing the maker of the film into a pre-production whine about his respectful treatment of the famous Chinese detective. Sioux Indians demonstrated against the book *Hanta Yo*, which contained passages on the ferocity of the Sioux. Under the guidance of many Sioux advisers, the television version will tone down the savagery and concentrate on the spiritual side of the tribe with a production entitled *Mystic Warrior*.

The feminist group Women Against Pornography zapped a Hanes   6 Hosiery commercial as sexist, which surprised the advertising agency involved. Men were indeed looking at a woman's legs, as they tend to do in "Gentlemen Prefer Hanes" commercials, but the story line of the ad was a female's successful attempt to join an all-male club over the stuffy objections of a Colonel Blimp type. In Congress, Mario Biaggi demanded hearings on the issue of whether two new productions of *Rigoletto* are offensive to Italian Americans. Both the English National Opera and the Virginia Opera Association are updating Verdi's tale of a contract killing from 16th century Mantua to 20th century New York City. Amid charges of "stereotyping," the opera executives backed down a bit: the Metropolitan Opera (host to the English company) dropped all references to the Mafia and Cosa Nostra, and the Virginia Opera inserted a program note apologizing for its bullet-marked poster. Cubans and Cuban Americans were officially affronted by the Al Pacino version of *Scarface*. Producer Martin Bregman, who is Jewish, felt compelled to point out that there are more crooked Jews than Cubans in the film. A Miami city commissioner helpfully suggested that Bregman could deflect criticism by making the protagonist an agent of Fidel Castro, sent to Florida to discredit Cuban Americans.

Even generic criminals with all-purpose names like Miller and   7 Greene can raise a hackle or two, at least if they appear in westerns: some members of the National Association for Outlaw and Lawman History argue that the lawmen were not as good or the outlaws as bad as presented in movies and on TV. Given the number of watchful pressure groups, it would seem the path of wisdom for film makers to make their villains middle-aged, middle-size heterosexual Anglo males. But even this is risky. Social Scientists Linda and Robert Lichter complain that prime-time TV criminals are usually "middle- or upper-class white males over age 30" and more apt to be rich than poor. The Lichters were acting as the hired guns for the Media Institute, a conservative, probusiness lobby. The institute, along with Mobil Oil Corp. and Accuracy in Media, would like to purge the tube of crooked businessmen.

The lobby for disabled people has been particularly strong, and   8
occasionally implacable. For the 1979 film *Voices*, a love story about a deaf woman and a would-be rock singer, MGM hired deaf actors and a deaf professor as a technical adviser. This was insufficient to placate the deafness lobby, which boycotted the film because it lacked captions and because the heroine was played by Amy Irving, who is not deaf. MGM plaintively said it had gone "to all ends" to find a deaf actress for the lead and wondered why it was being punished for producing a positive film about deaf people. Even a later version with captions added failed to satisfy the lobbyists. Jerry Lewis may think he is doing good work with his muscular dystrophy telethon, but he has been under fire for years from various disabled groups for featuring helpless children rather than self-sufficient adults, for inducing pity and for implying that the disabled cannot make it without outside help.

Much of the yelping at the media seems deeply trivial. A New York   9
coven of witches complained when ABC televised *Rosemary's Baby*. A marine biologist was bothered by the negative image of sharks in *Jaws*, and UFO enthusiasts groused when a woman was raped by a space alien on *Fernwood 2 Night*. Their point was that aliens do not go around raping people, and indeed there is little evidence that they do. The National Association to Aid Fat Americans mounted a stout protest against the Dom DeLuise movie *Fatso*. The group does not mind the word fat, but fatso is a red flag. NAAFA also took a swipe at the Diet Pepsi campaign for showing "emaciated, almost anorectic women." No rebuttal has been recorded, possibly because there is as yet no thin people's lobby to return the fire.

What would life have been like in Hollywood if there had been a   10
short people's lobby or a Hibernian Anti-Defamation League when Jimmy Cagney was shooting up the back lot at Warners'? Or when the Dracula movies were made? ("Neck sucking is another way of loving"—Vampire Liberation.) Though the past is hazy, the future is not. Here is how a few oldtime classics will doubtless be made to deflect all criticism:

Tom Sawyer. Indian Joseph, a deaf brain surgeon and weekend spelunker, is falsely accused of hanky-panky with Feminist Attorney

Becky Thatcher in the caves above Hannibal, Mo. Once cleared, Joseph and Thatcher team up with the Junior Chamber of Commerce to defend Tom Sawyer, a young entrepreneur defamed by antibusiness townspeople for allegedly exploiting Fence Painter Huck Finn. Prejudice against women, businessmen, Indians and deaf surgeons is delightfully exploded.

The Public Enemy's Kiss of Death. A mentally alert lady in a wheel-   12
chair, fresh from running the Boston Marathon, shoves Richard Widmark down a flight of stairs in justified retribution for centuries of male oppression. For much the same reason, Mae Clarke grinds half a grapefruit in the face of tall but sexist Breakfast Partner Jimmy Cagney. Though clad in a nightie, Ms. Clarke is shown carrying barbells and a briefcase to indicate she is not a sexual object. ("At last, a movie about strong, achieving women"—Alan Alda. "Thanks for exploding the myth about stairway safety"—Otis Elevator Co. "We resent the stereotyped connection between grapefruit and violence. Legal threat to follow"—Florida Citrus Commission.)

Mr. Dante's Inferno. Dante and Virgil tour the underworld, which   13
contains no one of Italian extraction and, in fact, no one of any ethnicity at all. They are shocked to find, however, that many sexual variationists, venture capitalists and members of other disadvantaged minorities are being cruelly punished for their alternative lifestyles. "This is right out of the Middle Ages," quips Dante. Virgil is quick to protest that many short people, lefthanders and vegetarians are among the tormented. A clever A.C.L.U. lawyer closes the place on a building-code violation.

Moby Dick. Captain Ahab, an emotionally well-adjusted and two-   14
legged maritime naturalist, pursues a generic gray whale with binoculars and a Peterson field guide. ("If this be 'obsession,' let's have more of it"—Save the Whales. "Call us happy. Can't wait for Moby Dick II"—Seafarers' International Union.)

The Lone Ranger. Crusading Reporter and leading Gay Activist   15
H.R. ("Tonto") Redmann goes under cover to unmask a deranged and excessively macho former lawman turned vigilante. Mr. Ranger is depicted as far from typical of most former lawmen, most heterosexuals and most white folks in general. His derangement is sensitively handled and shown to be the result of societal prejudice and a mistaken reading of the Miranda decision. All those perforated by Mr. Ranger's silver bullets are likewise portrayed sympathetically, and Tonto bans the use of the word outlaw as stigmatizing. ("A tale we can all identify with"—Native American Gays [NAG]. "O.K. with us"—Society of North American Retired Lawmen [SNARL]. "Shows we are all victims"—John De Lorean [JD].)

The Back of Notre Dame. Handsome Football Star J.J. Quasimodo,   16
on vacation in France, saves a self-sufficient but bound-and-gagged professional woman from a fiery death at the hands of a maddened

Parisian throng. Movie deftly makes the much needed social statement that people supposedly "handicapped" by lower back pain can easily perform impressive feats of rope swinging and feminist lifting. ("A bell ringer!"—the Rev. Theodore Hesburgh. "The first positive film about a man whose name ends in a vowel"—Representative Mario Biaggi. "Kudos for a great flick about Frogtown"—the Rev. Jesse Jackson.)

For Discussion and Writing

1. What does Leo say is the aim of organized lobbying groups in resisting or condemning stereotypes? What does Leo think of such efforts?
2. Leo cites many examples of the kind of touchiness he lampoons. Which of these make a valid point about stereotyping or unfair characterization, and which ones seem trivial or silly?
3. Why does Leo cite some make-believe examples toward the end of his essay? What effects may Leo be trying to achieve with such fictional illustrations? To what extent does he use humor and exaggeration to make a serious point?
4. Search out and write an essay about stereotyping on your campus. What are some common stereotypes you and others use? When, if ever, are such characterizations justified? How would you suggest people combat them?

Thinking and Writing about Chapter 1

1. In reading the three essays in this chapter, compare differences in the authors' basic purposes, strategies of development, and uses of language and tone. How do the more serious essays (Trippett and Krauthammer) differ in their effect from Leo's satirical piece?
2. Disputes over freedom of expression continue to fill public discussion. Where do you stand on the issue in general? Which values or beliefs underlie your views? Which arguments, on either side, do you find most persuasive or appealing? Why?
3. Write an essay in which you analyze the difficulties arising from the free-speech issue. Cite current examples (records, art work, books) that illustrate such problems, and propose your own solution to the issue of limiting or curbing free expression.

2

The Role of the Press

Another basic Constitutional guarantee that Americans prize highly is the freedom of the press, and, like freedom of expression, it has been the focus of disputes throughout our history. Should press freedom be absolute? When, if ever, must it be weighed against competing rights or freedoms? Should television journalists receive the same protection as do their colleagues in the print media? What is the role of the press in a free society?

These and many other allied questions have been the subject of *Time* essays dating back to the 1960s. In most cases, the writers have been solidly on the side of press freedoms—as one might expect in a magazine whose mission is journalistic. But those authors have also been forthright and honest in admitting the press's failings and limits, an attitude that helps keep that vital institution healthy.

In the pieces included here, longtime editor Henry Grunwald, in "The Press, the Courts and the Country," from July 1976, considers the relationship between the press, the judicial system, and the public. Then in two pieces, "When Journalists Die in War," from July 1983, and "Journalism and the Larger Truth," from July 1984, Roger Rosenblatt looks at the role of reporters in wartime and the nature of the journalistic enterprise.

The Press, the Courts
and the Country

Henry Grunwald

Are courts going too far in what is beginning to look like a 1
campaign to curb the press?

Most journalists would not yet agree with Allen Neuharth, head 2
of the Gannett newspaper chain, that in this respect, the Supreme Court
has moved "above the law." But the trend is clear and alarming, from
the denial of confidentiality of sources to surprise newsroom searches.
Not only the press is affected. The search decision can send the cops
into psychiatrists' or lawyers' offices as well. The latest court ruling that
pretrial hearings and possibly trials themselves may be closed to press
and public is reprehensible, among other reasons because it could lead
to collusion—behind closed courtroom doors—between judges, prose-
cutors and defendants. This ruling more than any other shows that the
conflict is not just between the courts and the press but the courts and
society.

Tension between power centers is useful in America. But the 3
judiciary ought to reflect about what it is doing. In important respects,
judges really are in the same boat as journalists, and ultimately in the
service of the same ideals. People who cheer the courts' moves against
the press are quite ready to condemn the courts in other areas. If the
press is seen as having too much power, so are the courts, and then
some.

The monstrous regiment of lawyers has rarely been more re- 4
sented. In a recent Harris poll about public confidence in various
institutions, law firms ranked eleventh on a list of 13. Even when
lawyers are miraculously transformed into judges, they do not regain
total trust. In the same poll, the Supreme Court came in sixth, while TV
news (somewhat surprisingly) ranked first and the press in general
ranked fifth, thus nosing ahead of the august court.

Distrust of the judiciary is nothing new in American history. 5
Thomas Jefferson in 1820 thought that the notion of judges as "the
ultimate arbiters of all constitutional questions" was "very dangerous"
and threatened the "despotism of an oligarchy." At times, the press

helped fan suspicion of judges; more recently it has functioned as an ally of the bench, as when the courts virtually administered school desegregation, and during Watergate.

Some historical perspective is necessary. The proud judiciary   6
traces its origins back far beyond the beginning of the printed word to times when the judge was king, and vice versa. Journalists, on the other hand, are relative newcomers, the spiritual descendants of itinerant printers, scribblers and (let's face it) rebels. Indeed, one of the reasons that journalists are so worried, even perhaps slightly paranoid, about the loss of their freedoms is that these rights have never been very secure, here or abroad.

In 16th century England, editors and "newswriters" were con-   7
stantly in danger of imprisonment or torture, even of beheading, hanging and burning at the stake, sometimes for refusal to reveal the source of confidential information. Until nearly the end of the 18th century, libel in Britain was readily used to jail journalists and others. John Walter, publisher of the young London *Times,* was confined for nearly a year and a half to Newgate Prison, from which he managed to run his newspaper.

Journalists fared somewhat better in America. Here, the press   8
played an essential part in bringing off the American Revolution. But that did not assure popularity. George Washington came to believe that the press should be firmly "managed" and kept in its place. Jefferson, kinder to the press than to the courts, disagreed and declared grandiosely that "nature has given to man no other means [than the press] of sifting out the truth either in religion, law, or politics." (In fairness, it should be noted that later he declared himself "infinitely happier" once he had stopped all his newspaper subscriptions.)

Still, journalism in America was a high-risk trade. Editors were   9
always in danger of being challenged to duels or horsewhipped or beaten up by gangs. During the War of 1812, one antiwar newspaper was actually blasted by a mob with a cannon. On the frontier, tarring and feathering editors was a popular pastime. Symbolically, of course, it still is. The press, its reach almost infinitely expanded by electronics, has come a long way since those days. Yet, the public, despite its daily if not hourly intimacy with the press, does not really understand it very well. That lack of understanding is reflected in the courts, although it goes far beyond matters of the law. In part, this is inevitable because the press is indeed a peculiar institution, full of paradoxes. To understand and judge—even to criticize it for the right reasons—a few broad points might be kept in mind.

 • The American press is better than ever. Yellow journalism per-   10
   sists, but largely on the fringes of the press and is pale compared

with what it was in the heyday of William Randolph Hearst. One episode: Drumming the U.S. to war against Spain, Hearst sent Artist Frederic Remington to Cuba. When Remington cabled that all was quiet, with no war in sight, Hearst fired back: "You supply the pictures, I'll supply the war." Arrogance of such magnitude is unheard of today. The sensationalist Joseph Pulitzer declared that accuracy is to a newspaper what virtue is to a lady, but the fact is that journalism today takes that maxim far more seriously than did the papers of Pulitzer's time.

True, the press still features triviality, gossip, scandal. It always   11
will. Charles Anderson Dana of the New York *Sun*—like Hearst and Pulitzer quite a phrasemaker and an exemplar of the era—declared that the *Sun* could not be blamed for reporting what God had permitted to happen. That was only partly a cop-out. While the press should not pander to base or grisly appetites, or merely "give the people what they want," neither should it be expected to change human nature (if that concept is still admissible). America's mainstream publications today, for all their faults, are far more broad-gauged, responsible, accurate— and self-critical—than ever before, or than any other in the world.

- The press should not be expected to be what it is not. Literary   12
  critics chide journalism for not being literary enough, historians
  for lacking historical accuracy, lawyers for not marshaling facts
  by the rules of evidence. But journalism is not literature, not
  history, not law. Most of the time it cannot possibly offer anything but a fleeting record of events compiled in great haste.
  Many news stories are, at bottom, hypotheses about what happened. Science, of course, works by hypotheses, discarding
  them when errors are discovered, and it does so, on the whole,
  without blame, even when a mistake costs lives. The press,
  which lays no claim to scientific accuracy, is not easily forgiven
  its errors. Admittedly, the press often rushes into print with
  insufficient information, responding to (and perhaps creating)
  an occasionally mindless hunger for news. A utopian society
  might demand that the press print nothing until it had reached
  absolute certainty. But such a society, while waiting for some
  ultimate version of events, would be so rife with rumor, alarm
  and lies that the errors of our journalism would by comparison
  seem models of truth.

The press was not invented by and for journalists. It is a result of   13
mass literacy and the instrument of a political system in which, for better or worse, all literate people—indeed even the illiterate—are

considered qualified voters. So the hunger for news is a hunger for power—not power by journalists, as is often suggested, but by the public. The press is a child of the Enlightenment and those who inveigh against it also attack, sometimes unconsciously, the values of the Enlightenment. It is no accident that the press grew as the concept of revealed truth declined. The press as we know it could not (does not) exist in societies that in all things accept the voice of authority.

• Profits should not make the press suspect. Many people (includ-   14
ing journalists and judges) are troubled by the fact that the press
performs a public service and yet makes profits. But this is
nothing the press should apologize for; on the contrary. The
press as a business is the only alternative to a subsidized press,
which by every conceivable measurement would be worse.
True, there are serious risks in the commercial aspects of the
press, but these are relatively minor compared with the situation a few generations ago, when weak and insecure newspapers all too easily succumbed to the checkbooks of political or
business pressure groups. Henry Luce argued that the press was
not really taken seriously and, in a sense, did not really become
free until it became a big business. Enterprising journalism is
expensive. (It costs more than $100,000 to keep a correspondent
in Washington, D.C., for one year. Paper, printing and distribu-
tion cost TIME magazine $120 million. The newspaper industry
spends $3 billion each year on newsprint alone.)

Questions about profits lead to questions about size. The spread   15
of newspaper chains and one-newspaper cities is, to be sure, a cause for
concern. Yet smallness as such is not necessarily good: it guarantees
neither quality nor independence. Bigness as such is not necessarily
bad: in most cases, large resources improve a publication. Nor does the
size of some enterprises keep new publications out. The number of
small publications is growing and their diversity is dazzling. The really
remarkable phenomenon of recent years is not so much the growth of
communications companies, but the spread of highly organized special
interest groups that have had considerable success in making themselves heard and seen.

• The press is not too powerful; if anything, it is not powerful   15
enough. Those who want to curb the press point out that it is no
longer the "fragile" thing it was when the First Amendment was
written. But neither is the Government. When Franklin Roosevelt took office, the federal budget, in 1979 dollars, amounted to
about $38 billion. In fiscal 1980, it will be around $530 billion.
When Roosevelt took office, the federal bureaucracy consisted

of 600,000 people. Today it adds up to 2,858,344. Such figures can only suggest that the growth of Government has been far more dramatic than the growth of the press that attempts to cover and monitor it. With innumerable Xerox machines and printing presses, through tons of publications, reports, tapes and films, countless Government flacks churn out enough information, and disinformation, to overwhelm an army of reporters. To a lesser extent this is true of other large institutions: corporations, unions, foundations, all of which try to manage the news and use the press for their ends.

The fact that the press is not accountable to any other power except   17
the marketplace clearly agitates a lot of people. This often takes the form of the hostile question to editors: Who elected you anyway? But some institutions in our society simply should *not* be subject to the usual political processes. As for the courts, whatever their intentions may be, they are not the place to cure the undeniable failings of the press.

Do recent court actions really make much of a difference to jour-   18
nalists in practice? Many judges doubt it, but let them try an experiment and take on a tough reporting assignment. Let them try to get complicated and controversial information from resisting sources and amid conflicting claims—without the judicial power to subpoena documents or witnesses—and have to testify under the disciplines of contempt or perjury. Let these judges then see how far they will get with their assignment if they are unable to promise an informant, who may be risking his job, assured confidentiality, or if they are hit by subpoenas, now said to be running at the rate of 100-plus a year, many of these mere "fishing expeditions."

To say this is not to claim an absolute privilege for journalists.   19
Newsmen should not ask the same standing that a lawyer or doctor has in dealing with clients or patients; lawyers and doctors after all are licensed, which is precisely what journalists will not and must not be. Obviously the American journalist enjoys unusual latitude and he must, therefore, bear unusual responsibility. He must expect a certain rough-and-tumble in his trade, and not wrap himself in the Constitution at every setback. By no means were all recent court rulings unmitigated disasters. The court in effect allows the press to print anything it can get its hands on. When the Supreme Court held that a newsman's state of mind and his preparations for a story were legitimate subjects of inquiry, this evoked visions of thought police; and yet it was only a consequence of an earlier pro-press ruling that a public figure, in order to be able to sue for libel, must prove "actual" malice and gross neglect on the part of the journalist. Most newsmen do not demand confidentiality of sources automatically, but only when naming sources or delivering notes is not strictly necessary to

meet the specific needs of a defendant. (Many judges in fact agree with this view.)

No serious journalist questions the need to balance the rights of a   20
free press against other rights in society, including the rights of defendants. But the degree of balance is what counts, and the balance is tilting
against the press. As a result, a backlash against the courts has begun
in Congress, with the introduction of many bills designed to shore up
the rights of journalists. That is a mixed blessing. Spelling out rights
that were assumed to exist under the general protection of the First
Amendment may very well result in limiting those rights. Most of the
press would much rather not run to Congress for protection against the
courts. Yet if the courts continue on their present course, journalists will
have little alternative.

Perhaps it is not too late for judges to restore some balance and to   21
discover that they do share with the press certain common interests, if
not a common fate. As New York's Irving R. Kaufman, Chief Judge of
the Second Judicial Circuit, has written: "Different as the press and the
federal judiciary are, they share one distinctive characteristic: both
sustain democracy, not because they are responsible to any branch of
Government, but precisely because, except in the most extreme cases,
they are not accountable at all. Thus they are able to check the irrespon-
sibility of those in power . . ."

Ultimately the question of freedom of the press comes down to   22
the question of freedom, period. Freedom exists both for good and bad,
for the responsible and the irresponsible. Freedom only for the good,
only for the right, would not be freedom at all. Freedom that hurts no
one is impossible and a free press will sometimes hurt. That fact must
be balanced against the larger fact that this freedom does not exist for
the benefit of the press but for the benefit of all. In the majority of
countries, judges are in effect only executioners and journalists are only
Government press agents. This reality should be kept in mind as the
courts deal with the American press and its rare and fragile rights.

For Discussion and Writing

1. In defending the press against what he sees as an assault upon First
    Amendment freedoms, Grunwald cites a number of supporting claims
    or assertions about journalism's role. What are these? According to the
    author, what is the function of the press in our country?
2. Grunwald places his argument in an historical context, loosely tracing
    the evolution of the press from 16th century England to the present.
    What does such historical information add to his claim that freedom of
    the press, for all its faults, is a freedom that exists "for the benefit of all"?

3. What is your sense of the press's function in today's world? Can you make distinctions between higher and lower forms of journalism? What specific suggestions might you make to professional journalists that would help the press be more effective?
4. Take any of Grunwald's claims—there are many—and support or rebut it. For example: "The press is not too powerful; if anything, it is not powerful enough" (16). Consider the assumptions about the press's role that you will take as a given, and the examples you'll use to support your case.

When Journalists Die in War

ROGER ROSENBLATT

Certain responses are to be expected whenever a journalist is 1
killed in a war. His employers will remark on his courage and devotion
to duty, his colleagues on his professionalism; from close friends and
family will come expressions of grief or anger. Occasionally, in the case
of celebrities, a President will offer a eulogy, as did Harry Truman for
Ernie Pyle, killed in the South Pacific in 1945: "No man in this war has
so well told the story of the American fighting man as the American
fighting man wanted it told." The standard was dubious, but the praise
sincere. For the public these moments pass rather quickly, like any death
in a war. Yet these killings are central to the function of journalism. In
odd ways, if briefly, they clarify the relationship among the news, those
who report it and the people who seek those reports.

The nature of this relationship was illustrated in the deaths last 2
week of two American journalists, Dial Torgerson and Richard Cross,
who were killed when their white, rented Toyota was struck by a
rocket-propelled grenade on a road in Honduras near the Nicaraguan
border. Nicaraguan soldiers apparently added machine-gun fire to the
damage of the grenade. This kind of story always startles people,
though it is hard to say why.

In part the surprise simply comes from the announcement of a 3
personalized death; two named and photographed victims in a war
automatically draw more attention than statistical casualties. Then, too,
there is something about the rhythm and character of their work: the
white moving line of the automobile perpendicular to the guns, the
pursuit of one profession bisecting another. There is the matter of their
being journalists, who as cultural figures are always accorded a special
(half revered, half resented) slot in the public mind, and of their being
foreign correspondents in particular, with all the folklore glamour
associated with that work. There is the influence of television, which
has aggrandized the whole profession. It may also be that these deaths
attract notice because they serve to remind people that risk entails the
possibility of failure. It is acutely shocking to learn that risk takers can
lose.

Of course, one must also allow for the possibility that the deaths   4
of journalists are important only to other journalists, the attention given
by the press being wholly disproportionate to true public interest. Yet
this seems not the case. For a hundred years, war reporters have
provided a basic service, apart from increasing the profits of their
employers. "If it is a solitary profession, it is also a kind of loving
involvement with history," Georgie Anne Geyer confessed in *Buying the
Night Flight: the Autobiography of a Woman Correspondent.* The involvement is the reader's equally, journalism being history on the run. When
the correspondent is removed, so is the citizen, who is then left to assess
the conduct of a war by official and authorized reports. Not that one is
ever sure that what the paper prints is what really happened, but the
presumption, however grumpily arrived at, favors the more disinterested observer.

For all the grandeur of the correspondent's responsibilities, how-   5
ever, he is usually the most unromantic of creatures. The exceptions
spring to mind because they are exceptions: John Reed dying for Mother
Russia, Richard Harding Davis, swaggering with his brace of pistols.
Most war reporters are quieter, almost sullen—frown-ridden loners
stretched out in weird hotel lounges, waiting wearily upon the return
of yet more troops from yet another major offensive or the disclosure
of an atrocity from yet another smooth-voiced press officer. Even those
who run with rebels in the tropics must find the perils repetitious after
a while, the colorful characters melting into abstractions. In these times,
a correspondent may move so quickly from Afghanistan to Beirut to
Ethiopia, it is a wonder that he is able to distinguish the names of towns
from Prime Ministers. Less a wonder is that these people sometimes
grow hard around the heart; when you've seen one mutilation, you've
seen them all. Still, as Arthur Koestler wrote of the war in Spain:
"Anyone who has lived through the hell of Madrid with his eyes, his
heart, his stomach, and then pretends to be objective, is a liar."

Is objectivity at last what the public seeks from its reporters?   6
Certainly, in matters as urgent as wars, no one wants impressionistic
sketches or first-person pleas for conciliation, but it may be that pure
objectivity is sought less than simple completeness, a good eye and ear
for detail. People often have a hard time dealing with facts that distort
their presumptions, but that is what they ask of their messengers: tell
everything. The difficulty in war reporting is that no one, on any side,
wants everything told. Everything includes cowardice, dishonor, the
breaking of codes. He who tells everything represents a greater menace
than the opponent's weaponry, which is why every sensible commander tries to keep correspondents away from the action. The best of
the lot are welcome nowhere.

Nor in fact is the public welcome in a war, except when one   7
assumes that it may be aroused in support of one's own side. Open as
they are, wars are essentially private acts, guilty violations of civilized
standards. "Now and then," wrote Ernest Bennett about "potting
Dervishes" in the Westminster *Gazette* in 1898, "I caught in a man's eye
the curious gleam which comes from the joy of shedding blood—that
mysterious impulse which, despite all the veneer of civilization, still
holds its own in a man's nature." If most generals had their way, wars
would probably be fought on other planets, free from inspection that
leads to judgment, which itself may join the hostile forces.

William Howard Russell, one of the first war correspondents,   8
wrote of the British hauteur in the Crimea: "Am I to tell these things or
hold my tongue?" He asked the question of the trade. Today one
normally expects that journalists will not hold their tongues, perhaps
because Russell and others did not, or perhaps because it is common
now to regard war as inglorious, even purposeless. In a sense, journalists always have been the enemies of war. From a tactical viewpoint,
one almost might say it lies in the interests of the participants to kill
them off, since inevitably they hold the enterprise up to the light.

When Torgerson and Cross died last week, so did the public, for   9
a moment, which may be the main reason one feels their deaths, and
the death of all war correspondents, with a sort of intellectual pain.
These curious people who take notes in the world's most murderous
places may do so mostly for themselves, for the thrill or the value of
being at the centers of experience. But they take to the wars for everyone
else as well, for those who may wish to be lulled by lies from time to
time but who in the long run do not wish to live as dupes or fools. For
them do the far-flung correspondents patrol the lines, seeking to report
how fares the dark.

For Discussion and Writing

1. According to Rosenblatt, why are the deaths of reporters in wartime
   "central to the function of journalism" (1), and how do they help clarify
   the relationship between events, journalists, and the reading public?
2. Rosenblatt describes the reporter's responsibilities as grand, yet he
   claims that journalists are "the most unromantic of creatures" (5). Is this
   a contradiction in terms? Why or why not? What picture of the journalist
   emerges from the author's characterization?
3. Why, according to the author, do the people who manage wars—the
   commanders—often try to keep correspondents away from the action?
4. Write an essay in which you attack or defend the claim that war
   reporting is necessary in a democracy, even though the news may
   damage the government's image in the public mind and thus erode
   support for the war effort.

Journalism and the Larger Truth

ROGER ROSENBLATT

When journalists hear journalists claim a "larger truth," they 1
really ought to go for their pistols. *The New Yorker's* Alastair Reid said
the holy words last week: "A reporter might take liberties with the
factual circumstances to make the larger truth clear." O large, large
truth. Apparently Mr. Reid believes that imposing a truth is the same
as arriving at one. Illogically, he also seems to think that truths may be
disclosed through lies. But his error is more fundamental still in assuming that large truth is the province of journalism in the first place. The
business of journalism is to present facts accurately—Mr. Reid notwithstanding. Those seeking something larger are advised to look elsewhere.

For one thing, journalism rarely sees the larger truth of a story 2
because reporters are usually chasing quite small elements of information. A story, like a fern, only reveals its final shocking shape in stages.
Journalism also reduces most of the stories it deals with to political
considerations. Matters are defined in terms of where power lies, who
opposes whom or what, where the special interests are. As a result, the
larger truth of a story is often missed or ignored. By its nature, political
thought limits speculative thought. Political realities themselves cannot
be grasped by an exclusively political way of looking at things.

Then, too, journalism necessarily deals with discontinuities. One
has never heard of the Falkland Islands. Suddenly the Falklands are the
center of the universe; one knows all there is to know about "kelpers"
and Port Stanley; sheep jokes abound. In the end, as at the beginning,
no one really knows anything about the Falkland Islands other than the
war that gave it momentary celebrity—nothing about the people in the
aftermath of the war, their concerns, isolation, or their true relationship
to Argentina and Britain. Discontinuities are valuable because they
point up the world's variety as well as the special force of its isolated
parts. But to rely on them for truth is to lose one's grip on what is
continuous and whole.

Journalism looks to where the ball is, and not where it is not. A 4
college basketball coach, trying to improve the performance of one of
his backcourt men, asked the player what he did when he practiced on

his own. "Dribble and shoot," came the reply. The coach then asked the player to add up the total time he dribbled and shot during a scrimmage game, how many minutes he had hold of the ball. "Three minutes in all," came the reply. "That means," said the coach, "that you practice what you do in three minutes out of 40 in a game." Which means in turn that for every player, roughly 37 out of a possible 40 minutes are played away from the ball.

Journalism tends to focus on the poor when the poor make news,   5
usually dramatic news like a tenement fire or a march on Washington. But the poor are poor all the time. It is not journalism's ordinary business to deal with the unstartling normalities of life. Reporters need a *story*, something shapely and elegant. Poverty is disorderly, anticlimactic and endless. If one wants truth about the poor, one must look where the ball is not.

Similarly, journalism inevitably imposes forms of order on both   6
the facts in a story and on the arrangement of stories itself. The structures of magazines and newspapers impose one kind of order; radio and television another, usually sequential. But every form journalism takes is designed to draw the public's attention to what the editors deem most important in a day's or week's events. This naturally violates the larger truth of a chaotic universe. Oddly, the public often contributes its own hierarchical arrangements by dismissing editors' discriminations and dwelling on the story about the puppy on page 45 instead of the bank collapse on Page One. The "truth" of a day's events is tugged at from all sides.

Finally, journalism often misses the truth by unconsciously erod-   7
ing one's sympathy with life. A seasoned correspondent in Evelyn Waugh's maliciously funny novel *Scoop* lectures a green reporter. "You know," he says, "you've got a lot to learn about journalism. Look at it this way. News is what a chap who doesn't care much about anything wants to read." The matter is not a laughing one. A superabundance of news has the benumbing effect of mob rule on the senses. Every problem in the world begins to look unreachable, unimprovable. What could one lone person possibly accomplish against a constant and violent storm of events that on any day include a rebellion of Sikhs, a tornado in Wisconsin, parents pleading for a healthy heart for their child? Sensibilities, overwhelmed, eventually grow cold; and therein monsters lie. Nobody wants to be part of a civilization that reads the news and does not care about it. Certainly no journalist wants that.

If one asks, then, where the larger truth is to be sought, the answer   8
is where it has always been: in history, poetry, art, nature, education, conversation; in the tunnels of one's own mind. People may have come to expect too much of journalism. Not of journalism at its worst; when one is confronted with lies, cruelty and tastelessness, it is hardly too much to expect better. But that is not a serious problem because lies,

cruelty and tastelessness are the freaks of the trade, not the pillars. The trouble is that people have also come to expect too much of journalism at its best, because they have invested too much power in it, and in so doing have neglected or forfeited other sources of power in their lives. Journalists appear to give answers, but essentially they ask a question: What shall we make of this? A culture that would rely on the news for truth could not answer that question because it already would have lost the qualities of mind that make the news worth knowing.

If people cannot rely on the news for facts, however, then journalism has no reason for being. Alastair Reid may have forgotten that the principal reason journalists exist in society is that people have a need to be informed of and comprehend the details of experience. "The right to know and the right to be are one," wrote Wallace Stevens in a poem about Ulysses. The need is basic, biological. In that sense, everyone is a journalist, seeking the knowledge of the times in order to grasp the character of the world, to survive in the world, perhaps to move it. Archimedes said he could move the world as long as he had a long enough lever. He pointed out, too, that he needed a ground to stand on.

For Discussion and Writing

1. Why is it not the role of journalism to seek "the larger truth"? In what way is such a mission in conflict with the limits and nature of reporting? Where are such larger truths to be found?
2. What are some of the limits Rosenblatt attributes to journalism? What does journalism provide for us, despite, or because of, its limits?
3. At the end of paragraph eight, Rosenblatt says: "Journalists appear to give answers, but essentially they ask a question: What shall we make of this? A culture that would rely on the news for truth could not answer that question because it already would have lost the qualities of mind that make the news worth knowing." What do you think he means?
4. Write an essay in which you address one of these ideas: A) Journalism's role is not to give us the big picture, but instead to let us see the details. Constructing the picture is up to us, individually, and that is as it should be. B) The press's claim that larger truths are not their job is a cop-out. Reporters should tell us what their stories mean, and what we're supposed to think about them.

Thinking and Writing about Chapter 2

1. The press has met opposition not only from the judiciary, as in Grunwald's essay, but from other branches of government. As recently as 1990-91, during the Persian Gulf War, press access was "managed" by the military, and journalists were limited to pool coverage, groups of reporters guided by military officers. What might Grunwald and Rosenblatt have to say about such limits on press freedom? Is there a case to be made for preventing the press from having free access to battle zones, combat, and so on?

2. The two authors in this chapter share some basic views about the value of journalism, and even its potentially heroic nature. What are these shared beliefs? Where, if at all, do Grunwald and Rosenblatt differ in their ideas about the press?

3. What does the press mean to you? What role does journalism play in your daily life? Where do you get the news—from newspapers, magazines, television, radio? Is journalism more than just the news? Write an essay in which you consider the importance, function, and appeal of journalism in your life.

3

Popular Culture

Throughout much of civilized history, people have made distinctions between the arts, ranking some higher than others. Classical music, for instance, has long been viewed as being more serious or sophisticated than folk or popular songs. And so it is with the other arts: painting is thought to be higher than cartooning, theater higher than movies, literature higher than drugstore fiction.

In America, such distinctions still hold true to some extent, with the world of high or serious art (opera, ballet, poetry) usually not seen as part of what has come to be called pop culture (rock and other forms of popular music, movies, television, comic strips, mass market fiction, and so on). And despite the widespread support for the higher arts in the U.S., pop culture appears to dominate in our society, with most of our attention focused on the latest special-effects blockbuster, the hottest best-selling novel or celebrity biography, the trendiest TV show or cartoon character. The tension between high and low exists even within pop culture itself, as critics seek to point out the best and the worst of mass culture has to offer, even turning high pop into a species of high art.

The three essays in this chapter address various aspects of pop culture in America. In "Disney: Mousebrow to Highbrow," from 1973, art critic Robert Hughes considers the nature of the imaginary world created by the Disney organization. In "We'll Always Have *Casablanca*," from 1982, Lance Morrow sings the praises of a classic American film. And in "The Triumph of Pap Culture," from 1984, Frank Trippett bemoans the "meatless mush" that he claims pop culture has become.

Disney: Mousebrow to Highbrow

ROBERT HUGHES

The staff cafeteria is immaculate, lit with fluorescence and   1
perked up by leaf-green supergraphics. Four dwarfs and a brown
nylon-shag bear stand at the counter, ordering chipped beef. Their
human faces, pinheads emerging from their neck-holes, look tiny,
naked and grumpy. Across a wide cinder-block corridor whose ceiling
is wreathed like a battleship's with gas pipes and power mains, more
ducks and mice are disappearing into the mask room. REMOVE YOUR HEAD
AND PLACE ON TABLE AFTER ENTERING, a notice commands; the racks are full
of familiar visages, the icons of one's childhood, Mickey and Pluto and
the others blown up to preternatural size, then guillotined; their eyes
goggle from the shelves like big affable poached eggs. There is even a
set of coolant waistcoats, their design a spin-off from NASA; they circulate
a chemical refrigerant round the body. In this humid and swampy
acreage of Florida, every hot duck on Main Street contains a hotter man
wildly signaling to be let out.

Farther down the corridor is the computer room, which controls   2
the "audio-animatronic" displays: banks of thick cassettes slotted into
a blinking steel wall, 14-track tape loops piling and swishing inside
their moon-shaped Plexiglas boxes, running across the heads like sepia
fettucine. Every second, millions of impulses skitter down the cables,
linking the Realworld beneath the podium to the Magic Kingdom: the
Bear Jamboree plunks and toots, holographic phantoms squeak and
gibber among the cobwebs of the Haunted Mansion, and in the ante-
chamber of the Moon Rocket in Tomorrowland, a robot scientist holds
a conversation with a scarcely less robotic Disney World hostess.

It was through these latitudes that Ponce de León stumbled in   3
1513, seeking the fountain of perpetual youth. It was not there. Now it
is. The Walt Disney World coat of arms—a terrestrial globe wearing
Mickey ears, set in a capital D—is no metaphor but a frank statement
of intention. The place is the last example of idealized, high-despotic
city planning, a rich hick cousin of all the imaginary and perfect
townships that architects from Filarete in the 15th century to Boullée in
the 18th wrought from their schematic, authoritarian fantasies but
never managed to build. Unlike Kublai Khan's pleasure dome, it exists

on a plane of unremitting kitsch, sustained by the most advanced technology ever brought to the service of entertainment.

One would be wrong to suppose that Disney—or the "imagineers" who carried this project forward after he died in 1966—planned his World from the outside in, starting with an audience and then successfully condescending to it. "I don't make films exclusively for children," Walter Elias Disney once remarked. "I make them to suit myself, hoping they will also suit the audience." As on film, so in the environments: Disney was nothing if not an expressionist, and he built the old Magic Kingdom in Anaheim, Calif., and the new one in Orlando to please himself. Disney World is a pure feat of self-projection in which neurosis and imagination are rendered equally concrete. One instinctive response is to turn away from Disney. After all, the promotional goo about magic, warmth and wonder that has been ladled over him and his works in the past 20 years would make even Bambi puke. But Disney's really interesting side was not the fabled rapport with children (from all accounts, he was about as innocent as Bobby Riggs and somewhat less likable) but the grip of organization—first in his art itself, and then in the area of business and social manipulation—which made Disneyland and Disney World possible. He turned himself from a cartoonist into the Old Master of masscult and from there became a utopian environmentalist.

By now there is no way of approaching the confused feedbacks between "high" and "mass" culture in America without running into Disney at nearly every twist of the discussion. And so, among culture critics—his traditional enemies—there has been a growth of very serious interest in Disney. As Peter Blake, editor of *Architecture Plus*, put it: "Walt Disney did not know that such things as vast urban infrastructures, multilevel mass-transit systems, People Movers, nonpolluting vehicles, pedestrian malls, and so forth were unattainable, and so he just went ahead and built them. In doing it he drew on all kinds of resources that no other city planner had ever before considered seriously, if at all . . . it seems unlikely that any American school of architecture will ever again graduate a student without first requiring him or her to take a field trip to Orlando."

Not so the art schools, but "Disney memorabilia"—the auction-room word for old Mickey Mouse watches—are moving from the camp boutiques to Parke-Bernet, and a New York art dealer named Bernard Danenberg has contracted with Walt Disney Productions to exhibit "cels" (the clear plastic sheets on which final animation drawings are made) from a new Disney cartoon, *Robin Hood*. This migration of Disney's iconography from masscult to the commercial fringes of "high" art (it happened to Norman Rockwell last year) will be prodded along by a 7½-lb. tome entitled *The Art of Walt Disney*, written by English

Art Critic Christopher Finch with the full cooperation of the Disney Archives and published, at $45, by Harry N. Abrams. The text has one defect: it is much too unctuous. Nevertheless the book reveals more clearly than anything written before the intricacy of the collaboration that went on in the studio in its earlier and better years. Finch resurrects from anonymity or near oblivion such artists and animators as Fred Moore, Bill Tytla and the abundantly gifted Albert Hurter, the presiding influence on *Pinocchio*. Hurter's pencil roughs and details exuded an essence of buckeye surrealism that got into gallery art only decades later—and then through Claes Oldenburg, who had himself worked at Disneyland.

But how can one describe the Disney collective's view of fine art? 7
Its taste, ultimately, was Walt's and his was not markedly subtle; he had no pretensions to high culture and if he had been encumbered with such longings the barnyard vitality of early Disney would have been lost. When fine-art quotes appear in Disney's films, they are either apocalyptic and expressionist or else genteel: little in between. Their storehouse is, of course, *Fantasia* (1940). The cold crags and demon-infested clouds of the *Night on Bald Mountain* sequence refer straight back to the hellscapes of late-medieval religious art. Like many another image in *Fantasia*, it is also filtered through Art Deco, the popular style of the '30s. Using Deco idioms was as far as Disney ever went in the direction of classicism, but it would be shaky to suppose he picked up the habit in a museum. By the same token, he may never have heard of Gustav Klimt or even Monet, but another section of *Fantasia*, the *Pastoral*, now looks like a shotgun marriage of the two, with Disney's plump, nippleless nymphs and plow-horse centaurs cavorting around the iridescent blooms and bubbles of a pond in Arcadia.

The appearance of abstract art in Disney's work was fleeting. 8
There was the *Toccata and Fugue* in *Fantasia*, with its pastel runs of animated Kandinsky. Now and then the studio would come up with an image that, while not really abstract, seems a distant reference to early European constructivism like the gush of music drawn as prismatic blocks issuing from the mouth of a dancing horn in *Make Mine Music* (1946). And, more distantly still, some of the Disney fantasies do run parallel to themes of high art, without displaying any awareness of their patrician *Doppelgängers*. The *Isle of Jazz* in *Music Land* (1946) is a brassy plebeian version of an almost archetypal image that in fine art reveals itself in Arnold Böcklin's *Isle of the Dead* and Watteau's *Embarkation for Cythera*: an island as kingdom of mood.

The point at which the flow reversed and Disney's iconography 9
began affecting high art can be identified almost to the frame: it happened when, in *Fantasia*, Mickey Mouse clambered up on the (real) podium and shook hands with the (real) conductor Leopold Stokowski. High and low art collapsed into one another. It was inevitably Mickey

who made Stokowski more of a star by the handshake, not the other way round. The gesture made Pop art possible and, after a gestation of nearly 20 years, it duly arrived in a flurry of mice: Roy Lichtenstein is said to have happened on his comic-strip idiom after his son asked him to prove he was a real artist by drawing a Mickey. Claes Oldenburg—whose obsessive and imperious fantasy about turning the whole environment into one Oldenburg is the closest thing high art has to what Disney World achieves—has based whole series of sculptures, multiples and drawings on the Mouse.

What this fitful leakage across the culture gap meant was set forth   10 by Richard Schickel in *The Disney Version* (1968), a book that is still the best dissection of Disney. "It is the business of art to expand consciousness, while it is the business of mass communication to reduce it. At best this swiftly consummated reduction is to a series of archetypes; at worst it is to a series of simplistic stereotypes." Disney's use of fine-art images usually came down to stereotype, for it worried him not to have things clear-cut. He understood business but not richness, which is why the interiors and garden sequences of the prince's castle in *Cinderella* came out with the nasty polystyrene glamour (twinkledust and all) of the Fontainebleau lobby in Miami Beach.

Since the '50s—since *Bambi* in 1942, some would say—the reduc-   11 tion has gone even further, acting on Disney's earlier work in a steady process of self-cannibalization that increases to the extent that the early Disney is seen as high art. The animals get cuter and more anthropomorphic, the forest glade more compulsively spotless, the characters blander; and having deprived Mickey of his rattishness, Donald Duck of his foul and treacherous temper, the Disney studio had no qualms about ruining *Alice in Wonderland* or Kipling's *Jungle Book* for the kids as well. Yet within the natural bounds of his style, especially up to the late '30s and his masterpiece *Pinocchio*, Disney repeatedly pulled sequences and single images that seem destined to survive as long as the history of cinema itself: the hilarious ballet of hippos, crocodiles and bemused ostrich in *Fantasia*, the terrifying image of little Jiminy Cricket perched on the eyeball of Monstro the Whale in *Pinocchio*, the sight of Dopey with diamonds screwed into his face like monocles, whirling his multiplied eyes within their facets. Such things are the real stuff, and any smart five-year-old can distinguish them from the cyclamate guck of late Disney.

But the specific works are less important than the atmosphere   12 Disney created. Art, or some kinds of it (visionary, surrealist, erotic), has the power to expand the limits of fantasy. Disney could not push those too far without ceasing to be Mr. Clean, the celluloid geneticist who ingeniously bred the anus and genitals out of the animal kingdom, the trusted entertainer whose mandate was to give children the dreams adults like them to have. And so his achievement became a large shift in the limits of unreality, which is not by any means the same thing as art. The shows and puppetry at Disney World, like the recent Disney films, are quite without power to stimulate the imagination. The old symbolism of Carnival is lost and buried; Disney cleaned it up, and in the process illuminated a law that might well bear his name—that when illusion becomes too perfect, one loses interest and instead focuses on the backstage machinery. The real magic of the Magic Kingdom is everything a paying visitor doesn't see: the stupendous technology behind these dinky scaled-down Main Street façades, artificial lakes and unsubmersible Jules Verne submarines on rails. In this, Disney's 50th anniversary year, it appears that the Mouse has labored and brought forth a very odd mountain indeed.

For Discussion and Writing

1 Hughes begins his critique of the Disney aesthetic with a descriptive portrait of Walt Disney World, in Florida. What is the effect of this opening strategy? What is Hughes' apparent attitude toward his material? How does the opening set the tone for the rest of the essay?

2. Hughes evaluates Disney as an example of "the confused feedbacks" (5) between high and mass culture in America. How does Disney's work illustrate such a relationship? What does "this fitful leakage across the culture gap" (10) mean?

3. Hughes calls Disney a "trusted entertainer whose mandate was to give children the dreams adults like them to have" (12). What do you think he means? Is the statement a fair appraisal of the kind of material for which Disney productions are known?

4. We've all grown up with the world Disney created and may find it hard to be objective about that world. As an exercise, though, imagine that you are a visitor from another culture, one unfamiliar with Disney cartoons, movies, or theme parks. Write an essay in which you attempt to describe or make sense of Disney's vision for your friends back home. In an alternate writing idea, take another imaginary world from pop culture, such as television's "The Simpsons," and critique it, looking at its values, characters, themes.

We'll Always Have Casablanca

Lance Morrow

It's still the same old story. The Lisbon plane always descends 1
like a kid's toy landing on the living-room rug. Stick-figure Nazis with
animal faces (Strasser a wolf, his aide a fat little pig in glasses) come
strutting off. That night at Rick's they chorus *Die Wacht am Rhein,* the
stein-swinging bully song that is the Nazis' idea of a good time in a
nightclub. The defiantly answering *Marseillaise* stirs the soul and raises
its Pavlovian goose bumps for the 15th time. They still pronounce "exit
visa" weirdly: "exit vee-zay."

Casablanca is exactly 40 years old. It opened in New York in late fall, 2
1942. At the time, the real Germans were locked around Stalingrad, and
the French scuttled their fleet in Toulon Harbor rather than surrender it
to the Reich. In Hollywood's version, civilization was dressed in an
off-white suit: Victor Laszlo, played by Paul Henreid. Henreid is still
alive. So, for that matter, is Ronald Reagan, whom Jack Warner originally
wanted for the part of Victor. (All wrong, too American, as wholesome
as a quart of milk.) But Humphrey Bogart and Ingrid Bergman and Peter
Lorre and Sydney Greenstreet and Claude Rains and Conrad Veldt are
all dead. The movie they made has achieved a peculiar state of permanence. It has become something more than a classic. It is practically
embedded in the collective American unconscious.

What accounts for the movie's enduring charm? *Casablanca* is, of 3
course, a masterpiece of casting. Not only the leads but the lesser
players as well are perfect, each one a small, vivid miracle of type.
Fetching up their names is an old game for the trivialist: Sam (Dooley
Wilson), the bartender Sascha (Leonid Kinsky), the waiter Carl (S.Z.
Sakall), the jilted Yvonne (Madeleine LeBeau), the Bulgarian couple (Joy
Page and Helmut Dantine), the pickpocket (Curt Bois), the croupier
(Marcel Dalio).

More people know more lines from *Casablanca,* possibly, than from 4
any other movie. They recite the best ones. They splash around in the
sentimentality. They sing along in the way that Churchill used to
rumble the lines of *Hamlet* from his seat in the audience at the Old Vic.
They stooge around: imagine Howard Cosell in the part of Rick Blaine

and recite the lines in Cosellian cadence: "Of all the gin joints in all the towns in all the world, she walks into mine."

The movie is a procession of perfect moments. Its dialogue is an   5
exquisite fusion of the hard-boiled and a shameless, high-cholesterol sentimentality. The lines inspire a laughing, capitulating kind of affection. One cherishes them: *What waters? We're in the desert . . . I was misinformed . . . Was that cannonfire? Or was it my heart pounding? . . . Kiss me! Kiss me as though it were the last time! . . . Play it, Sam. Play As Time Goes By . . . I saved my first drink to have with you . . . Round up the usual suspects . . . We'll always have Paris.* It has inspired bits of business: Sydney Greenstreet bowing graciously to Ingrid Bergman in the Blue Parrot and then with brutal abstraction swatting a fly, which for the instant becomes the moral equivalent of any refugee in *Casablanca.* Or the alltime triumphant moment of literal-minded symbol-banging exposition: Claude Rains dropping the bottle of Vichy Water into a wastebasket and giving it a kick, the charming collaborator virtuous at last.

Casablanca is, among other things, a fable of citizenship and ide-   6
alism, the duties of the private self in the dangerous public world. It is a thoroughly escapist myth about getting politically involved. Perhaps today the escapism overwhelms the idea of commitment. Local TV stations run *Casablanca* on election nights, so that Americans can avoid watching news reports about their democracy in action.

One can concoct mock-academic theories about *Casablanca.* One   7
can lay the sweet thing down on a stainless-steel lab table and dissect it with instruments Freudian or anthropological. A doctoral thesis might be written on the astonishing consumption of alcohol and cigarettes in the movie. At that rate, everyone would have died of cirrhosis and lung cancer by V-E day.

Another paper might examine *Casablanca* as the ultimate rational-   8
ization of, and sublimation of, adultery. One woman, two men. Woman has affair with man not her husband. But wait: it's all right, she thought the husband was dead. And these are desperate times, good and evil are clashing everywhere. A woman can get confused.

It is *poshlost*, as the Russians say, an overheated lunge toward the   9
profound, to think of *Casablanca* in terms of deeper allegory. Still, it is hard to resist delving for Jungian archetypes, primal transactions of the kind that lurk in, say, the Oedipus story (*Here's looking at you, Mom!*). Much of *Casablanca's* constituency is collegiate anyway. Generations of Harvard students have wandered out of the Brattle Theater in a state of sappy exaltation. The movie's audience is too large to be described as a cult, but the religious vibration in that word may be oddly right.

Semioticians, who study the significance of signs and symbols,   10
have discussed *Casablanca* as a myth of sacrifice. One can have fun with that. Consider it this way: America is the Promised Land, the place of safety and redemption. Rick Blaine has been cast out of America, for

some original sin that is as obscure as the one that cost Adam and Eve their Eden. Rick flees to Europe, which is the fallen world where Evil (the Nazis, Satan) is loose. He meets and beds the widow of Idealism. Idealism (meaning Victor) is dead, or thought dead, but it rises from the grave. Rick, losing Ilsa, falls obliviously into despair and selfishness: "I stick my neck out for nobody." He becomes an idiot in the original Greek sense of the word, meaning someone indifferent to his duties as a citizen.

Rick's Café Americain is the state of the stateless. Rick sets himself   11 up as a kind of chieftain or caliph in his isolated, autonomous, amoral fiefdom, where he rules absolutely. Victor and Rick are splintered aspects, it may be, of the same man. Ultimately, the ego rises above mere selfish despair and selfish desire. It is reborn in sacrifice and community: "It doesn't take much to see that the problems of three little people don't amount to a hill o' beans in this crazy world." Idealism and its bride ascend into heaven on the Lisbon plane; Rick goes off in the fog with Louis, men without women, to do mortal work in this world for the higher cause.

About *Casablanca* there clings a quality of lovely, urgent innocence.   12 Those who cherish the movie may be nostalgic for moral clarity, for a war in which good and evil were obvious and choices tenable. They may be nostalgic for a long-lost connection between the private conscience and the public world. *Casablanca* was released three years before the real moment of the fall of the modern world: 1945. That year, the side of good dropped nuclear bombs on cities full of civilians, and the world discovered Auschwitz. We have not yet developed the myths with which to explain such matters.

For Discussion and Writing

1. In praising *Casablanca*, Morrow claims that the film has become "practically embedded in the collective American unconscious" (2). What reasons does he give to support this assertion?
2. Morrow cites a number of possible interpretations of the *Casablanca* story. What are these? If you know the film, which interpretation seems closest to the mark? Would you offer your own?
3. In what way, according to Morrow, is *Casablanca* a film about idealism and innocence?
4. Write an essay in which you either praise or fault a popular film (classic or recent). If possible, view the movie again before writing about it, paying careful attention to its elements of casting, dialogue, dramatic effect, specific scenes or moments, storyline, film technique, special effects, soundtrack and so on. In your essay, try to be as specific as possible in supporting your critical position with evidence from the film.

The Triumph of Pap Culture

Frank Trippett

Summertime is the season for sanctioned cultural slumming, or 1
so holds a seldom examined article of American folklore. The basic
notion is hinted at by language that appears all the time in cultural
journalism—"summer entertainment," "summer movies," "summer
reading." Such phrases suggest that it is all right for respectable Americans to indulge their appetites for cultural cotton candies when it is too
hot to digest quality stuff. Anybody caught at the beach reading something other than Proust or Nabokov is thus assured of amnesty.

The folklore is sound as far as it goes, but it does not go nearly far 2
enough. Cultural slumming is certainly big in the summer, but nowadays it hardly lets up in the fall, winter and spring either. The American
craving for cultural junk has become a yen for all seasons. Book buyers
did not wait until summer to turn *Miss Piggy's Guide to Life* and *101 Uses
for a Dead Cat* (ugh!) into bestsellers, and disc jockeys will not stop
broadcasting "easy listening" schmaltz when autumn arrives. The rush
for fatuous books on diets and moneymaking never lets up, and of the
endless boom in frothy tales like Harlequin Books and Silhouette Romances, Book Marketing Executive Kay Sexton of Chicago says: "People are absolutely addicted."

In fact, pop (for popular) culture has become—to borrow the word 3
that means childish, meatless mush—mostly pap culture, a.k.a. trash,
kitsch and schlock. In the ten alltime top moneymaking movies, most
of fairly recent vintage, the pap quotient is stunning; the list includes:
*Star Wars, Jaws, The Empire Strikes Back, Grease, The Exorcist, The Godfa-
ther, Superman* and *The Sting.* The same is true of the very hottest novels
(among them: *The Godfather, The Exorcist, Jaws, Jonathan Livingston
Seagull* and *Love Story*) and of the top nonfiction books of the past ten
years (*The Late Great Planet Earth, Chariots of the Gods, Your Erroneous
Zones, The Joy of Sex*). And almost everybody knows the pap quotient
of television: *Hee Haw* is still going strong.

Though the prevalence of lightweight cultural matter may not be 4
surprising, its universal acceptance is nonetheless striking. Two decades ago, the priests of high culture railed at the possible harm to mind,
spirit and aesthetics that might result from the proliferation of junky

cultural works—"Masscult," to use the sinister word that Critic Dwight Macdonald put on the lot of it. Said Macdonald: "It is not just unsuccessful art. It is non-art. It is even anti-art." Now cultural pap is bigger than ever, but the champions of high culture seldom bother to protest any more. Pap has triumphed as an American staple, and now so abounds that it tends to be noticed, like the air, only when it contains some particularly noxious pollutants.

Pop pap, to be sure, draws occasional fire. A new film version of *Tarzan, the Ape Man* opened last week to great volleys of critical derision and scorn. And rightly so, since this version of *Tarzan*—directed by John Derek and starring his wife Bo Derek as Jane—spoils a perfectly good pap yarn by trying to transform it from a juvenile adventure story into a piece of erotica. In contrast, the hottest new "summer" movie, *Raiders of the Lost Ark*, has won loud applause from most critics and all audiences because it does precisely what pap is supposed to do. *Raiders*, a compilation of cliff-hanging adventures of the sort formerly featured in weekly movie serials, is designed to appeal to the child—even the child in the adult spectator.

By definition, cultural pap plays to the child in everybody. It can offer only entertainment, diversion, maybe distraction, without any promise of redeeming cultural value. When a work offers more—exaltation or the possibility of elaborate aesthetic responses—it has ceased to be pap; it verges on becoming art. Unlike art, pap is easy to absorb, which is precisely why it is perennially popular—and not only in low places. Dwight Eisenhower relished his Zane Grey westerns just as Ronald Reagan relishes such epics by Poet Robert Service as —*The Shooting of Dan McGrew* and *The Cremation of Sam McGee.* John Kennedy enjoyed Ian Fleming's James Bond yarns, and Lyndon Johnson found it nice to have Muzak piped into the White House. And why not? Pap, though bipartisan, is inherently democratic.

Yet pap has its standards, and they are often as elusive and controversial as those of high culture. "Someone's kitsch is somebody else's masterpiece," says Film Critic Vincent Canby. Author Judith Krantz alluded to the book *Alien,* when it had the nerve to knock her own kitschy *Scruples* out of top spot on the bestseller list, as "a 270-page piece of schlock." Every piece of pap has its own critics and partisans, as every consumer of the product realizes sooner or later. Humorist Russell Baker is not being merely funny when he writes: "I am a glutton for trash. I love it in almost all forms except television. I can race through two or three smutty novels and a half-dozen gossip magazines and hear the Top 40 playing on the stereo in the background while the television viewer is wasting three hours and getting nothing but the tepid, watered-down stuff afforded by three or four sitcoms and an evening soap opera."

Clearly, the U.S. has evolved a special pap-culture aesthetic. Some- 8
times it is as intricate as the aesthetic theory that Litterateur D.B.
Wyndham Lewis applied to poetry. "There is bad Bad Verse and good
Bad Verse," said Lewis, and a great many Americans now say pretty
much the same thing about pap. In fact, the devotees of good bad pap,
particularly in the film form, add up to a subculture within the pop-pap
culture. This fact has even given rise recently to commercial festivals of
bad movies featuring films like *The Terror of Tiny Town,* a 1938 western
with a cast of midgets. Books like *The Golden Turkey Awards* (1980) and
The Fifty Worst Films of All Time sell tens of thousands of copies. The *Dial*
magazine earlier this year offered an article titled "Five Great Bad
Movies." Author John Malone discussed *Duel in the Sun, Elephant Walk,
The Naked Jungle, The Rains of Ranchipur* and *Legend of the Lost,* and
ventured guidance on how to tell a good bad movie from a bad bad
movie. Says Malone: "A great bad movie must be in color."

Actually, despite all the intricate aesthetic distinction, good bad 9
pap appeals to some whimsical people for the same reason that simple
good pap appeals to others: entirely as a source of fun. Many observers
fear that the explosion of pap in the media-ridden 20th century might
harm society's more serious culture. So far, as Sociologist Herbert Gans
points out in *Popular Culture and High Culture,* there has been no evidence to support such worries. Ultimately, pap is an annoyance and a
hazard only to those who take it seriously—which, perhaps significantly, seldom includes those who enjoy it.

For Discussion and Writing

1. In the first two paragraphs, Trippett uses several insulting terms to
   describe pop culture: cultural slumming, cultural cotton candies, cultural junk. How does he support such a negative characterization of
   mass entertainment?
2. What, according to Trippett, is the chief difference between art and pap?
   What is pap's central appeal?
3. What is Trippett's final assessment of pop culture's significance? Does
   his conclusion seem consistent with his opening remarks?
4. Using examples of pop culture with which you're familiar (day- or
   primetime TV, movies, romance or adventure fiction, comic books, and
   so on) write either in defense of or against the values such material
   seems to embody. Some examples: portrayals of violence, relations
   between men and women, children, heroism, status or materialism.

Thinking and Writing about Chapter 3

1. Though two of the three essays here are generally against pop culture, even Hughes and Trippett have something good to say about it. How does Hughes praise Disney? What virtue does Trippett see in mass art? Does Morrow have anything negative to say about *Casablanca*?
2. Compare and contrast the authors' prose styles and attitudes in these three essays. Which of the three is the most disdainful of pop culture? Which writers use humor to balance their critiques?
3. Compile a list of recent or classic pop culture artifacts, grouped according to the best and worst among them. What standards will you use to evaluate these works? What makes for quality popular art or culture, and what makes for junk? Write an essay setting forth your ideas, supported by your examples.

4

TV: The Medium and the Message

While television as a technology dates back to the early decades of the 20th century, as a cultural force it did not come into its own until it displaced radio, in the late 1940s and early 1950s, as the principal medium of mass entertainment. With the growth of the first broadcast networks, the expansion of the programing day (until now, when television is a continuous, pervasive presence), and the financing of the industry through paid advertising, television has become the most influential of all media. It provides us with the news, helps to set the national political agenda, reflects the styles and manners of the day, and, through its ceaseless commercialism, bombards us with an endless stream of images and exhortations to consume every imaginable product generated by the world economy.

But do we really see what television is showing us? What messages, if any, lie behind the dazzling electronic surface?

In the essays in this chapter, *Time* writers take a critical look at television and its implications for our society. In "Is There Intelligent Life on Commercials?," from April 1973, Stefan Kanfer writes as a visitor from outer space, trying to understand the strange nature of TV advertising. In "The Politics of the Box Populi," from June 1979, Lance Morrow analyzes television's cultural significance. And in "History? Education? Zap! Pow! Cut!," from May 1990, Pico Iyer considers the "postliterate" world the medium may be helping to create.

Is There Intelligent Life on Commercials?

Stefan Kanfer

TO: ZB*33 + X
FROM: 45 = K29-$\frac{1}{4}$
RE: EXPLORATION OF MINOR PLANET

We had intended to observe this little ball "RTH" for a longer   1
period. But we developed engine trouble over Omega, and by the time
we entered orbit, we were only getting six light-years to the gallon. In
our brief visit, however, we discovered what generates those high-
frequency signals that have been jamming our radio telescopes. It is a
small box called TEEVEE, present in nearly every dwelling in the YEW-
ESS, a small land area between two oceans.

TEEVEE is the display window of the national store. Its merchan-   2
dise, like all valuable goods, is displayed against a plush but vapid
background. This background is called PROGRAMMING and is of no
importance. The key elements of the broadcast day (and night) are
called SPOTZ. These SPOTZ are 30 seconds to 60 seconds long and cost
their manufacturers about $500 per second. Programs, by contrast, cost
$50 per second.

From observing SPOTZ we are able to report the following con-   3
clusions:

- The YEWESS is a vastly troubled land, emerging from a com-   4
plex, ambiguous struggle against an implacable foe. The name
of this enemy is WETNESS. New scientific weapons, however,
go on like a powder and give unprecedented protection. Thus,
for the first time in this soul-searing conflict, there is the fragile
promise of peace.

- To amuse themselves YEWESSERS also sing and dance. To this   5
end, the SPOTZ, which are also called commercials, sell them
an entertainment called NOSTALJYA. According to the an-

45

nouncements, the top numbers for 1973 include *The Hut-Sut Song, Moonlight Serenade* and *The Woodpecker Song.* The year's most highly regarded artists are the Andrews Sisters and Snooky Lanson, singers; Sammy Kaye and Glenn Miller, bandleaders; and Woody Woodpecker, a bird.

- These ingenious people are bothered by many plagues. When   6
the distress appears, the person moves in ten quick, jerky motions and booms: "No headache is going to make me yell at my son [or daughter]." Thereupon the victim takes a miraculous white tablet, which dissolves in the stomach faster than another tablet. Just 3.1 seconds later, this incredible pill enables the victim to change his outlook and handle the most difficult household chores with ease. Other tablets simultaneously drain all eight sinus cavities, rearrange the background music and style the hair in 3.2 seconds.

- If pain persists or recurs, YEWESSERS always see a physician.   7

- YEWESSERS are of various hues, but mix freely with no trouble   8
whatsoever. In every SPOT involving the young, there is a ratio of 1.5 black children to 4.9 white ones. Their smiles are constant and blinding. At adult cocktail parties, the commercial ratio is 2.2 black couples to 6.8 white. They smile with equal candlepower.

- Some YEWESSERS dwell in apartments, where they live on   9
either side of a flimsy medicine cabinet. All others live in white split-level houses. The males are cranky in the morning and astonished when the coffee is not bitter or the breakfast is palatable. Then they beam and demand to know the name of the product, which they repeat nine times. The wives then proceed to their day, which consists of eight hours of unmitigated jealousy and fear. The jealousy is exhibited at wash time. During this period they stare enviously at their neighbor's laundry, which is always whiter—and the colored things brighter—than their own. With wide eyes, they then proceed to learn a series of mysterious monosyllables, among them Biz, Fab, Cheer, Dash, All and Bold. They do not exhibit fear until nightfall, or on weekend afternoons. At these points the MOTHER-IN-LAW arrives for a white-glove inspection of the home. This includes a revealing scrutiny of the kitchen (with its telltale odors), the male's collar (with its inevitable ring) and the salad (too vinegary). On the next visit, 3.8 seconds later, all is perfection, thanks to the intervention of a remarkable product that scents the air, sanitizes the collar, emulsifies the dressing, rearranges the background music and restyles everyone's hair.

- Children are encouraged to visit their father's place of business. 10 There they interrupt proceedings with a ritual cry: "Only one cavity!" Children may also be seen in the early morning, when they ingest the seven essential vitamins every child needs for perfect health. Toward evening they grow pale and cough until a powerful potion brings speedy relief.

- YEWESSERS each chew 180 lbs. of gum a year. This was de- 11 duced from the size of the gum package (roughly 3 ft. in length).

- All YEWESS pets are fussy but highly literate eaters who metic- 12 ulously examine the labels of their canned food before dining.

- YEWESSERS sing while eating and drinking. The song is usu- 13 ally an apostrophe to hamburger or a dithyramb dedicated to cola, uncola or the beverage the citizens are forbidden to quaff on-camera: beer.

- After the singing and eating, the YEWESSERS are remorseful 14 and repair to salons, where they shed unsightly pounds and inches with the aid of wonder-working machines.

- An elaborate etiquette prevails at supermarkets. Consumers are 15 encouraged to squeeze the white bread and forbidden to squeeze toilet tissue. They are also urged to look for chickens by name, beef by price and coffee by reputation.

- All waitresses, dishwashers and plumbers supplement their 16 incomes by peddling products to customers. These products range from paper towels to soaps, and are invariably superior to the leading brand.

- The YEWESS is really two nations. Citizens of one prefer the 17 Pink Pad; citizens of the other buy the Blue one.

- The automobile is the greatest friend nature ever had. Cars are 18 affectionately named for animals (cougar, mustang, falcon, impala); gasolines keep engines clean; and there are seldom more than three vehicles on the road at any time.

19

At this point in the time-space continuum, we found it necessary to re-enter the intergalactic void for our millennial tune-up. As for your query: Is there intelligent life on RTH? Having peered at length at the little windows, our answer must be negative. How about a visit to Jpiter? The only SPOTZ there are the ones caused by meteors.

For Discussion and Writing

1. In his essay, Kanfer adopts what is sometimes called an anthropological perspective—that is, he looks at something familiar through alien eyes. Why does he use such a strategy? What does he gain by it?
2. Kanfer's attitude is playful, satirical. What does he seem to be saying about the society reflected in the commercials he mocks?
3. Although Kanfer was writing in 1973, nearly twenty years ago, much of what he implies about TV commercial style and content still holds true. Can you cite examples of current TV ads that parallel the ones he mocks? How are television advertising styles different today?
4. Write your own satirical or serious treatment of current television commercials. What do you notice about the way ads are made, about the way characters are portrayed, about the kinds of values and preoccupations people seem to display in such advertising?

The Politics of the Box Populi

Lance Morrow

No one has ever decided what television is really supposed to be *for*. Is the wondrous box meant to entertain? To elevate? To instruct? To anesthetize? The medium, in its sheer unknowable possibilities, seems to arouse extreme reactions: contempt for its banal condition as the ghetto of the sitcom, or else grandiose metaphysical ambitions for a global village. The tube is Caliban and Prospero, cretin and magician. "What makes television so frightening," writes Critic Jeff Greenfield, "is that it performs all the functions that used to be scattered among different sources of information and entertainment." Television could, if we let it, electronically consolidate all of our culture—theater, ballet, concerts, newspapers, magazines and possibly most conversation. It is a medium of eerie and disconcerting power; one college professor conducted a two-year study that asked children aged four to six: "Which do you like better, TV or Daddy?" Forty-four percent of the kids said that they preferred television. 1

An old question keeps recurring: Who should control so pervasive a force? A Civil Rights Commission report last winter on the role of minorities on television complained that women, blacks and others, including Hispanics, Pacific Island Americans, American Indians and even Alaskan natives are underrepresented in or virtually absent from TV dramas. Composed in a spirit of bureaucratic pedantry, the report suggested that the Federal Communications Commission should lean on the networks a bit by formulating rules that would "encourage greater diversity." 2

The argument is simplest if it turns on TV purely as entertainment, with no intent larger than diversion. On that basis, the laissez-faire system of the ratings possesses absolute logic: the people decide, voting with their channel selectors. What works as diversion will presumably be highest rated and therefore most successful. But there is a fallacy here: a laissez-faire principle of rule by ratings would be admirable if a wide variety of choices existed. Too many network shows are devoted almost entirely to exploring new dimensions of imbecility. That seems an old and boringly elitist criticism of TV, but it acquires fresh force, 3 even urgency, if one sits through a few hours of *Supertrain, The Ropers* and *The $1.98 Beauty Show.*

Television drama—leaving aside the question of TV news, whose   4
effects are a different phenomenon altogether—becomes more complicated when it is considered as a medium of persuasion, the little
electronic proscenium alive with potentially sinister ideological glints.
In years past, American TV has been considered a moderately conservative influence. From the suburban complacencies of Ozzie and Har-
riet through the vanishing six-gun authority of Sheriff Matt Dillon, TV
entertainment seemed an elaborate gloss on the status quo.

A sometime television writer, Ben Stein, claims, on the contrary,   5
to see in TV entertainment an infestation of liberal chic. In *The View from
Sunset Boulevard,* Stein argues that, each night in its prime-time sitcom
diet, the vast American TV audience receives near lethal doses of
liberalism from a small band of some 200 Hollywood writers and
producers, who exercise a preposterously disproportionate influence in
TV's almost subliminal channels of opinion making.

The message of this liberal chic, according to Stein, is, among other   6
things both antibusiness and antimilitary. The thrust of CBS's top-rated
M*A*S*H, for example, is that the Army is constantly trying to get as
many people killed as possible, to burn down villages, to separate loved
ones. Small towns fare badly on the tube, according to Stein. The *Bad
Day at Black Rock* syndrome applies: repeated episodes of peaceful,
postcard towns in which something terribly evil is afoot.

Despite this interpretation, most programs obey no pat formula.   7
Battlestar Galactica, for example, seems to teach a rigorously militaristic
sort of watchfulness; the peacemakers tend to be soft fools with good
intentions. On the durable detective show *Hawaii Five-0,* the hero Mc-
Garrett exhibits some of J. Edgar Hoover's least attractive qualities.
Many shows are almost entirely innocent of meaning: What is the
political content of *Mork & Mindy*? What can the bizarre *Incredible Hulk*
signify except perhaps an adolescent's fantasies of puissance and rage?

In fact, it would be extremely difficult for a Sunset Boulevard   8
conspiracy to retail a coherent party line even if it wished. Says Michael
Jay Robinson, a political scientist at Washington's Catholic University:
"Programming is really a sausage—created by grinding together the
values of the producers, a few dozen formula plots, network perceptions about audience, and the implied guidelines given by the censors,
affiliates, FCC and even the National Association of Broadcasters. And,
obviously, the ratings." The National PTA exerts a heavy influence
against violence. Since kids so often control the dial, the low audience
age dictates a certain level of abject foolishness.

. . .

The operating politics of television has an unexpected subtlety.   9
Through the mid- and late '70s, a procession of shows like *All in the Family, Maude, Three's Company* and *Laverne & Shirley* has promoted a progressive, permissive, liberalized attitude toward such previously untouchable subjects as premarital sex and homosexuality. But, as Robinson suggests, a complex crisscross may have occurred: while television may indeed have coaxed Americans to shift leftward in social matters, the nation seems at the same time to have moved a bit to the right politically. These movements aside, it may well be that television's greatest consequence has been to impart sheer velocity to ideas and fads. From antiwar protests to disco dancing, such trends tend to start on the coasts and then get transfused with astonishing speed into the life of the heartland between. TV thus serves to obliterate regional and local distinctions, to create national social values.

This powerful national theater does not often rise to its responsi-   10
bilities. A certain grotesque *Gong Show* brand of schlock-peddling could be forgiven if it were not for the stupefying dimensions of the American TV habit. The average household's TV set runs six hours a day. Although television does useful service in informing and entertaining, its strange power is bound to arouse a great deal of spiritual disquiet. People may expect too much of TV. It will never replace the printed word as an instrument of thought. Its entertainment side may ultimately be rescued from mediocrity by technological diversifications into cable TV, video-tape recorders, video disc and other elaborate equipment. The new technology will bring a greater selection—and thus a wider, though more personal, choice—to the audience. It is possible, of course, that this could mean that a public already besotted with the tube might become even further enslaved by it.

For Discussion and Writing

1. Morrow defines the politics of television, its subtle or unstated influences or messages. What does he say these are? Do you think it makes sense to speak of TV as a single thing, or should its apparent diversity be a factor in any analysis? Is there "good" or "bad" TV?
2. The fact that many of Morrow's illustrations are dated, more than a decade old, helps confirm one of his essential points: that TV speeds up the spread, and thus the wearing out, of ideas and fads. Cite several recent trends in TV programming—fads that have already burned out, and directions that seem to have a future.
3. At the close of his essay, Morrow speculates that new technologies (cable, VCRs, and so on) may further enslave television viewers. To what extent do you consider yourself enslaved by TV? What role does

television play in your life? Do you use it for specific purposes—or does it use you?

4. Write a supportive or negative critique of television as a social or cultural influence. To what extent does it add to or detract from our lives as individuals and members of families and communities? Is TV a medium of "eerie and disconcerting power" or, as one critic, Newton Minow, said some thirty years ago, a "vast wasteland"?

History? Education? Zap! Pow! Cut!

PICO IYER

In his new novel, *Vineland*, Thomas Pynchon, that disembodied 1
know-it-all hiding out somewhere inside our nervous system, performs
an eerie kind of magic realism on the McLuhanite world around us. His
is an America, in 1984, in which reflexes, values, even feelings have been
programmed by that All-Seeing Deity known as the Tube. Remaking us
in its own image (every seven days), TV consumes us much more than
we do it. Lovers woo one another on screens, interface with friends, cite
TV sets as corespondents in divorce trials. And the children who have
grown up goggle-eyed around the electric altar cannot believe that
anything is real unless it comes with a laugh track: they organize their
emotions around commercial breaks and hope to heal their sorrows
with a PAUSE button. Watching their parents fight, they sit back and wait
in silence for the credits. History for them means syndication; ancient
history, the original version of *The Brady Bunch*.

All this would sound crazy to anyone who didn't know that it was 2
largely true. As the world has accelerated to the fax and satellite speed
of light, attention spans have shortened, and dimension has given way
to speed. A whole new aesthetic—the catchy, rapid-fire flash of images—is being born. Advertising, the language of the quick cut and the
zap, has quite literally set the pace, but Presidents, preachers, even
teachers have not been slow to get the message. Thus ideas become
slogans, and issues sound bites. Op-ed turns into photo op. Politics
becomes telegenics. And all of us find that we are creatures of the screen.
The average American, by age 40, has seen more than a million television commercials; small wonder that the very rhythm and texture of his
mind are radically different from his grandfather's.

Increasingly, in fact, televisionaries are telling us to read the 3
writing on the screen and accept that ours is a postliterate world. A new
generation of children is growing up, they say, with a new, highly visual
kind of imagination, and it is our obligation to speak to them in terms
they understand. MTV, *USA Today*, the PC and the VCR—why, the acronym
itself!—are making the slow motion of words as obsolete as picto-
graphs. The PLAY button's the thing. Writing in the New York *Times* not
long ago, Robert W. Pittman, the developer of MTV, pointed out just how

much the media have already adjusted to the music-video aesthetic he helped create. In newspapers, "graphs, charts and larger-than-ever pictures tell the big story at a glance. Today's movie scripts are some 25% shorter than those of the 1940s for the same length movies." Even TV is cutting back, providing more news stories on every broadcast and less material in each one.

There is, of course, some value to this. New ages need new forms, and addressing today's young in sentences of Jamesian complexity would be about as helpful as talking to them in Middle English. Rhetoric, in any case, is no less manipulative than technology, and no less formulaic. Though TV is a drug, it can be stimulant as well as sedative. And the culture that seems to be taking over the future is a culture so advanced in imagemaking that it advertises its new sports cars with two-page photographs of rocks (though the Japanese, perhaps, enjoy an advantage over us insofar as their partly ideogrammatic language encourages them to think in terms of images: haiku are the music videos of the printed word). Nor would this be the first time that technology has changed the very way we speak: the invention of typography alone, as Neil Postman writes, "created prose but made poetry into an exotic and elitist form of expression." No less a media figure than Karl Marx once pointed out that the *Iliad* would not have been composed the way it was after the invention of the printing press.

Yet none of this is enough to suggest that we should simply burn our books and flood the classroom with TV monitors. Just because an infant cannot speak, we do not talk to him entirely in "goos" and "aahs"; rather, we coax him, gradually, into speech, and then into higher and more complex speech. That, in fact, is the definition of education: to draw out, to teach children not what they know but what they do not know; to rescue them, as Cicero had it, from the tyranny of the present. The problem with visuals is not just that they bombard us with images and information only of a user-friendly kind but also that they give us no help in telling image from illusion, information from real wisdom. Reducing everything to one dimension, they prepare us for everything except our daily lives. Nintendo, unlike stickball, leaves one unschooled in surprise; TV, unlike books, tells us when to stop and think. "The flow of messages from the instant everywhere," as Daniel Boorstin points out, "fills every niche in our consciousness, crowding out knowledge and understanding. For while knowledge is steady and cumulative, information is random and miscellaneous." A consciousness born primarily of visuals can come terrifyingly close to that of the tape-recorder novels of the vid kids' most successful voice, Bret Easton Ellis, in which everyone's a speed freak and relationships last about as long as videos. Life, you might say, by remote control.

If today's computer-literate young truly do have the capacity to process images faster than their parents, they enjoy an unparalleled opportunity—so long as they learn to process words as well. They could become the first generation in history to be bilingual, in this sense, fluent onscreen as well as off. We need not, when we learn to talk, forget to communicate in other ways. But only words can teach the use of words, and ideas beget ideas. So just as certain tribes must be taught how to read a TV set, we must be taught how to read the world outside the TV set. Much better, then, to speak up than down, especially when speech itself is threatened. Nobody ever said that thinking need be binary. Nobody, that is, except, perhaps, a computer.

For Discussion and Writing

1. Iyer begins his essay with a reference to author Thomas Pynchon's description of TV as an "All-Seeing Deity" that controls its mindless viewers, and Iyer says that the characterization is "largely true" (2). Do you agree? Why or why not? How would you defend TV against the claim that it turns its audience into passive, "goggle-eyed" zombies?
2. According to Iyer, although TV may be justified as a new form for a new age, visual images have at least one serious drawback. What is this, and what does Iyer claim it may lead to?
3. Iyer implies that in a postliterate world, people care less about words and have a harder time mastering language and ideas. In your own experience, has the presence of TV helped or hindered your appreciation of spoken and written language? What positive effects has TV had on you, and how may it have damaged your education or personal growth?
4. Write an essay in which you defend or attack this proposition: Primary and secondary education should help teach children to become "TV literate"—that is, to understand how visual media work, how programmers and advertisers use TV to influence viewing and consumer behavior, and how viewers can learn to control their own viewing habits.

Thinking and Writing about Chapter 4

1. Comparing the descriptions of TV in Morrow's and Iyer's essays, how has the medium changed between the 1970s and the 1990s? What new elements or styles distinguish it from those of earlier years? (Think, for example, of the older shows or commercials you may have seen in reruns on various cable channels. How do they seem different from today's programming in style, pace or technique?)

2. Do you think that the writers and producers of TV shows and commercials have a certain political perspective (liberal, independent, conservative) that they're trying to push? Which shows or commercials, if any, attempt to appeal to political attitudes? Which ones seem utterly without political slants?

3. Write an essay under the title "A Guide to Intelligent TV Viewing." If you were to give advice to someone trying to bring a TV habit under control, or trying to find the best that TV had to offer, what would you say? Is it possible to be selective and intelligent in one's use of TV, or is that somehow a contradiction in terms?

5

The Joys of Books

What you hold in your hand is a book—one of many billions in existence throughout the world. But what is a book? What do books really mean to us? Certainly many of us take them for granted, hardly noticing what a remarkable and sometimes magical invention they are. Books have many purposes, from the lowly to the exalted, and they are fated to varying degrees of permanence or oblivion. But few would deny that the *idea* of books is central to the way we organize our knowledge of the world and convey it to others, whether those books be instructive, speculative, imaginary, transient or timeless.

Education would be impossible without books, as would the development of civilization. It was writing, after all, that put human history on the map.

In this chapter's essays, three writers consider the value of literary study and pleasure, the meaning of books in our lives. In "The Odd Pursuit of Teaching Books," from March 1983, Roger Rosenblatt investigates the sometimes mysterious role of the teacher in making books live in the minds of students. In "A Holocaust of Words," from May 1988, Lance Morrow expresses his view that the values and pleasures books provide us are unique and irreplaceable. And in "Private Eye, Public Conscience," from December 1988, Pico Iyer gives an affectionate appreciation of detective novelist and screenwriter Raymond Chandler.

The Odd Pursuit of Teaching Books

ROGER ROSENBLATT

Douglas Bush died on March 2 at the age of 86, after 46 years as   1
professor of English literature at Harvard and a life of devotion to
Paradise Lost. The obituary in the New York *Times* made him out a gentle
crank, quoting a complaint of Bush's that too many students attend
universities these days, and thus cannot be adequately educated—the
sort of hackneyed wail that Bush himself would never have dwelt on
or even considered right plucked from a greater, kindlier context.
Bush's world was the greater, kindlier context. Like Samuel Johnson he
knew everything worth knowing. Like Johnson, too, he was born to
teach books. Few people are. It is an odd pursuit. Literary study stands
at the center of modern education, but when one tries to determine what
happens in the relationship among book, student and teacher, the
teacher grows shadowy, eventually vanishes.

Of course, teachers of every subject suffer from obsolescence, that   2
being almost a tool of the trade if one's students are to build on what
they learn, even to the point of rejecting it at the onset of independent
thinking. Good teachers yearn to be obliterated. Good teachers of
literature have little choice in the matter. The *Hamlet* they pry open for
the 19-year-old will not be the *Hamlet* that student reads at age 50. The
play will have changed because the reader's experience will have recast
it—the noble, tormented boy of one's youth reappearing in middle age
as something of a drip.

But even at the moment that a teacher of literature is doing his job,   3
the work is hard to put a name to. What precisely is it that you did,
Professor Bush? Every teacher knows the boredom and terror of that
question. A teacher of French teaches French, a teacher of piano, piano.
But a teacher of Proust, Austen, Donne, Faulkner, Joyce? Are not the
writers the teachers themselves? Oh, one can see the need for a tour
guide now and then: notes, terms, some scraps of biography. But surely
the great books were written for people, and if they require the presence
of middlemen, then they could never have been so great in the first
place. So goes the cant.

In point of plain fact, a teacher of literature may do several quite   4
different things, especially these days when universities house their

own schools of thought on the subject. Some teach the formal aspects of literature, some the sociology of literature, some the politics. There are those who teach because literature tells them what it means to be human; others who hold that literature means whatever one wishes it to mean; still others who say it means nothing at all. Defenders of each fort sometimes make the newspapers, where, in argument with one another, they sound like crazed religious warriors. In a sense, the answer to "What do you do?" is "This and that." And it may be that just as there are books and books, so are there various ways of apprehending them, and thus no core of the subject to teach.

Still, something central seems to be conveyed in the teaching of   5
literature beyond a particular point of view, something in the attitude of the teacher toward both his students and the books: his concentration, his appreciation, occasionally his awe. Awe can be a powerful pedagogical instrument, the sight of someone overwhelmed overwhelming by refraction. True, the relationship of teacher to the work of art is that of a middleman, but in the best circumstances the middleman becomes a magnifying glass ("Do you see *this*?"). Instead of intruding between Yeats and his reader, he shows Yeats in the light, reveals not only poetry but how poetry comprehends the world, thus lending his students the eyes of the poet. At full strength, the teacher is an artist himself, and not just for restorations. Treating the book as an event, he manipulates it the way the writer manipulated reality, making of literature what the writer made of life.

Curiously, this high point is precisely where the question of the   6
teacher's usefulness sometimes turns bitter. A book says something ennobling; a teacher makes that clear. It ought to follow that students are ennobled, but the opposite often occurs. In his essay "Humane Literacy," George Steiner brooded, "We know that some of the men who devised and administered Auschwitz had been taught to read Shakespeare or Goethe, and continued to do so. This compels us to ask whether knowledge of the best that had been thought and said does, as Matthew Arnold asserted, broaden and refine the resources of the human spirit." One might wonder why a teacher of literature should worry about being unable to regulate moral actions, when no such self-recrimination haunts the teacher of, say, physics. But a work of literature, unlike a physical law, has moral content to begin with, and the teacher's inability to transfer that content may seem either a failure of his own understanding or a basic flaw of the craft.

What concerns such a teacher, the scrupulous teacher, is that he is   7
dealing solely with words—the words of others, which are not his property, and his own words in their behalf. The matter is abstract, thus unnerving. Every word is an idea, and that may offer consolation or encouragement. But ideas are also merely represented by words, and

when the teacher, who is the purveyor and curator of words, strides into the classroom and spills the words on his desk, he has no control over them, no way to enforce intelligence, charity, love, wit, or any of the elements of which the books he values are made.

So what is it he does in that mysterious classroom when the thick 8 wood door shuts behind him and the rows of too young faces turn and rise like heliotropic plants, eager for a sign? "Today we consider Kafka." Is that in fact what "we" are considering today? Or are we considering the teacher considering Kafka, and if that is the case, what exactly is to be considered—the learned scholar stocked deep with information about "irony" and "metaphor," or the still deeper mind, which has confronted Kafka alone in a private dark, and which Kafka has confronted in turn? "How does one say that [D.H.] Lawrence is right in his great rage against the modern emotions, unless one speaks from the intimacies of one's own feelings, and one's own sense of life, and one's own worked-for way of being?" asked Lionel Trilling. The testimony is always personal. Behind the spectacles and the fuzzy coat, the teacher teaches himself.

In the end it may come to a matter of character. John Ruskin said 9 that only a good man can make a good artist, but that notion is disproved all the time. Good teaching, however, is another matter. No one knows how virtuous a person Milton was, but the speculation becomes irrelevant when applied to *Paradise Lost*, which, like every work of art, assumed a life of its own as soon as it was finished. The writer let it go. But the teacher of *Paradise Lost* cannot let it go; he becomes its life. Whether he sees the work as a brilliant display of versification or as the story of man's fall from grace, the poem is a sacred text, the source of his intellectual or moral faith. His students thus behold the poem and the faith together, and are bound to like *Paradise Lost* in part because they admire his strength of belief.

This faith in literature cannot be easy to acquire. A teacher of books 10 must learn to live before becoming good at his work, since literature demands that one know a great deal about life—not to have settled life's problems, but at least to recognize and accept the wide, frail world in which those problems have a home. The achievement of such perspective involves a penalty too. He who has gained that generous view inevitably moderates the books in his charge, domesticates their subversiveness, puts out the fire. As moderator he becomes a caricature, as teachers of English in fiction are always portrayed as caricatures. Who's afraid of Virginia Woolf's professor? The practice of giving apples to teachers may have originated as an unconscious mockery of their lack of experience and danger, of their apparent refusal to risk the loss of paradise.

And yet the power they generate can be enormous. Remember?   11
One may not know exactly what happens in those classrooms, but one
knows that it did happen, long after the fact, after all the classrooms
and the schools are left behind. Two, perhaps three, teachers in a lifetime
stick in the mind, and one of them is almost always a teacher of
literature. He remains not as presiding deity but as a person, someone
impassioned about words on paper. Perhaps he knows that words are
all we have, all that stand between ourselves and our destruction. The
teacher also intervenes. Robert Hollander Jr. of Princeton described a
class of R.P. Blackmur's, who taught Hollander the Dante he now
teaches others: "The lecture gasped, tottered and finally settled ruin-
ously into total silence. He stood there, I thought, debating whether or
not to chuck it all up, leave the room (with 20 minutes still to run before
the bell), perhaps even to leave the earth." Danger enough.

Courage too, of a sort. Who but a teacher of books dares claim as   12
his province the entire range of human experience, intuition no less than
fact? Who else has the nerve? And what does he do with this vast
territory he has staked out for himself? He invites us in, says in effect
there has never been anything written, thought or felt that one need be
afraid to confront. A teacher of books may favor this or that author or
century, but fundamentally his work is the antithesis of prejudice. Take
it all, he urges; the vicious with the gentle. Do not run from anything
you can read. Above all, do not become enraged at what is difficult or
oblique. You too are difficult, oblique and equally worth the effort.

It may be that such people remain with us because they were   13
always with us from the start. Basically the enterprise of teaching
literature is a hopeful one, the hope residing with the upturned faces.
First faith, then hope. If words are merely words after all, then the
teacher of books may be the world's most optimistic creature. No matter
how he may grumble about life's decay, it is he who, year after year,
trudges up the stone steps of old, dank buildings, hauls himself before
the future, and announces, against all reason of experience, that "the
World was all before them."

With those words, Milton approached the end of his long moral   14
poem, and when Douglas Bush came to read those words aloud before
his Harvard classes, there was nothing in his voice that betrayed a
personal reverberation to the grand dismay the words contain. Bush
showed none of Blackmur's visible force or Trilling's visible elegance,
though like them he believed in the good that words and people are
capable of. On the last day of courses at Harvard, it is the custom for
students to applaud the teachers they most appreciate. After years of
suffering this embarrassment, Bush would begin to pack up his books
in the last minutes of the hour, so that he could time his exit from the
room right at the bell. Thus when the moment arrived, and Bush was

already halfway down the steps, it appeared that the students were clapping on and on for someone not there. But he was there.

For Discussion and Writing

1. Rosenblatt frames his essay around the career of Douglas Bush, a Harvard literature teacher, and begins by questioning the importance of Bush's, or any teacher's role in acting as a "middleman" (3) between author and reader. What is the effect of such a strategy, and how does Rosenblatt address his own question? What is the teacher's role?
2. In characterizing "scrupulous" teachers (7), Rosenblatt says that their "testimony is always personal. Behind the spectacles and the fuzzy coat, the teacher teaches himself." What do you think he means? Why is teaching books such a personal undertaking?
3. Rosenblatt also attributes courage to the teacher of literature. Why does he think the profession heroic? Do you agree?
4. Rosenblatt talks about the two or three teachers we may remember most strongly, and bets that one of them will have been a teacher of literature. Remember the teachers in your life, and write an essay about which one(s) had the greatest impact on you. Were they teachers of books? What was it about these men or women that stuck with you?

A Holocaust of Words

Lance Morrow

The library in Leningrad burned for a night and a day. By the time the fire was out at the National Academy of Sciences, 400,000 books had been incinerated. An additional 3.6 million had been damaged by water. In the weeks since the fire, workmen have been shoveling blackened remains of books into trash bins and hanging the sodden survivors on lines to dry in front of enormous electric fans. 1

The mind cracks a little in contemplating a holocaust of words. No one died in the fire. And yet whenever books burn, one is haunted by a sense of mourning. For books are not inanimate objects, not really, and the death of books, especially by fire, especially in such numbers, has the power of a kind of tragedy. Books are life-forms, children of the mind. Words (in the beginning was the Word) have about them some of the mystery of creation. 2

Russians have always loved their books profoundly. Literature has sometimes sustained the Russians when almost everything else was gone. During the siege of Leningrad, the city's population, frozen and starving down to the verge of cannibalism, drew strength by listening to a team of poets as they read on the radio from the works of Pushkin and other writers. "Never before nor ever in the future," said a survivor, "will people listen to poetry as did Leningrad in that winter—hungry, swollen and hardly living." Today Russians will fill a stadium to hear a poetry reading. 3

There is of course some irony in the Russian passion for books. Knowing the power of written words, Russian authority has for centuries accorded books the brutal compliment of suppression. It has slain books by other means than fire. Book publishing first flourished in Russia under Catherine the Great, and yet it was she who used local police, corrupt and ignorant, to enforce the country's first censorship regulations. Czar Nicholas I conducted a sort of terrorism against certain books and writers. He functioned as personal censor for Pushkin and banished Dostoyevsky to Siberia. Revolution only encouraged the Russian candle-snuffers. Lenin said, "Ideas are much more fatal things than guns," a founder's *nihil obstat* that culminated in the years of poet 4 destruction (Osip Mandelstam, Marina Tsvetaeva) and book murder under Stalin.

For generations of Russians, books have been surrounded by   5
exaltation and tragedy. In a prison camp in the Gulag during the 1960s, the poet and essayist Andrei Sinyavsky hid hand-copied pages of the *Book of Revelations* in the calf of his boot. He wrote, "What is the most precious, the most exciting smell waiting for you in the house when you return to it after half a dozen years or so? The smell of roses, you think? No, mouldering books."

Vladimir Nabokov carried his love of Russian into exile: "Beyond   6
the seas where I have lost a sceptre,/ I hear the neighing of my dappled nouns,/ Soft participles coming down the steps,/ Treading on leaves, trailing their rustling gowns . . ."

Americans don't take books that seriously anymore. Perhaps   7
Russians don't either: their popular culture has begun to succumb to television. In America one rarely encounters the mystical book worship. Everything in the West today seems infinitely replicable, by computer, microfilm, somehow, so that if a book chances to burn up, there must be thousands more where that came from. If anything, there seem to be entirely too many words and numbers in circulation, too many sinister records of everything crammed into the microchips of FBI, IRS, police departments. Too many books altogether, perhaps. The glut of books subverts a reverence for them. Bookstore tables groan under the piles of remaindered volumes. In the U.S. more than 50,000 new titles are published every year. Forests cry out in despair that they are being scythed so that the works of Jackie Collins might live.

It was the Dominican zealot Girolamo Savonarola who presided   8
over the Bonfire of the Vanities during Carnival in Florence in 1497. Thousands of the Florentine children who were Savonarola's followers went through the city collecting what they deemed to be lewd books, as well as pictures, lutes, playing cards, mirrors and other vanities, and piled them in the great Piazza della Signoria of Florence. The pyramid of offending objects rose 60 feet high, and went up in flames. One year later Savonarola had a political quarrel with Pope Alexander VI, was excommunicated, tried and hanged. His body was burned at the stake. Savonarola went up in smoke.

The Leningrad library fire was a natural disaster. Deliberate book   9
burning seems not only criminal but evil. Why? Is it worse to destroy a book by burning it than to throw it into the trash compactor? Or to shred it? Not in effect. But somehow the irrevocable reduction of words to smoke and, poof!, into nonentity haunts the imagination. In Hitler's bonfires in 1933, the works of Kafka, Freud, Einstein, Zola and Proust were incinerated—their smoke a prefiguration of the terrible clouds that came from the Nazi chimneys later.

Anyone who loves books knows how hard it is to throw even one   10
of them away, even one that is silly or stupid or vicious and full of lies.
How much more criminal, how much more a sin against consciousness,
to burn a book. A question then: What if one were to gather from the
corners of the earth all the existing copies of *Mein Kampf* and make a
bonfire of them? Would that be an act of virtue? Or of evil?

Sometimes it seems that the right books never get burnt. But the   11
world has its quota of idiotic and vicious people just as it has its supplies
of books that are vicious, trashy and witless. Books can eventually be
as mortal as people—the acids in the paper eat them, the bindings decay
and at last they crumble in one's hands. But their ambition anyway is
to outlast the flesh. Books have a kind of enshrining counterlife. One
can live with the thought of one's own death. It is the thought of the
death of words and books that is terrifying for that is the deeper
extinction.

For Discussion and Writing

1. Early in the essay, why does Morrow spend several paragraphs talking
   about the Russian passion for books? How does this support his essential point that books transcend human life and "have about them some
   of the mystery of creation"?
2. Morrow says that Americans "don't take books that seriously anymore"
   (7). What reasons does he give for our lack of "mystical book worship"?
3. In paragraph 10, Morrow raises the hypothetical question: Would it be
   an act of good or evil to gather all the world's copies of *Mein Kampf*
   (Hitler's autobiographical manifesto) and burn them? What do you
   think? What if we were to substitute for Hitler's book any volume that
   is "silly or stupid or vicious and full of lies"?
4. Write an essay in which you consider the following questions: Which
   books do you treasure? Why do you value them? What have they meant,
   and continue to mean, to you? What would your life be like if you had
   never read them?

Private Eye, Public Conscience

Pico Iyer

I lit another cigarette and looked at the dental-supply company's   1
bill again. The minutes went by with their fingers to their lips. Then
there was a small knocking on wood. It was a blond. A blond to make
a bishop kick a hole in a stained-glass window. She smelled the way the
Taj Mahal looked by moonlight. She gave me a smile I could feel in my
hip pocket. "Cops are just people," she said irrelevantly. "They start out
that way, I've heard."

The lines above come from four different novels by Raymond   2
Chandler. Yet all of them seem to issue from our memories or dreams,
or at least the ones in which we picture ourselves, alone in the office,
dreaming of cool blonds and stiff whiskeys (or cool whiskey and stiff
blonds). Raymond Chandler was ghostwriter to the sound track our
lives so often imitate. The figure of the tough-but-tender hero cracking
wise to cover up his soft spots; the lethal blond and the flick-knife
dialogue on which the movies (and so the rest of us) still feed—all of
them seem to have been copyrighted by the onetime oil executive who
only began writing at the age of 45. In seven novels and in the screen-
plays he wrote for Billy Wilder and Alfred Hitchcock, Chandler scripted
much of the unshaven poetry and arsenic idealism that form us now,
and haunt us still, in Mickey Spillane beer ads and smoky urban videos,
from Jack Nicholson's Chinatown to Joan Didion's Malibu.

Chandler is not, of course, the only American writer with a cente-   3
nary this year who worked in a British bank, steeped his writing in the
classics and explored the breakdowns of the age in cadences so memorable that he seems to have taken up a time-share ownership of
Bartlett's. But T.S. Eliot was an American who found his voice in
England, and in books. Chandler, by contrast, was an honorary Brit who
smuggled two foreign substances into Hollywood—irony and morality—and so gave us an unflinchingly American voice, the kind we hear
in the rainy voice-overs of our mind. Few would suggest that Chandler
is a more significant literary figure than Eliot. But quality and influence
are mysteriously related, and Chandler has inspired more poses and
more parodies, perhaps, than any other American writer of the century

save Hemingway. Eliot merely articulated the deepest spiritual and emotional issues of the times; Chandler put them on the sidewalk.

Chandler's most immortal creation—co-produced by Humphrey   4
Bogart—was the quixotic figure of the gumshoe, Philip Marlowe, private eye and public conscience, sitting behind his pebbled-glass door with an office bottle and a solitary game of chess. What made Marlowe special was simply the fact that he was nothing special, no genius like Sherlock Holmes, no *Connoisseur* model like James Bond. Just an underpaid drudge with, as one mobster says, "no dough, no family, no prospects, no nothing"—except a habit of making other people's worries his own, and a gift for walking in on corpses he knows just well enough to mourn.

Chandler's greatest invention, however, may well have been   5
Marlowe's constant adversary, California. Nobody has ever caught so well the smell of eucalyptus in the night or the treacherous lights and crooked streets of the L.A. hills. In Hollywood, city of false fronts and trick shoots, Chandler found the perfect location for investigating artifice, and with it the shadow side of the American dream of reinventing lives. The one time Marlowe enters a Hollywood stage, it is from the back, and that, in a sense, is his customary position: seeing glamour from behind, inspecting illusions from the inside out, a two-bit peeper spying on the rich man's costume ball from the service entrance. His is a Hollywood filled with missing persons, bit players who are living a long way from the lights: gigolos, gold diggers and snooping old women, remote-controlled punks and "the kind of lawyers you hope the other fellow has." Chandler found gurus, juju addicts, pornographers and abortionists before most people knew they existed.

It is no coincidence, then, that Chandler's most famous weapon   6
was the simile, the perfect device for describing a world in which everything is like something else, and nothing is itself. And the unrelenting sun of California only intensified the shadiness. By the end of his career, in fact, Chandler was pulling off a series of bitter twists and brilliant turns on the paradoxes of illusion: the prim secretary from Manhattan is, in truth, from Manhattan, Kans., and turns out to be a tight little chiseler, while the movie-star vamp has a fugitive innocence the more theatrical for being real. Chandler's greatest technical flaw—his way, ironically, with plots—arose from the simple fact that he felt the only real mystery worth investigating was morality, and why only the innocent confess, while murderers are brought to no justice but their own.

There was, of course, an element of romantic sentimentalism in   7
much of this, as Chandler well knew. It was no coincidence that he called his first detective "Mallory." Chandler identified all too closely with his "shop-soiled Galahad," struggling to maintain a code of honor

in a Hollywood that had never heard of the Marquis of Queensberry rules. Chandler knew the sting of being typecast as a small-time operator ("The better you write a mystery," he complained, "the more clearly you demonstrate that the mystery is not really worth writing"). Yet what he knew most of all, as one of Hollywood's great theoreticians, was that a writer cannot afford to be too removed from the streets, and that what the public needs is a shot of romantic realism. T.S. Eliot was a civil man, and a public-minded writer, and so it is only right that his anniversary be marked in public ceremonies; Chandler was the laureate of the loner, and so his admirers recall him now in quieter ways, alone, unnoticed, with a light on in their darker corners.

For Discussion and Writing

1. According to Iyer, what are some of Chandler's lasting influences on today's writers and filmmakers?
2. In appraising Chandler, Iyer analyzes his use of several of the essential elements in fiction: character, setting, language, plot. What does he say about each of these? Why does he open the essay with a selection of Chandler's sentences?
3. Iyer says that Chandler wrote from a sense of "romantic realism," about a contemporary hero "struggling to maintain a code of honor" (7). Which fictional characters from today's literature or film embody heroic ideas? Are you drawn to them as imaginary models of your own behavior? Why or why not?
4. Using Iyer's essay as a guide, write an appreciation of your favorite author, concentrating on his or her special qualities, the values the books embody, the things for which the writer is likely to be remembered.

Thinking and Writing about Chapter 5

1. All three writers in this chapter speak of literature and writing in moral terms, as a matter of good versus evil. From Rosenblatt's perspective, why is the teaching of books a moral act? For Morrow, why are books to be loved and protected, and mourned when they are lost? In Iyer's view, what is it about Raymond Chandler's work that speaks to our moral selves?

2. Implicit in these essayists' discussions of books and writing are certain assumptions about the relationship between literature and life. One such idea is that books are a unique and especially important expression of the human mind and heart, that books fulfill a need that no other art can. What is it about the experience of reading books that is different from other forms of intellectual activity—such as listening to a lecture or watching a film?

3. Write an essay in which you try to persuade someone unaccustomed to reading books (as opposed to magazines or newspapers) to adopt the habit. Don't preach, but try to make a convincing case for the joys, rewards, or other benefits of serious reading.

6

Human Nature

One of the central preoccupations of the arts and humanities is the observation of human beings. Painters and sculptors create images of the human form; writers tell stories or compose poems about human experience; musical artists give melodic contours to the human spirit; historians and philosophers ponder the essential qualities of human civilization and nature. And in our own lives, in our own ways, we spend a great deal of our energy and attention on our fellow creatures, being in families and other kinds of relationships, observing people with curiosity and interest in the course of the day, thinking about and forming our own character—deciding what kind of person we wish to be—as we grow.

It's no surprise, then, to find human nature, its weaknesses and strengths, a consistent theme in *Time* essays. The three pieces in this chapter consider what might be called problems in human nature, though writers have also addressed more noble characteristics.

In "The Fine Art of Putting Things Off," from June 1974, Michael Demarest writes about procrastination, finding in it some surprising virtues. In "Back to Reticence!" from February 1980, Lance Morrow laments the decline in American public conduct, and the rise of anger and hostility in everyday life. And in "Of Weirdos and Eccentrics," from January 1988, Pico Iyer compares two universal human types, asking what they may imply about society.

The Fine Art of Putting Things Off

MICHAEL DEMAREST

"Never put off till tomorrow," exhorted Lord Chesterfield in 1749, "what you can do today." That the elegant earl never got around to marrying his son's mother and had a bad habit of keeping worthies like Dr. Johnson cooling their heels for hours in an anteroom attests to the fact that even the most well-intentioned men have been postponers ever. Quintus Fabius Maximus, one of the great Roman generals, was dubbed *"Cunctator"* (Delayer) for putting off battle until the last possible *vinum* break. Moses pleaded a speech defect to rationalize his reluctance to deliver Jehovah's edicts to Pharaoh. Hamlet, of course, raised procrastination to an art form. 1

The world is probably about evenly divided between delayers and do-it-nowers. There are those who prepare their income taxes in February, prepay mortgages and serve precisely planned dinners at an ungodly 6:30 p.m. The other half dine happily on leftovers at 9 or 10, misplace bills and file for an extension of the income tax deadline. They seldom pay credit-card bills until the apocalyptic voice of Diners threatens doom from Denver. They postpone, as Faustian encounters, visits to barbershop, dentist or doctor. 2

Yet for all the trouble procrastination may incur, delay can often inspire and revive a creative soul. Jean Kerr, author of many successful novels and plays, says that she reads every soup-can, and jam-jar label in her kitchen before setting down to her typewriter. Many a writer focuses on almost anything but his task—for example, on the Coast and Geodetic Survey of Maine's Frenchman Bay and Bar Harbor, stimulating his imagination with names like Googins Ledge, Blunts Pond, Hio Hill and Burnt Porcupine, Long Porcupine, Sheep Porcupine and Bald Porcupine islands. 3

From *Cunctator's* day until this century, the art of postponement had been virtually a monopoly of the military ("Hurry up and wait"), diplomacy and the law. In former times, a British proconsul faced with a native uprising could comfortably ruminate about the situation with Singapore Sling in hand. Blessedly, he had no nattering Telex to order in machine guns and fresh troops. A U.S. general as late as World War 4 ll could agree with his enemy counterpart to take a sporting day off, loot the villagers' chickens and wine and go back to battle a day later. Lawyers are among the world's most addicted postponers. According to Frank Nathan, a nonpostponing Beverly Hills insurance salesman, "The number of attorneys who die without a will is amazing."

Even where there is no will, there is a way. There is a difference, 5 of course, between chronic procrastination and purposeful postponement, particularly in the higher echelons of business. Corporate dynamics encourage the caution that breeds delay, says Richard Manderbach, Bank of America group vice president. He notes that speedy action can be embarrassing or extremely costly. The data explosion fortifies those seeking excuses for inaction—another report to be read, another authority to be consulted. "There is always," says Manderbach, "a delicate edge between having enough information and too much."

His point is well taken. Bureaucratization, which flourished amid 6 the growing burdens of government and the greater complexity of society, was designed to smother policymakers in blankets of legalism, compromise and reappraisal—and thereby prevent hasty decisions from being made. The centralization of government that led to Watergate has spread to economic institutions and beyond, making procrastination a worldwide way of life. Many languages are studded with phrases that refer to putting things off—from the Spanish *mañana* to the Arabic *bukra fil mishmish* (literally "tomorrow in apricots," more loosely "leave it for the soft spring weather when the apricots are blooming").

Academe also takes high honors in procrastination. Bernard Sklar, 7 a University of Southern California sociologist who churns out three to five pages of writing a day, admits that "many of my friends go through agonies when they face a blank page. There are all sorts of rationalizations: the pressure of teaching, responsibilities at home, checking out the latest book, looking up another footnote."

Psychologists maintain that the most assiduous procrastinators 8 are women, though many psychologists are (at $50-plus an hour) pretty good delayers themselves. Dr. Ralph Greenson, a U.C.L.A. professor of clinical psychiatry (and Marilyn Monroe's onetime shrink), takes a fairly gentle view of procrastination. "To many people," he says, "doing something, confronting, is the moment of truth. All frightened people will then avoid the moment of truth entirely, or evade or postpone it until the last possible moment." To Georgia State Psychologist, Joen Fagan, however, procrastination may be a kind of subliminal way of sorting the important from the trivial. "When I drag my feet, there's usually some reason," says Fagan. "I feel it, but I don't yet know the real reason."

In fact, there is a long and honorable history of procrastination to 9 suggest that many ideas and decisions may well improve if postponed. It is something of a truism that to put off making a decision is itself a decision. The parliamentary process is essentially a system of delay and deliberation. So, for that matter, is the creation of a great painting, or an entrée, or a book, or a building like Blenheim Palace, which took the Duke of Marlborough's architects and laborers 15 years to construct. In the process, the design can mellow and marinate. Indeed, hurry can be the assassin of elegance. As T.H. White, author of *Sword in the Stone*, once wrote, time "is not meant to be devoured in an hour or a day, but to be consumed delicately and gradually and without haste." In other words, *pace* Lord Chesterfield, what you don't necessarily have to do today, by all means put off until tomorrow.

Editor's Note: To create the appropriate mood, the author of the above Essay put off writing   10
it for 16 successive weeks, and the editors delayed editing it for several more.

For Discussion and Writing

1. Is Demarest serious in his apparent praise of procrastination? How does he attempt to justify this supposed fault as a natural inclination?
2. What virtues does he see in procrastination? When may it have healthy or welcome effects?
3. Demarest cites several examples of procrastination to illustrate how common a human trait it is. What are these? Can you think of any of your own?
4. How would you argue against Demarest's claim that procrastination is, or can be, a good thing? When is it potentially harmful, irresponsible, or just stupid? Write an essay in which you take the other side of the argument, using concrete examples to support your position.

Back to Reticence!

.

LANCE MORROW

> *Cultivated to a high degree by art and science, we are*
> *civilized to the point where we are overburdened with all*
> *sorts of social propriety and decency.*
>
> —Immanuel Kant, 1784

Jimmy Connors does not labor under Kant's burden. Sometimes   1
when the tennis gets intense, Connors grabs his crotch and shakes it for
the crowd. He pelts the linesmen and judges with rotten language. He
shoots his finger. The umpire usually responds with the flustered and
ineffectual dismay of a curate who has discovered the servants copu-
lating in his study.

This sort of court behavior, also indulged in by John McEnroe and   2
Ilie Nastase, is what kindergarten teachers call "age inappropriate." It
is punk tennis, the transformation of a formerly pristine game into the
moral equivalent of roller derby. The spectacle is symptomatic of something that has befallen the American's idea of how one ought to behave.
What would once have been intolerable and impermissible public
conduct has now become commonplace. If it is not exactly accepted,
then at least it is abjectly and wearily endured.

Social habit in the U.S. has taken decisive turns toward the awful.   3
Since the end of World War II, Americans have been steadily relinquish-
ing their inhibitions about the social consequences of their actions. They
have lost a crucial sense of community, even while highways, jets,
satellite TV signals and leisure travel have brought them physically
closer together. The social environment has grown polluted along with
the natural; a headlong greed and self-absorption have sponsored both
contaminations. Somehow, Americans have also misplaced the moral
confidence with which to condemn sleaziness and stupidity. It is as if
something in the American judgment snapped, and has remained so
long unrepaired that no one notices any more.

The daily grind of the offensive is both tiring and obscurely   4
humiliating. It is impossible to watch the nightly news on network
television without being treated to a stream of 30-second treatises on

74

hemorrhoids, tampons, feminine deodorant sprays and constipation. "I want to talk to you about diarrhea," says the earnest pitchman. T shirts, sweatshirts and bumper stickers proclaim their aggressive little editorials. Some are mildly funny (a woman's T shirt, for example, that says SO MANY MEN, SO LITTLE TIME). But often they are crude with a faintly alarming determination to affront, even sometimes to menace. They are filled with belligerent scatology. Something or other always SUCKS.

Constitutionally protected grossness—edible underwear, the vi- 5 brators in the drugstore window, massage parlors, sex merchandised in its pervasive richness—has spread the pornographic spirit widely. The Twelfth Night Masque, the oldest private subscription ball in Chicago and hitherto a bastion of Midwestern decorum, has suffered a recent rash of crudity. Last year some guests showed up at the ball dressed as hemorrhoids when President Carter was so afflicted; two years before, when the masque theme was "The Father of Our Country," a number of Lake Shore socialites appeared as penises or sperm. No one proposes calling out a SWAT team to deal with this sort of whoopee-cushion wit. It is not sullenly antisocial, like the blaring radios the size of steamer trunks that adolescents haul onto public buses to cook up a small pot of community rage, or the occasional pistols that got waved in gas lines.

Much of today's offensiveness began in the guise of a refreshing 6 virtue: honesty. The doctrine of "letting it all hang out" got propagated in the headlong idealism of the late '60s. The result is a legacy of insufferable and interminable candor. The idealism has vanished into the mainstream of the culture or into thin air. We are left with the residue of bad habits, ugly noises and moral slackness.

As in some burlesque science fiction, the nation seems to have 7 been injected with a truth serum designed to make people bore one another to death; it has given them a compulsion to confide embarrassing intimacies, has led them on to endless emotional ostentations, as if, as Saul Bellow once wrote, "to keep the wolf of insignificance from the door." A man sits down at a New Jersey dinner party, beside a woman he met half an hour before, and hears in elaborately explicit detail from soup through coffee, how the woman and her husband managed to conquer their sexual incompatibility with the help of a sex therapist. A magazine writer not long ago met the new young husband of Novelist Erica Jong at a party and realized with a disagreeable little jolt that she knew from Jong's novel *How to Save Your Own Life* just how large the husband's penis was.

The book racks are filled with volumes of confession and revenge. 8 People rush to destroy their own privacy, possibly judging that loneliness is worse. In the past ten or twelve years, everything has tumbled out of the closet in a heap. Some homosexuals parade themselves like walking billboards, the placement of the keys and handkerchiefs in their back pockets acting as a semaphore to signal the specific secrets of their sexual tastes.

The depressing quality of much American public behavior—from   9
Connors to T shirts—is its edgy meanness. Bad enough that it is calculatedly cheap. Worse is the stolid nastiness of it, the rock in the snowball, the compulsion to affront. Even relentless candor—wounding friends or family by telling them their defects in the name of honesty—is a symptom not only of stupidity but also of unkindness and buried anger.

There are doubtless profound cultural reasons for such anger: the   10
aggressive self-regard of the era now perhaps passing, the centrifugal individualism, the loss of authority, the sense of alienation from "the System," a precipitous disenchantment that tended to discredit all rules, including those of social behavior. It is possible that the price of a certain amount of personal liberty is excess and mess, all the frictions and bad smells generated by social change and people exercising their constitutional rights. Jefferson had an idea that democracy should be genteel, but it did not work out that way. And today, there is no point in growing as mistily sentimental as a Soviet realist hack about the pleasures of right thinking and conformity.

Still, it is possible that the '80s are going to demand some virtues   11
unknown in the '60s and '70s—self-control, self-discipline, stoicism, decorum, even inhibition and a little puritanism. It may be time for a touch of reticence. Coercion cannot produce such attitudes, but the mood of the time may. Americans may find themselves agreeing in some paraphrase of Elihu Root when he walked through a squalid Siberian village as Woodrow Wilson's emissary in the first Soviet revolutionary dawn. "I'm a firm believer in democracy," he said, as he skeptically eyed his surroundings. "But I do not like filth."

For Discussion and Writing

1. Morrow's essential claim, based upon evidence from 1980, is that American public conduct has declined sharply, "toward the awful" (2–3). Which examples does he offer to support this claim?
2. Morrow seeks not only to offer examples of bad conduct, but to ask how it came to be. What causes does he attribute to the decline in American social conduct?
3. Morrow's essay also considers the larger meaning of a decline in public behavior. What does he say it may indicate about our society, and about the nature of democracy?
4. Write an essay in which you consider examples of bad, rude, thoughtless, antisocial behavior. What do you think about such conduct? How would you propose to curb it? Does it have any useful place in civilized society?

Of Weirdos and Eccentrics

PICO IYER

Charles Waterton was just another typical eccentric. In his 80s 1
the eminent country squire was to be seen clambering around the upper
branches of an oak tree with what was aptly described as the agility of
an "adolescent gorilla." The beloved 27th lord of Walton Hall also
devoted his distinguished old age to scratching the back part of his head
with his right big toe. Such displays of animal high spirits were not,
however, confined to the gentleman's later years. When young, Waterton made four separate trips to South America, where he sought the
wourali poison (a cure, he was convinced, for hydrophobia), and once
spent months on end with one foot dangling from his hammock in the
quixotic hope of having his toe sucked by a vampire bat.

James Warren Jones, by contrast, was something of a weirdo. As 2
a boy in the casket-making town of Lynn, Ind., he used to conduct
elaborate funeral services for dead pets. Later, as a struggling preacher,
he went from door to door, in bow tie and tweed jacket, selling imported
monkeys. After briefly fleeing to South America (a shelter, he believed,
from an imminent nuclear holocaust), the man who regarded himself
as a reincarnation of Lenin settled in Northern California and opened
some convalescent homes. Then, one humid day in the jungles of
Guyana, he ordered his followers to drink a Kool-Aid-like punch
soured with cyanide. By the time the world arrived at Jonestown, 911
people were dead.

The difference between the eccentric and the weirdo is, in its way, 3
the difference between a man with a teddy bear in his hand and a man
with a gun. We are also, of course, besieged by other kinds of deviants—
crackpots, oddballs, fanatics, quacks and cranks. But the weirdo and
the eccentric define between them that invisible line at which strangeness acquires an edge and oddness becomes menace.

The difference between the two starts with the words themselves: 4
eccentric, after all, carries a distinguished Latin pedigree that refers,
quite reasonably, to anything that departs from the center; weird, by
comparison, has its mongrel origins in the Old English *wyrd*, meaning
fate or destiny; and the larger, darker forces conjured up by the term—
Macbeth's weird sisters and the like—are given an extra twist with the

slangy, bastard suffix -o. Beneath the linguistic roots, however, we feel the difference on our pulses. The eccentric we generally regard as something of a donny, dotty, harmless type, like the British peer who threw over his Cambridge fellowship in order to live in a bath. The weirdo is an altogether more shadowy figure—Charles Manson acting out his messianic visions. The eccentric is a distinctive presence; the weirdo something of an absence, who casts no reflection in society's mirror. The eccentric raises a smile; the weirdo leaves a chill.

All too often, though, the two terms are not so easily distin-   5
guished. Many a criminal trial, after all revolves around precisely that gray area where the two begin to blur. Was Bernhard Goetz just a volatile Everyman, ourselves pushed to the limit, and then beyond? Or was he in fact an aberration? Often, besides, eccentrics may simply be weirdos in possession of a VIP pass, people rich enough or powerful enough to live above convention, amoral as Greek gods. Elvis Presley could afford to pump bullets into silhouettes of humans and never count the cost. Lesser mortals, however, must find another kind of victim.

To some extent too, we tend to think of eccentricity as the prerog-   6
ative, even the hallmark, of genius. And genius is its own vindication. Who cared that Glenn Gould sang along with the piano while playing Bach, so long as he played so beautifully? Even the Herculean debauches of Babe Ruth did not undermine so much as confirm his status as a legend.

Indeed, the unorthodox inflections of the exceptional can lead to   7
all kinds of dangerous assumptions. If geniuses are out of the ordinary and psychopaths are out of the ordinary, then geniuses are psychopaths and vice versa, or so at least runs the reasoning of many dramatists who set their plays in loony bins. If the successful are often strange, then being strange is a way of becoming successful, or so believe all those would-be artists who work on eccentric poses. And if celebrity is its own defense, then many a demagogue or criminal assures himself that he will ultimately be redeemed by the celebrity he covets.

All these distortions, however, ignore the most fundamental dis-   8
tinction of all: the eccentric is strange because he cares too little about society, the weirdo because he cares too much. The eccentric generally wants nothing more than his own attic-like space in which he can live by his own peculiar lights. The weirdo, however, resents his outcast status and constantly seeks to get back into society, or at least get back at it. His is the rage not of the bachelor but the divorcé.

Thus the eccentric hardly cares if he is seen to be strange; that in   9
a sense is what makes him strange. The weirdo, however, wants desperately to be taken as normal and struggles to keep his strangeness to himself. "He was always such a nice man," the neighbors ritually tell reporters after a sniper's rampage. "He always seemed so normal."

And because the two mark such different tangents to the norm, their incidence can, in its way, be an index of a society's health. The height of British eccentricity, for example, coincided with the height of British power, if only, perhaps, because Britain in its imperial heyday presented so strong a center from which to depart. Nowadays, with the empire gone and the center vanishing, Britain is more often associated with the maladjusted weirdo—the orange-haired misfit or the soccer hooligan.   10

At the other extreme, the relentless and ritualized normalcy of a society like Japan's—there are only four psychiatrists in all of Tokyo—can, to Western eyes, itself seem almost abnormal. Too few eccentrics can be as dangerous as too many weirdos. For in the end, eccentricity is a mark of confidence, accommodated best by a confident society, whereas weirdness inspires fear because it is a symptom of fear and uncertainty and rage. A society needs the eccentric as much as it needs a decorated frame for the portrait it fashions of itself; it needs the weirdo as much as it needs a hole punched through the middle of the canvas.   11

For Discussion and Writing

1. Iyer begins his essay with two anecdotes, brief narrative or descriptive stories. One focuses on Charles Waterton, an eccentric, the other on cult leader Jim Jones, a weirdo. What do these illustrations add?
2. Iyer's method is, at least in part, to compare eccentrics and weirdos, looking for distinctions between them. What differences does the author attribute to each human type?
3. Both eccentrics and weirdos live in society, but each has a different relationship with it. How does each relate to the society around him or her, and how does each act as an index to that society's health?
4. Write an essay in which to apply Iyer's comparison to people you know well, such as fellow students, family members, friends. Without mentioning names, but using concrete examples, try to define and compare qualities of eccentricity and weirdness.

Thinking and Writing about Chapter 6

1. Human nature is vastly complex, and three essays can hardly begin to describe its difficulties and diversity. As you observe your fellow human beings, what do you notice most? What human traits and characteristics would you put at the center of a definition of human nature?

2. One of the traditional disputes about human behavior is the question of nature or nurture. That is, are human beings born the way they are, or are they made by society and environment? How do you think the three authors here would answer this question? Which evidence, in each of their essays, indicates a tilt toward one side or the other of this argument?

3. Write an essay about human nature in which you seek to define its chief characteristics, isolate positive or negative traits, compare or contrast similar human types, or classify aspects of human behavior into a system of categories.

7

The Drug Culture

Most of us may think of the drug culture as a recent phenomenon, dating from the late 1960s, when LSD, marijuana, and other substances came into widespread use. Historians have shown, though, that drug use (including alcohol) has been prevalent in the United States from the beginning of the republic, and certainly that the use of natural drugs as medicine is an ancient practice. Still, today we do seem to find ourselves living in a world where an enormous variety of illegal drugs are available, in common use among all social classes, and, in far too many instances, associated with appalling violence, corruption, and social disintegration.

What should we do about the drug problem? Should we make all drugs legal and live with the consequences? Should we continue to fight an often futile war against illegal drugs? Should we seek some sort of compromise, legalizing "softer" drugs such as marijuana in the hope that the harder ones will disappear?

The essayists in this chapter address several, among a great many, aspects of the drug issue. In "LSD," from June 1966, an anonymous writer considers a then relatively new synthetic chemical, first used by the U.S. Army in notorious secret experiments, which would go on to play a major role in forming the drug and music culture of the 1960s. In "Glass Houses and Getting Stoned," from June 1988, Michael Kinsley reflects upon the subsequent generation of drug use and the impulse that continues to drive it. And in "Feeling Low over Old Highs," from September 1989, Walter Shapiro expresses his sense of guilt over being part of a drug-using generation.

L S D

Three letters, on a drawing of three cubes, appeared not long ago   1
on a fence at the University of Wisconsin with the slogan: YOUR CAMPUS
TRAVEL AGENT—ONE TRIP IS WORTH A THOUSAND WORDS. Just about everyone
at Wisconsin knew what kind of "trip" that was: the voyage into "inner
space," the flight into or out of the self, provided by LSD.

More than half a century ago, the noted American neurologist,   2
Weir Mitchell, chewed some of the mescal buttons of the peyote cactus
and reported that he felt "as if the unseen millions of the Milky Way
were to flow in a sparkling river before my eyes." He predicted "a
perilous reign of the mescal habit when this agent becomes attainable."
To some, it seems that the perilous reign has begun—not through
Mitchell's bitter buttons but through their enormously more powerful
relative, lysergic acid diethylamide.

The U.S. has lately become familiar with the accounts of some   3
users who report dazzling states of heightened awareness or mystical
experiences worthy of St. Teresa of Avila; others claim insights that have
changed their lives. In John Hersey's latest novel, *Too Far to Walk*, the
Devil feeds Faustus LSD ("The closest equivalent to infinity in sheer
living"). There have also been stories of "bad trips"—writhing night-
mares that end in the nearest psychiatric ward. Occasionally LSD is a
one-way trip. Since the recent flood of sensational publicity about LSD
has let up somewhat, it is possible to assess the phenomenon more
calmly. LSD is certainly not the means of instant, universal bliss that its
most extreme and most ludicrous proponents make it out to be. Nor is
it an indication of diabolical decadence or proof that, as Critic Leslie
Fiedler predicted some time ago, the U.S. is changing from a "whisky
culture to a drug culture." But LSD is considerably more than a mere
fad.

The Food and Drug Administration estimates that "tens of   4
thousands" of college students are using it or have tried it. In Los
Angeles, a recent survey showed as many as 200 victims of bad trips in
the city's hospitals at one time. In New York City, Dr. William Frosch of
Bellevue Hospital and New York University Medical Center guesses
that the number of steady users in the city has doubled from 5,000 to

10,000 during the past year. A Hollywood mogul, a Broadway producer and a noted drama critic all agree that 60% of stage and screen performers are using it. Los Angeles has a dance joint called The Trip, and until recently featured one called Lysergic a Go-Go. "Acid heads" are apt to "turn on" in walk-up pads and ride-up penthouses—but seldom in slums, where people want their escape straight rather than disguised as "insights" or "breakthroughs." LSD so far is strictly a middle-class phenomenon.

The Supply

Last month two Senate committees held hearings on the uses and abuses of LSD. In testimony, the Food and Drug Administration and the National Institute of Mental Health opposed federal legislation that would have made mere possession of LSD a crime—although California and Nevada have since passed such statutes. Restrictive legislation, say Administration officials, would only cut off the supply for legitimate research. (This has already partially happened because of LSD's notoriety.) Besides, it is argued, the situation can be handled by merely sharpening existing rules, to prohibit the unregistered manufacture, traffic and sale of LSD and its basic ingredient, lysergic acid.

The acid, which is difficult to make (it is derived from ergot, a cereal fungus), continues to be smuggled in from Canada, Mexico and Europe. Given the acid to start with, LSD is relatively easy to cook up for anyone with a working knowledge of chemistry. Essentially, what is required is a batch of lysergic acid dissolved in some other chemicals plus a solution of diethylamine (a volatile liquid used in processes like vulcanizing). The two batches, cooled to freezing and stirred together, result in a solution that contains LSD. The trick is to extract the LSD from the solution. This can be done with the help of chloroform, benzine, a vacuum evaporator or steam bath, and a glass gadget known as a chromatographic column (available in any chemistry supply shop).

LSD is generally black-marketed in impregnated sugar cubes, costing from $2.50 to $5 for 100 micrograms, enough for an eight- to ten-hour trip. Another way of transporting small quantities is to mix them in water, soak the solution up in a handkerchief and let it dry—to be cut up later into squares, which LSD users chew. LSD is hard to track down because the compound is colorless, tasteless and odorless, and so potent that a gram, equal to one million micrograms, or 10,000 trips, could be stashed in a single cigarette. So far, illegal LSD is manufactured largely by amateurs, but potential profits represent a strong temptation for organized crime. Tougher legislation will probably make LSD scarcer and therefore more expensive.

The Psychiatric Hope

Through the ages, men have sought out drugs to dull their phys-   8
ical aches and pains or to alleviate, like the nepenthe Homer describes,
their mental ones. More treasured still have been the substances used
to bring mortal flesh into the presence of the divine. Such was the
mysterious soma, mentioned in a Sanskrit chronicle. Nomads on the
Kamchatka Peninsula lofted themselves into the dazzling world of the
gods with the mushroom *Amanita muscaria*), and discovered that the
visions of one eater could be passed to as many as five others if each
one drank the urine of the man before him. In South America, long
before Columbus, witch doctors took cohoba snuff to converse with
gods and the dead.

"Hallucinogenic" or "psychedelic" (literally, "mind-manifesting")   9
drugs come in three groups. The mild ones are morning-glory seeds,
nutmeg and marijuana. The moderately potent ones are the mescaline
of Weir Mitchell's experiment, psilocybin (derived from the Mexican
Indians' "sacred mushroom"), bufotenine (a constituent of *Amanita
muscaria*, and dimethyltryptamine (found in cohoba). By itself on the
third level is LSD. It has 100 times the potency of psilocybin and 7,000
times that of mescaline, which is itself considerably more powerful than
marijuana.

The pharmacology of LSD is not yet fully understood. The tracing   10
of injected radioactive LSD shows that only an infinitesimal amount
ever reaches the brain—and that is gone before the effects begin to be
felt. It is generally thought, therefore, that LSD does not act directly but
triggers an unknown series of metabolic processes. These in turn somehow affect the midbrain, seat of the intimate interchange between
emotional response, awareness of external and internal stimuli, and the
sympathetic and parasympathetic nervous systems. Tranquilizers or
barbiturates halt LSD's effects, while stimulants like amphetamine tend
to elevate them. LSD is no aphrodisiac. It is not physically habit-form-
ing, but it can be psychologically habituating.

The drug was developed in 1938 by Dr. Albert Hofmann, a re-   11
search chemist at the Sandoz laboratories, at Basel, Switzerland, who
was trying to find a new stimulant for the nervous system. He did not
know what he had done, however, until five years later, when he
accidentally inhaled a minute amount and became dizzy and delirious,
with "fantastic visions of extraordinary vividness accompanied by a
kaleidoscopic play of intense coloration."

One of the first theories about LSD was that it was a psychotomi-   12
metic—a mimicker of psychoses. The idea offered hope of finding a
chemical cure for schizophrenia, as well as of increasing the
psychiatrist's empathy with a schizophrenic by giving himself "mad-

ness in miniature" and thereby knowing what his patient was going through. Some of the LSD-induced symptoms are indeed similar to psychoses—the feeling of being outside one's body, for instance, or of coming apart. But the all-important difference is that the LSD taker almost always knows that the hallucination he is experiencing is caused by the drug and is not real.

The psychiatric hopes for LSD were followed by the spiritual ones. 13 British-born Orientalist Alan Watts, who spent six years as an Episcopal priest, says flatly that "LSD is quite emphatically a new religion. The God-is-dead thing is not unconnected. The standard brands have not been delivering the goods. This is technological mysticism."

The first big impetus toward this sort of mysticism came from the 14 late writer-mystic Aldous Huxley, who in *The Doors of Perception* (1954) furnished a superseductive account of his experience under the influence of mescaline. Huxley recalled that earlier mystics had used fasting or self-flagellation to achieve a spiritual state. Nowadays, he argued, such measures are no longer necessary, since we know "what are the chemical conditions of transcendental experience."

Fasting and flagellation, sensory deprivation and repetitive 15 prayer, may indeed have produced chemical or metabolic changes as preconditions of samadhi, satori, or the beatific vision. It has even been suggested that many extremes of asceticism were developed because, for some reason, drugs ceased to be available. But, to the orthodox Christian, "technological" or "chemical" mysticism is either blasphemous or absurd. The man who gets to a mountaintop in a funicular has the same view as the man who climbs the peak, but the effort of getting there is important too; the vision is not all, and manuals of contemplation often advise against paying too much attention to "beauty." Indeed the Christian concept of grace—never earned, never under man's control—seems to nullify the idea that a man can attain a mystical experience by taking a pill. Psychedelic mystics tend to look toward the Eastern religions, in which, as one puts it, "you rap [have rapport] with the world; you rap with dogs and trees and everything makes sense."

Dropping Out of life

The leading American psychedelic guru—and martyr—is Timo- 16 thy Leary, 45, who began to experiment with the drugs in 1960 when he was a psychologist working at Harvard's Center for Research in Personality. Harvard fired him and an associate when their project seemed to get out of hand. Leary then moved his experiments to the vicinity of Acapulco but was expelled by the Mexican government. Early this year a Texas judge sentenced him tentatively to 30 years in jail and a $40,000 fine for transporting half an ounce of marijuana and failing to pay tax on it (he is out on bail). He still runs the International Foundation for Internal Freedom (I.F.I.F. for short), which is dedicated to making LSD and psilocybin as available as chewing gum.

Leary calls himself a Hindu, and he uses Eastern symbolism along   17
with psychedelic experience to reject the outward-looking, "goal-directed" American attitude (disciples like to quote him to the effect that "Buddha was a dropout"). Leary is overfond of using the word "game" to put down the concerns men usually take seriously. Not that he would eliminate game playing: he says he only wants the games recognized for what they are. In practice, however, this requires a degree of judgment far beyond the capabilities of most mortals. Many a youthful LSD user, newly impressed with what suddenly seems to him the irrelevance of his activities, has dropped out of school a few weeks before he is due to graduate, soon thereafter he is dropping out of life as well, cultishly convinced that he and his psychedelic set are superior because they have Seen and they Know.

LSD has two major effects. For one thing, it tends to shatter and   18
dissolve the usual web of associations and habit patterns. A telephone, for instance, is suddenly nothing but a black plastic object of a certain shape—how outrageous and funny to see someone pick it up and talk to it as though it were a person. The boundaries that normally separate things from each other, or from oneself, may be dissolved also. This may cause the impression that one's limbs and torso are liquefying and flowing away (horror!); or that one is in such close rapport with others in the room that one can read their thoughts (love!); or that the barriers of logic have disappeared to reveal a tremendous insight, for instance, that death and life are the same (truth!).

The other major effect of psychedelic compounds is a vastly   19
increased suggestibility. Say "I'm so happy!" and savor the ecstasy; say "Miserable me!" and feel the hot tears of self-pity. This souped-up sensitivity may account for the apparent vividness of ordinary colors under the influence of the drugs, though tests show that vision is actually impaired slightly. It certainly reinforces the horrors.

LSD cultists say that sessions should be carefully prepared, under   20
the guidance of an experienced "leader." Leary calls this "perhaps the most exciting and inspiring role in society. A leader is a liberator, one who provides illumination, one who frees men from their lifelong internal bondage."

Diagnostic X Ray

Such rhapsodizing is pure, pretentious guff to most of the psychi-   21
atrists and psychologists who have worked with LSD, psilocybin and mescaline; they consider it the kind of happy talk that exerts a strong

appeal on just the sort of unstable people most likely to be injured by the drugs. Under the influence of LSD, nonswimmers think they can swim, and others think they can fly. One young man tried to stop a car on Los Angeles' Wilshire Boulevard and was hit and killed. A magazine salesman became convinced that he was the Messiah. A college dropout committed suicide by slashing his arm and bleeding to death in a field of lilies. Says Los Angeles Psychiatrist Sidney Cohen, one of the country's leading LSD experts: "If we can tolerate unsupervised use of LSD, why not Russian roulette? Or why not let children play with hand grenades?"

Chicago Psychiatrist Dr. Marvin Ziporyn, who has administered   22
LSD to some 50 patients since 1960—besides taking it himself, along with his attorney wife—sees LSD's laying bare of the personality in purely diagnostic terms. "LSD is, if you like, a psychiatric X ray," he says. "With LSD you have no greater vision of the universe than you did before. It no more expands your consciousness than an X ray expands your lungs when you see them on the screen. All you do is get a better look."

Some researchers, while sneering along with Dr. Ziporyn at the   23
view of LSD as instant mysticism, feel that the psychedelic drugs may eventually do more than merely give the psychiatrist a better look. There is evidence that it may be effective in rehabilitating alcoholics and narcotics addicts. Several doctors, among them Eric Kast of the Chicago Medical School, have reported LSD useful in relieving both the pain and anxiety of dying patients. Kast theorizes that the dissolution of antici- pation, the concentration on the present moment, which may be bene- ficial to the dying, is also what appeals to some of the young, for whom so much of life is deferred. "LSD impairs anticipation, and that's the sole characteristic that puts us on top of the animal heap," says Kast. "If people no longer feel the need to calculate the necessary delays before acting, then chaos could result." Often, relief over the lifted burden comes into conflict with a lingering sense of responsibility, and this, Kast suspects, is the cause of many a bad trip.

No responsible authority favors use of LSD without close scien-   24
tific supervision. On the other hand, no responsible authority wants to stop research into the potentially vast possibilities of LSD and other "mind drugs." New substances are already forecast, notably a "smart pill," derived from RNA, to speed up the learning process; this has given rise to the slightly uneasy crack that in a few years "people won't ask you what books you're reading, but what drugs you're taking." Some of the drugs may be bubbling even now in the retorts of Dr. Hofmann, who was back in the Basel lab last week after receiving from Stockholm's Karolingska Institute an honorary degree for the discovery of lysergic acid diethylamide.

For Discussion and Writing

1. As a door into the past, "LSD" gives us a sense of the thinking during the early days of what has become a national drug culture. What do you notice about the content, attitude, and tone of this essay that indicates how people felt about experimental or "recreational" drugs in 1966?
2. The author of "LSD" claims that the drug has two major effects. What are these? Why has the essayist included so much background information in the piece? What does this add to your understanding of the drug?
3. Does this essay take a strong stand for or against the use of LSD? What is the writer's attitude toward medicinal or therapeutic drugs?
4. What is your sense of the drug culture in the late 1960s to early 1970s? What influences did drugs seem to have on music, behavior, styles of dress or popular art? Write an essay in which you give your impressions of that period as they have been formed by your exposure of music, popular history, and the stories of friends and acquaintances.

Glass Houses and Getting Stoned

Michael Kinsley

*Using marijuana is . . . like what happens when a person
with fuzzy vision puts on glasses. Listening to a familiar
piece of music, such as a Bach orchestral suite, the mind is
newly conscious of the bass line; listening to a
conversation, the mind is more aware of the nuances of
each voice . . .*

—Charles Reich, *The Greening of America*

Right, and don't forget the taste of food, and . . . 1

In the great debate over legalizing recreational drugs, the least 2
convincing assertion of the pro-legalizers is that drug use might not
even increase as a result. I can state for certain that drug use would
increase. I don't use drugs now. If they were legal, I would use them.
Or rather, if marijuana were legal, I would use it occasionally instead
of the legal drug I now use regularly, alcohol. To be sure, increased
respect for the law is not the only reason so many middle-class, mid-
dle-age people have abandoned marijuana: you're also no longer so
carefree about where your mind might take you on automatic pilot,
especially in public. But society's official disapproval is a substantial
deterrent. Without it, many of us would sneak the odd toke or two.

The dishonesty at the heart of the drug debate is the refusal of both 3
sides to acknowledge the pleasure of getting high, a pleasure most
participants in the debate probably have experienced themselves without damaging effect. That in itself is no reason to legalize marijuana, let
alone more serious drugs. But sensible policy cannot be made without
taking it into account.

After last year's revelation that Judge Douglas Ginsburg, Presi- 4
dent Reagan's brief nominee to the Supreme Court, had smoked marijuana, there was a parade of politicians confessing that they too had
"experimented with" the evil weed. They all insisted that this was a
youthful indiscretion that they deeply regretted, and they all were
awarded little stars for courage and frankness. But where is the politi-

cian with the true courage to admit that he enjoyed smoking dope and does not especially regret it?

Both sides of the legalization debate cite the example of alcohol, without really understanding it. Pro-legalizers say other drugs are no worse than alcohol and it's hypocritical for society to spend millions trying to ban the use of "drugs" while other millions are spent promoting the use of Scotch. Anti-legalizers say, hypocrisy or not, we're stuck with the social costs of alcohol but that doesn't mean we need to add other drugs to the vicious stew.

But alcohol is not legal out of tragic necessity, just because Prohibition was a practical failure. Alcohol is legal because Americans *like* to drink. Almost all drinkers indulge their habit in moderation, with no harmful effect. Quite the reverse: alcohol is a small but genuine contribution toward their pursuit of happiness. Society has decided that the pleasure of drinking is worth the equally genuine cost to society and pain to many individuals of alcoholism, automobile accidents and so on. What's more, this social decision is correct. The world would *not* be a better place without booze, even if that were possible. The pursuit of happiness has its legitimate claims in the social calculus.

The mainstream argument for legalization is pragmatic: the war against drugs has failed, and the cost to society of keeping them illegal is greater than the cost of learning to live with them. Out at the fringes of respectability is the libertarian argument: people have the right to control their own lives, even to wreck their own lives, if that is their choice. Unmentioned as a reason for legalizing drugs, though widely believed and acted on as a practical matter by most Americans, is what might be called the Dionysian argument. Look, it says, the desire for an occasional artificial escape from the human condition is part of the human condition. It is not ignoble. In fact it's healthy. Yes, yes, within limits.

Please don't get the wrong idea. The author of this essay is no one's idea of a wild Dionysiac. That, in a way, is the point. The desire to get high occasionally is not restricted to a small self-destructive minority. It's shared by the most boring and respectable citizens.

The goal of sensible social policy should be to channel this natural human desire in safer directions, not to snuff it out, which is neither possible nor desirable. Thinking about the drug problem in this way focuses special attention on the role of marijuana. Current policy steers people like you and me, fellow bourgeois TIME readers, away from marijuana and toward alcohol. Is that a good idea? I'm not sure. Legalizing marijuana might steer the users of crack, heroin, PCP, etc., toward grass instead. Whether that's a good idea seems much clearer.

To repeat: the mere fact that getting high on marijuana brings pleasure to the vast majority of its adult users is not sufficient reason to legalize it. The majority of people probably could drive safely at 75 or

80 m.p.h., but we can't custom-make the rules for each individual and it's the minority at greatest risk we have to worry about. If a significant minority cannot use marijuana safely, if grass frequently leads to more dangerous drugs, if it has dangerous long-term side effects of its own, if the problems of keeping it from children are insurmountable, these are all important and possibly determinative considerations. But society's ability to weigh these factors is hobbled by its inability to accept the obvious truth: like alcohol's, marijuana's function as a pleasure drug is a plus, not a minus in the calculation.

In trying to make this case, it may seem like an unnecessary, 11 self-imposed handicap to start off with a quote from *The Greening of America*, the definitive expression of the 1960s zeitgeist and possibly the most foolish book ever to be serialized in *The New Yorker* and debated on the New York *Times* op-ed page (though that is a bold claim). But just 18 years ago, a book rhapsodizing about the pleasures of getting high got the kind of serious attention reserved more recently for *The Fate of the Earth* and *The Closing of the American Mind*. This is a sharp reminder of how far we've veered in the other direction, to the point where the Dionysian impulse is considered an illegitimate subject for social policy, except for the question of how far we dare to go in smothering it.

For Discussion and Writing

1. Kinsley begins his essay with a disarmingly honest statement of his own attitude toward one common drug. What is the effect of such an admission? Why is honesty an issue in the debate over drug policy?
2. How does Kinsley justify his assertion that "The world would *not* be a better place" without alcohol (6), and, presumably other pleasurable drugs? What is "the Dionysian impulse"?
3. What does Kinsley say the goal of a sensible drug policy should be? What kinds of standards would he use to determine whether or not a drug should be legal?
4. Kinsley grounds his argument in the assumption that people have a natural desire to "escape from the human condition" through drugs. Write an essay in which you argue in defense of or against the claim that "it's natural to want to get high once in a while." Should such an impulse be viewed as A) healthy, B) unfortunate but natural, or C) deviant—against acceptable human behavior?

Feeling Low over Old Highs

WALTER SHAPIRO

For the most part, I stopped smoking marijuana in the mid-1970s 1
because I grew bored with ending too many social evenings lying on
somebody's living-room rug, staring at the ceiling and saying, "Oh,
wow!" This renunciation was not a wrenching moral decision, but
rather an aesthetic rite of passage as my palate began to savor California
Chardonnay with the avidity I once reserved for Acapulco Gold. Yet as
an aging baby boomer, my attitudes remain emblematic of that high-
times generation that once freely used soft drugs and still feels more
nostalgic than repentant about the experience.

This permissive mind-set colors my instinctive response to cur- 2
rent drug problems. The initial breathless media reports of the crack
epidemic aroused all my journalistic skepticism, and I groused that the
antidrug frenzy seemed like *Reefer Madness* revisited. On those infre-
quent occasions when friends and acquaintances still pass around a
bootleg joint, my reaction remains benign tolerance. Just a few weeks
ago, when marijuana made a furtive appearance at my wife's 20th high
school reunion in upstate New York, I viewed this throwback gesture
as a quaint affectation, almost as if the class of '69 had all shown up in
tie-dye T shirts instead of business suits and cocktail dresses.

Many may scorn these confessions as evidence of immaturity, 3
unreliability and even moral laxity. But we are all the product of our life
experiences, and I, like so many of my peers, cannot entirely abandon
this *Lucy in the Sky with Diamonds* heritage. Normally I only share these
slightly outré sentiments with close friends. But such views have become a public issue with drug czar William Bennett's attacks on my
generation's self-indulgence, coupled with George Bush's prime-time
address to the nation on drugs. For in identifying those responsible for
the cocaine crisis, the President pointedly included "everyone who
looks the other way." Am I really a fellow traveler in this epidemic of
addiction? Do my affectionate, albeit distant, ties to 1960s-style permissiveness render me as culpable as Bennett claims? Or is my comfortable,
middle-class life so far removed from inner-city crack houses and the
Colombian drug cartel that any allegation of causal nexus represents
little more than politically motivated hyperbole?

The honest answer, which both surprises me and makes me squirm, is that to some degree Bennett and Co. are right. My generation, with its all too facile distinctions between soft drugs (marijuana, mild hallucinogens) and hard drugs (heroin and now crack), does share responsibility for creating an environment that legitimized and even, until recently, lionized the cocaine culture. This wink-and-a-nod acceptance, this implicit endorsement of illicit thrills, has been a continuing motif in movies, late-night television and rock music. My personal life may rarely intersect with impoverished drug addicts, but the entertainment media created in the image of people like me easily transcend these barriers of class, race and geography. [4]

And what should the Woodstock alumni association tell its offspring? Conversations with friends, especially those raising teenagers, suggest that adults with colorful pharmacological histories face unique problems in following the President's exhortation to "talk to your children about drugs." For such parents, family-style drug education often comes down to awkward choices like lying about their own past, feigning a remorse that they do not feel, or piously ordering their children to read lips rather than re-enact deeds. More subtle messages can get lost in the adolescent fog. One 17-year-old I know well seems to misinterpret his parents' preachments about the particularly addictive nature of cocaine to mean, choose prudently from the cornucopia of other drugs available at your local high school. How much easier the burden must be for a parent who can honestly instruct his children, "Don't tell me about peer pressure. Remember, I got through the '60s without drugs." [5]

Such self-righteousness is inappropriate for those of us with a less sterling record of resisting temptation. Thus I stand, a bit belatedly, to concede my guilt in contributing in a small way to the drug crisis. Maybe the '60s were a mistake, maybe I too frequently condoned the self-destructive behavior of others, maybe I was obtuse in not seeing a linkage between the marijuana of yesteryear and the crack of today. I hope that this admission, which does not come easily, will animate my behavior. But while I am willing to shoulder some of the blame on behalf of my generation, I trust that the other equally respectable co-conspirators in America's two-faced war on drugs will acknowledge their own complicity. [6]

The list, alas, is long. Begin with public officials who have exploited the issue for 20 years, advocating phony feel-good nostrums like the current fad for drug testing in the workplace, as if mid-level bureaucrats were society's prime offenders. Joining the politicians in the dock are those antidrug crusaders who have either squandered credibility with exaggerated scare talk or strained credulity with prissy pronouncements. The media are culpable as well, for sensationalized cov- [7]

erage that has often served to glamorize the menace they are decrying. Then there are the social-policy conservatives who purport to see no connection between the flagrant neglect of the economic problems of the underclass and the current crack epidemic. And sad to say, well-intentioned parents can also contribute to the hysteria by viewing drugs as the sole cause of their children's problems, rather than as a symptom of family-wide crisis.

For drug use, as Bennett argues, is indeed a reflection of the   8
nation's values. And as long as American society continues to place a higher premium on titillation than truth and on callousness than compassion, the latest attack on drugs may prove, like all the failed battle plans of the past, to be mostly futile flag waving.

For Discussion and Writing

1. Shapiro opens his discussion with several paragraphs of personal material, in which he talks about his age, his drug-using past, his social class. What purpose does such autobiographical detail have in his argument supporting (former) drug czar William Bennett's attack on the 1960s generation?
2. Who else does Shapiro blame as "respectable co-conspirators in America's two-faced war on drugs"? How are they also responsible for creating the climate he condemns?
3. Given what you know about drug use in this country, do you agree that a specific generation or period of social change should be blamed for causing the drug problems? What other causes might also contribute to the widespread use of illegal drugs?
4. Write a personally expressive essay about your own feelings, attitudes, doubts, or beliefs about the drug culture. Speculate about possible causes, justifications, solutions. Is drug use the most important social issue facing us today? What other national problems might be even more serious?

Thinking and Writing about Chapter 7

1. Both Kinsley and Shapiro use humor in their treatment of drug use. Who or what are the targets of their jokes? What is the effect of these lighter moments? Is humor appropriate when writing about such a serious subject? Why or why not?
2. Compare Kinsley's and Shapiro's attitudes toward the drug issue. Where, specifically, do they differ? Do they share any common views?
3. Through interviewing or a brief questionnaire, conduct an informal survey among your fellow students in which you try to determine attitudes toward drug policy. Compile the results in an informative essay, using brief quotations from your subjects to illustrate student views.

8

Violence in American Life

Turn on the television tonight, or read the newspaper, or watch a movie, and what are you likely to see? Violence, murder, mayhem. Violent behavior—beatings, killings, bombings, wars, even genocide— is so commonplace in the world that we may hardly even notice it. We enclose ourselves in a cocoon of personal goals, ambitions, relation- ships, seeking order in an obviously chaotic and dangerous universe. Maybe human violence is just an extension of some kind of cosmic brutality, creation and destruction on an infinite scale.

Still, that doesn't solve the very difficult and disturbing problem of violence in our midst—and it doesn't make us any less reluctant to avoid unlighted city streets or to leave our doors unlocked at night. Violence seems a uniquely American preoccupation, something we endlessly lament and glorify.

In this chapter's essays, three *Time* writers address the issue of American violence. In "Psychology of Murder," from April 1972, Vir- ginia Adams seeks to understand the nature and causes of a pervasive and ghastly social problem. In "The Male Response to Rape," from April 1983, Roger Rosenblatt analyzes male psychology in the context of violent sexual crimes. And in "Crime and Responsibility," from May 1989, Charles Krauthammer mounts an impassioned attack on a young gang accused of raping and nearly beating to death the woman who became known only as "the Central Park jogger."

Psychology of Murder

VIRGINIA ADAMS

For all its sinister drama, the Mafia's bloodletting accounts for 1
only an insignificant fraction of the killings that occur every year in the
U.S. The rising toll sometimes seems to validate H. Rap Brown's mor-
dant dictum: "Violence is as American as cherry pie." In 1970 there were
16,000 criminal homicides in the nation—one every 33 minutes. With
the carnage mounting—up 8% from the previous year and 76% over the
decade—the U.S. is maintaining its long-held, unhappy distinction of
leading advanced Western nations in the rate at which its citizens
destroy one another. Philadelphia, for example, with a population of
2,000,000, has the same number of homicides annually as all of England,
Scotland and Wales (pop. 54 million).

This murderous preeminence, fostered by the nation's longstand- 2
ing habit of violence, occurs against a background of street crime,
political assassination and an almost obsessive violence in movies and
television. It has led many behavioral scientists to begin talking about
a national "crisis of violence." In the U.S., warns Psychiatrist Thomas
Bittker, "violence is practiced as if it were productive." It may have been
so for the Stone Age hunter of mammoths, but in the era of H-bombs it
is not only non-productive but distinctly suicidal. Man has become so
dangerous to himself that his continued existence has been called into
doubt.

Saul Bellow's Mr. Sammler reflected gloomily that killing is "one 3
of the luxuries. No wonder that princes had so long reserved the right
to murder with impunity." Yet there has always been a democracy of
homicide. Ever since Cain slew Abel, murder has been a classless crime.
The East Harlem father who hurls his children from the roof is paral-
leled across the Hudson in the affluent New Jersey suburbs: a Westfield
insurance salesman named John List was indicted last winter on a
charge of shooting his wife, mother and three children and ranging four
of the bodies side by side in his mansion's empty ballroom.

Although murder is part of the fabric of history, it has assumed an 4
alarming quality in America today. It is a new truism that violence has
become what sex used to be, the object of morbid fascination. A sort of

blind Mansonism hangs in the air—an incomprehensible glorification of death and destruction.

However common it has become, murder is still the crime com- 5
mitted by others: men and women dissociate themselves from murderers by assuming that all killers are psychotic. But most are not. Psychiatrists do not know precisely how those who have killed are different from those who have not. In contrast to the Mafia's business killing, for example, murder among laymen is generally a very personal matter. In three out of four cases, the murderer and victim know each other; in one out of four, they are related by blood or marriage. An estimated five out of six killers are men, and 60% of murderers are blacks—as are 55% of victims. In 1970, 43% of the suspects arrested for homicide were under 25; 10% were younger than 18. Nearly half (45%) of all killings occurred in the South, which has about 30% of the nation's population. But the murder rate was highest in big cities: 17.5 murders for every 100,000 inhabitants, compared with 6.4 in rural areas and only 3.8 in the suburbs.

The sheer availability of firearms is undoubtedly a stimulus to 6
murder. There are perhaps 115 million privately owned guns in the U.S., almost one for every male between 14 and 65. Indeed, guns are used in 65% of all U.S. killings. Twenty percent of the victims are dispatched by knife, while poison is rarely used. In Manhattan, there have been two recent cases of murder by bow and arrow, and some years ago another New Yorker attempted murder by rattlesnake. As Princess Sita observed in *Ramayana*, the ancient Indian epic of nonviolence: "The very bearing of weapons changeth the mind of those that carry them."

Most nonprofessional killings are impulsive—done in a flash of 7
anger triggered by a minor insult or a quarrel over money, love or sex. Many are committed by people who, Sociologist Stuart Palmer says, "tend to be overconforming most of the time"—which may help to explain their extreme violence when their rebellious impulses finally break out. Often the killer does not intend to kill; in at least 20% of the cases, he is acting in self-defense.

Sometimes murder can be indirect, an act that Psychoanalyst Joost 8
Meerloo calls psychic homicide: consciously or unconsciously, the murderer pushes someone into suicide. Meerloo cites an engineer who had struggled "all his life with a harsh, domineering and alcoholic father." On a final visit, he took along a bottle of barbiturates, suggesting that they could "cure" his father's addiction. In combination with alcohol, the prescription was fatal.

The impulse to murder seems to be universal, but the reasons that 9
men and women yield to it are as varied and mysterious as human history. To most psychiatrists, murder usually implies a defect in the killer's ego. Sometimes, of course, the motive appears to be nothing

more complicated than the desire for material gain. In family murders, a frequent motive is the killer's conviction that no one, not even his wife, understands him. Says Psychiatrist Frederick Melges: "He may expect empathy without communicating his feelings. Paradoxically, attempts at communication may lead to the discovery that the partner does not understand." If that happens, he may feel embittered, deserted and alone, and may strike out in sudden rage at the thwarting of his expectations. A number of criminals, Psychiatrist George Solomon believes, "feel that the only attention they can evoke is punishment," and for them "murder may be a way to be killed." Long before being convicted of murdering his landlady, whom he liked, a New York sculptor named Robert Irwin told a psychiatrist: "I was going to kill somebody so that I would be hung."

Even this crime is less terrifying than what Poet Robert Penn 10 Warren calls "blank, anonymous murder," the motive-less, gratuitous atrocity. In Warren's words: "An old man on a park bench reading his papers, smoking his morning cigar, is dead suddenly because some kid decided to kill him." These days, says Theodore Solotaroff, editor of *New American Review,* "a kind of anarchic murder is in the air."

Anarchic murder is not new. It occurred during the European 11 plague epidemics of the 16th century, when hooligans plundered at will, sometimes cutting the throats of the sick. It was common during the Thirty Years War in the 17th century, when troops ravaged the countryside indiscriminately. New or old, wanton slaughter recalls the question posed by Nietzsche's red judge: "Why did this criminal murder?" Nietzsche's reply: "His soul wanted blood; he thirsted after the bliss of the knife."

. . .

Not many contemporary thinkers would accept this view of man 12 as essentially savage. True, Freud once believed that human beings are born with an aggressive instinct and that "the aim of all life is death," but he later abandoned the idea. Currently, Ethologist Konrad Lorenz insists that aggression and violence are inevitable because they were bred into man by natural selection during prehistoric times. But there is widespread disagreement with this theory. Psychiatrist Fredric Wertham, for example, considers the Lorenz view "nonsense," calling it "not explanation but rationalization."

Frustration frequently touches off aggressive behavior. It can take 13 many forms, and often arises from a feeling of physical, social or intellectual inferiority. It can also result from physical and psychological brutality inflicted during childhood. Describing one parental attack, a mother told Sociologist Palmer, "I thought the boy was done for. His father knocked him from one end of the house to another like a man gone insane." Observes Palmer: "Perhaps it was coincidence, perhaps it was not. But when he was 24, that same boy beat to death a man 30 years older than himself."

Sometimes the frustration that fires aggression is highly imper- 14 sonal. Yale Psychoanalyst Robert Jay Lifton links at least some violence to general frustration, anger and anxiety over countless "little deaths"—the failure of national morality, the breakdown of family life and feelings of alienation in a mobile population. Boredom, too, drives people to look for meaning in nihilistic violence, to accept the philosophy "I kill, therefore I am."

Most behavioral scientists believe that aggressive behavior is 15 learned, often by observation, and some are convinced that violence on TV fosters violent behavior in both children and adults. Along with eleven other researchers who carried out studies for the U.S. Surgeon General, Psychologist Robert Liebert asserts that, for healthy as well as disturbed children, "a clear and important link has been shown between TV violence and aggressive behavior." As for the theory that watching TV violence drains off the viewer's own savage impulses, Political Scientist Ithiel de Sola Pool maintains that "if there is any kind of cathartic effect, it is swamped by the incitement effect." A few experts consider the TV-violence controversy something of a red herring. "Even if we did away with all the violence on TV we would have solved nothing," says Psychoanalyst Ner Littner. "There is no such thing as a single simple cause or a single simple solution. Searching for scapegoats allows us to avoid facing the problem of why we are violent, and also postpones the solution."

. . .

In the opinion of many behavioral scientists, historians and phi- 16 losophers, the Viet Nam War, more than any previous conflict, has helped to foster violence at home. One evidence of the war's impact is indicated by a recent national survey of attitudes toward the Calley case. According to Harvard Psychologist Herbert Kelman, many Americans regard Lieut. Calley's behavior at My Lai as normal. That suggests, Kelman concludes, that an alarmingly large segment of the population might be willing to employ extreme violence if ordered to do so.

Even more ominous is the trend toward the philosophical and 17 artistic glorification of violence and death. Following Sartre, many young people believe that "violence is man re-creating himself," and that savagery is a kind of purifying force bearing, as Historian Richard Hofstadter puts it, "the promise of redemption." Murder has always been a central theme in the arts. There were killings (off-stage) in the Greek theater. The Shakespearean stage was often littered with bodies by the fifth act. As early as the 19th century, American writers like Melville and Poe were beginning to show what Historian David Davis had called "undisguised sympathy for sublime murders and amoral supermen moved by demonic urges." That sympathy seems to have deepened recently, especially among movie directors. Arthur Schlesinger Jr. speaks of "a pornography of violence," and Critic Pauline Kael complains that "at the movies, they are desensitizing us." She objects to a film like *Straw Dogs* because it equates violence and masculinity. Few psychiatrists would argue with her. Nor would they disagree with critics who object that filmed violence has become the ultimate trip, the stimulus for mind-blowing sensations wilder than any induced by LSD.

Some behavioral scientists, philosophers and aestheticists believe 18 that violence in the arts is not bad *per se* and that it may, in fact, be the best means of inspiring a horror of violence. Brutality in films, asserts Robert Lifton, "can illuminate and teach us about our relationship to violence." *The Godfather*, he believes, provides that kind of illumination by brilliantly contrasting the Corleone family's sunny private life and its brutally dark professional life. Critic Robert Hatch rejects that view, calling the movie a "chronicle of corruption, savage death and malignant sentimentality" that wreaks harm by forcing the viewer "to take sides in a situation that is totally without moral substance." It was chilling, he says, "to hear an audience roar its approval when a young gangster on 'our' side blew the brains out of two gangsters on 'their' side."

That easy empathy with cinema slayings, together with a growing 19 tolerance of real-life brutality, suggests a dismaying conclusion: beneath the surface, Americans may be less alarmed by murder—and more attracted to it—than they care to admit. Just as an individual must become aware of his problems before they can be solved, the nation, too, will have to acknowledge its unhealthy fascination with murder as the first step toward coming to terms with it.

For Discussion and Writing

1. Adams characterizes American violence in 1972, a full generation ago. What parallels do you see with violence today? Compare recent crime statistics to the ones Adams cites (paragraphs 5–6). What conclusion do you draw?
2. Adams cites several causes of murderous violence in American society. What are these? Do you believe that some people have a murderous instinct, that they thirst after "the bliss of the knife" (11)?
3. Toward the end of her essay, Adams links the violence in society with its expression in popular arts such as film. What does she conclude

about the fact that Americans find movie murder entertaining, and that there seems to be "a growing tolerance of real-life brutality"?

4. Writing from a personal perspective, speculate whether your exposure to cinematic or televised violence (real or fictional) had made you less disturbed by it. Do you find violence troubling or alarming? When viewing it as fiction, is it entertaining? Why do you think so? Can we separate the violence we consider as imaginary from what we know to be real?

The Male Response to Rape

ROGER ROSENBLATT

Between the book reviews and the science notes, the third gang rape of the past two months. This one occurred in the Charlestown section of Boston, where seven young men have been charged with kidnaping a 17-year-old girl and raping her repeatedly for seven hours in an apartment belonging to one of the men. The incident followed the more widely publicized attack in New Bedford, Mass., some weeks earlier, in which four men raped and tormented a woman for two hours on a pool table in Big Dan's bar, while onlookers cheered. That one was preceded by yet another at the University of Pennsylvania; there a young woman has charged that she was gang-raped by five to eight fraternity brothers during a party. Class distinctions need not apply. If one is tempted to construct a hypothesis around shiftless young Irishmen in a poor city neighborhood or the unemployed Portuguese in a depressed fishing port, sociology is obliterated by the party boys from the U. of P., no different in kind or action, just privilege. All subhumans are created equal.

Reading of such incidents, women are horrified because inevitably they identify both with the victims in particular and with the entire condition of victimization, of which gang rape may be the harshest instance. But why do men recoil so strongly? The straightforward answer is that the vast majority of men disapprove of rape, and their disapproval is intensified when a gang is involved. Yet the idea of gang rape is repugnant to men for reasons of identification as well. Few men would associate themselves with those who actually "did it to her." But quite more than a few know what it is to be caught in the middle of an all-male show of power and coercion, and thus to be complicit, even at the fringes, in something their consciences abhor.

Gang rape is war. It is the war of men against women for reasons easy to guess at, or for no reasons whatever, for the sheer mindless display of physical mastery of the stronger over the weaker. In the wake of the reports from Charlestown, New Bedford and the University of Pennsylvania, conjectures are bound to arise about the frustration of contemporary man at the growing independence of women, and there may be some truth to that. But men have never needed excuses to commit rape in gangs. The Japanese in China, the Russians in Germany, the Pakistanis in Bangladesh. Read accounts of what some American soldiers did to Vietnamese village girls of 13 and 14 in places like My Lai, and it seems clear that the subject of gang rape goes a good deal deeper than modern man's humiliation.

One psychological theory has it that these acts are homosexual rituals: men in groups desire each other, yet are ashamed of their urges, and so they satisfy themselves by convening at a common target. Another theory holds that there are situations where men so seek to prove their masculinity to one another that they will do anything, including murder. An American soldier in Viet Nam described how, for no other reason than that a comrade led the way, he shot to death a girl he had raped. Sex and violence have an eerily close kinship as it is. Rape itself may be a form of murder, the destruction of someone's will and spirit. No wonder those same soldiers in Viet Nam spoke of dragging girls into the woods "for a little boom-boom." To "bang" a woman remains part of the idiom. The sound is a gun, the body a weapon. In a "gang bang," murder becomes a massacre.   4

Upon learning of such things at a distance, most men feel not only revulsion, but also a proper urge to enact society's revenge. Lock the bums away forever. At the same time, they can still imagine what it feels like to be present at the atrocities, even for the briefest instance; every life has analogues of its own. The essential circumstance is that of the mob, always a terrifying entity, whatever its goal. One thinks of lynch mobs before rape mobs, but all mobs have the same appearances and patterns, the same compulsion to tear things down or apart. The object of passion is sighted and pursued. The mob rises to a peak of pure hate, does what it does, then slinks away, its energy spent. Perhaps every mob commits rape in a way. Anybody who has ever seen a mob in action senses its latent sexuality—the collective panting, the empty ecstasy. Even at the outskirts, the voyeur participates. Eventually he may run or protest, but for at least one long moment he is helpless to move.   5

It is that moment of seemingly hypnotized attention most men know and dread. It is a moment in which they are out of control as individuals—not merely outside the law, but out of biological order. Something stirs, an ancient reflex, as if they are dragged back through history to a starting point in evolution. The mob is a pack, its prey the female. Her difference is the instigator, her frailty the goad. Rape what you cannot have. Plunder what you can never know. Mystery equals fear equals rage equals death. It is she who stands for all life's threats, she who released animal instinct in the first place. Once aroused, why stop to reason or sympathize? The savage surfaces, prevails.   6

Of course, this happens only occasionally, in the heat of battle or Big Dan's bar or Charlestown or the Alpha Tau Omega house, where   7 boys were boys. But gang rape does not need to recur frequently to remind men of their own peculiar frailty. And that reminder brings terror, not the terror of the victim, to be sure, but one as benumbing in its way: that of acknowledging one's natural potential for violence and destruction. Rape need not be involved. Was not that you, so many years ago, standing on the sidelines while that other boy was bullied in the playground? Or you in the crowd that razzed the old drunk in the park? Or you in the rear when they set fire to the cat? Child's play, possibly, but boy's play primarily; and the child becomes the man. If you have cast off most of the cruelty of boyhood, still some of the fascination with cruelty remains. The fascination is a form of cruelty itself, expressionless, primeval, a fisheye in the dark.

No, that is not you boozing it up in the Charlestown apartment, or you, college boy, or you, Portuguese sailor. But isn't that *you*, propped neatly behind the desk, growling ever so faintly under your no-starch-in-the collar, reading intently of all the shocking gang rapes? 8

At the beginning of *Julius Caesar*, before Caesar's assassination, Casca has a premonition of disaster that he reports to Cicero: "Against the Capitol I met a lion, who glared at me, and went surly by." The implication is that in every civilization, however lofty, a lion always roams the streets; the jungle never entirely disappears. What most men fear is a lion in the soul. Women, too, perhaps, but not in the matter of rape. That is male terrain, the masculine jungle. And no man can glimpse it, even at a distance, without fury and bewilderment at his monstrous capabilities. 9

For Discussion and Writing

1. Throughout his essay, Rosenblatt uses graphic and often powerful language to describe and analyze male violence against women. What is the effect, for instance, of his opening lines? His analysis of the kinship between sex and violence in the language of rape (4)? His sexual metaphor in paragraph 5?
2. Rosenblatt defines gang rape in terms of mob psychosis (3–6). Does the comparison in any way absolve men of responsibility in the act of rape? Why or why not?
3. Toward the end of his essay, Rosenblatt uses his discussion of gang rape to imply something larger and perhaps even more disturbing about the male psyche. What is it? Why does he shift, in this passage, and address the reader as "you"?
4. Rosenblatt implies that all men harbor the capacity to commit violence against women, that all have "monstrous capabilities." Do you agree? Writing from your perspective as a man or woman, address Rosenblatt's claim, using evidence from your own knowledge and experience to support your case.

Crime and Responsibility

CHARLES KRAUTHAMMER

"I'm depraved on account I'm deprived."

—West Side Story

Twelve years ago, Bonnie Garland, a pretty, upper-class Yale   1
student, was murdered. Her estranged boyfriend went up to her bedroom one night and with a hammer cracked her head open "like a
watermelon," as he put it. Murders are a dime a dozen in America. But
the real story here, the real horror, chronicled in painful detail by
Willard Gaylin (in *The Killing of Bonnie Garland*), was the aftermath:
sympathy turned immediately from victim to murderer, a Mexican
American recruited to Yale from the Los Angeles barrio. Within five
weeks he was free on bail, living with the Christian Brothers and
attending a local college under an assumed name. Friends raised
$30,000 for his defense. "From my investigation," wrote Gaylin, "it is
clear that more tears have since been shed for the killer than for the
victim."

Now in New York City another awful crime. A 28-year-old jogger   2
was attacked in Central Park by a gang of teens from nearby Harlem.
Police say the boys hunted her down, beat and raped her savagely and
left her for dead. At week's end she remained in a coma.

In New York the instinct to "Garland" the monstrous—to exten-   3
uate brutality and make a victim of the victimizer—is more attenuated
than in the Ivy League. The New York tabloids, the moral voice of the
community, are full-throated in their vilification of the monstrous "wolf
pack." It is their social betters, those from the helping professions, who
have lost their moral compass. It is they who would Garland this attack
if they could.

These children are "damaged," explains forensic psychologist   4
Shawn Johnston. "They are in pain inside . . . acting out their pain on
innocent victims. In the case of the Central Park beating, they picked a
victim that was most likely to shock and outrage. That speaks to how
deep their anger and despair is."

"We have to be honest," explains psychologist Richard Majors.   5
"Society has not been nice to these kids."

"They're letting out anger," explains Alvin Poussaint, the Harvard   6
educator and psychiatrist. "There's a lot of free-floating anger and rage
among a lot of our youth."

Rage? Upon arrest, police said, the boys joked and rapped and   7
sang. Asked why he beat her head with a lead pipe, Yusef Salaam was
quoted by investigators as saying "It was fun." The boys have not yet
been taught to say they did it because of rage, pain and despair, because
of the sins whites have visited upon them and their ancestors. But they
will be taught. By trial time, they will be well versed in the language of
liberal guilt and exoneration.

How could boys have done something so savage. We have two   8
schools. The "rage" school, which would like to treat and heal these
boys. And the "monster" school, which would like to string them up.

I'm for stringing first and treating later. After all, the monster   9
theory, unlike the rage theory, has the benefit of evidence. What distinguishes these boys is not their anger—Who is without it?—but their
lack of any moral faculty. Acts of rage are usually followed by reflection
and shame. In this case, these characteristics appear to be entirely
missing.

The boys were not angry. They were "wilding." Wilding is not   10
rage, it is anarchy. Anarchy is an excess of freedom. Anarchy is the
absence of rules, of ethical limits, of any moral sense. These boys are
psychic amputees. They have lost, perhaps never developed, that psychic appendage we call conscience.

Conscience may be inbred, but to grow it needs cultivation. The   11
societal messages that make it through the din of inner-city rap 'n' roll
conspire to stunt that growth. They all but drown out those voices
trying to nurture a sense of responsibility, the foundation of moral
character.

For example, the ever fatuous Cardinal O'Connor could not resist   12
blaming the park assault on, well, society. We must all "assume our
responsibility," he intoned, "for being indifferent to the circumstances
that breed crimes of this sort." What circumstances? "Communities
which know nothing but frustration."

When the Rev. Calvin Butts Ill of Harlem's Abyssinian Baptist   13
Church was asked by cbs about the attack, he spoke of "the examples
that our children are faced with." Such as? We've had Presidents resign,
foreign Prime Ministers resign in disgrace. We've had Oliver North lie
publicly on television . . . And many of our youngsters, across racial
lines, see that and then act it out."

Richard Nixon. Noboru Takeshita and Ollie North may have   14
much to answer for in the next world, but the savaging of a young

woman in Central Park is not on the list. The effect of such preposterous links is to dilute the notion of individual responsibility. Entire communities are taught to find blame everywhere but in themselves. The message takes. New York *Newsday* interviewed some of the neighbors of the accused and found among these kids "little sympathy for the victim." Said a twelve-year-old: "She had nothing to guard herself; she didn't have no man with her: she didn't have no Mace." Added another sixth-grader: "It is like she committed suicide."

There is a rather large difference between suicide and homicide. 15
For some, the distinction is not obvious. They must be taught. If not taught, they grow up in a moral vacuum. Moral vacuums produce moral monsters.

Young monsters. The attackers are all 14 to 17. Their youth is yet 16
another source of mitigation. In addition to class and racial disadvantage, we must now brace ourselves for disquisitions on peer pressure, adolescent anomie and rage.

Spare us the Garlanding. The rage in this case properly belongs to 17
the victim, to her family and to us.

For Discussion and Writing

1. Krauthammer's essay is strongly worded and filled with rage. What are the targets of his anger? Do you think he is correct? Do you agree with his utter lack of sympathy for those who committed the attack?
2. Where do you think the author's language is most effective or powerful? Where might it be faulted for excess?
3. Is there a contradiction in Krauthammer's accusing the gang of "lack of any moral faculty" and at the same time advocating that they be "strung up"? How do you react to the author's implicit defense of lynch mob psychology?
4. Using Krauthammer's essay as a model, use impassioned language to attack a current problem of social violence about which you feel strongly. Possible subjects: date rape, the death penalty, child abuse, drunk driving, gun control.

Thinking and Writing about Chapter 8

1. Compare and contrast the attitudes these three writers take toward their subjects. Which of them seems to be most emotionally involved? To what extent does such passionate expression help to clarify, or to obscure, the difficult issues surrounding violence in our culture?
2. If America is truly a violent society, why do you think it is? Why should life in the United States be any more violent than in other democratic or industrial nations? Are the causes to be found in our history as a rebel country, in our age-old racial injustices, in the "sheer availability of firearms," as Virginia Adams says? Or is it a mistake to think that Americans' fascination with violence is any greater than elsewhere in the world, where terrorism, political assassination, torture, and mass murder also can be commonplace?
3. If you have had personal experience with violence of any kind, whether to yourself or another, write an essay in which you express your feelings about the event and your understanding of what it meant to you. How has it altered your outlook on life, your daily behavior, you relations with other people?

9

The Battle for Racial Equality

During the Civil Rights Movement of the early 1960s, when issues of racial justice seized the American public mind, there was a moment when it seemed that a great new era had been opened. Congress and the Johnson administration passed landmark legislation ensuring voting rights and equal opportunity, and blacks and whites worked together to reshape national life. But then, with the assassination of Martin Luther King, Jr., in 1968, and the subsequent riots, and with the recessions and energy crises of the 1970s and 1980s, the euphoria of King's dream faded, and the hard daily battles of politics and economics reasserted themselves.

Today, we find race still at the forefront of public debate, now joined, however, in an increasingly complex social soup, by other minority-, ethnic-, age-, and gender-related issues. It seems that everywhere we turn—in our communities, on the campuses, in the nation at large—people are in opposition to one another, arguing about rights, obligations, duties, historical grievances, equitable social policy. What has happened to the old American idea of the melting pot—people of widely diverse heritage and belief coming together to build a new world? Was it ever really true, and, if it was, will it ever return?

The essays in this chapter address the issue of race, especially the historical tension between blacks and whites. In "The Great Black and White Secret," from March 1981, Roger Rosenblatt looks through the complexity of race relations to find elemental and often ignored common ground. In "The Powers of Racial Example," from April 1984, Lance Morrow considers the nature of influential models within the black community. And in "Reparations for Black Americans," from December 1990, Charles Krauthammer proposes what he calls "a historic compromise."

110

The Great Black and White Secret

ROGER ROSENBLATT

In James Baldwin's first novel, *Go Tell It on the Mountain* (1952), there is a brief early scene in which Baldwin's 14-year-old black hero, John Grimes, takes a headlong run down a hill of melting snow: "At the bottom of the hill, where the ground abruptly leveled off onto a gravel path, he nearly knocked down an old white man with a white beard, who was walking very slowly and leaning on his cane. They both stopped, astonished, and looked at one another. John struggled to catch his breath and apologize, but the old man smiled. John smiled back. It was as though he and the old man had between them a great secret."

At least part of their great secret is that they both live in the same country. White and black have shared that secret for a long time now, and have done an efficient job of keeping it from each other. The smile that connected John Grimes and the old man, while pleasant enough for the occasion, was historically speaking a lapse of judgment, a slip of the heart. If Baldwin had been writing news instead of fiction, John might never have thought to apologize, and the old man might have swung his cane like a war club.

Now that would make a scene one could more easily believe in. After all, it repeats itself constantly one way or another these days— black and white giving each other the fisheye in elevators; making great sudden arcs on the sidewalk; or even less subtle, the dinner party conversation between black and white that zeroes in on The Black and White Question like a surface-to-air missile. The lily-white athletic club. The coal-black radio station. It is odd to think that this is where the civil rights movement of the 1960s has wound up, or down. But as any strict constructionist will adjure, the civil rights laws were enacted to allow for equal chances, not equal smiles; so it should hardly shock the system to learn that, on the bulk of the evidence, official and personal, the American social scene is less mixed now than ever. In the March issue of FORTUNE, Roger Wilkins sees blacks and whites separated by a widening "social chasm." Recent reports of the U.S. Commission on Civil Rights and of the National Urban League concur.

The formal causes of this separation are no great secret to anyone—busing, housing, crime, the normal distances between the too rich and the too poor. Terms like white flight and steering have become so comfortable in the national argot that one almost forgets that they are weapons. Affirmative action has helped split black and white as well, particularly black and blue collar and black and Jew, on the issue of quotas. Then too there are the white lies told daily in the universities by faint-hearted, if well-meaning, professors writing false recommendations for unprepared black students for jobs in which they are bound to fail; the professors then are lost in dismay when the students fail and resent the lie. All these things and more, including white racism, whose unredeemed resilience may be read in the revival of the Klan, or scrawled above the nation's urinals, where it belongs.

Yet, even if all the familiar impediments to social integration were suddenly to be lifted from the country, few nowadays believe that black and white would rush toward each other automatically, unhesitantly. The differences between black and white America run awfully deep. And the deepest of them are not found in surveys or in statistical studies, or even in the most open conversations. Where they do crop up, as they always have, is where they are taken least seriously: in the fiction and poems of black writers, where as art they may be both revealed and camouflaged simultaneously. That passage in *Go Tell It on the Mountain,* for instance. Moving as it is, it makes the point that despite their shared smile and great secret, the black boy and the white man do not speak or meet again.

A similar scene occurs in Chester Himes' *If He Hollers Let Him Go* (1945). Himes' hero, Bob Jones, takes his girlfriend to an exclusive restaurant, where the waiters stick them off in a corner and where other customers ogle the black couple as if they were birds in a zoo. Jones' girlfriend is mortified. He trembles between panic and rage. Looking around the room, he sees a white ensign and a "very blond girl" sitting with an older couple, evidently the parents of one of them. Jones and the ensign have been casually admiring each other's girlfriend, and when their eyes meet neither shows hostility, "only a mild surprise and a sharp interest." Forgetting his situation momentarily, Jones suddenly has a "wistful desire to be the young ensign's friend." Then he catches the "frosty glare" of one of the elders at the ensign's table, which kills the moment and restores reality. That scene could be written today.

To use art as evidence for arguments about the real world is a tricky business because artists are supreme individuals as well as supreme liars. Yet if one surveys the body of black American writing from Reconstruction to the present, a remarkably consistent picture of black America, of America itself, springs to life. The mythology of that literature is a historical fact, the nation's worst—slavery. Besides the moral damage that slavery did the nation, it also created a cultural framework at once so distorted and solid that we live within it still.

Its central distortion was that the enslaved man was not a man; he   8
was the opposite of a man, whatever that might be. His very color was
a sign of deviation, a sign to be carried by generations after him, like
the mark of Cain. There are a dozen scenes in black American novels
where a child is going along happily until someone (often a school-
teacher) points out the "difference" in his life, which is also the difference of his future. At that revelation the child flees in panic to a mirror
in order to stare at himself, to see himself for the first time as the white
world sees him, as something "other," a vision of the negative.

From that point on, his life becomes a series of oppositions. A   9
young black girl like Janie of Zora Neale Hurston's novel *Their Eyes Were
Watching God* (1937) may see that she is beautiful, but how can black be
beautiful if the standard of beauty is to be white, blond, fair? How can
black be good if cleanliness (whiteness) is next to godliness, if Satan is
the Prince of Darkness, if there are blackguards and blackmail, black
thoughts and black deeds? To be in the dark is one thing, but to see the
light is quite another. Images of whiteness can be terrible too, of course
(the white whale, whited sepulchers, death on a pale horse), but these
are fairly concrete things compared with the general designation of
black as the color of evil or chaos. Young John Grimes is named for dirt.
He observes the dirt around him, and recalls the book of *Revelations (22:
11):* "He who is filthy, let him be filthy still."

All this is kid stuff compared to the final opposition, which is to   10
be dehumanized completely. Slavery at its worst did that job most
efficiently, but when slavery was no longer available, something else
evidently had to take its place. In his autobiography, *Black Boy* (1945),
Richard Wright tells a story of himself as a teen-ager working in an
optical factory in Memphis. Some local white men tried repeatedly to
goad Wright and Harrison, another black boy who worked for a rival
company, into a fight by telling each that the other hated him. When
that lie failed, the men offered the boys $5 apiece to step into the ring.
The boys hesitated, but eventually accepted, for the money, agreeing
between themselves to pull punches. On a Saturday afternoon in a
basement before a frenzied white audience, Wright and Harrison went
at each other, stripped to the waist. They jabbed faintly at first; then one
hit too hard; then the other. Finally they had to be pulled apart, having
beaten each other to the point of exhaustion. After the fight, full of
shame, they would not speak. What the white men had originally
contended was so after all. The boys actually did hate each other. The
lie became the truth.

When lies come true, there are not too many places where one can   11
get a grip on life. The idea of time in black writing, for example, of time
as an index of progress, or as a context of history, has either no meaning

or a dangerous one (Ralph Ellison's 1952 novel, *Invisible Man,* struggles to escape from time). The idea of Christianity is also suspect because the church, while an instrument of salvation, is also an instrument of social containment, a taming device. The idea of home is elusive and treacherous, with one's home being traced either to a ghetto or to a Southern plantation or, as in Toni Morrison's *Song of Solomon* (1977), into the past, where there are more dreams than roots. Is the U.S. itself home? That is no easy problem for a people from whom much of the country's bounty has been withheld, yet who are far more native sons than most whites.

For its part, the white world, which both made and denied that   12 home, has behaved within its own set of distortions. Out of its abiding guilt it has created a code of self-protecting lies, including a sexual phantasmagoria about blacks that has resulted in everything from cheap jokes to lynchings. (In black novels, heroes fear the accusation of rape far more than that of murder.) Guilt has also created stereotypes. In a poem on the comic actor Willie Best, LeRoi Jones listed the unlaughable characteristics: "Lazy/ Frightened/ Thieving/ Very potent sexually/ Scars/ Generally inferior/ But natural rhythms." White America has also created itself—a world that, when depicted in a novel like William Melvin Kelley's *dem* (1967), comes off as pallid, literally colorless, and trapped. In *Drylongso,* an oral history collected by John Langston Gwaltney and published last July, Jackson Jordan Jr., a nearly 90-year-old black North Carolinian, puts it to white people rather kindly: "Pretending to know everything or just pretending to be better than you know you are must be a terrible strain on anybody."

As for the strain on the black man and woman, it shows in various   13 ways. Paul Laurence Dunbar, the black dialect poet, explained, "We Wear the Mask." That is one way of surviving; as a con man, a common figure in black fiction. Another way is to "disappear," to pass for white or otherwise become anonymous. The *Invisible Man* disappeared altogether, forging a life of an existential fact: since he was invisible to the white world anyway, why not go whole hog? The third way—separation—brings America back from fiction to reality. In a sense, separation often seems the most reasonable choice. After all, black Americans have a richly independent culture quite apart from the one that has been imposed upon them, a culture made up of its own music, language, a common past. With a history of such guilt and hate between them, why should black and white persist in a sham? Why should they not go their separate-but-equal ways?

In fact they should, if there were such a thing as being able to   14 choose one's friends and lovers with absolute freedom. The lingering question, however, is: Are these choices actually made freely, or are they so encumbered by past associations and events that separatism is merely expedient? Certainly it is safer and more convenient for black and white to retain their color lines. But if these lines are retained not by choice but rather by fear, then the acts of division are not freely made. Indeed, they are as unnatural and distorted as anything that ever characterized the relationship.

Whether blacks and whites actually have something to gain from 15 social integration is yet to be proved. It is all very well to mumble about the glorious prospect of cultural exchange, but no one is sure that such exchanges breed enhancement. A loftier argument is that the nation, as a whole, would be improved. Perhaps. The old democratic vista of Whitman and Emerson, the transcendentalist democracy of one for one and one for all sounds quite fine; it always has. Since that goal has never been achieved, however, one may argue that it is simply another tenet of American hypocrisy, or, less harshly, that it is a goal incompatible with the realities of human nature.

Still, it is also human nature to underestimate the realities of 16 human nature. The fact is that fragments of social integration are achieved every day, like it or not. They occur every time black and white happen to catch each other without armor—white not wearing its white, nor black its black—in those elevators, at those dinner parties, at work—in careless stumbles into unguarded affection, like Baldwin's pair. Despite the "social chasm," those moments may now be occurring more frequently than ever, though they fail to be recorded. Eleanor Holmes Norton, former head of the Equal Employment Opportunity Commission, calls ours the "cross-over generation." Could be. The cross-over would certainly be worth a try.

Yet for that to happen, it will take not only time and patience but 17 a certain alertness. A black boy smiles at a white man who smiles back. The moment is construed as accidental. It is not accidental. It is their essential relationship, only made to appear accidental by cruel history, fears and stupidity. The boy who smiles at the man recognizes him; recognizes the man recognizing the boy. Either they can choose to treat that act as a mere acknowledgment, as a separate-but-equal nod, or they can elaborate on it—dress it up, fill it out, talk. They know perfectly well what life is like when they do not do that; that is no great secret. The great secret is that they may need each other.

For Discussion and Writing

1. According to Rosenblatt, what is the great secret between black and white Americans? How might acknowledgment of this secret help bridge the gulf between the races?

2. Rosenblatt says that slavery "created a cultural framework at once so distorted and solid that we live within it still" (7). What do you think he means? How do the distortions caused by slavery continue to affect relations between blacks and whites?
3. To support his analysis of racial tensions, Rosenblatt looks at the literature of black writers: James Baldwin, Chester Himes, Zora Neale Hurston, Richard Wright, Ralph Ellison, Toni Morrison, and others. Why does he look to these authors for guidance, and what kinds of ideas do they express?
4. Rosenblatt implies that current tendencies toward black and white separation are a failure of the civil rights movement, which sought to do away with the concept of "separate but equal." Do you agree with Eleanor Holmes Norton that the "social chasm" between black and whites can and should be crossed? What can individuals do to ease racial tensions? Based on your own experience, write an essay in which you address the issue of race relations and its challenges.

The Powers of Racial Example

LANCE MORROW

The ghost of Tiresias told Ulysses to carry an oar upon his 1
shoulder and walk inland until he met a traveler who did not know
what an oar was. Thus Ulysses, exhausted by the sea, would recognize
that he was safely home.

Some day, possibly, the American racial odyssey will end, and 2
racial hatred, like the oar, will be an item of bafflement and curiosity:
What was the point of all that, anyway? Why was it so fierce, so
enduring?

In recent months, the nation has taken a few steps on the inland 3
march. Some of them were merely tokens of motion, but considered
together, they amount at least to an interesting procession of symbols.
The first black American astronaut went into space. For the first time a
black was crowned Miss America. Blacks now are the mayors of four of
the largest American cities: Los Angeles, Chicago, Philadelphia and
Detroit. Congress proclaimed a national holiday to honor Martin Luther
King Jr., and a conservative Republican President endorsed the idea.

And, in the most significant display, the first black presidential 4
candidate (or the first with a serious following), King's disciple, Jesse
Jackson, sits side by side in debate with the two white Senators running
for the Democratic nomination. Whatever errors he has made elsewhere
in the campaign (stupid, private references to Jews as "Hymie," his
close relationship to a poisonous character who heads the Nation of
Islam), Jackson has sometimes sounded in the debates like the only
grownup in the race. In any case, the spectacle of a young black man
treated equally with two whites in a fight for the most powerful office
on earth would have been unthinkable in the U.S. a generation ago.

During the '70s, a powerful white politician in New York was 5
discussing the realities of his trade. He shook his head in disgust.
"Forgot the black vote," he said. "Blacks don't vote." They do now, as
New York discovered last week. George Wallace learned the lesson
sometime earlier and later found himself out courting the blacks whom
he had once symbolically blocked at the schoolhouse door.

It is fitting that Jackson should be the man to enspirit the black 6
electorate. For years he has been the one black leader whose attention

was focused clearly on the dramatic stage on which the last act of the American racial melodrama will eventually be enacted. That stage is located in the black mind.

The journey of American blacks has been a series of epic passages: 7
the "Middle Passage" from Africa . . . the long passage through slavery to the Emancipation Proclamation . . . the false dawn of Reconstruction . . . the terrorist Klan era with its night-riding death squads . . . the passage north to South Side Chicago and Detroit and Harlem . . . then *Brown* vs. *Topeka* and desegregation and the Martin Luther King era and the Great Society. What is unfolding now may be thought of in years to come as the Jesse Jackson era for black America. Whatever Jackson's role in the journey, the ultimate passage to be accomplished is the internal passage, the psychological passage.

To say that the last battle must be fought in the minds of blacks   8
themselves strikes some as a perverse exercise of white man's jujitsu, a way of blaming the victim. If psychology is involved, surely it is the white mind that must change, not the black. Anyway, the problems of blacks are not psychological but harsh and external, and if anything, getting worse. There are many black Americans, of course, and it is difficult to make large generalizations, psychological or otherwise. But statistics can take the overall readings. The median income of blacks is only 55% that of whites. Black unemployment is, as usual, twice that for whites. Many black families are stable, but more than half of black babies are born to unwed mothers. The lives of American blacks are sicklier and shorter than those of whites. And so on.

Yes. But as Jackson knows, the ultimate victory over the problems   9
begins in the will and morale and imagination of blacks. The residue of the slave mentality still eats at that morale, still drips acids on the self-esteem. The external arrangements of things (Jim Crow and all the rest) seeped many generations ago into the heart and left there an annihilating anger and, sometimes, a self-loathing. Blackness has found it difficult to esteem itself in the imperiously white contexts of things. Besides, some of the arrangements designed to help poor blacks have simply replicated the patterns of the plantation. It is the same old configuration of subservience and *noblesse oblige*, of dependence and resentment and contempt, the part of the (benevolent) master played by the Federal Government, and the blacks still living in the slave quarters (ghettos) on the white man's dole.

In the service of black morale, symbols are immensely important.   10
"Tokenism" has a bad name, but tokens have their uses. People become only what they can imagine themselves to be. If they can only imagine themselves working as menials, then they will probably subside into that fate, following that peasant logic by which son follows father into a genetic destiny. If they see other blacks become mayors of the largest

cities, become astronauts, become presidential candidates, become Miss Americas and, more to the point, become doctors and scientists and lawyers and pilots and corporate presidents—become successes—then young blacks will begin to comprehend their own possibilities and honor them with work.

For years Jesse Jackson has stood in front of high school audiences 11 and led them in psychological cheers: "I am . . . somebody!" The theme is not original with Jackson. Marcus Garvey, for example, thundered the idea: "Up, you mighty race, you can accomplish what you will!" That is a perfectly American thought, although usually addressed to individuals, not races. The U.S. has always been an immense struggle of the wills of the people who came here, a struggle of cultural and moral energy and discipline. The American Indians' story represents an immense tragedy, a catastrophic demoralization, almost a cultural extinction. Then one sees certain Korean Americans, with their sharp commercial energy, their Confucian family discipline and, often, very rapid rise (in one generation) from vegetable stand to Harvard Medical School. American blacks still struggle between the two states of mind, the one leading toward disintegration, the other toward success and acceptance.

It may be many years before the U.S. elects a black President—or 12 for that matter, a Mexican-American President or a Korean-American President. But it now becomes thinkable for a black child to entertain a fantasy that used to be advertised as every white boy's dream: that he might grow up to be President.

Hunger and joblessness are not psychological, but the beginning 13 of the solution is. Symbols can bring change. They have real power in the world. "Firsts" proceed and become seconds and thirds, until they are no longer phenomenal but routine. As that happens, more American blacks will become, in a sense for the first time, citizens of the United States.

For Discussion and Writing

1. Morrow claims that blacks have made recent progress in American public life. Which evidence does he cite to support his point?
2. What does Morrow mean by "the power of racial example"? What does he mean when he says (8) that "the last battle must be fought in the minds of blacks themselves"? Do you agree with his assumption, attributed to Jesse Jackson, that "the ultimate victory over the problems begins in the will and morale and imagination of blacks"? Why or why not?

3. Black Americans "still struggle between two states of mind," Morrow says (11). What are these two states? How may symbols be powerful forces to help resolve this struggle?
4. Morrow assumes that strong models, heroes of a kind, help mold our behavior. Do you agree? Write an essay in which you characterize a person who influenced you, or one whom you have tried to emulate. If possible, choose a racial or ethnic figure, either someone known to you personally or on the national scene.

Reparations for Black Americans

CHARLES KRAUTHAMMER

"**N**obody's asking for reparations. I'm asking you to give us the crumbs from the table," said Craig Washington, one of five black Congressmen from the South, on the floor of the House. What crumbs? More and stronger affirmative action as mandated by the Civil Rights Act of 1990.

George Bush, an aristocrat who hates to deny crumbs to anyone, vetoed the bill anyway, on the ground that it encouraged racial quotas. But the bill was more than just bad legislation. It was a sign of intellectual bankruptcy in our thinking about race. As race relations worsen, as ethnic divisions harden, as an ex-Nazi pulls nearly as many votes in Louisiana as did the 1988 Democratic presidential candidate, the country has run out of ideas.

Take the Civil Rights Act of 1990. It makes it easier for minorities to sue the boss if the employee roster does not meet some statistical measure of racial balance. A nightmare for employers, a bonanza for lawyers, a crumb for blacks. How many, after all, would be helped by such legislation, and at what cost?

There is no denying that affirmative action has started some blacks on the ladder of advancement and thus helped create a black middle class. There is equally no denying that because it violates the rights of some people purely on the grounds of race, it has exacerbated racial resentments.

But as Shelby Steele argues, preferential treatment for blacks has an even more pernicious cost: it creates corrosive doubt in the eyes of both whites and blacks about the worth of any black achievement. However much people may deny it, no one can see a black professor or doctor without having the thought run through his mind: Did he make it on his own or did he get through on a quota? These doubts gratuitously reinforce in both blacks and whites a presumption of racial inferiority.

Moreover, the idea that affirmative action is just a temporary remedy is a fraud. With every new civil rights act, like the one just attempted and soon to be reintroduced in the 102nd Congress, ethnic quotas and race consciousness become more deeply woven into American life. The current uproar over race-based college scholarships reminds us just how divisive the issue can be.

What is to be done? Representative Washington has it exactly   7
backward. Forget the crumbs, demand reparations. It is time for a
historic compromise: a monetary reparation to blacks for centuries of
oppression in return for the total abolition of all programs of racial
preference. A one-time cash payment in return for a new era of irrevocable color blindness.

Why reparations? First, because they are targeted precisely at   8
those who deserve them. By now affirmative action has grown to
include preferential treatment for Hispanics, women, the handicapped
and an ever-expanding list of favored groups. This is absurd. By what
moral standard should, say, a Marielito, already once rescued by America, enjoy a preference over, say, an Italian-American vet or an Irish cop?
A Richmond ordinance struck down two years ago by the Supreme
Court assigned 30% of city subcontracts to firms owned by minorities,
defined as "Blacks, Spanish-speaking [citizens], Orientals, Indians, Eskimos or Aleuts." Richmond, capital of the Confederacy, is not known
for its mistreatment of Eskimos. Yet under the law, Richmond would
have had to prefer an Alaskan Eskimo to a local white in city contracting.

Let us be plain. Richmond's sin—America's sin—was against   9
blacks. There is no wrong in American history to compare with slavery.
Affirmative action distorts the issue by favoring equally all "disadvantaged groups." Some of those groups are disadvantaged, some not.
Black America is the only one that for generations was officially singled
out for discrimination and worse. Why blur the issue?

Reparations focus the issue most sharply. They acknowledge the   10
crime. They attempt restitution. They seek to repay some of "the
bondsman's 250 years of unrequited toil." They offer the wronged some
tangible means to elevate their condition.

For that very real purpose, reparations should be more than   11
merely symbolic. Say, $100,000 for every family of four. That would cost
the country a lot—about 50% more than the cost of our S&L sins—but
hardly, for a $6 trillion economy, a bankrupting sum. (A 10-year 75¢ gas
tax, for example, would pay the whole bill.) Recession may not be the
best time to start such a transfer, but America will come out of recession.

The savings to the country will be substantial: an end to endless   12
litigation, to the inefficiencies of allocation by group (rather than merit),
to the distortion of the American principle of individualism, to the
resentments aroused by a system of group preferences. The fact is, we
already have a system of racial compensation. It is called affirmative
action. That system is not only inherently unjust but socially demoral-

izing and inexcusably clumsy. Far better an honest focused substitute: real, hard, one-time compensation.

But is not cash-for-suffering demeaning? Perhaps. But we have 13 found no better way to compensate for great crimes. Germans know that the millions they have dispersed to Holocaust survivors cannot begin to compensate for the murder of an entire civilization. Yet for irremediable national crimes, reparations are as dignified a form of redress as one can devise.

Racial preferences, on the other hand, are a demeaning form of 14 racial tutelage. Better the identity of a debt repaid, however impersonally, than the warm glow of condescension that permeates affirmative action.

It is time to reclaim the notion of color blindness before it is too 15 late. A one-time reparation to blacks would help real people in a real way. It would honor our obligation to right ancient wrongs. And it would allow us all a new start. America could then rededicate itself to Martin Luther King Jr.'s proposition that Americans be judged by the content of their character, not by the color of their skin.

For Discussion and Writing

1. Taking a stand against government-mandated hiring of racial minorities (affirmative action programs), Krauthammer criticizes racial quotas on several grounds. What are his objections? Do you agree that "preferential treatment for blacks . . . creates corrosive doubt in the eyes of both whites and blacks about the worth of any black achievement"?
2. What does Krauthammer propose in place of such government programs? Why does he make such a proposal, and what does he claim will be its benefits?
3. How does the author justify cash payment as a legitimate form of compensation for America's mistreatment of blacks?
4. Krauthammer argues both in favor of reparations and against affirmative action. What is your view of government regulation of minority hiring? Write an essay in which you give serious consideration to the perspective of minority workers seeking employment. Should social justice be a factor in employer-employee relations?

Thinking and Writing about Chapter 9

1. Each of these essays refers to the formative experience of blacks in America: slavery. Compare the author's treatment of slavery as a continuing cause of black-white problems. How can something that was supposed to have ended in the previous century still be a factor in the way blacks and whites think about and relate to one another?
2. To what extent is racial or ethnic discrimination an issue in your life? Do you come from a community in which such tensions exist? What sort of racial or ethnic values did you grow up with, and how have those values changed? Are you hopeful, or pessimistic, about the future of race relations? Why?
3. Write a persuasive moral argument in which you speak to the reader's possible racial bias. What might you say to a person you knew to be racially prejudiced? How might you start to convince that man or woman to change attitudes, assumptions, behavior?

10

Sexual Politics

Authors James Thurber and E. B. White once collaborated on a book satirizing relationships between men and women. Published in 1929, *Is Sex Necessary* took a decidedly male slant, but was accurate in its assumption that men and women at least have the potential to be ceaseless adversaries. The so-called war between the sexes has had its truces—romantic periods when love seems to conquer all—but in recent years the friction between competing interests, desires, and definitions of self seem once again to be rubbing feelings raw. There are good reasons for this, as people in a free society seek to improve their lot in life, and as women seek to overthrow generations of literal second-class citizenship.

Conflicts between men and women aren't the only issues involved in sexual politics, however. The gay rights movement, following closely on the heels of the women's movement of the 1960s and '70s, also has brought the plight of an oppressed minority into the public realm.

In this chapter, *Time* writers investigate three different aspects of these volatile contemporary disputes, issues that continue to occupy our attention. In "Women's Lib: Beyond Sexual Politics," from July 1971, Ruth Brine appraises what the women's movement has accomplished and proposes what the next step should be. In "Homosexuality: Tolerance vs. Approval," from January 1979, John Leo considers implications of the gay rights movement. And in "What Do Men Really Want?," from the Fall 1990 special issue, Sam Allis reports on the burgeoning men's movement and a reappraisal of contemporary masculinity.

Women's Lib: Beyond Sexual Politics

Ruth Brine

One would think that Kate Millett or Germaine Greer were   1
feeding the gentlemen their lines. More than 300 earnest women—ranging from Black Congresswoman Shirley Chisholm to Writer Gloria
Steinem to Betty Smith, former vice chairman of Wisconsin Republicans—met in Washington last week to form a National Women's Political Caucus. Its goal: to seek out and promote candidates of either sex,
preferably women, who will work to eliminate "sexism, racism, violence and poverty." And what was the reaction in San Clemente?
Discussing a newspaper photograph of four of the caucus leaders,
Secretary of State William Rogers remarked that it looked "like a
burlesque." The President replied: "What's wrong with that?"

. . .

Faced with that kind of crude, belittling response, it is no wonder   2
that women are often provoked to sharp recriminations, and sometimes
to stretching a point beyond reason. For example, along with setting
themselves the admirable goal of organizing politically, a few speakers
at the Women's Caucus also made some farfetched assertions. "We
must humanize America and save her," said Betty Smith, implying that
it is up to women to do the job. Author Steinem railed at the "masculine
mystique belief" in the inevitability of violence. If recriminations are in
order, one could with some justice blame women for passively tolerat-
ing that violence, since for some time now they have constituted more
than half of the electorate. To imply that they are more humane and
peace-loving than men is to make not only a dubious claim but a sexist
one.

The occasionally exaggerated rhetoric of the feminists would not   3
matter, except that it could discredit an important movement that still
has a long way to go. Are suburban wives really comparable to the
inmates of Nazi concentration camps? So Betty Friedan argued eight
years ago, groping for strong words in *The Feminine Mystique* to stir up
the feminist movement after its 43-year relapse following ratification of
the 19th amendment. Now, having achieved some success, the movement might be expected to show greater responsibility. Instead, in

126

countless books and "consciousness raising" sessions, hyperbole seems to have become its hallmark. "The majority of women drag along from day to day in an apathetic twilight," states Germaine Greer unequivocally in *The Female Eunuch*. She warns that "women have very little idea of how much men hate them." The draconian arbiter of *Sexual Politics*, Kate Millett, has mentioned the "envy or amusement" she noticed in certain men when Richard Speck murdered eight nurses.

Extremism in any movement—despite its attention-getting value—scares off potential followers, and makes it all too easy for dissenters to attack or ridicule its aims. Women's Lib is no exception. There is the further danger that female chauvinism will mislead and confuse the women themselves, particularly younger ones who have little experience to give them ballast. Consider, for example, the consequences of distorting or exaggerating three of the movement's most enlightening propositions:

1) Certain kinds of behavior and occupations have been expected of women from birth; it is therefore difficult for them to become autonomous individuals.

Elizabeth Janeway, 57, a novelist and mother of two sons who stands somewhat apart from the movement, provides a low-keyed discussion of this valid notion in a new book called *Man's World; Woman's Place* (William Morrow; $8.95). Unlike Millett, who drew on fiction, or Greer, whose examples came mostly from pop culture, Janeway borrows from academic sociology to explain how society maintains itself by means of roles and myths. One of her basic themes, applicable to either sex, is that individuals find it easier to adopt a ready-made self than to create one.

But social shifts can make familiar roles and myths archaic. Most Americans still believe that a woman's chief function is to be housewife and mother. In fact, 43% of American women today are in the labor force and 75% of these work full time, most of them because they have to support themselves or their families. Others work because they want a vocation with utility and meaning that their homes do not always provide—especially for a lifetime.

This does not mean that women have fundamentally changed; it is home and family that have been altered beyond recognition. The "virtuous woman" of *Proverbs* never thought about a "career," but she bought fields, planted vineyards, made fine linen and sold it. A few centuries ago, rural estates were, in effect, agricultural and industrial cooperatives, and women took their place beside men as managers of farms and workshops. Now there are few comparable possibilities for productive work at home; moreover the proportion of a woman's life devoted to care of her children, thanks to her longevity and the sharp reduction in the size of her family, has dwindled. Nonetheless, it is still considered somewhat unfeminine, even "abnormal," for a woman to stress her career; and to be regarded as abnormal today, Janeway points out, is almost as damaging as it was to be thought heretical in the Age of Faith.

. . .

Today's women should certainly see the traditional role as only   9
one possibility in their lives, and then feel free to accept or reject it. But are they conditioned by culture to accept it? Or at least influenced as powerfully as Women's Lib claims? Does overemphasizing this point discourage women from striking out for themselves? If cultural conditioning accounts for everything, there would be no Women's Lib. To devastate some feminists with whom she disagrees, Germaine Greer suggested that their theories were "devised by minds diseased by the system." If conditioning were all, Greer's mind would be no less diseased.

Liberated women should put cultural conditioning in its place,   10
along with Freud's notion of biology as destiny, which the movement's best ideologues have so brilliantly attacked. They might even, for a moment, pay heed to the archenemy. In *The Prisoner of Sex*, Norman Mailer suggests that "some necessity may exist in human life to rise above what is easiest and most routine for it. Humans-with-phalluses, hardly men at birth, must work to become men, not be—as Millett would have it—merely conditioned into men; and humans-with-vaginas, not necessarily devoted from the beginning to maternity, must deepen into a condition which was not female automatically, must take a creative leap into becoming women." The latter is not a popular ambition at the moment, but liberated women should not throw out the baby with the bath water. The important tip from Mailer is that to become anybody at all (certainly to become autonomous), one must make a creative leap beyond one's conditioning, not count on it or blame it.

2) Only by learning how society has hobbled her can a   11
woman heal herself.

The text of many consciousness-raising sessions seems to have   12
been taken from Søren Kierkegaard: "What a misfortune to be a woman! And yet the misfortune, when one is a woman, is at bottom not to comprehend that it is one." In other words, a woman is lucky only if she understands how unlucky she is.

Certainly there was no chance of changing society's attitudes   13
toward women until they dared to see themselves and their problems clearly. Yet how deeply and how long do they have to look? Many

women, especially those over 30, feel a sense of disbelief on reading the new chronicles of sexist injustice. There are some passages that seem to be authentic, that jibe with their experience and feelings, but on the whole, no. To take the diatribes at face value can lead to incapacitating bitterness. The central question was posed rather poignantly by a columnist in *Rat*, the radical women's underground newspaper "How to change pain into strength again?" she asked.

One of the most frequently invoked analogies in the movement is   14
that "woman is a nigger." Apart from its triteness (we now have students as niggers, and workers as niggers—everything but blacks as niggers), there is some question as to how apt the comparison is. Women are not segregated from their male "oppressors": moreover, women constitute 51% of the population, not 11%, as blacks do.

Nonetheless, Shulamith Firestone claims that it is worse to be a woman than to be a black. In *The Dialectic of Sex*, she contends that "feminists have to question not just all of Western culture, but the organization of culture itself, and further, even the very organization of nature. For we are dealing with an oppression that goes back beyond recorded history to the animal kingdom itself." What she means by "oppression," it turns out, is the necessity for females to bear offspring. Firestone is logical enough to see that only test-tube babies will save women from this predicament. But is it really necessary for women to go back, beyond history or forward to test tubes to gain social and economic equality?

3) Most men treat women as sexual objects.   16

This notion is now embraced by 57% of American women under   17
25, according to a recent poll by *McCall's* of 20,000 females. Many women who do not agree with the proposition still applaud the movement's rebellion against the *Playboy* philosophy. Even girls that girl-watchers watch are bored at being considered nothing more than Bunnies or potential bedmates and are delighted to reject the cosmetic look imposed by male tastes. Germaine Greer says that she is "sick of peering at the world through false eyelashes, so everything I see is mixed with a shadow of bought hairs." She should certainly remove them, even less radical women would agree.

Having made some valid points about the indignity of being   18
considered only sexual objects, a few of the feminists have unfortunately gone on to exaggerate the proposition. They now claim that women are almost universally victims of rape. Never since the Sabine women were put upon by the Romans has there been as much furor about this crime as in the past year or so. This outcry has less to do with violence in American cities than with the radicals' all-embracing definition of the offense. Last April, they organized an all-day "rape

workshop" in Manhattan, where they discussed such topics as "rape in marriage" and "the psychology of rapist and victim." (Child care was provided.) For women who cannot bring themselves to feel raped, there is a spectrum of lesser outrages to dwell upon, like being whistled at or ogled. Manhattan's *Village Voice* recently printed an essay "On Goosing" by Liberationist Susan Brownmiller, who furiously denounced all such male attentions as heinous insults, reminiscing painfully about her most memorable gooses from age 13 on and calling them "a long and systematic continuum of humiliation."

What should women do about lovers who treat them only as 19 sexual objects? Kate Millett suggests that women are virtually powerless before such men—Lady Chatterley before Mellors, for example. In celebrating the "transformation of masculine ascendancy into a mystical religion," D.H. Lawrence presents "sexual politics in its most overpowering form," she wrote. Katherine Anne Porter, no feminist at all but a perceptive novelist, analyzed the situation quite differently. "It is plain," she wrote in an essay eleven years ago, "that Lady Chatterley will shortly be looking for another man; I give Mellors two years at the rate he is going, if sex is really all he has to offer her, all she is able to accept. For if sex alone is what she must have, she will not abide with him."

More mischief lies in the Great Clitoral Controversy. Movement 20 radicals, misinterpreting Masters' and Johnson's laboratory experiments, declare that the clitoris is the key to womanly orgasm. They denounce Freud and his notion of the superior role of the vagina. Certainly women are entitled to any sort of orgasm they like. But girls who are now being enjoined to "Think clitoris!" are being sold a mechanistic view of sex that is almost as dehumanizing as the phallic consciousness of *Playboy*.

It is time for the movement to abandon sexual politics for real 21 politics. U.S. women have less political representation than their counterparts in many other Western democracies, and indeed less than they used to have. Maine's Margaret Chase Smith is the sole female Senator, and there are only eleven women compared with 422 men, in what New York Congresswoman Bella Abzug has derisively called the House of Semi-Representatives (she was also referring to its small number of young people and members of minority groups). In appointive positions, the record is even worse: women hold only 1.5% of the 3,796 top federal jobs. As a promising first step, the National Women's Political Caucus has already begun to organize groups in 26 states and Washington, D.C.

What, specifically, can politicized women do? Some will be fight- 22 ing for job equality (including pay), child-care centers or tax relief for mothers who have to work, and further liberalization of abortion laws, and safer means of contraception than the Pill. They will also pressure universities, still largely male sanctuaries, to admit women on an equal basis with men both as teachers and as graduate students. Sensibly, last week's Women's Caucus subordinated such specific, feminist aims in favor of such larger, humanistic goals as better housing and a national health-care system that might cut down America's infant mortality rate, now a shocking 14th among developed nations.

Achieving any of these goals will not be easy. They will, in fact, be   23 impossible to attain unless American women, both in and out of politics, demand a lot more of themselves and their daughters. In her classic treatise on womanhood, Simone de Beauvoir accused "the second sex" of exhausting its courage in dissipating mirages and stopping at the threshold of reality. She may be right. If they really want to liberate themselves and to create the kind of world they talk about, women must start thinking less about consciousness-raising and more about stepping across that threshold.

For Discussion and Writing

1. What is Brine's essential objection to the rhetoric of the women's movement in 1971? Which examples does she cite to support her claim?
2. Which aspects of the women's movement does Brine favor? What is her response to each of the three "enlightening propositions" the feminist movement has put forth?
3. What do you think Brine means when she says (18) that "it is time for the movement to abandon sexual politics for real politics"? What does she recommend for the feminist political agenda? In the time since this essay was written, have such goals for the most part been met or unmet?
4. Does Brine's essay seemed dated to you, or are some of the issues she raises still controversies or continuing matters of concern for women and men who support feminist goals? Write an essay in which you critique Brine's three central ideas from your own perspective as a man or woman. How do you see yourself in relation to feminist politics? Involved, indifferent, opposed?

Homosexuality:
Tolerance vs. Approval

JOHN LEO

Homosexuality is . . . (check one): 1) unnatural and
perverse, 2) a simple sexual preference, 3) a result of
childhood trauma, 4) learned behavior, morally neutral, 5)
a problem of genes or hormones, 6) a private matter that is
none of the public's business.

As answers to this question would prove, the nation has never   1
been so confused on the subject of homosexuality as now.

In general, there has been a marked growth of tolerance. In the   2
1960s, when an aide to President Johnson was arrested for committing
a homosexual act, he was expected to resign in disgrace—and did. This
year a Congressman who apologized for trying to buy sex from a
teen-age boy won his party's support, and re-election. Homosexual
publishing is booming, and gays now receive far more sympathetic
coverage in the media. Gay bars and bathhouses operate unmolested
in large communities and small. Police who were once notorious for
harassing homosexuals are now likely to be found playing good-will
softball games with gays. Although sodomy laws are still on the books
in many states, there is clearly little will to enforce them. The recent
attempt to pass major punitive legislation against gays—California's
Proposition 6—was soundly defeated.

At the same time, there is a strong reaction against the homosexual   3
rights movement. Polls show resistance to homosexuals as schoolteachers, and to laws that seem to enshrine homosexuals as a specially
protected minority. Still, now that homosexuals, and their opponents,
are pressing for various laws, many Americans are questioning their
own gut feeling that homosexuality is wrong. Many are downright
ashamed or guilty about this aversion. Is their feeling merely instinct
and prejudice? Or are there valid, respectable reasons for distaste for
homosexuality and its public claims?

132

The most basic opposition to homosexuality seems to arise from religion. In the Judaeo-Christian tradition, homosexual acts are considered sinful. Leviticus calls homosexuality "an abomination," and St. Paul condemns the practice three times. Homosexuals and their allies in the churches argue that these proscriptions are culture-bound and no longer apply. One argument is that the ancient Hebrews associated homosexuality with the competing Canaanite religion and with the vengeance of conquering armies, which routinely sodomized the vanquished as a gesture of contempt. Some Christians suggest that St. Paul was attacking a loveless sexuality and a refusal by heterosexuals to procreate. Another argument, received with some incredulity by conservative church members, is that Jesus Christ would have endorsed homosexual mating if he had been culturally able to envision Christians incapable of being attracted to the opposite sex. 4

What about other cultures? The only worldwide survey of sexual behavior, published in 1951 by Psychologist Frank Beach and Anthropologist Clellan Ford, found that 49 out of 76 societies approved some form of homosexuality. Yet this approval extended only to sharply limited expressions of homosexuality, such as ritual acts, puberty rites and youthful premarital affairs. Beach and Ford found no society where predominant or exclusive homosexuality was affirmed. 5

Even cultures and people not religiously oriented can object to homosexuality on broadly moral grounds. True, Kinsey considered bisexuality natural. Most researchers think that homosexuality, like heterosexuality, is learned behavior, the product of subtle interaction between a child and the significant people around the child. This argument now carries such weight in the academic world that researchers seem reluctant to investigate the origins of homosexuality without also investigating the origins of heterosexuality. 6

The main problem with this position is that heterosexuality requires no complicated explanation. Even though most heterosexual acts do not lead to reproduction, sex between a man and woman has an obvious biological function. Homosexuality has no such function, and cannot ever have it. The push of evolution and the survival of human culture are geared to heterosexual mating. 7

Another reason for opposing homosexuality—and one long considered very liberal—is that it represents a sickness, or at least some form of biological or emotional disorder. Evidence to date casts doubt on the theory that homosexuality is biologically based. Freud, who believed that homosexuality was the fruit of early psychic stress, considered it to be a developmental arrest rather than an illness. As he wrote to the mother of an American homosexual, "It is assuredly no advantage, but it is nothing to be ashamed of, no vice, no degradation, it cannot be classified as an illness." Freudians have spun off dozens of 8 theories of homosexuality, many of them focusing on mother fixation in males and a fear of aggression from other males.

In the hands of his successors, Freud's view hardened into the theory that homosexuality was pathological. But the rise of the Gay Liberation movement and the decline of popular support for the theories of psychoanalysis have seriously eroded the hard line Freudian view. Militant gays have been strikingly successful in portraying Freudianism as a kind of conservative priestcraft devoted to enforcing the heterosexual status quo. When the gay rights movement demanded that the American Psychiatric Association remove the "sick" label from homosexuals, the association was in no mood to disagree. First, the homosexual lobby had demonstrated, in the words of one Freudian, "that there is a large ambulatory population of homosexuals out there who do not need psychiatric help." And second, the lobbyists argued, with heavy effect, that the "sick" label is the linchpin of society's oppression of homosexuals.

In a highly political compromise, the A.P.A. adopted a statement declaring that "homosexuality, *per se,* cannot be classified as a mental disorder." The operative term, *per se,* left homosexuals free to think that they had been declared "normal" and traditional psychiatrists free to think that homosexuality, though not a disorder itself, was, or could be, a symptom of underlying problems. To compound the confusion, the association felt that it had to list homosexuality somewhere, so it created a new diagnostic category, "sexual orientation disturbance," for homosexuals dissatisfied with their sexuality. This diagnosis can only be applied with the patient's consent. It is a bit like dermatologists voting to ordain that acne is indeed a skin blemish, but only if the acne sufferer thinks it is. Though the A.P.A. vote seems to have pushed a great many therapists toward a more benign view of homosexuality, a strong body of psychiatric opinion still insistently holds that homosexuality reflects psychic disturbance. Last year an informal poll of 2,500 psychiatrists showed that a majority believed that homosexuals are sick.

Personality tests comparing heterosexuals and homosexuals have not been of much help in resolving the confusion. Seven recent studies of lesbians and straight women, for instance, conclude, variously, that: lesbians are not more neurotic but prone to anxiety; more neurotic; more depressed; less depressed; not more neurotic; not necessarily more neurotic; and less neurotic. The recent Kinsey Institute study of homosexuals, published as the book *Homosexualities,* reported that a minority of gays are indeed deeply disturbed, but that the majority function about as well as heterosexuals.

In the welter of conflicting studies, researchers tend to agree on at least one point: homosexuals report more problems with their par-

9

10

11

12

ents—unloving attitudes by at least one parent and parental conflict—than comparable groups of heterosexuals. This finding has been consistent among researchers who find homosexuals sick and those who find them well. Psychologists Seymour Fisher and Roger P. Greenberg, in their book *The Scientific Credibility of Freud's Theories and Therapy,* debunk much of Freud, but conclude that he was right about the fathers of male homosexuals. "In study after study," they write, "this father emerges as unfriendly, threatening or difficult to associate with."

Another area of agreement in the studies: there seem to be many   13
more male than female homosexuals. Kinsey estimated that there are two to three times as many males, and, though the actual figures are obviously unknowable, later researchers have roughly agreed. This evidence points away from the theory that homosexuality is a random variation (which ought to be randomly distributed by sex) and toward the theory that it is heavily related to special problems of male development, which appears to be more complicated and disaster-prone than that of the female. In this view, homosexuality is one of many unconscious strategies chosen by some children under great pressure, primarily pressure created by parents. It is, in short, nothing to despise, nothing to celebrate.

Many people disapprove of homosexuality because of the as-   14
sumption, long popular among some historians, that it is a sign of decadence and because of the fear of "contagion." About this, the evidence is, at best, mixed. The first point depends on what one means by decadence. The open, even glaring display of homosexuality may be seen simply as another sign of generally relaxed rules, which apply to heterosexual behavior as well. As for the "seduction of the innocent," there is little evidence that homosexual teachers, for example, are any more a threat to young pupils than heterosexual teachers. In most children, sexual orientation—the "learned" behavior that the psychologists talk about—is fixed early in life, probably by age five. In the rare cases when that orientation is not set until school age, it is doubtful that a homosexual teacher will have much impact. In fact, children raised by homosexual parents almost always grow up heterosexual. On the other hand, common sense observation shows that in many fields homosexuals do function as admired role models, and that growing social acceptance allows potential homosexuals to follow their bent rather than trying to suppress it.

In sum, there are plenty of "respectable," valid reasons, including   15
reasons of taste, for opposing homosexuality. That is very different from trying to justify the persecution or oppression of homosexuals, for which there is no case at all. The trouble, however, is that for most heterosexuals the issue is not tolerance but social approval—the differ-

ence between placards that read I'M PROUD OF MY GAY SON and I'M PROUD MY SON IS GAY. Every oppressed group seeks a positive image, and some gays argue that homosexuals will never be truly free until society produces a positive image of homosexuality. That is precisely what the majority of Americans are unwilling to grant, however much they regret the past oppressions of homosexuals.

Many people who do not consider homosexuality either sinful or   16
sick are still not prepared to say that it is merely a matter of preference, just as good as—if not better than—other forms of sexual behavior. This question of social approval lurks behind the debate over gay teachers. Many parents believe that if current laws dictate the hiring of gay teachers, future ones may require that homosexuality and heterosexuality be discussed in sex education classes as equally desirable choices. Richard Emery, a civil liberties lawyer in Manhattan, suggests just that. Gay Activist Bruce Voeller says he believes that parents who try to push their children toward heterosexuality are guilty of an unjustified use of "straight power." This is understandable minority-group politics. And it is just as understandable if parents reply that this argument is absurd, and that they want to spare their children the kind of shocks and pressures that seem to be involved in homosexuality.

The same kind of fear is operating in the debate over gay rights   17
laws. Though polls show increasing tolerance of homosexuality, opposition to laws that might be read as endorsements of homosexuality or special treatment for gays is clearly rising. As if to clinch the point that Americans are leaning in both directions at once, homosexual activists report that when rights laws are defeated, as they were in Miami, discrimination against homosexuals declines.

Homosexuals counter that increased tolerance is not enough, that   18
the nation owes them protective laws like those passed in favor of blacks and women. A good many liberals have bought this argument, partly out of feelings of guilt over past cruelties to homosexuals. But it is possible to doubt that homosexuals are a class of citizens entitled to such legislation. The government's function is not to guarantee jobs or apartments for every disaffected group in society but only to step in where systematic or massive discrimination requires it. That is clearly not the case with homosexuals, who, unlike blacks and women, are already well integrated into the economy. Homosexuals ("We are everywhere") claim that they represent 10% of every profession—police, fire fighters, teachers, surgeons, even the psychiatrists who voted on the mental health of homosexuals.

The homosexual complaint is a claim that homosexuals should   19
not have their private behavior judged when it enters the public arena. No group in America enjoys that protection under the law. "It's a life-style question," said one opponent of a gay rights law in Eugene, Ore. "We've never seen legislation passed to protect a life-style." Sim-

ple-minded prejudice is, of course, a standard feature of many hiring decisions. But, in a free society, employers and landlords are granted considerable latitude in taking into account all publicly known aspects of an applicant's character and behavior.

The problem is that laws passed for blacks and women are not   20 currently viewed as rare exceptions to the general rule that employers and landlords can hire or rent to whom they please. Instead, such laws have come to be regarded as a basis for extending the same legal guarantees to a wide array of other aggrieved groups. The handicapped, for instance, have been included as protected persons in much legislation. Alcoholics may be next. In fact, a professor has sued Brooklyn College on grounds that he was let go because of alcoholism. The Government has entered the suit on the professor's side, arguing that alcoholics should be considered handicapped persons under the 1973 Rehabilitation Act. If he wins the suit, it will be illegal for federally assisted colleges to prefer teetotaling teachers over alcoholics. Enough. The Government has better things to do than proliferate categories of unfireable citizens. Like Masons, millenarians and est graduates, homosexuals must take their chances in the marketplace, just as everyone else does.

It is true that America has a great deal to be ashamed of in its   21 treatment of homosexual citizens. It owes them fairness, but not the kinds of legislation sought by gay groups. In their franker moments, homosexual activists refer to gay rights laws as educational efforts and many heterosexuals have no wish to be part of such efforts. The best public policy toward homosexuals is no public policy at all—no sodomy laws, no special interventions pro or con. On matters of consensual adult sex, the law is, or should be, blind.

For Discussion and Writing

1. Written near the peak of the gay rights movement, Leo's essay may offend some readers. What might be the likely reaction of those in the gay community? What traditional objections to homosexuality does Leo list, and how persuasive are they?
2. Leo wants to distinguish between tolerance and outright endorsement of gay life. What is the difference between these two positions, and why does Leo support one but not the other?
3. What does Leo say should be the government's position with respect to gay rights? How does he justify his recommendation?
4. Given the evidence in Leo's essay, do you think public attitudes toward homosexuality have changed noticeably since 1979? Write a personally expressive treatment of the subject of gay rights, considering questions of tolerance, approval, fairness. What factors still make this issue so controversial?

What Do Men Really Want?

SAM ALLIS

Freud, like everyone else, forgot to ask the second question: What   1
do *men* really want? His omission may reflect the male fascination with
the enigma of woman over the mystery of man. She owns the center of
his imagination, while the fate of man works the margins. Perhaps this
is why so many men have taken the Mafia oath of silence about their
hopes and fears. Strong and silent remain de rigueur.

But in the wake of the feminist movement, some men are begin-   2
ning to pipe up. In the intimacy of locker rooms and the glare of large
men's groups, they are spilling their bile at the incessant criticism, much
of it justified, from women about their inadequacies as husbands,
lovers, fathers. They are airing their frustration with the limited roles
they face today, compared with the multiple options that women seem
to have won. Above all, they are groping to redefine themselves on their
own terms instead of on the performance standards set by their wives
or bosses or family ghosts. "We've heard all the criticism," says New
York City-based television producer Tom Seligson. "Now we'll make
our own decisions."

In many quarters there is anger. "The American man wants his   3
manhood back. Period," snaps John Wheeler, a Washington environmentalist and former chairman of the Vietnam Veterans Memorial
Fund. "New York feminists [a generic term in his lexicon] have been
busy castrating American males. They poured this country's testoster-
one out the window in the 1960s. The men in this country have lost their
boldness. To raise your voice these days is a worse offense than urinat-
ing in the subway."

Even more prevalent is exhaustion. "The American man wants to   4
stop running; he wants a few moments of peace," says poet Robert Bly,
one of the gurus of the nascent men's movement in the U.S. "He has a
tremendous longing to get down to his own depths. Beneath the turbu-
lence of his daily life is a beautiful crystalline infrastructure"—a kind
of male bedrock.

Finally, there is profound confusion over what it means to be a   5
man today. Men have faced warping changes in role models since the
women's movement drove the strong, stoic John Wayne-type into the

sunset. Replacing him was a new hero: the hollow-chested, sensitive, New Age man who bawls at Kodak commercials and handles a diaper the way Magic Johnson does a basketball. Enter Alan Alda.

But he, too, is quickly becoming outdated. As we begin the '90s, the zeitgeist has changed again. Now the sensitive male is a wimp and an object of derision to boot. In her song *Sensitive New Age Guys,* singer Christine Lavin lampoons, "Who carries the baby on his back? Who thinks Shirley MacLaine is on the inside track?" Now it's goodbye, Alan Alda; hello, Mel Gibson, with your sensitive eyes and your lethal weapon. Hi there, Arnold Schwarzenegger, the devoted family man with terrific triceps. The new surge of tempered macho is everywhere. Even the male dummies in store windows are getting tougher. Pucci Manikins is producing a more muscular model for the new decade that stands 6 ft. 2 in. instead of 6 ft. and has a 42-in. chest instead of its previous 40.

What's going on here? Are we looking at a backlash against the pounding men have taken? To some degree, yes. But it's more complicated than that. "The sensitive man was overplayed," explains Seattle-based lecturer Michael Meade, a colleague of Bly's in the men's movement. "There is no one quality intriguing enough to make a person interesting for a long time." More important, argues Warren Farrell, author of the 1986 best seller *Why Men Are the Way They Are,* women liked Alan Alda not because he epitomized the sensitive man but because he was a multimillionaire superstar success who also happened to be sensitive. In short, he met all their performance needs before sensitivity ever entered the picture. "We have never worshiped the soft man," says Farrell. "If Mel Gibson were a nursery school teacher, women wouldn't want him. Can you imagine a cover of TIME featuring a sensitive musician who drives a cab on the side?"

The women's movement sensitized many men to the problems women face in society and made them examine their own feelings in new ways. But it did not substantially alter what society expects of men. "Nothing fundamental has changed," says Farrell. Except that both John Wayne and Alan Alda have been discarded on the same cultural garbage heap. "First I learned that an erect cock was politically incorrect," complains producer Seligson. "Now it's wrong not to have one."

As always, men are defined by their performance in the workplace. If women don't like their jobs, they can, at least in theory, maintain legitimacy by going home and raising children. Men have no such alternative. "The options are dismal," says Meade. "You can drop out, which is an abdication of power, or take the whole cloth and lose your soul." If women have suffered from being sex objects, men have suffered as success objects, judged by the amount of money they bring home. As one young career woman in Boston puts it, "I don't want a

Type A. I want an A-plus." Chilling words that make Farrell wonder, "Why do we need to earn more than you to be considered worthy of you?"

This imbalance can be brutal for a man whose wife tries life in the   10
corporate world, discovers as men did decades ago that it is no day at
the beach, and heads for home, leaving him the sole breadwinner.
"We're seeing more of this 'You guys can have it back. It's been real,' "
observes Kyle Pruett, a psychiatrist at the Yale Child Studies Center. "I
have never seen a case where it has not increased anxiety for the man."

There has been a lot of cocktail-party talk about the need for a   11
brave, sensitive man who will stand up to the corporate barons and take
time off to watch his son play Peter Pan in his school play, the fast track
be damned. This sentiment showed up in a 1989 poll, conducted by
Robert Half International, in which about 45% of men surveyed said
they would refuse a promotion rather than miss time at home. But when
it comes to trading income for "quality time," how many fathers will
actually be there at the grade-school curtain call?

"Is there a Daddy Track? No," says Edward Zigler, a Yale psychol-   12
ogist. "The message is that if a man takes paternity leave, he's a very
strange person who is not committed to the corporation. It's very
bleak." Says Felice Schwartz, who explored the notion of a Mommy
Track in a 1989 article in the *Harvard Business Review*: "There isn't any
forgiveness yet of a man who doesn't really give his all." So today's
working stiff really enjoys no more meaningful options than did his
father, the pathetic guy in the gray flannel suit who was pilloried as a
professional hamster and an emotional cripple. You're still either a
master of the universe or a wimp. It is the cognitive dissonance between
the desire for change and the absence of ways to achieve it that has
reduced most men who even think about the subject to tapioca.

Robert Rackleff, 47, is one of the rare men who have stepped off   13
the corporate treadmill. Five years ago, after the birth of their third
child, Rackleff and his wife JoEllen fled New York City, where he was
a well-paid corporate speechwriter and she a radio-show producer.
They moved to his native Florida, where Rackleff earns a less lavish
living as a free-lance writer and helps his wife raise the kids. The drop
in income, he acknowledges, "was scary. It put more pressure on me,
but I wanted to spend more time with my children." Rackleff feels
happy with his choice, but isolated. "I know only one other guy who
left the fast track to be with his kids," he says. "Men just aren't doing
it. I can still call up most of them at 8 p.m. and know they will be in the
office."

Men have been bombarded with recipes to ripen their personal   14
lives, if not their professional ones. They are now Lamaze-class regulars
and can be found in the delivery room for the cosmic event instead of

pacing the waiting-room floor. They have been instructed to bond with children, wives, colleagues and anyone else they can find. Exactly how remains unclear. Self-help books, like Twinkies, give brief highs and do not begin to address the uneven changes in their lives over the past 20 years. "Men aren't any happier in the '90s than they were in the '50s," observes Yale psychiatrist Pruett, "but their inner lives tend to be more complex. They are interested in feeling less isolated. They are stunned to find out how rich human relationships are."

Unfortunately, the men who attempt to explore those riches with   15
the women in their lives often discover that their efforts are not entirely welcome. The same women who complain about male reticence can grow uncomfortable when male secrets and insecurities spill out. Says Rackleff: "I think a lot of women who want a husband to be a typical hardworking breadwinner are scared when he talks about being a sensitive father. I get cynical about that."

One might be equally cynical about men opening up to other men.   16
Atlanta psychologist Augustus Napier tells of two doctors whose lockers were next to each other in the surgical dressing room of a hospital. For years they talked about sports, money and other safe "male" subjects. Then one of them learned that the other had tried to commit suicide—and had never so much as mentioned the attempt to him. So much for male bonding.

How can men break out of the gender stereotypes? Clearly, there   17
is a need for some male consciousness raising, yet men have nothing to rival the giant grass-roots movement that began razing female stereotypes 25 years ago. There is no male equivalent for the National Organization for Women or *Ms.* magazine. No role models, other than the usual megabillionaire success objects.

A minute percentage of American males are involved in the handful   18
of organizations whose membership ranges from men who support the feminist movement to angry divorcés meeting to swap gripes about alimony and child-custody battles. There is also a group of mostly well-educated, middle-class men who sporadically participate in a kind of male spiritual quest. Anywhere from Maine to Minnesota, at male-only weekend retreats, they earnestly search for some shard of ancient masculinity culled from their souls by the Industrial Revolution. At these so-called warrior weekends, participants wrestle, beat drums and hold workshops on everything from ecology to divorce and incest. They embrace, and yes, they do cry and confide things they would never dream of saying to their wives and girlfriends. They act out emotions in a safe haven where no one will laugh at them.

At one drumming session in the municipal-arts center of a Boston   19
suburb, about 50 men sit in a huge circle beating on everything from tom-toms to cowbells and sticks. Their ages range from the 20s to the

60s. A participant has brought his young son with him. Drummers nod as newcomers appear, sit down and start pounding away. Before long, a strong primal beat emerges that somehow transcends the weirdness of it all. Some men close their eyes and play in a trance. Others rise and dance around the middle of the group, chanting as they move.

One shudders to think what *Saturday Night Live* would do with   20 these scenes. But there is no smirking among the participants. "When is the last time you danced with another man?" asks Paul, a family man who drove two hours from Connecticut to be there. "It tells you how many walls there are still out there for us." Los Angeles writer Michael Ventura, who has written extensively about men's issues, acknowledges the obvious: much of this seems pretty bizarre. "Some of it may look silly," he says. "But if you're afraid of looking silly, everything stops right there. In our society, men have to be contained and sure of themselves. Well, f__ that. That's not the way we feel." The goal, continues Ventura, is to rediscover the mystery of man, a creature capable of strength, spontaneity and adventure. "The male mystery is the part of us that wants to explore, that isn't afraid of the dark, that lights a fire and dances around it."

One thing is clear: men need the support of other men to change,   21 which is why activities like drumming aren't as dumb as they may look. Even though no words are exchanged, the men at these sessions get something from other men that they earnestly need: understanding and acceptance. "The solitude of men is the most difficult single thing to change," says Napier. These retreats provide cover for some spiritual reconnaissance too risky to attempt in the company of women. "It's like crying," says Michael Meade. "Men are afraid that if they start, they'll cry forever."

Does the search for a lineal sense of masculinity have any rele-   22 vance to such thorny modern dilemmas as how to balance work and family or how to talk to women? Perhaps. Men have to feel comfortable with themselves before they can successfully confront such issues. This grounding is also critical for riding out the changes in pop culture and ideals. John Wayne and Alan Alda, like violence and passivity, reflect holes in a core that needs fixing. But men can get grounded in many ways, and male retreats provide just one stylized option, though not one necessarily destined to attract most American men.

What do men really want? To define themselves on their own   23 terms, just as women began to do a couple of decades ago. "Would a women's group ask men if it was O.K. to feel a certain way?" asks Jerry Johnson, host of the San Francisco-based KCBS radio talk show *Man to Man.* "No way. We're still looking for approval from women for changes, and we need to get it from the male camp."

That's the point. And it does not have to come at women's ex-   24
pense. "It is stupid to conclude that the empowerment of women means
the disempowerment of men," says Robert Moore, a psychoanalyst at
the C.G. Jung Institute in Chicago. "Men must also feel good about
being male." Men would do well, in fact, to invite women into their
lives to participate in these changes. It's no fun to face them alone. But
if women can't or won't, men must act on their own and damn the
torpedoes. No pain, no gain.

For Discussion and Writing

1. Why, according to Allis, are men today supposedly angry and speaking
   out about sexual politics? What complaints are they voicing? What
   kinds of earlier male images have men apparently rejected, and what
   have they adopted for the 1990s?
2. If the women's movement helped men understand what it is like to be
   a woman in society, Allis says, it didn't change what society expects
   from men. What kind of issues or problems, according to Allis, do men
   continue to face? Are societal stereotypes an obstacle for men as well as
   for women?
3. How are some men currently attempting to rediscover or redefine their
   masculinity? Do you think a "men's movement" is necessary or holds
   much promise? Why or why not?
4. What do you think men want? Writing honestly, from your own perspective, try to define essential qualities of maleness, but avoid sweeping or categorical statements about "all men." You might want to isolate
   several types of masculinity, or to distinguish between definitions of
   men as they are and men as you would like to see them become.

Thinking and Writing about Chapter 10

1. Have older or more traditional ideas about men and women resurfaced in recent years? Comparing the essays by Brine and Allis, for example, what do you notice about changes in attitudes, behavior, values between 1970 and 1990?

2. Overheard in the library stacks: two male college students talking about men and women. One says, "I know women deserve the same rights and opportunities as men, but I still like to hold the door for them. I still want to treat women like ladies." Is this statement self-contradictory, inconsistent—or can men and women share equal rights and opportunities, while at the same time treating each other as sexual beings with profound differences? How do you think most men and women these days want to be treated by one another?

3. Are sexual politics—struggles about power, gender, freedom, responsibility, behavior—matters that concern you or with which you find yourself (even reluctantly) involved? Which issues seem the most directly problematic for you? How do you go about coping with them? Write an essay in which you detail your views on the relationships between men and women and each others' expectations.

11

Issues in Education

Chances are that if you're reading this you're in a college classroom, library or dorm. You're a student, probably new to campus, perhaps wondering about just what your education will mean to you, how you want to use it, and what the future may bring when you've gone on to the working world.

American education, by many counts one of the great achievements of a democratic society, is by no means a perfect system, and it continues to be plagued by a number of natural if unresolved and often thorny problems. Is educational quality as high as it should be? Are educational doors open to all citizens? Do programs exist to meet the diverse needs of an increasingly segmented population? What kinds of educational policies and standards must we maintain? How will education help to transform our society in the future?

The authors in this chapter consider a variety of educational issues from several perspectives. In "Against a Confusion of Tongues," from June 1983, William A. Henry III analyzes the current debate over teaching foreign students in the native languages, and argues against the notion of a permanently bilingual culture. In "Confessions of an Ivy League Reject," from April 1990, Walter Shapiro writes self-revealingly about educational snobbery, and about how his painful rejection by Harvard and its ilk eventually led to useful personal growth. And in "Teach Diversity—with a Smile," from April 1991, Barbara Ehrenreich argues forcefully in favor of embracing a multicultural perspective in higher education.

Against a Confusion of Tongues

William A. Henry

"We have room for but one language here, and that is the English language, for we intend to see that the crucible turns our people out as Americans and not as dwellers in a polyglot boarding house."

—Theodore Roosevelt

In the store windows of Los Angeles, gathering place of the world's aspiring peoples, the signs today ought to read, "English spoken here." Supermarket price tags are often written in Korean, restaurant menus in Chinese, employment-office signs in Spanish. In the new city of dreams, where gold can be earned if not found on the sidewalk, there are laborers and businessmen who have lived five, ten, 20 years in America without learning to speak English. English is not the common denominator for many of these new Americans. Disturbingly, some of them insist it need not be.

America's image of itself as a melting pot, enriched by every culture yet subsuming all of them, dates back far beyond the huddled yearning masses at the Baja California border and Ellis Island, beyond the passage in steerage of victims of the potato famine and the high-minded Teutonic settlements in the nascent Midwest. Just months after the Revolution was won, in 1782, French-American Writer Michel-Guillaume-Jean de Crèvecoeur said of his adopted land: "Individuals of all nations are melted into a new race of men." Americans embittered by the wars of Europe knew that fusing diversity into unity was more than a poetic ideal, it was a practical necessity. In 1820 future Congressman Edward Everett warned, "From the days of the Tower of Babel, confusion of tongues has ever been one of the most active causes of political misunderstanding."

The successive waves of immigrants did not readily embrace the new culture, even when intimidated by the xenophobia of the know-nothing era or two World Wars. Says Historian James Banks: "Each nationality group tried desperately to remake North America in the image of its native land." When the question arose of making the U.S. multilingual or multicultural in public affairs, however, Congress stood firm. In the 1790s, 1840s and 1860s, the lawmakers voted down pleas to print Government documents in German. Predominantly French-speaking Louisiana sought statehood in 1812; the state constitution that it submitted for approval specified that its official language would be English. A century later, New Mexico was welcomed into the union, but only after an influx of settlers from the North and East had made English, not Spanish, the majority tongue.

Occasional concentrations of immigrants were able to win local   4
recognition of their language and thereby enforce an early form of affirmative action: by 1899 nearly 18,000 pupils in Cincinnati divided their school time between courses given in German and in English, thus providing employment for 186 German-speaking teachers. In 1917 San Francisco taught German in eight primary schools, Italian in six, French in four and Spanish in two. Yet when most cities consented to teach immigrant children in their native Chinese or Polish or Yiddish or Gujarati, the clearly stated goal was to transform the students as quickly as possible into speakers of English and full participants in society.

Now, however, a new bilingualism and biculturalism is being   5
promulgated that would deliberately fragment the nation into separate, unassimilated groups. The movement seems to take much of its ideology from the black separatism of the 1960s but derives its political force from the unprecedented raw numbers—15 million or more—of a group linked to a single tongue, Spanish. The new metaphor is not the melting pot but the salad bowl, with each element distinct. The biculturalists seek to use public services, particularly schools, not to Americanize the young but to heighten their consciousness of belonging to another heritage. Contends Tomás A. Arciniega, vice president for academic affairs at California State University at Fresno: "The promotion of cultural differences has to be recognized as a valid and legitimate educational goal." Miguel Gonzalez-Pando, director of the Center for Latino Education at Florida International University in Miami, says: "I speak Spanish at home, my social relations are mostly in Spanish, and I am raising my daughter as a Cuban American. It is a question of freedom of choice." In Gonzalez-Pando's city, where Hispanics outnumber whites, the anti-assimilationist theory has become accepted practice: Miami's youth can take twelve years of bilingual public schooling with no pretense made that the program is transitional toward anything. The potential for separatism is greater in Los Angeles. Philip Hawley, president of the Carter Hawley Hale retail store chain, cautions: "This is the only area in the U.S. that over the next 50 years could have a polarization into two distinct cultures, of the kind that brought about the Quebec situation in Canada." Professor Rodolfo

Acuña of California State University at Northridge concurs. Says Acuña: "Talk of secession may come when there are shrinking economic resources and rising expectations among have-not Hispanics."

Already the separatists who resist accepting English have won   6
laws and court cases mandating provision of social services, some government instructions, even election ballots in Spanish. The legitimizing effect of these decisions can be seen in the proliferation of billboards, roadside signs and other public communications posted in Spanish. Acknowledges Professor Ramon Ruiz of the University of California at San Diego: "The separatism question is with us already." The most portentous evidence is in the classrooms. Like its political cousins, equal opportunity and social justice, bilingual education is a catchall term that means what the speaker wishes it to mean.

There are at least four ways for schools to teach students who   7
speak another language at home:

1) Total immersion in English, which relies on the proven ability   8
of children to master new languages. Advocates of bilingual education argue that this approach disorients children and sometimes impedes their progress in other subjects, because those who have already mastered several grades' worth of material in their first language may be compelled to take English-language classes with much younger or slower students.

2) Short-term bilingual education, which may offer a full curricu-   9
lum but is directed toward moving students into English-language classes as rapidly as possible. In a report last month by a Twentieth Century Fund task force, members who were disillusioned with the performance of elaborate bilingual programs urged diversion of federal funds to the teaching of English. The panel held: "Schoolchildren will never swim in the American mainstream unless they are fluent in English."

3) Dual curriculum, which permits students to spend several years   10
making the transition. This is the method urged by many moderate Hispanic, Chinese and other ethnic minority leaders. Says Historian Ruiz: "The direct approach destroys children's feelings of security. Bilingual education eases them from something they know to something they do not."

4) Language and cultural maintenance, which seeks to enhance   11
students' mastery of their first language while also teaching them English. In Hispanic communities, the language training is often accompanied by courses in ethnic heritage. Argues Miami Attorney Manuel Diaz, a vice chairman of the Spanish American League Against Discrimination: "Cultural diversity makes this country strong. It is not a disease."

The rhetoric of supporters of bilingualism suggests that theirs   12
may be a political solution to an educational problem. Indeed, some of
them acknowledge that they view bilingual programs as a source of jobs
for Hispanic administrators, teachers and aides. In cities with large
minority enrollments, says a Chicago school principal who requested
anonymity, "those of us who consider bilingual education ineffective
are afraid that if we say so we will lose our jobs." Lawrence Uzzell,
president of Learn Inc., a Washington-based research foundation, contends that Hispanic educational activists are cynically protecting their
own careers. Says Uzzell: "The more the Hispanic child grows up
isolated, the easier it is for politicians to manipulate him as part of an
ethnic voting bloc."

The signal political success for bilingualism has been won at the   13
U.S. Department of Education. After the Supreme Court ruled in 1974
that Chinese-speaking students were entitled to some instruction in a
language they could understand, the DOE issued "informal" rules that
now bind more than 400 school districts. Immersion in English, even
rapid transition to English, does not satisfy the DOE; the rules compel
school systems to offer a full curriculum to any group of 20 or more
students who share a foreign language. The DOE rules have survived
three presidencies, although Jesse Soriano, director of the Reagan
Administration's $138 million bilingual program, concedes, "This is
money that could be spent more effectively." About half of students
from Spanish-speaking homes drop out before the end of high school;
of the ones who remain, 30% eventually score two or more years below
their age group on standardized tests. But it is hard to demonstrate the
value of any bilingual approach in aiding those students. In 1982 Iris
Rotberg reported in the *Harvard Education Review:* "Research findings
have shown that bilingual programs are neither better nor worse than
other instructional methods." Indeed, the DOE's review found that of all
methods for teaching bilingual students English and mathematics, only
total immersion in English clearly worked.

One major problem in assessing the worth of bilingual programs   14
is that they often employ teachers who are less than competent in either
English or Spanish, or in the specific subjects they teach. In a 1976 test
of 136 teachers and aides in bilingual programs in New Mexico, only
13 could read and write Spanish at third-grade level. Says former
Boston School Superintendent Robert Wood: "Many bilingual teachers
do not have a command of English, and after three years of instruction
under them, children also emerge without a command of English."
Another complicating factor is the inability of researchers to determine
whether the problems of Hispanic students stem more from language
difficulty or from their economic class. Many Hispanic children who

are unable to speak English have parents with little education who hold unskilled jobs; in school performance, these students are much like poor blacks and whites. Notes Harvard's Nathan Glazer: "If these students do poorly in English, they may be doing poorly in a foreign language."

Even if the educational value of bilingual programs were beyond   15
dispute, there would remain questions about their psychic value to children. Among the sharpest critics of bilingualism is Author Richard Rodriguez, who holds a Berkeley Ph.D. in literature and grew up in a Spanish-speaking, working-class household; in his autobiography *Hunger of Memory*, Rodriguez argues that the separation from his family that a Hispanic child feels on becoming fluent in English is necessary to develop a sense of belonging to American society. Writes Rodriguez: "Bilingualists do not seem to realize that there are two ways a person is individualized. While one suffers a diminished sense of private individuality by becoming assimilated into public society, such assimilation makes possible the achievement of public individuality." By Rodriguez's reasoning, the discomfort of giving up the language of home is far less significant than the isolation of being unable to speak the language of the larger world.

The dubious value of bilingualism to students is only part of   16
America's valid concern about how to absorb the Hispanic minority. The U.S., despite its exceptional diversity, has been spared most of the ethnic tensions that beset even such industrialized nations as Belgium and Spain. The rise of a large group, detached from the main population by language and custom, could affect the social stability of the country. Hispanic leaders, moreover, acknowledge that their constituents have been less inclined to become assimilated than previous foreign-language communities, in part because many of them anticipated that after earning and saving, they would return to Puerto Rico, Mexico, South America or Cuba. Says Historian Doyce Nunis of the University of Southern California: "For the first time in American experience, a large immigrant group may be electing to bypass the processes of acculturation." Miami Mayor Maurice Ferré, a Puerto Rican, claims that in his city a resident can go from birth through school and working life to death without ever having to speak English. But most Hispanic intellectuals claim that their communities, like other immigrant groups before them, cling together only to combat discrimination.

The disruptive potential of bilingualism and biculturalism is still   17
worrisome: millions of voters cut off from the main sources of information, millions of potential draftees inculcated with dual ethnic loyalties, millions of would-be employees ill at ease in the language of their workmates. Former Senator S.I. Hayakawa of California was laughed at for proposing a constitutional amendment to make English the

official language of the U.S. It was a gesture of little practical consequence but great symbolic significance: many Americans mistakenly
feel there is something racist, or oppressive, in expecting newcomers to
share the nation's language and folkways.

Beyond practical politics and economics, separatism belittles the   18
all-embracing culture that America has embodied for the world. Says
Writer Irving Howe, a scholar of literature and the Jewish immigrant
experience: "The province, the ethnic nest, remains the point from
which everything begins, but it must be transcended." That transcendence does not mean disappearance. It is possible to eat a Mexican meal,
dance a Polish polka, sing in a Rumanian choir, preserve one's ethnicity
however one wishes, and still share fully in the English-speaking common society. Just as American language, food and popular culture
reflect the past groups who landed in the U.S., so future American
culture will reflect the Hispanics, Asians and many other groups who
are replanting their roots. As Author Rodriguez observes after his
journey into the mainstream, "Culture survives whether you want it to
or not."

For Discussion and Writing

1. Why does Henry think it disturbing that some newly arrived Americans
   reject the English language as a "common denominator" by which they
   may be integrated into the larger society? What, according to Henry, is
   the principal cause that helps fuel the drive for bilingualism? If bilingualism should triumph, what sorts of consequences does he foresee?
2. One revealing aspect of Henry's essay is that the bilingualism issue is
   hardly new. Trace Henry's background material, citing examples of
   earlier conflicts over language and heritage in the U.S.
3. What are the main arguments Henry mounts against bilingualism? Do
   you agree with him? Why or why not?
4. Henry cites author Richard Rodriguez, who, based on personal experience, claims that it's better to give up the language of home than to
   remain isolated from the mainstream culture. Write an essay, perhaps
   using experience as evidence, in which you defend or attack this idea.
   Must the bilingualism issue be framed as an either/or question, or is
   there some middle ground, some compromise, that the two sides might
   reach?

Confessions of an Ivy League Reject

WALTER SHAPIRO

Twenty-five years ago this month, Harvard said no. So did Yale, 1
Princeton, Dartmouth, Columbia and Williams. I can still see my 18-
year-old self standing by the mailbox in stunned disbelief, holding six
white envelopes. Six anorexically thin white envelopes. The precise
wording of the form letters has been lost to history, but I can still conjure
up their face-saving phrases like "many strong candidates" and "very
difficult decisions." Reading them one right after another, it seemed like
an Ivy League chorus was cheerfully wishing me "the best of luck with
your college career." Best of luck, that is, as long as I enrolled somewhere else.

Even with good grades and high test scores, I should have known 2
that I was courting rejection by the sheer act of applying. The odds of
getting into schools like Harvard and Dartmouth that year were worse
than 1 out of 4. Perhaps if I had lived somewhere distant like Indiana
or California, I might have found comfort in raging against the injustice
of East Coast élitism. My problem was that by my senior year in high
school, I was already an insufferable East Coast snob. So by the social
standards of suburban Connecticut in the mid-1960s, the multiple
rejections consigned me to the outer darkness, destined to be shunned
on commuter trains, blackballed at country clubs and never allowed to
buy a home in a community with four-acre zoning. I would have to plod
through life stigmatized by the knowledge that I had been judged "Not
Ivy League material."

Such adolescent angst was, of course, ludicrous. Every life has its 3
disappointments; rejection by the college of your choice is probably
more serious than not finding a date for the prom and less grievous than
your mother throwing out a collection of 1950s baseball cards. Even
then I was aware that my safety school was far better than most. So I
stoically trudged off to the University of Michigan, a college that
seemed majestically impervious to the damaged goods it was receiving.
Michigan more than fulfilled its part of the bargain; the lingering gaps
in my education (the inability to commune with head waiters in flawless French, tone-deaf ignorance of classical music, and scientific training that stopped with *Mr. Wizard*) are entirely my own fault. At 43 I can

safely conclude that the lack of an Ivy League imprimatur has neither marred my career nor deprived me of any social entrée that I would have enjoyed.

Why then, a quarter of a century later, do I still find painful the   4
memory of those six undernourished envelopes? Why do I periodically peek into college-rating handbooks to see how Michigan is faring against the Ivy League? And why do I sometimes blanch when friends innocently suggest lunch at the Harvard Club?

This lingering sensitivity, which I am chagrined to confess, has   5
been exaggerated by the cities where I have lived and the work that I do. Both New York and Washington revere the Ivy League like Club Med worships tanned bodies and a strong backhand. Odd how when visiting the Midwest I drop the University of Michigan into conversation with an avidity I rarely display back East. Lawyers and physicists may often rate colleagues by the quality of their professional education, but an enduring adult fascination with undergraduate pedigrees remains acute in the fields I know well, such as journalism and politics, where it is still possible to achieve success through talent, luck and a good B.A. degree. For example, at the Washington *Post* in the early 1980s, so thick were the references to bright college days in Cambridge, Mass., that I sometimes felt I was working at the *Harvard Crimson* alumni association. Peggy Noonan in her best-selling White House memoir, *What I Saw at the Revolution,* loudly complains that her colleagues in the Reagan Administration "were always asking me what college I went to." Noonan, sensitive to the status slights that accompany her Fairleigh Dickinson degree, theorizes that in a fluid environment like the White House, people pop the Ivy League question to categorize one another while simultaneously underscoring their own importance, as in "Yes, she does seem bright; she went to Radcliffe, but before my wife."

My instinct is to join Noonan in her populist fury against the   6
"Harvardheads" in government. But rationally I know that at my age (and Noonan's) such resentment is silly. For millions of college-educated men and women like us, whose undergraduate histories do not automatically inspire awe, the struggle is over—and we won. For we have reached the stage in life where what we have learned and what we do with it are all that should matter. In fact, aside from the pride of parents who emblazon their children's college crests on the rear windows of their Accords and Audis, it is hard to find much objective evidence that a thick envelope from the Ivy League possesses the power to transform lives. I recently asked half a dozen sociologists whether there is any way to measure the career advantages that come with a prestigious undergraduate degree. Their consensus was yes, of course, Princeton and Yale alumni are disproportionately successful, but it is

unclear whether this superiority is due to the factors that originally impressed the admissions committees or the supposed added value of their élite education. It was the old nature-vs.-nurture debate transported to the tables down at Mory's.

Applied to my own life, their message seems clear. I am pretty   7
much the same person I would have been had Harvard said yes—or had Dartmouth written apologetically to say that the envelopes had been switched at birth and I was really a prince, not an educational pauper. Yet I wonder. My own sense is that those rejection letters changed me in ways that I am still hard-pressed to define. Total defeat is never easy, especially when it comes so suddenly so young. Sometimes I fear the experience eroded my self-confidence. But mostly I prefer to think it toughened me, taught me humility, trained me to value what I accomplished on my own and—most important— tempered my tendencies toward snobbery. Not a bad haul from six form letters mailed a quarter-century ago.

For Discussion and Writing

1. From his opening anecdote to his concluding sentence, Shapiro uses himself as his prime example of what can happen to a student who suffers a major college rejection. What sense of the author as a person comes through his self-revealing essay? Does he seem embittered, cynical about those who did manage to get into Ivy League schools, embarrassed that he cannot claim an Ivy League imprimatur? How would you describe his attitude toward himself and his material?
2. Shapiro deals with the tendency to be status-conscious and snobbish about where one attended college. Why does he still feel the pain of his Ivy League rejections? Were considerations of status and reputation part of your decision about where to attend college?
3. What does Shapiro say he had learned about himself in light of his rejection? Do you believe him?
4. Whether or not you share the author's experience of rejections by a coveted school, write a personal essay about a rejection or another painful school experience and about what educational effects it had in your life.

Teach Diversity—with a Smile

Barbara Ehrenreich

Something had to replace the threat of communism, and at last 1
a workable substitute is at hand. "Multiculturalism," as the new menace is known, has been denounced in the media recently as the new
McCarthyism, the new fundamentalism, even the new totalitarianism—take your choice. According to its critics, who include a flock of
tenured conservative scholars, multiculturalism aims to toss out what
it sees as the Eurocentric bias in education and replace Plato with
Ntozake Shange and traditional math with the Yoruba number system.
And that's just the beginning. The Jacobins of the multiculturalist
movement, who are described derisively as P.C., or politically correct,
are said to have launched a campus reign of terror against those who
slip and innocently say "freshman" instead of "freshperson," "Indian"
instead of "Native American" or, may the Goddess forgive them,
"disabled" instead of "differently abled."

So you can see what is at stake here: freedom of speech, freedom 2
of thought, Western civilization and a great many professorial egos. But
before we get carried away by the mounting backlash against multiculturalism, we ought to reflect for a moment on the system that the
P.C. people aim to replace. I know all about it; in fact it's just about all
I *do* know, since I—along with so many educated white people of my
generation—was a victim of monoculturalism.

American history, as it was taught to us, began with Columbus' 3
"discovery" of an apparently unnamed, unpeopled America, and
moved on to the Pilgrims serving pumpkin pie to a handful of grateful
red-skinned folks. College expanded our horizons with courses called
Humanities or sometimes Civ, which introduced us to a line of thought
that started with Homer, worked its way through Rabelais and reached
a poignant climax in the pensées of Matthew Arnold. Graduate students
wrote dissertations on what long-dead men had thought of Chaucer's
verse or Shakespeare's dramas; foreign languages meant French or
German. If there had been high technology in ancient China, kingdoms
in black Africa or women anywhere, at any time, doing anything worth
noticing, we did not know it, nor did anyone think to tell us.

Our families and neighborhoods reinforced the dogma of 4
monoculturalism. In our heads, most of us '50s teenagers carried
around a social map that was about as useful as the chart that guided
Columbus to the "Indies." There were "Negroes," "whites" and "Orientals," the latter meaning Chinese and "Japs." Of religions, only three
were known—Protestant, Catholic and Jewish—and not much was
known about the last two types. The only remaining human categories
were husbands and wives, and that was all the diversity the monocul-
tural world could handle. Gays, lesbians, Buddhists, Muslims, Malay-
sians, Mormons, etc. were simply off the map.

So I applaud—with one hand, anyway—the multiculturalist goal 5
of preparing us all for a wider world. The other hand is tapping its
fingers impatiently, because the critics are right about one thing: when
advocates of multiculturalism adopt the haughty stance of political
correctness, they quickly descend to silliness or worse. It's obnoxious,
for example, to rely on university administrations to enforce P.C. standards of verbal inoffensiveness. Racist, sexist and homophobic
thoughts cannot, alas, be abolished by fiat but only by the time-honored
methods of persuasion, education and exposure to the other guy's—or,
excuse me, woman's—point of view.

And it's silly to mistake verbal purification for genuine social 6
reform. Even after all women are "Ms." and all people are "he or she,"
women will still earn only 65¢ for every dollar earned by men. Minorities by any other name, such as "people of color," will still bear a hugely
disproportionate burden of poverty and discrimination. Disabilities are
not just "different abilities" when there are not enough ramps for
wheelchairs, signers for the deaf or special classes for the "specially"
endowed. With all due respect for the new politesse, actions still speak
louder than fashionable phrases.

But the worst thing about the P.C. people is that they are such poor 7
advocates for the multicultural cause. No one was ever won over to a
broader, more inclusive view of life by being bullied or relentlessly
"corrected." Tell a 19-year-old white male that he can't say "girl" when
he means "teen-age woman," and he will most likely snicker. This may
be the reason why, despite the conservative alarms, P.C.-ness remains
a relatively tiny trend. Most campuses have more serious and ancient
problems: faculties still top-heavy with white males of the monocul-
tural persuasion; fraternities that harass minorities and women; date
rape; alcohol abuse, and tuition that excludes all but the upper fringe
of the middle class.

So both sides would be well advised to lighten up. The conserva- 8
tives ought to realize that criticisms of the great books approach to
learning do not amount to totalitarianism. And the advocates of multiculturalism need to regain the sense of humor that enabled their prede-

cessors in the struggle to coin the term P.C. years ago—not in arrogance but in self-mockery.

Beyond that, both sides should realize that the beneficiaries of multiculturalism are not only the "oppressed peoples" on the standard P.C. list (minorities, gays, etc.). The "unenlightened"—the victims of monoculturalism—are oppressed too, or at least deprived. Our educations, whether at Yale or at State U, were narrow and parochial and left us ill-equipped to navigate a society that truly is multicultural and is becoming more so every day. The culture that we studied was, in fact, *one* culture and, from a world perspective, all too limited and ingrown. Diversity is challenging, but those of us who have seen the alternative know it is also richer, livelier and ultimately more fun.

For Discussion and Writing

1. What is "monoculturalism" as Ehrenreich defines it? How does it differ from multiculturalism? Why does Ehrenreich applaud multicultural-ism "with one hand"? What is her objection to some of those who push such political correctness to extremes?
2. Ehrenreich writes with a biting wit and sarcastic, mocking tone. Why does she adopt an irreverent stance toward her material? What does she gain by it as a persuasive strategy?
3. What does Ehrenreich recommend as a response to the campus dispute over multicultural education?
4. Write an essay in which you attack or defend Ehrenreich's essential claim: Diversity may be challenging, full of problems but it's much "richer, livelier and ultimately more fun" than the alternative. If possi-ble, use as supporting evidence your own campus's attitudes, or those from high school, toward cultural and educational diversity.

Thinking and Writing about Chapter 11

1. Compare Henry's and Ehrenreich's essays in their attitudes toward educational diversity. How might Henry respond to his colleague's call for multicultural teaching? How might Ehrenreich react to Henry's opposition to bilingualism? Are the two issues identical or are there important distinctions between them?
2. Both Shapiro and Ehrenreich use humor to enliven their treatment of serious subjects. How would you characterize Shapiro's voice and manner as against Ehrenreich's?
3. The essays in this chapter raise three among many educational issues. Think about how education affects your own life, and about which problems, in addition to the ones discussed here, seem most compelling. Write an essay in which you address a specific issue, define it, analyze it, and propose a remedy. Some similar topics: College financing, campus politics, balancing study with other activities, anti-learning peer pressure.

12

The World of Sport

Scratch the surface of the average American and you'll likely find a sports nut. Sports is a multi-billion-dollar business, an enormous source of television programing, an abiding entertainment for millions of fans. It is a force that shapes higher education, directs the flow of much leisure spending, and provides employment, in one form or another, for a significant portion of the population.

Why do we love sports so much? Why are there riots when sports teams win pennants and league titles? Why do stadium skyboxes cost as much as New York penthouses? Why are ticket scalpers able to gouge spectators with obscene prices for choice seats? For some viewers, sports are one among many sources of excitement, stimulation, diversion. Others delight in sports for their moments of athletic beauty and skill. And for some, the world of sport is a grand and timeless arena, a mythic realm apart from everyday life.

The three essays in this chapter address the world of sport—our love for it, its potential violence, its silliness. In "The Greatest Game," from April 1973, Stefan Kanfer offers an homage to the all-American pastime. In "Doing Violence to Sport," from May 1976, Kanfer looks at the underside of professional televised games. And in "What's in a Nickname," from January 1987, John Leo provides a delightful banquet of team names and their sometimes bizarre rationales.

The Greatest Game

STEFAN KANFER

SLOW? Players have been known to sleep *during* a game. Un-   1
focused? It begins when the hockey rinks are frozen and ends when
footballs are tossed in snow flurries.

Archaic? Its greatest heroes are locked in the mythic past, an epoch   2
located roughly between the Jurassic era and World War II.

Unfashionable? Of all major team sports, it is the only one that is   3
not played against a clock.

By all rational standards, baseball should have gone the way of   4
the bison and the convertible by now. But there are no rational standards in love. Besieged by Masters tournaments, Olympics, track meets
and Super Bowls, the fans have kept baseball incredibly popular. In a
recent Harris poll, they were asked which championship event they
would prefer to attend. Results:

1. World Series: 23%   5

2. Super Bowl: 20%   6

3. Kentucky Derby: 10%   7

4. Indianapolis 500: 10%   8

5. College bowl game: 8%   9

Why should baseball, with its sluggish metabolism and lack of   10
crunch, retain its hold on the national imagination? The answer lies
partly in its seasonal associations. No one is immune to the vernal
equinox. The same jump of the blood occurs on ghetto streets and Little
League diamonds, in bleachers and in front of the TV screen. Baseball
implies an earthly benignity: clear skies, vacations and, above all, no
school.

Secondly, there is the peculiarly intellectual quality of the game,   11
with its geometric layout and its deep well of tradition. Philip Roth,
whose new book *The Great American Novel* concerns the fortunes of a
homeless baseball team, recalls: "Not until I got to college and was
introduced to literature did I find anything with a comparable emotional atmosphere and as strong an esthetic appeal . . . baseball, with its
longeurs and thrills, its spaciousness . . . its peculiarly hypnotic tedium,

its heroics, its nuances, its 'characters,' its language, and its mythic sense of itself, was the literature of my boyhood."

Almost from the beginning, novelists have gone to bat for the   12
game. Ring Lardner saw baseball as the great American comedy—look through the knothole and you found uniformed counterparts of Huck Finn and Charlie Chaplin.

The magic works for spectators as well as novelists. In *The Summer*   13
Game, Roger Angell celebrates a field that never was: the Interior Stadium. "Baseball in the mind . . . is a game of recollections, recapturing and visions . . . anyone can play this private game, extending it to extraordinary varieties and possibilities in his mind. Ruth bats against Sandy Koufax or Sam McDowell . . . Hubbell pitches to Ted Williams. Baseball, I must conclude, is intensely remembered because only baseball is so intensely watched."

No other sport *can* be so intensely watched. There is no jumbled   14
scrimmage that must be clarified with instant replay. The ball may approach home plate at 100 m.p.h. or crawl down the third-base line like a crab. A 400-ft. fly ball may fall foul by two inches. As in chess, power radiates from stationary figures. Yet on a given pitch, ten men may be moving. Clearly, this is a game to be scrutinized.

With all the intensity, there is something more. Baseball's deepest   15
fascination lies in twin aspects of the game: records and time. In other sports, the past is a laugh. Teen-age girls are breaking Johnny Weismuller's old Olympic marks. The four-minute mile has been shattered beyond repair. Pole vaulters, broad jumpers, skiers, quarterbacks, golfers, chess players—they have all rewritten the record books until yesterday's hero is exposed as a man with feat of clay. Only baseball has retained so many of its idols. No one has come close to Joe DiMaggio's 56-game hitting streak of 1941. The Ted Williams of 1941 was the game's last .400 hitter. Pitcher Cy Young's record of 511 victories has held for two generations. This permanence extends to the game's oddballs, men like Casey Stengel, who once tipped his hat to the crowd and released a bird that was nesting in his hair; Bobo Holloman, who pitched only one complete game in the majors—and that one a no-hitter. There are players whose names alone could render them immortal: Eli Grba, Fenton Mole, Eppa Rixey, Wally Pipp, Napoleon Lajoie. All these men, the immortals and the "flakes," exist like the game beyond the erosions of style and time.

Down on the playing field, another version of time exists,   16
Einsteinian in its complexity. Other sportsmen keep an eye on the minute hand, hoping to "kill" the clock. In baseball, time is subservient to circumstance. An inning may last six pitches or 80 minutes. Official games have gone 4$\frac{1}{2}$ innings, and 26. That timelessness is at once the game's curse and its glory. At the conclusion of his disastrous World

Series with the Mets, Baltimore Manager Earl Weaver philosophized, "You can't sit on a lead and run a few plays into the line and just kill the clock. You've got to throw the ball over the goddam plate and give the other man his chance." Then he paused and concluded: "That's why baseball is the greatest game of them all."

Or is it? Surely football is closer to the *Zeitgeist*, with its chatter of　17 "long bombs" and marches downfield. Surely basketball with its constant scoring, or hockey with its eruptions of violence, is America's ideal spectator sport. The conservative, hidebound sport of baseball can offer no such qualities; scoring is rare, violence a matter of tempers, not policy. The game is an echo of a vanished pre-TV, prewar America, a bygone place of leisure and tranquility.

Baseball was doomed when the Black Sox scandal revealed that　18 the World Series of 1919 was fixed by gamblers. It was finished when it refused to admit black players—gifted men who were forced to play in brilliant, threadbare leagues where only the ball was white. It was dead when attendance wavered and franchises fled hysterically to Seattle, Kansas City, Atlanta, Oakland.

The game survived it all. How? Is it because of the inexhaustible　19 promotional gimmicks, the bat and ball and senior citizens days; the all-weather artificial turf; the dazzling uniforms? Is it the metaphysics and momentum that still continue from the zenith of the '30s and '40s? Or is it that this supposedly stolid, permanent game has imperceptibly accommodated change—that in each era it has accepted physical, textual and social alterations that a decade before had seemed impossibly revolutionary? Is it that, in the end, no other sport is so accurate a reflection of the supposedly stolid, permanent—and ultimately changeable—country that surrounds the interior and exterior stadiums?

For Discussion and Writing

1. What does Kanfer say are some of baseball's most appealing qualities? Cite some of the examples he uses to illustrate his point. Do you agree with him that baseball is "the greatest game"? Why or why not?
2. In what ways does baseball "echo a vanished pre-TV, prewar America, a bygone place of leisure and tranquility"? Are such characterizations the romantic rhetoric of magazine writers, or is there some truth in the claim that baseball is essentially the same game it was more than one hundred years ago, in the late 19th century?
3. Toward the end of his essay, Kanfer speculates about why baseball has survived and prospered over so many generations. Why does he think it has?
4. What is your favorite sport? Using Kanfer's essay as a model, write an extended definition and analysis of it, praising its virtues and seeking to understand its appeal.

Doing Violence to Sport

STEFAN KANFER

The knuckleball comedy *The Bad News Bears* does not play all its scenes for laughs. In one gritty confrontation, a coach stomps out to the mound and strikes a twelve-year-old to the ground. The moment seems pure fake-believe; in fact it is a Little League echo of Major propensities. Since the start of this year's baseball season, aggression has been the order of the day.

Last week New York Yankee Lou Piniella slid into Boston Red Sox Catcher Carlton Fisk with enough force to trigger a wild on-field brawl—and bloody fights in the stands. One result: Pitcher Bill Lee was so severely hurt that he may be out for the rest of the season. At an Atlanta Braves-Houston Astros game, a controversial first-base call brought the entire Braves bench storming onto the field. The men in blue were forced to leave the stadium with other men in blue—a police escort. In perhaps the ugliest confrontation of this strange young season, Cardinal Pitcher Lynn McGlothen readily forgave himself after hitting two New York Met batters. Proclaimed McGlothen: "If a pitcher feels he has been intimidated by a hitter, he has the right to throw at him."

The same sort of "right" is being exercised in basketball. Boston Celtic Coach Tom Heinsohn rushed onto the court recently in an effort to attack an opposing player. During the N.B.A. play-offs between the Phoenix Suns and Golden State Warriors, Ricky Sobers and Rick Barry momentarily gave up basketball for boxing. Last month hockey suffered a serious disgrace when four Philadelphia Flyer players were arraigned in Toronto on charges of assault and carrying "dangerous weapons"—hockey sticks—during games that resulted in blood on the ice, disorder in the stands and players in the infirmary. Similar Flyer scrimmages have elicited McGlothen-like statements from the opposition of that fight-prone team: "I never have trouble getting up for games against Philadelphia," says Montreal Canadien Defenseman Larry Robinson. "When you play the Flyers, there are more opportunities to hit people."

Perusing these declarations, gazing at these confrontations, the spectator has every right to conclude that anarchy has been loosed in

163

the world of sport, that the center cannot hold—nor can the guard, the forward, the pitcher or the referee. Naked aggression seems on the surface to underline the statement of Political Scientist James Q. Wilson: "People actually get hurt in televised sports programs, and the hurt cannot even be justified by a higher cause. By some standards, it is the most shocking form of violence, done merely for sport or fun."

. . .

Is sport becoming a series of organized assaults? Is the new violence an indicator of a lawless epoch, a broken mirror-image of the country at large? The conclusions are not as obvious as they seem. Professional sport is in fact no more violent than it used to be. The beanball has been with us since baseball began. Back in 1920, Cleveland Indian Ray Chapman was killed by Yankee Carl Mays' fastball. Twenty years ago Giant Pitcher Sal Maglie was given the sobriquet "the Barber" because of the close shaves his fastball gave the faces of hitters. Don Drysdale, a Dodger star of the '60s, was famed as a fastballing head-hunter. Basketball, theoretically a non-contact sport and one pleasantly peopled with college types, long had its "hit" men, players like Boston's Jungle Jim Loscutoff, whose primary role was to intimidate opponents.

Even the eruptions of hockey can be misperceived. Says New York Islander Official Hawley Chester: "Hockey is actually not as tough as it used to be years ago when there were only six professional teams. The competition was very tough." Then why does the sport seem so bloody? "There's more coverage of isolated incidents. Television and the press have accentuated the violence."

Chester's rationale cannot be dismissed as mere puck passing. Only 12,000 saw the Chapman tragedy; today a man kicking dirt on the shoes of an umpire is seen by millions of viewers. University of California Sociologist Harry Edwards, a former college track star, adds that "the violence in sport is magnified by television. The fan can identify with violence in terms of what he would like to do with the forces he cannot control." And in a recent paper in the medical journal *Pediatrics*, three physicians reported an "Evel Knievel syndrome"—imitation of exhibitionism in sport. "Televised violence," explains the paper, "especially during sporting events and news reporting, is increasingly indicated in imitative and aggressive behavior exhibited by children."

Those children have had plenty of opportunities to view crunches from closeup angles. Replaying highlights of games that viewers had not seen, ABC *Monday Night Baseball* showed at length the on-field fracas of the Chicago Cubs–San Francisco Giants game nine days after it occurred. Football cheap shots and beanball brawls, hockey fistfights and basketball square-offs—exercises of passion that transgress the rules—are a minor part of any sports event. Yet they are given long and detailed attention, instant and incessant replay.

Therein lie the true hazards of contemporary athletic violence. The debunking of the athlete-as-hero is hardly new. Such disaffected jocks as Dave Meggyesy and Jim Bouton have uncovered more clay feet than there are statues. The facile comparison of football and the Viet Nam War was one of the shibboleths of the '60s. Even the littlest leaguers know that professional sport is hard, fast and punishing. But now there is something more than imagery at stake: a danger that the whole perception of games is being altered. 9

. . .

In his classic study of man at play, *Homo Ludens,* Historian Johan Huizinga described it as "a free activity standing quite consciously outside 'ordinary life,' " animated by "the impulse to create orderly form." Once the idea of order goes, so goes the game itself—and its fans. A report commissioned by the Ontario provincial government on hockey violence in Canada concluded: "When the evidence strongly indicates that there is a conscious effort to sell the violence in hockey to enrich a small group of show business entrepreneurs at the expense of a great sport (not to mention the corruption of an entire generation's concept of sport) then one's concern grows to outrage." 10

The outrage is well placed. Few fans weep for the professional athlete, even when he is hospitalized. He is young, heavily muscled and even more heavily compensated. A six-figure income does much to assuage pain and indignity. The essential concern is with that "entire generation's concept of sport." A fan, an owner or a player who comes to believe a pitcher has the right to injure a batter may as well believe that Bobby Fischer has a right to kick over the chessboard when he is threatened, or that order itself is an outmoded idea. When moral rules are bent, more than sport is mangled. In the end, it is not the players who are cheapened and injured, nor even the event itself. It is the children and adults who watch and then repeat what they see on the playground and in the stands—and perhaps in their lives. *The Bad News Bears* is not yet a sports documentary. But what if it becomes one? Would any title be more fitting than that of another movie: *End of the Game?* 11

For Discussion and Writing

1. Does Kanfer object to violence in sport? What is his view of it, and where does he place at least partial blame for the problem?
2. What does Kanfer say is the larger issue or consequence of sports violence?

3. Do you agree with Kanfer (5) that "professional sport is in fact no more violent than it used to be"? Can you cite examples to support your view?
4. Defend or attack the notion that violent outbursts are not a significant problem in professional sports. Are they, or should they be, a natural part of the game? Or are they violations of the code of sportsmanlike conduct—violations of the spirit of sporting competition—that must be curbed through fines, suspensions, and other penalties?

What's in a Nickname?

JOHN LEO

Everyone knows that sports teams must have nicknames, but selecting an appropriate one is fraught with peril. Alabama, for instance, may be proud of the Crimson Tide, but it sounds like a bloodbath or a serious algae problem. Notre Dame's famous jocks are ossified as the Fighting Irish, though Hibernian-American athletes are about as rare in South Bend as they are on the Boston Celtics. Nothing exposed the nickname crisis more starkly than the 1982 NCAA basketball championship game played between the Georgetown Hoyas and the North Carolina Tar Heels. Even if you know what a hoya or a tarheel is, the only sensible strategy is to forget it. (For those overwhelmed by a need to know, hoya is short for *Hoya saxa!*, a garbled Greek and Latin cheer meaning "What rocks!," and tarheel originated during the Civil War as a disparaging term for folks from the Carolina pine forests.) Few knew what the Fort Wayne Zollner Pistons were when a pro basketball team played under that name. (They were players owned by Fred Zollner, who also happened to own a piston factory in Fort Wayne.) The early vogue of naming a team for a person seems to have come to an end with Paul Brown, the original coach of the Cleveland Browns. Fans who found the cult of personality distasteful at least were grateful that he wasn't named Stumblebrenner.

The Zollner Pistons eventually became the Detroit Pistons, showing that some nicknames travel well. The Brooklyn Dodgers, named for the difficulty of evading trolley cars in the famous borough, are now the Los Angeles Dodgers, where evading mayhem on the freeways is equally hard. The name Los Angeles Lakers, however, makes no sense at all, though it did when the team was in Minnesota. Utah, with its Mormon tradition, could easily have accepted the New Orleans football team (the Saints, as in Latter-Day Saints and saints who go marching in). Instead it got the New Orleans basketball team, now known as the Utah Jazz, which makes about as much sense as the New Orleans Tabernacle Choir.

In general, nicknames are supposed to come from two categories: animals that specialize in messy predation (lions, sharks, falcons and so forth) or humans famous for rapine and pillage (pirates, buccaneers,

Vikings, conquistadors, bandits, raiders, etc.). The image of mangled flesh must be evoked, but tastefully, one reason why there are no teams named the Massacres or the Serial Murderers. The aim, of course, is to borrow ferocity, but there are signs of change. Some years ago, students at Scottsdale Community College in Arizona voted to name their team the Artichokes and picked pink and white as the team colors. Authorities balked, but three years later students got half a loaf: the team is the Artichokes, but the colors are blue and white. Last year a similar nickname struggle took place. By 5 to 1, students at the University of California at Santa Cruz voted to call school teams the Banana Slugs in honor of a slimy yellow gastropod that swarms over the seaside campus on rainy days. Lest anyone miss the message, pro-Slug students said they meant to twit the "football mentality" of other California schools.

Not every team, of course, can be accused of seeking overly aggressive names. The New York University Violets or the Swarthmore Little Quakers do not induce terror. At Transylvania College, the team nickname is not the Neck Biters but the Pioneers. Women's teams are caught between the quaint feminine names of the old days (Colleens, Lassies) and the carnage-producing names of male teams. The defunct Women's Pro Basketball League had the Fillies and the Does, but leaned toward unisex names (Pioneers, Stars, Pride, Diamonds and Hustle). Most colleges, however, simply put the word lady in front of the men's nickname: the Lady Dragons or the Lady Monarchs. The Midwest Christian Lady Conquerors are deeply awe-inspiring, perhaps a bit more so than the Hofstra Flying Dutchwomen or the Iowa Wesleyan Tigerettes.

In major league baseball, most of the aggressive nicknames, like Pirates and Tigers, are attached to older franchises. Now that the game is played by college-trained millionaires, the newer teams have been more sedately named after seagoers and spacegoers (Mariners, Astros), birds (Blue Jays), religious figures (Angels, Padres) or a dimly remembered world's fair (Expos).

While the nicknames of many older pro football teams enshrine civic boosterism (Packers, Steelers, Oilers), newer names include most of the violent ones. The United States Football League produced the Invaders, Maulers, Gamblers, Gunslingers and Outlaws. As one irritated analyst put it, this group "sounds like the roster from a Hell's Angels' convention."

The growth areas for team names are the military-industrial complex (Jets, Supersonics, Generals, Astros, Bombers, Rockets) and the more nostalgic violence of cowboys and Indians (Braves, Redskins, Chiefs, Indians, Outlaws, Cowboys, Wranglers and Rangers).

Copycat names (Oakland Raiders, Oakland Invaders) are also popular. After the New York Mets came the football Jets, basketball

Nets, the team-tennis Sets and the Off-Track Betting Bets (known locally as the Debts). There was even some loose talk of a water-polo squad to be known, inevitably, as the Wets, and a women's basketball team, the Pets. This sort of second-hand glory is an old story in sports, dating back at least to football's Detroit Lions' and Chicago Bears' attempting to identify with the established baseball teams, the Detroit Tigers and Chicago Cubs. Another kind of identity problem forced the Cincinnati Reds, America's oldest professional sports team, to change their name to the Redlegs during the height of the cold war. One Cincinnati sportswriter objected on the ground that since the Moscow Reds were the newcomers, they should be asked to change *their* name.

Every now and then a franchise attempts a punning name. A   9 hockey team in Georgia was known as the Macon Whoopees, and the Los Angeles Rams cheerleaders were once called the Embraceable Ewes. The name Buffalo Bills is a pun of sorts. So was the name of the late American Basketball Association team, the St. Louis Spirits. (Get it? *The Spirit of St. Louis*?) Perhaps one day we will have the Norman (Okla.) Conquests or the Greenwich Village Idiots.

One trend is to name teams for malevolent forces, such as the Blast,   10 Sting, Blizzard and Blitz. Three team names celebrate disasters that destroyed much of their native locale: the Golden Bay Earthquakes, Chicago Fire and Atlanta (now Calgary) Flames. Such a breakthrough in reverse civic pride may yet induce other cities to celebrate their local disasters. Just think. The Boston Stranglers, the New York Muggers, the Washington Scams, the Los Angeles Smog . . .

For Discussion and Writing

1. Is there a pattern in team nicknames? What kinds of names seem to be favored? Why? What other types of names does Leo consider?
2. Leo's essay is if nothing else an amazing catalogue of names, and it may have the cumulative effect of making sports seem goofy, silly or downright trivial. Do you think he means his discussion to make affectionate fun of sport?
3. How important are sports teams and their names in expressing the identity of their home schools or cities? Why do you think fans take sports rivalries so seriously? What would be your reaction if your favorite team were sold to another city, or its name changed? Would it be the same team, or a different one?
4. Try your hand at writing a light or humorous essay about sports. Sample topics: an appreciation of a bumbling team, disastrous moments in your sports career, "America's ridiculous obsession with sports superstars," sports figures we love to hate.

Thinking and Writing about Chapter 12

1. Many writers, the two here included, have been drawn to sport as a source of mythic material—the world of sport as a place of heroic battle, tragic loss, metaphorical or otherwise significant landscapes. When you think about sport, what does it mean to you? Are you drawn to it for reasons apart from the obvious ones (action, excitement, entertainment)? What do you appreciate most about sport—and where do you see its flaws?
2. One of the continuing controversies surrounding professional sports is its commercialization, and the enormous salaries paid to sports figures. What are your views on these issues? Is the world of sport in America primarily a business? Should it be? Are professional athletes overpaid?
3. Write an essay in which you address the issue of collegiate athletics, either on your campus or in general. Are student athletes being used by the universities—to keep alumni entertained, to keep the school's sports profile high? Should students receive athletic scholarships? Should marginal or academically unqualified students be admitted to play college sports? Should the role of the student-athlete be redefined?

13

Challenges of Democracy

In 1974, historian Daniel Boorstin, echoing the great psychologist Sigmund Freud, published a book entitled *Democracy and Its Discontents,* and many today would say that a revised version, with yearly updates, might be called for. Since its resurgence in modern form in the eighteenth century, democracy has been the subject of endless debate by social critics, political theorists, philosophers, and ordinary citizens. What is democracy, exactly, and how is it supposed to work? There are, it seems, an infinite number of answers.

What we do know is that democracy is far from perfect, yet it continues to spread, in various forms, throughout the world—even, in recent years, to Eastern European countries that had been in the grip of communist governments for decades. We know that it is a messy and open-ended political process—one, therefore, that keeps transforming itself even as it defies consistent analysis. And we know that, for all its obvious and often maddening flaws, few of us would trade liberty for a more orderly but inevitably repressive system.

Over the years, *Time* has published many essays about democracy, the following three among the best. In "The Menace of Fanatic Factions," from October 1978, Frank Trippett looks at a political phenomenon that has only grown in the years since. In "Another Look at Democracy in America," from June 1986, Paul Gray, writing as the 19th century French observer Alexis de Tocqueville, updates that author's landmark study of democratic life. And in "Democracy Can Goof," from November 1988, Michael Kinsley tries to clarify what he sees as a central misunderstanding in the public view of democratic elections.

The Menace of Fanatic Factions

FRANK TRIPPETT

"Liberty is to faction what air is to fire." When he wrote those   1
words, James Madison clearly expected the faction-ridden nation he
helped found to go right on producing special-interest groups constantly pressing for advantage. But even the prescient coauthor of the
Federalist papers might be amazed at the abundant fulfillment of his
vision by Americans of the late 1970s. The nation has entered a period
of ascendant factionalism, a time when the larger desires of society can
scarcely be heard for the insistent clamor of its numberless segments.

It is the era of the strenuous clique and the vociferous claque, of   2
artful pressure groups and willful activists who effectively control
many things by veto and filibuster. Factions of all sizes and configura-
tions, alike only in self-service and single-mindedness, tend to dominate virtually every salient issue of the day, be it abortion, water
conservation, nuclear power or the location of bridges and express-
ways. Draw an issue anywhere and contenders will rally on both sides,
or several sides, shouting up influence out of all proportion to their
numbers. These days every political and social issue tends to be seen as
a consuming cause, and Americans who throw themselves into public
controversies increasingly tend to become single-issue champions—
crusaders.

Groups pushing one cause only are growing both in number and   3
political importance. They tend, in a time of fading political parties, to
dominate the debate of all problems and often prevail in the resolution.
They have become the undertakers for the professional politician's
career and the manipulators of legislative bodies. What they cannot
achieve by law they are often willing to achieve by defiance. They have,
most of them, an aversion to cooperation, conciliation and compromise.

Historically, the U.S. has been at pains to make sure that small   4
factions are not pushed around by any overbearing majority. Today,
such is the fragmented atmosphere of public discourse, that it is sometimes hard to remember that majority will or consensus exists, and,
indeed, these seem to crystallize less and less often nowadays. When
truckers dislike a nationally mandated speed limit, they turn into an
instant faction and willfully protest the law with massive slowdowns.

172

Los Angeles motorists, irritated by an experimental expressway lane for car poolers, defeat it not with persuasion and argument but by circumventions and defiant traffic blockages. It has become commonplace to see popular sentiment disdained, frustrated and sometimes decisively defeated by willful factions of minuscule size.

What members of these factions forget is that they are citizens not 5 of a cause but of a country of many causes. The adamant attitude that gives some motorists victory on the expressway may well propel some other faction to triumph on another issue—environment, conservation, name it—in a way the motorist might deplore.

Take the gun-control issue. Though polls have long shown over- 6 whelming popular support for handgun registration and regulation, opponents repeatedly triumph in state legislatures and Congress. Thus the pro-gun lobby, embodied in the National Rifle Association, stands as a pluperfect example of the single-issue factions. The N.R.A.'s traits and methods—passionate, uncompromising zeal combined with keen organization and ruthless skill at pressure tactics—are widely copied.

Thoughtful resolution of many a current national issue has been 7 thwarted or confounded by single-minded groups. Dissatisfied with different particulars of President Carter's proposed energy policy, extremists against decontrol ganged up to block it—or any reasonable compromise—for 18 months. Zealots on both sides have also muddied the real issues surrounding the Equal Rights Amendment. Small bands of protesters and a few smart lawyers have tied up construction of nuclear-power plants, although polls repeatedly show that two-thirds or more of the public favor them. The maneuverings of a confusing profusion of factions have put off any meaningful overall doctoring of the almost universally criticized tax system; the tax reduction bill that was emerging from Congress last week was, not surprisingly, a hodgepodge of revisions sought by a miscellany of special-interest factions. The public credo of the new factionalism is as self-centered as the private philosophy that pervades the so-called Me Decade: Do-it-my-way-or-not-at-all.

This fanatical attitude and the vindictiveness that goes with it 8 have given rise to the one-issue politics that is conspicuous in this election season. Too many voters decide for—or more often against—a candidate on the basis of his stand on a single question. For example, New York Governor Hugh Carey's future may well ride not on his respectable record in office but on his stand against capital punishment. Single issues, and particularly those heavy with questions of social value and morality, are deciding political destinies in more and more jurisdictions. Such a trend can only narrow the scope of debate and diminish the already insufficient willingness of leaders to give thought—and voice—to the question of the larger general welfare.

The rise of factionalism has occurred right along with some gen- 9
eral diminishing of the traditional American respect for the sensibilities
of others. Under the reign of permissiveness (made possible only by the
acquiescence of a majority of Americans), a handful of pornographers
flaunt their wares heedless of the public incidentally offended, and
pimps herd their whores along city streets with the same tyrannical
disregard for those they might offend. It has become commonplace for
owners of gigantic transistor radios to lug them onto public transportation (against taste and some city laws), blaring as though the world
were a private concert hall. Under the skin they are kin to the nudists
who invade public beaches from time to time to exhibit what a great
many people would as soon not see. Such segments of society may not
amount, technically, to factions, but they surely display a kindred
do-it-my-way arrogance. The same spirit has suddenly turned smokers
and non-smokers into acrimonious adversaries in many places.

Large and small pressure groups or activist groups are exercising 10
their new muscle legally even when they stray beyond the bounds of
civility, as they frequently do. Nobody questions their right to behave
as they do, and even critics who recall with distaste the triumph of the
zealous temperance crusade that, in 1919, got the Prohibition amendment passed could cite occasions when dedicated dissident groups
have served the nation's higher interests admirably. Indeed, today's
factional enthusiasm is usually tracked to two such instances: the civil
rights movement and the anti-Viet Nam War movement.

Both were launched by numerical minorities, both ultimately 11
succeeded and both taught the larger American public lessons about
the efficacy of organization, demonstration, passionate dramatics and
exploitation of the mass media. The tacticians of those movements,
dealing with fateful and fundamental issues, could plausibly justify
using every available technique, including civil defiance. The trouble is
that not only the techniques but the fervid spirit of the rights and
antiwar movements are being adopted for general application in almost
all social and political controversies. Some groups of Long Island
residents howled and demonstrated effectively for a while against the
Concorde's landing in New York as if it were a fresh incursion into
Cambodia. In North Carolina, where wets and dries fuss interminably
over the issue of legalizing liquor by the drink, all partisans tend to hurl
themselves into the fray as though life and death depend on whether
brown-bagging survives or goes by the boards. When the zealous spirit
prevails, all perspective seems lost.

Burgeoning factionalism has a healthy side: it draws fresh people 12
into public activity. Yet no matter how well it satisfies particular narrow
causes, sooner or later it must damage larger public values. Eventually,
as Political Scientist Norman Ornstein of Washington's Catholic Uni-

versity puts it, "You have too many decision makers and too many groups trying to exercise a veto over decisions, and with that you reach a paralysis in government." In the extreme, there could be worse things than paralyzed government. There could come a breaking of that basic spirit of accommodation and mutual respect that, in the final analysis, is the very heart of American democracy—but not an abstract matter of "goodness." Everybody's self-interest is ultimately undermined when the capacity for give-and-take and conciliation erodes.

For Discussion and Writing

1. What does Trippett say has happened to democratic debate in contemporary America? How does he define factions, and which characteristics does he attribute to them?
2. What is Trippett's main objection to factionalism in American democracy? Does he offer any counter-examples—instances of factionalism as a virtue in political life?
3. Which essential characteristic of American democracy does Trippett fear becomes eroded with the rise of factionalism? Do you agree?
4. Write an essay in which you attack or defend this proposition: Pressure-group politics is a natural expression of pluralistic society (a society made up of many diverse groups); we should worry less about factionalism itself, and more about how to bring groups with common interests together.

Another Look at Democracy in America

Alexis de Tocqueville, as told to Paul Gray

I did not intend to revisit the United States, nor can I say what power has transported my spirit hither. I must speculate that my presence here implies a responsibility related to the one I assumed more than 150 years ago, when I spent nine months traveling in this country. I was 26, and the nation had enjoyed barely 50 years of independence. America impressed me as a place where the experiment in Democracy, the social revolution that so agitated my contemporaries, was being most peaceably and generally conducted. So, in *Democracy in America,* I attempted to explain how a multitudinous people contrived to govern themselves and live together under terms of equality—a thing the world had never before witnessed. I ventured not only to assess the effect of the American political system on the habits and enjoyments of citizens beholden to no power excepting themselves, but also, extrapolating from my evidence, to suggest what might spring from the new way of life I observed in America.

Now, a stranger again on these shores, I survey a landscape whose surface has changed almost beyond recognition. To rehearse these alterations would be tedious, so let us quickly grant what we all know: the 24 states and 13 million inhabitants of 1831 have swelled to 50 and 240 million; scientific advances have stretched beyond my power of foresight; the United States is no longer an infant among nations but the most powerful entity on earth.

Yet the more things change, as a saying in my native language has it, the more they remain the same. America still excites the world's hopes and fears; it continues to attract immigrants, disquietude and hatred. The experiment that struck me so forcefully when I and my host country were young continues with undiminished vigor and uncertainty. To see this tumultuous process anew fills me with hope, misgivings and the desire to make a few more remarks on the ways this great land may yet fulfill or betray its destiny. In what follows, I will have occasion to repeat some of my own words; for the past 1½ centuries, scarcely anyone commenting on America at any length has failed to quote Tocqueville. I ask the same indulgence.

The Disappearing Tyranny of the Majority

At the time I wrote *Democracy in America,* one of the strongest fears   4 was that this form of government would be tantamount to mob rule. I suggested how the American system could prevent or mitigate the tyranny of the majority. This process went further than I anticipated. Now I am hard put to find any majority in America at all. There are, to pick but one example, more women in the United States than men; yet since gaining suffrage in 1920 they have failed to win decisive power at any level of government. I attribute this to the fact that women, like men, do not see themselves as part of a mighty army but as Democrats or Republicans, married or single, old or young, heterosexual or things my 19th century upbringing forbids me to name. In fact, few individuals seeking redress or public attention claim the advantage of numbers on their behalf. On the contrary: they petition from weakness as the surest method of attaining their goals. The proliferation of vociferous minorities has doubtless resulted in the righting of many wrongs. It has also led to a noticeable decline in the civility of public discourse. The United States has become at once more equitable, and clamorous, than before.

The Precarious First Amendment

It struck me as self-evident that freedom of expression was the   5 cornerstone of all democratic liberties and that censorship of the press, in particular, would soon be seen by all Americans as folly and the sure road to despotism. I now realize that my confidence was premature. Government agencies continue to threaten news organizations that publish information known to everyone, including bitter adversaries, but the American people. Certain women strive to ban, as violations of their civil rights, portrayals of members of their sex that they find insulting. People who attempt to restrict what others are allowed to read do not imagine themselves as enemies of Democracy. I must allow that they pay ideas the backhanded tribute of fearing their power. But the proper antidote to obnoxious or wicked concepts is exposure, not suppression. The urge to censor betrays a disregard for the intelligence of others. To mistrust the judgment of one's fellow citizens is to question, ultimately, their ability to govern themselves.

The Power of the Automobile

Mass-produced automobiles put freedom of movement within　6
the reach of nearly all Americans. Nothing, in theory, could be more
democratic than that. But as I see and hear America now, I marvel at the
apparent enslavement of a robust people to their machines. Nearly
everyone must live within earshot of the snarling, thunderous din of
traffic. People who motor to their places of employment must make
allowances for the time they will spend sitting still in long lines and for
the time they will have to devote to finding a place to put their automobile once they arrive. To be spared such an ordeal would seem a
blessing, but to suggest to an American that he give up his automobile
is to invite incredulous laughter.

And of Television

Citizens who are able to set out on the road to see their country　7
are also at liberty to remain home and have their country, indeed much
of the world, transmitted to them by television. There is much to admire
in this remarkable invention and more than a little cause for concern.
On the one hand, television unites in common perceptions a disparate
people spread across a broad continent. Such an immediate and inclusive forum would seem an unquestioned boon to Democracy. Such is
not entirely the case. Although television appears to reflect marvelous
diversity, it in fact fosters uniformity. Varieties of American speech,
fashions and opinions are modified toward sameness by the examples
of what millions of Americans watch. It also seems to me that television
achieves part of its power by appealing to human weaknesses. The
habit of viewing it does not encourage reflection or contemplation. The
eye is trained to crave novelty, while the brain rests or slumbers.
Political debate, which during my last visit seemed a passion and a
recreation among Americans, has shrunk to brief bursts of pleasant
images. And television's ascent has coincided with a measurable decline in the ability of young people to read. Democracy cannot function
without an informed citizenry. The paradox of television in forwarding
such a goal seems clear: barring extraordinary circumstances, it can best
summon the attention of most of the nation by presenting trivialities.

On Charity and the State

"The state almost exclusively undertakes to supply bread to the　8
hungry, assistance and shelter to the sick, work to the idle, and to act as
the sole reliever of all kinds of misery." I wrote this description not of
America but of the European nations of my own age; I ardently hoped

that the self-reliant energies stimulated by Democracy would render such well-intended but despotic administrations of charity forever a thing of the past. Yet America today presents the spectacle of an enormous machinery for the dispensing of support. Indeed, the monies spent for this purpose by government at all levels each year exceed what the nation spends annually on its self-defense. I am sad but not surprised to report that this unimaginably expensive machine does not work. There are indications that the poor are growing in number. Dependence on government help has rendered many of them unwilling or unable to pursue productive roles. The enigma is striking: a system that everyone, beneficiaries included, dislikes; a torrent of money that leaves the social landscape ever more sere. I thought that Democracy could do better than this, and I retain that expectation.

On the Decline of the Word Public

"A stranger is constantly amazed," I wrote after my first visit, "by the immense public works executed by a nation which contains, so to speak, no rich men." America now contains many rich men, and the very word public seems to have sunk into strange opprobrium. I suspect that these two phenomena are related. As the number and size of fortunes have swelled, the people who possess such wealth have naturally sought means to distinguish themselves from the common run of their fellow citizens. Private wealth in America is seldom used to purchase ostentatious grandeur. Instead, great money buys the freedom not to mingle indiscriminately with those of inferior resources. The rich prefer not to avail themselves of services that are provided to the multitude. The consequences of this retreat by the wealthy from hoi polloi have been unsettling. Those who no longer require public amenities soon begrudge the funds required to maintain them. Public schools, which their children do not attend, come to seem wasteful and unnecessary; public transportation, which they do not ride, is changed from an adornment of well-regulated society into a subject of scorn. Such attitudes among the rich would not, by themselves, be decisive. But they are adopted by millions of others who hope to become rich and purchase splendid isolation for themselves. In the scramble to pursue this goal, the comfort of the public concerns fewer and fewer people. And those who have no choice but to use general facilities no longer feel glad of the convenience but trapped, resentful and abusive.

Of Industry and Commerce

"Not only are manufacturing and commercial classes to be found in the United States, as they are in all other countries, but, what never occurred elsewhere, the whole community is simultaneously engaged in productive industry and commerce." Producing goods now seems to interest the populace less than it did then, with the result that America imports more goods from other nations than it ships out. I am at a loss to explain this change. I can only point to one development that strikes an outsider as extraordinary. Huge companies devote great energy to buying and selling one another. The American genius for commerce has discovered a method for generating vast profits without the inconvenience of making anything of value.

On the Condition of Blacks

I had few expectations that whites and blacks would ever exist   11
easily and peacefully together here: "If ever America undergoes great revolutions, they will be brought about by the presence of the black race on the soil of the United States; that is to say, they will owe their origin, not to the equality but to the inequality of condition." I am heartened that this matter turned out better than I imagined. Wherever I turn, I see blacks in positions of authority and prominence. My initial exposure to television leads me to conclude that the most beloved person in the country is a black man named Bill Cosby. Though America has freed itself from the most visible manifestations of racial injustice and intolerance, I cannot truly say that whites and blacks have resolved all of their differences. Few whites any longer are willing to display open prejudice, but this silence does not always reflect their true feelings. Blacks, for their part, often have conflicting emotions about succeeding in America; gratifying rewards may come, but not the conviction of full acceptance in society. Complicating these tensions is the existence of a class of blacks who seem permanently excluded from the opportunities of American life. Concentrated most visibly in the decaying centers of older cities, these people produce a disproportionate amount of violence, crime and fear. These depredations are bad enough, but worse still is the prospect of wasted lives and generations: children born out of wedlock in turn bearing children who have neither the training nor the chance to break the cycle of their hopelessness. Unless blacks and whites learn how to address this problem with appropriate frankness and sensitivity, I fear that a small portion of disaffected people may make life so intolerable for all that a terrible correction will enforce safety at the expense of liberty.

America remains an inexhaustible subject, and the most I can offer   12
is scattered readings of history still in the process of being written. If my remarks strike any as too critical, I am sorry but not apologetic. As I wrote once: "Men will not receive the truth from their enemies, and it

is very seldom offered to them by their friends." I am a friend of Democracy. My birth and training inclined me to aristocratic interests, but my heart led me to America. It is still the place among all others where the play of human nature is allowed the greatest latitude, for good and ill. It is still the place that can make itself even better by deciding to be so.

For Discussion and Writing

1. Gray, writing as Alexis de Tocqueville, makes several comparisons between the society of 1831 and that of today. What are the chief similarities he finds? What are the differences?
2. "Tocqueville" observes many features of modern America. What does he say about each of them?
3. Gray writes in imitation of an earlier English prose style. What do you notice when comparing it to the style of most of the other essays in this book?
4. Like Kanfer, in his essay ("Is There Intelligent Life on Commercials?") in Chapter 4, Gray adopts an anthropomorphic perspective—writes as an alien visitor—in this case a man from an earlier time. Using Gray and Kanfer as models, write an essay in which you describe today's democratic habits and practices from an outside perspective. Topic ideas: voting, election campaigns, political advertising, conventions.

Democracy Can Goof

MICHAEL KINSLEY

It looks as if my candidate for President is going to lose this election. If so, he will be constrained to be graceful about it. Not laboring under any such constraint, I am free to say that the voters—or at least a majority of them—are idiots, betrayers of their country's future, misperceivers of their own best interests, ignorant about the issues, gulled by slick lies. Unless, of course, there's an upset. In that case, the voters have magnificently exercised their ingrained popular wisdom, vindicated the faith of the Founding Fathers, demonstrated the innate genius of democracy, etc., etc., etc. I knew it all along. Regarding my candidate for Senator, kindly reverse those two explosions of prejudice.

It's widely considered a breach of democratic etiquette to question the collective wisdom of the electorate. To suggest that the voters are wrong, let alone to characterize their error in more melodramatic terms, opens you up to charges of élitism. The contention that people have been misled or manipulated, wrote one smug supporter of the probable winner shortly before the election, "reveals an extraordinary contempt for the political intelligence of the public."

The electorate's decision is held to be self-validating. However knowledgeable or ignorant, focused or distracted, reflective or scatterbrained they may be individually, the voters collectively are always wise. Political pundits who have been concentrating for months on the shallowest and most mechanistic aspects of the election campaign—tactics, commercials, "likability" and so on—will switch gears on Election Day and begin interpreting the "message" of the election in the most grandiose philosophical terms. Reports of the candidates' strategies for appealing to various groups or regions of the country will be replaced by theories about what an undifferentiated mass called "the people" was trying to say. These theories will often be of such exotic sophistication that no single one of the people, let alone all of the people, could possibly have thought of them before voting.

Foremost among the theorizers will be supporters of the winner, who will reject any notion that their man's victory might be due to their own vigorous exertions of the previous few months. It was, instead, they will argue, a fundamental and clearheaded rejection of the

1

2

3

4

"values" represented by the loser. And the neutral political observers will agree: an election loss is supposed to force losers to reconsider not merely their political strategy but their fundamental beliefs.

Yet why should this be so? As a matter of logic, it makes no sense. Serious beliefs derive from serious reflection, over a long time. A serious thinker should always be open to counterarguments from those who disagree, but the mere fact of disagreement, however widespread, shouldn't count for much.

The real insult to democracy, it seems to me, is to treat it as some sort of tennis game where victory is the definitive judgment on the players. And the real insult to the electorate is the patronizing attitude that it is a sort of lumbering collective beast, immune from error because it reaches its judgments through some mystical process that is beyond rational discourse, rather than an amalgam of individuals, each one fully capable of being right and being wrong.

The commentator who sneers that it shows "contempt for the political intelligence of the public" to suggest that the voters may have been duped is a highbrow intellectual who wouldn't dream of reaching his own political judgments based on the information and level of argument offered to the voters by his candidate. (Or mine, for that matter.) Who is showing real contempt for the public? Those who question the infallible wisdom of the majority, or those who hold the voters to a lower intellectual standard than they hold themselves to? Who is more "élitist"?

I extend every voter who votes differently from me the courtesy of serious disagreement: I think you're wrong. You may well have been misled or underinformed or intellectually lazy, or you may be highly informed and thoughtful but have a faulty analysis, or you may have acted out of narrow, unpatriotic self-interest, or you may just be a fool. But whatever the reason, you blew it. In my opinion. And I take democracy seriously enough that my own decision on how to vote was the result of a lengthy intellectual process that is not going to reverse itself overnight on Nov. 8 just because a majority of voters disagrees with me. Finally, although I am always open to dissuasion about my political beliefs, and more than open to suggestions on how to make those beliefs more salable to others, I have enough respect for the political intelligence of the public that I hope a majority may come to agree with me the next time around.

One problem with American politics is that it is dominated by people—the candidates usually and their advisers almost invariably— who don't hold any belief deeply enough to withstand evidence that the majority believes the opposite. Sincerely holding unpopular beliefs is something you accuse your opponent of, an accusation that is generally false.

The theory of democracy is not that the voters are always right.   10
Nothing about voting magically assures a wise result, and for a citizen
to dissent from the majority's choice in an election is no more élitist than
for a Supreme Court Justice to dissent from his or her colleagues'
judgment in some case. The proper form of democratic piety was nicely
expressed by Senator Warren Rudman during the Iran-*contra* hearings
(explaining why the illegal secret funding of the *contras* offended him,
although he favored *contra* aid himself). "The American people," he
said, "have the constitutional right to be wrong." You can value and
honor that right without cheering every exercise of it.

For Discussion and Writing

1. According to Kinsley, why is it illogical to think that the losers in a
   democratic election should abandon not only their political strategy but
   also their basic beliefs?
2. What does Kinsley claim are the "real" insults to democracy and the
   electorate? What is Kinsley's implied answer to the rhetorical question
   ("Who is showing real contempt for the public?") in paragraph 7?
3. Why is it a misunderstanding of the democratic process to think that
   elections are not about right and wrong? If the theory of democracy, as
   Kinsley says, is not that the voters are always right, what is it?
4. How important is voting in a democracy? Many voters today view the
   election process as a waste of time—something over which they can
   have no influence. What do you think? Write an essay about voters'
   rights, obligations or responsibilities, taking a strong stand on either
   side of the issue.

Thinking and Writing about Chapter 13

1. Which common ideas or beliefs do you find among these three essayists? Do they share a similar vision of the democratic process? Where do they seem to differ?
2. Each of these essays considers potential or real weaknesses in democracy. Trippett cites the fragmenting of the body politic into ever smaller one-issue factions; Gray lists a number of current problems, including technology's impact; and Kinsley laments voter ignorance and philosophical misunderstanding of basic democratic concepts. Given the many failings of our system, what proposals would you offer to help make the process work better, more efficiently, more intelligently?
3. Write your own philosophical essay about your understanding of democracy. You might want to try an extended definition of its essential characteristics, divide your treatment between strengths and weaknesses, or draw comparisons between conflicting views of democratic principles. Try to keep your essay concrete, with examples to illustrate your general points.

14

Youth &
Family Life

Few societies in history have been as youth- or child-oriented as the United States. Perhaps because America was itself the child of Europe, because the forces that drove the country toward expansion and world dominance were youthful energy and freedom, our society developed peculiar and sometimes contradictory attitudes toward being young. On the one hand, we seem to worship youth, devoting enormous wealth to a culture of adolescent entertainment, style, and often unrestrained liberty. On the other, more than a few adults apparently resent young people for the very things they stand for, the things adults may have lost.

Can parents worship their children and at the same time long to be as free and unencumbered as they are? What happens when older generations turn away from children, or when they actively abuse them? What happens to the society at large when the family breaks apart?

The writers in this chapter address several vital questions about parents and children and the relationships between them. In "Wondering If Children Are Necessary," from March 1979, Lance Morrow analyzes the late 1970s' drift away from child rearing toward a prolonged adult adolescence. In "The Young: Adult Penchants—and Problems," from April 1981, Frank Trippett sees in the youth of that same period a stunted adolescence and premature adulthood. And in "The Freedom of the Damned," from October 1986, Roger Rosenblatt reflects on the notorious New York murder of Jennifer Levin, 18, by Robert Chambers, 19, and what it may illustrate about contemporary parental attitudes toward young adults.

Wondering If Children Are Necessary

LANCE MORROW

In the *Leave It to Beaver* suburban world of the American '50s, the family and the child were enveloped in a cherishing mythology. Americans, it was even said, had grown obsessively kiddified; they were child-worshipers who sentimentalized their offspring in a complacent land of Little League and Disney. Toward the end of the Eisenhower years, the literary critic Leslie Fiedler wrote a lively diatribe about the "cult of the child," which he denounced as "this most maudlin of primitivisms."

Today some Americans worry that in the last decade or so the U.S. has veered to the opposite extreme, that it has developed a distaste for children that sometimes seems almost to approach fear and loathing. If that is true, the United Nations' International Year of the Child, just beginning, comes at an ironic time. The premise of the International Year, of course, is not so much that the world's children are disliked or unwelcome as that too many of them are undernourished, badly housed and ill educated. The First World and the Third World have somewhat different perspectives on children.

Those who detect a pervasive, low-grade child-aversion in the U.S. find it swarming in the air like pollen. They see a nation recoiling from its young like W.C. Fields beset by Baby Leroy. Of the 50,000 parents who responded to a query by Advice Columnist Ann Landers a while ago, a depressing 70% said that, given the choice again, they would not have children; it wasn't worth it. Although a few states have laws forbidding discrimination by landlords against families with children, huge apartment complexes and even entire communities have policies to keep the brats out. A Georgia couple that endorsed a detergent in a TV commercial were assaulted by angry telephone calls and letters denouncing them for having six children. All over the country, school budgets are being killed in tax revolts. That may be more an indication of disastrous inflation and a protest against bad educational systems than a specifically anti-child gesture, but such refusals suggest something about a community's priorities.

Specialists in the field now estimate that there are at least 2 million cases per year of child abuse, not 1 million as thought earlier. Even granting that the statistic seems inflated because more cases are re-ported now, experts think that there has been a substantial real increase in the practice. Last year's Supreme Court decision allowing teachers to spank children in school, thinks Yale Psychologist Edward Zigler, sets an example for institutional abuse, an offense that is even more wide-spread than abuse by parents. The business of child pornography flourishes. In Los Angeles the police estimate that 30,000 children, many of them under the age of five, are used each year as objects of pornog-raphy. A number of them are actually sold or rented for the purpose by their parents. Perhaps both child abuse and child pornography can be regarded as merely aberrational; some child abuse is actually a bent expression of too *much* caring, and kiddie porn (both the selling of it and the taste for it) may be just a ragged, ugly leftover of the sexual revolution. Still, the profound hostility accumulated in all that child abuse and pornography could be used to wage a medium-sized war.

The much belabored and quite real self-absorption of the '70s   5
implies, by definition, a corollary lack of interest in children. There are many forms of narcissism, of course; one of the lesser arguments of militant non-propagationists has been that children are an ego trip, begotten for the pleasure of watching one's own little clone toddle around. But today having children often seems to have been trivialized to the status of a life-style—and an unacceptable one. The obsession with being young and staying young has led to the phenomenon of almost permanently deferred adulthood. "I know 50-year-olds who are still kids," says Social Analyst Michael Novak. "They're in the play-ground of the world: single, unattached, self-fulfilling, self-centered. People are trying to make little Disney Worlds of detachment for themselves." For such people, parenthood is an intrusion of responsi-bility, of potential disappointment and, ultimately, of mortality. The kids are a *memento mori*. It can be profoundly disturbing, in a narcissistic time, to have about us, yapping and demanding and growing relent-lessly, the generation that is going to push us off the planet.

But behind these symptoms of distaste for children, many com-   6
plicated mechanisms of change are working. It can be both inadequate and misleading to argue that the nation's adults have become less hospitable to children. In their history, Americans have passed through periods of appalling cruelty and stupidity toward children. To the early Calvinists, a child was a lump of pure depravity. In Massachusetts Bay Colony, it was against the law for children to play. Things were not much better after behavioral psychologists undertook to dictate the treatment of children. Dr. J.B. Watson, an earlier generation's Dr. Spock, insisted in 1928 that children must be treated with cold scientific de-tachment. "Never hug and kiss them," he advised.

All of that elaborate—and sometimes cruel—attention to the sub- 7
ject of children in the past presupposed one thing: their inevitability.
The great changes in attitudes toward children today may revolve
around three factors: 1) Whereas children in earlier, rural settings were
economically valuable, needed for their labor, today they are a painfully
expensive proposition (according to one estimate, the average middle-
class family spends $100,000 to raise a child); 2) Children are no longer
considered a necessary and inevitable part of marriage; and 3) For
reasons of feminism and/or sheer economic need, more women than
ever before are working. In fact, of those women who do have children,
more than half have jobs outside the home. These developments have
produced a very complicated series of readjustments, the social machine fine-tuning itself in hundreds of subtle ways.

Around the beginning of the '70s came a convulsion of disgust at 8
what some regarded as the tyrannical conventions of the American
family. Both the need for population control and the urgency of
women's rights impelled various writers to launch polemics against
having kids. It was not an antichild so much as an antiparent movement. Among the voices raised against the tyrannies of automatic
motherhood was that of Betty Rollin, who is now a correspondent for
NBC News. "Motherhood is in trouble, and it ought to be," she wrote.
"A rude question is long overdue: Who needs it?" The feminist Ellen
Peck recruited Critic John Simon, TV Performer Hugh Downs and
others to form the National Organization for Non-Parents ("None is
fun"), devoted to the ideology of non-propagation.

Something interesting has happened to a few of the N.O.N. be- 9
lievers. They have grown older and changed their minds. Now Rollin
says she "feels like I've missed something" by not having a child. A
number of women who in their 20s concentrated on their careers
decided in their 30s, as they began to contemplate the impending
biological limit of their childbearing years, to have at least one child
while there was time. Says Novelist Anne Roiphe (*Up the Sandbox*):
"We're seeing a whole rash of people having babies just in the nick of
time. There's a difference between what one says at 20 and what one
says at 38." Roiphe persuasively argues that the dogmas against children—or at least, against having children—are undergoing revision.
"There has indeed been a swing of thought against children, but it was
against this whole idea that one *must* have a family," she says. "Now I
think it's probably going to swing back. All the excesses of the women's
movement, including that one shouldn't 'look nice' and so on, are all
going to be sifted through."

A doctrinal attitude toward children—for or against—is not the 10
prevailing approach of most Americans. Michael Novak suggests that

only the "idea elite," the 10% of the population in well educated, upper-income groups whose work centers on education, the professions, communications or some such—may harbor ideological or even environmental biases against children. That group could not have accounted by itself for the almost uninterrupted decline in the U.S. birth rate in the '70s. It is very likely that the economics of child rearing has had much to do with the trend toward smaller families, which has been encouraged by legal abortions.

Jerome Kagan, a Harvard professor of developmental psychology,   11
doubts that there is a generalized American antipathy toward children. Says he: "With the exception of the Japanese, American parents spend more money on books on child rearing, more time at lectures about children than any parents in the world—and it's been growing." Robert Coles, a child psychiatrist best known for his five-volume *Children of Crisis*, thinks that, if anything, children are unwholesomely overvalued by many parents: "They are the only thing the parents believe in. They don't believe in God, or in any kind of transcendence, and so they believe in their children. They are concerned with them almost in a religious way—which I think is unfortunate—as an extension of themselves. That is quite a burden for a child to experience. In that sense, it is not cruelty to children. It is paganism."

Almost no one can discuss children rationally; having children   12
and raising them successfully is an essentially irrational act. It obeys a profound and sometimes self-punishing logic like salmon thrashing upriver to spawn, an impulse encoded in the race's will to go on. All kinds of aversions to and adorations of children occur simultaneously now. The young are battered and cherished, subjected to violent extremes of malnourishment and indulgence. Children are so swaddled in myth and delusion that Marian Wright Edelman, director of the Children's Defense Fund in Washington, argues that Americans should try not to posture about them but instead look hard at statistics: The U.S. has the 14th highest infant mortality rate in the world; 10 million U.S. children have no regular source of basic medical care; 600,000 teen-agers a year, most of them grotesquely unprepared for the experience, give birth to children.

Yet more American women than ever in history now have a choice   13
about whether or not to give birth and how often. That is the most encouraging part of the new situation of children. Couples who wait to have children will probably be more mature in handling the ordeal of parenthood. Those who do not want children will not so often, as in the past, be forced to endure them. Very gradually, it may become more probable that those children who are born are also wanted.

The nation now seems to be achieving some new psychological   14
equilibrium about families and children. The wild swoop from the

excessively domestic '50s to the fierce social unbucklings of the '60s and early '70s left confusion and wreckage. A lot of menacing nonsense got flashed around and mingled with difficult truths. Generations bared their teeth at one another. Parents discovered, as if for the first time, how much their children could hurt them; some of the apparent aversion to children is a leftover fear of that palpable, demonstrated, maddening power that the young possess. Today, many new parents start with the lowest expectations about having children—everyone has told them how sick the family is—and then awake in astonished delight to find that the experience is (or can be) wonderful. It is possible that the U.S., with its long history of elaborate delusions about children, is beginning to grow up on the subject.

For Discussion and Writing

1. According to Morrow, how had attitudes toward children changed from the 1950s to the late 1970s? In what way has having children been "trivialized"?
2. To what does Morrow attribute causes of the 1970s' change in attitudes toward children? Is the '70s view still in force, do you think, or has there been a subsequent shift in such attitudes?
3. Rather than claiming universal child aversion, Morrow offers a more complex, realistic, and even paradoxical view of how children are regarded in American life. What is this view? In what way is Morrow optimistic about the future of American family life?
4. As well as you can determine, what are today's attitudes toward marriage and child rearing? Do you find yourself in agreement with them, or opposed? What are your views? Write an essay in which you express your opinion about marriage and family, explaining why you think as you do. Or you may want to try writing an argumentative essay in which you attempt logically to persuade someone your age to come over to your side of the issue.

The Young:
Adult Penchants—and Problems

FRANK TRIPPETT

Suddenly they were back in the news, if briefly: young people   1
marching with placards and upraised fists to protest U.S. military
intervention in El Salvador. Naturally the demonstrations stirred memories of the Viet Nam War. But they were also a striking reminder of
something else: how little American youth has made its presence felt in
recent years.

Compared with their predecessors, Americans in the pre-adult   2
age brackets have, for the past ten years, been nearly invisible. Those
predecessors, to be sure, were something special. They were the most
active and activist generation of young people ever to come down the
American pike. They were also, being baby-boom youngsters, the most
numerous. In terms of both numbers and aggressive venturousness
they all but dominated the stage of U.S. social change during the 1960s.

The young in those years did more than merely hold the attention   3
of the nation; they became a national obsession. Adults sometimes
imagined themselves lost on the wrong side of that much repeated
cliche, the "generation gap." From hairstyles to civil rights, the young
made their presence felt in almost every aspect of national life. And as
the decade ended they provided the great body of the visible opposition
to the Viet Nam War. Their activity peaked in the angry campus protests
that followed the killing of four students during antiwar demonstrations at Kent State University in 1970. Soon after that, to the shock of
many of their elders who expected them to persist and grow as a
permanent political force, the young moved offstage.

Theirs would have been a hard act to follow, had anybody tried.   4
As things turned out, nobody did. In the decade since, with the war
ending and the draft no longer a threat, youngsters as a whole have not
showed much inclination to give themselves to public causes even as
voters, let alone as crusaders. While they occasionally barge into the
national consciousness during such rites as their pre-Easter pilgrimage
to Fort Lauderdale, Fla., they seem to live mostly outside adult view.

As a result, they have given the larger society no clear impression of what they are like.

What they are not like is certainly clear enough. They are not like   5
their predecessors, those activists of the '60s. Professional youth watchers have described the young of the '80s as being more traditional, more religious, less rebellious than earlier youths. Also more pessimistic, more serious, more worldly-wise. Says Psychology Professor Harry Schumer of the University of Massachusetts: "They are returning to private goals. What matters is the here and now." James Barry, director of admissions at St. Ambrose College in Davenport, Iowa, says: "The good old days [of mobilized youth] never happened to them. They hardly even talk about the '70s. It's just now. And now isn't so hot."

The voices of the young tend to corroborate these views. Says   6
David Greene, 17, of Worcester, Mass.: "We're a generation of pragmatists. There's less pie in the sky for us today. So whatever works we'll do it." Christian Nurse, 16, a sometime short-order cook in Boston: "We've got to look out for ourselves. Nobody else will—the politicians or whatever. The main thing is taking care of your business, having a job and knowing what to do with the check at the end of the week."

The young, of course, are far too numerous to be so blithely   7
lumped into one thing or another; the 13-to-21 age group, though a diminishing fraction of the total population, still totals some 32 million. They are also too diverse. Still, every generation is distinguishable by the trait-marks of its mainstream members.

The peculiar thing about today's young is that so many of their   8
characteristics sound like those of—adults. This is particularly true of their cynicism and their hard-boiled self-centeredness. Says Dr. Saul Brown, director of the department of psychiatry at Cedars-Sinai Medical Center in Los Angeles: "Teen-agers have grown up on Watergate, and they feel those in power are out for themselves. Many seem to feel, 'Let me get what I can now!'" Says Joan Schuman, director of Massachusetts' bureau of student services: "It is their selfishness that strikes me most of all. The predominant theme is 'What's in it for me?' and 'I don't care what happens to my fellow man.'"

Today's young indeed resemble adults in their aspirations and   9
even in their problems. Their foremost aspiration is often to get a job that will keep them going, and a growing number work while in school. Says Thomas Fulton, assistant superintendent of the Pleasantville (N.Y.) school system: "So many seniors work that it's taking away from the total high school environment." Their very grownup worries are about the uncertainty of the future in general and the danger of nuclear destruction in particular; almost none believe in the possibility of any worthwhile survival of nuclear war. Though one recent study showed a slight decline in the use of marijuana among high school seniors,

excessive drinking is an ever growing problem (an estimated 5.3 million 14- to 17-year-olds are problem drinkers). So is teen-age sex (a million or so pregnancies occur each year among teen-agers).

The breakdown of the traditional family has made many of the 10 young feel that they are left with too much adult-like freedom. The increased number of families with both parents working, as well as the high divorce rate and the number of one-parent households, has deprived the young of guidance they consciously desire. The casual character of many modern divorces leaves affected youngsters not only without adequate control but without adult models to respect. Says Michael Peck, director of the Suicide Prevention Center in Los Angeles: "Parents are leaving homes because they want an alternative life-style, and that is just not very convincing to a child. In effect, the parent is saying, 'I'm more adolescent than you,' which is a terrible blow to the child." On the other hand, what some parents do give the child might be better withheld. Says Atlanta Psychiatrist Alfred Messer: "The 'me' attitudes of many adults are now filtering down to lower age groups. Teen-agers don't have enough good ego models."

The situation of the young today, contrasted with earlier genera- 11 tions, raises the question of whether some fundamental revision of youth's special estate in U.S. society may have occurred. It has been a long while since Americans rhapsodized about youth in the way of, say, Thomas Wolfe, who saw it as a wonderful time of existence, full of "the strange and bitter miracle of life." Indeed, America has directed less and less sentiment toward youth as parents and authorities have more and more relinquished to the young what were once seen as adult folkways and vices. Youth, or adolescence, as a special, privileged stage of life, crystallized a relatively short time ago—around the turn of the century. Is it possible that society, moved first by alarm about its children and then by disenchantment, has subtly begun the process of disestablishing youth simply by turning everybody to adult ways promptly at puberty?

For Discussion and Writing

1. Trippett makes an implicit comparison to a previous generation—the youth of the 1960s. How did this generation differ from the later one? Does Trippett judge the '70s–'80s generation harshly, or is he sympathetic?

2. What attitudes and characteristics define the generation Trippett writes about? To what does he compare them? Is his a fair or reasonable appraisal?

3. If Trippett's claims are accurate, what does he worry that they will mean for the future of adolescence in American society? Have such worries been justified in the decade since the essay appeared? Are they justified now?

4. Write an essay in which you attempt to characterize or define the essential qualities—both strengths and weaknesses—of your generation. What makes you tick? What social or historical influences have helped to shape you? How do you view yourself in relation to previous generations? What are your hopes and ambitions for the future?

The Freedom of the Damned

ROGER ROSENBLATT

Not long before dawn on Aug. 26, Robert E. Chambers Jr., 19, 1
and Jennifer Dawn Levin, 18, strolled into New York City's Central Park
behind the Metropolitan Museum of Art. Something happened between
them. Chambers allegedly strangled Levin, then remained nearby as
morning rose and the body was discovered and removed. Even shock-
proof New York sat up straight and stared. Something about a killing
on a summer night in the park, the brooding sweetness of the shadowed
grass. Something more about two upper-middle-class teenagers walking casually into a nightmare reserved for naturalistic American novels:
sensational grief, sensational murder trial, relentless public glare.

This sort of story was not supposed to happen to privileged 2
children who command the city with their lusty self-assurance; who
shop at Benetton's and Bergdorf's, have plenty of style, plenty of
clothes; who do not leave home without American Express. But they do
leave home. Breezy, noisy, they lope about the fashionable streets like
flocks of orphans in Brazil or in Beirut, like the earth's poorest children—hanging out, swooping into saloons where no one looks twice at
the doctored ID cards; the kids' money is good. Don't blame the
saloonkeepers, say the sociologists. Blame the moral carelessness that
parents pass off as the gift of freedom as they cut their children loose
like colorful kites and wish them an exciting flight.

What is this perversion of freedom about? In an enthralling series 3
of articles on the Levin killing, Samuel G. Freedman of the New York
Times observed that rich parents and poor parents are alike in their
promiscuous freedom giving. The poor let their children hustle for
subsistence. The rich buy them off. It is as if parents are afraid to touch
the people they created; and in a sense this may be so. By the time
parents are old enough to have adolescent children, they often are
undergoing second-adolescent turmoils of their own. The elder teen-
ager beholds the younger and sees his biography in the making—tumultuous prelude to a tumultuous middle. The prospect unnerves him;
he disowns it.

Or parents may be confounded by the fact that children are 4
blatantly freer than they are themselves. A subculture of young people

196

slide about the house, so much more alert than their parents to changes in music, movies, codes of dress; quick as terriers; loose as geese; all things that age is not. The power of parents lies in experience and work. The power of children lies in the freedom from those things. Parents, who cannot retrieve that sort of freedom, may regard it with bewilderment, even resentment. They keep their distance.

The central trouble seems simply that too many parents have   5 forgotten that freedom gains meaning from restraint. In this they are creatures of their times. For thousands of years, various, and very different, definitions of freedom—Aristotelian, Cartesian, Augustinian, Kantian—have all related freedom to significant choice. Over the past 20 years, the idea of freedom has evolved like a mutated animal, involving the absence not only of significant choice but of moral or rational restraints. Without a context of limitations, freedom has become dangerous and meaningless. If freedom has no restraints and embraces everything, then it risks becoming tyranny, since logically it must include tyranny among the things it embraces.

So senseless a definition could prevail only in a time when there   6 are few social penalties for destructively free behavior. The crime of murder carries demonstrably severe penalties, and so requires no continuous statement of community disapproval. But for the great range of *social* crimes, for everything from gossip to greed, no sanctions exist except those that a community informally may agree to impose: banishment, disgrace, curtailment of income. In the world these days, social crimes rarely are penalized and often are rewarded. Investment companies receive relatively small fines for major theft. Insider traders are glorified as clever. A best-selling writer plagiarizes another writer's work. He pays some dollars in a civil suit. But beyond this, his earning power is not diminished, his stature in his community is, if anything, enhanced.

What all this means to anyone watching—say a child—is that   7 character no longer is related to destiny. If a community cares only for that sinister cliché the bottom line, then there is no community pressure on individuals to behave fairly and honorably. In a world of bottom lines, why should anyone—say a child—bother to improve a soul?

The fact is that no wide social community exists, no village of   8 common thought, in which personal freedom may be judged, guided and made valuable. That is not true of political freedom. Throughout last July's Liberty Weekend, Americans trumpeted their personal freedoms from every stage, mainly because those freedoms have contributed to making a fruitful collective entity, a country. It may be argued that the most important purpose of political freedom is to tend toward community, since individual freedom allows one to grow toward an appreciation of others, a sense of common tragedy and the exercise of generosity. Yet, as soon as a community develops, individual freedom begins to be restricted. The result is the perpetual American balancing act, which applies to disputes on AIDS, drug testing, abortion, school prayer, to any issue or condition that would blow off the national roof were there no continuing, deliberate compromise between personal liberty and citizenship.

Odd that the basic balance of forces sustaining the country seems   9 to have been abandoned by the American family, which is a naturally closer community and potentially a happier one. The consequences of excessive family freedom need not be as dramatic as in the Levin killing. Little murders are committed daily in homes where Mom and Dad sit planted in front of pieces of paper or *The Cosby Show*, while the children lie still as dolls on their beds and gaze at ceiling fixtures, like stations in a dream. See how free everybody is. The only things missing are the essentials: authority, responsibility, attention and love.

If parents really are afraid to touch their children, they must be   10 afraid of these essentials too, as attitudes that confine their own free lives. They are afraid of the wrong things. Between parent and child there is no monster like silence. It grows even faster than children, filling first a heart, then a house, then history. The freedom children seek is the freedom from silence. The freedom they are given too often is the freedom of the damned, with which they may strangle themselves late on a summer night, in a city, in a park, where they have gone to be alone.

For Discussion and Writing

1. In your own words, describe the parental attitude that Rosenblatt condemns. In what way does the Chamber-Levin murder story illustrate Rosenblatt's point?
2. What happens, according to Rosenblatt, when community and parental sanctions on "destructively free behavior" disappear? Instead of benign neglect, what healthy human qualities does the author say parents should express toward their children?
3. What does Rosenblatt mean by his key phrase, "the freedom of the damned"? What kind of freedom is it that is damnation by another name?
4. Rosenblatt says that freedom can become dangerous and meaningless without limitations, that "freedom gains meaning from restraint" (5). Do you agree that children, even older adolescent ones, want or need their parents to set certain limits? From your own experience, or as a more general argument, write an essay about the tension between freedom and restraint, and the realistic needs young adults have for parental boundaries.

Thinking and Writing about Chapter 14

1. Looking at all three essays, which common themes do you find about relationships between contemporary parents and children? Do the authors agree on basic ideas, or do they have significant differences?
2. Where do the authors here lay blame for the problems of family and youth? To what extent are adolescent children themselves to blame for some of the difficulties they and their parents face today?
3. Based on what you know in your own and friends' experience with family life, growing up, and so on, how accurate are these writers' descriptions of turmoil and conflict in the American home? Do they exaggerate, or have they even gone far enough in critiquing the major issues or problems facing parents and children? Where would you agree or disagree? Where would you expand these treatments to include other ideas? Write a reflective essay in which you explore your own views of these large issues.

15

The American Character

The United States began in the self-conscious attempt of the Colonists to separate themselves from British and European civilization—to create a new world, a heavenly "city on a hill." And since that beginning, Americans have argued about whether the country's original direction has remained on course. Are we a healthy society, a moral country, still living up to the standards set down by the Founders? Or have we lost our way, gone into a kind of Roman Empire slide toward social decline and chaos? In other words, are we basically okay as a nation, or have we become "decadent"?

Of course there are arguments to be made on both sides of such large issues. During the Reagan years, when the president told us it was "morning again" in America, the national mood was upbeat, optimistic, confident that an earlier sense of mission and direction had been reborn. Some would say, however, of that same period, that the country was self-indulgently arrogant, cruelly insensitive to those who were not already wealthy or on their way to riches. The question of national decadence or health seems to be in the eye of the beholder.

In the three pieces in this chapter, all by essayist Lance Morrow, we see that even the beholder may change his opinion. In "The Fascination of Decadence," from September 1979, Morrow takes a detailed look at a complex and problematic idea as it relates to American life. In "Have We Abandoned Excellence?," from March 1982, he investigates a similar notion, arguing against the grain. And in "In the Land of Barry and the Pilots," Morrow uses two recent news stories to indicate a metaphor for life in the 1990s—and a noticeable shift in his views on the national character.

The Fascination of Decadence

Lance Morrow

*I like the word decadent. All shimmering with purple and
gold. It throws out the brilliance of flames and the gleam
of precious stones. It is made up of carnal spirit and
unhappy flesh and of all the violent splendors of the Lower
Empire; it conjures up the paint of courtesans, the sports
of the circus, the breath of the tamers of animals, the
bounding of wild beasts, the collapse among the flames of
races exhausted by the power of feeling, to the invading
sound of enemy trumpets.*

—Paul Verlaine, circa 1886

It was partly the spectacle of Western decadence that aroused the 1
Ayatullah Khomeini to orgies of Koranic proscription. Alcohol, music,
dancing, mixed bathing all have been curtailed by the Iranian revolution. Americans find this zealotry sinister, but also quaint: How can
almost childish pleasures (a tune on the radio, a day at the beach)
deserve such puritanical hellfires? But Americans are also capable of a
small chill of apprehension, a barely acknowledged thought about the
prices that civilizations pay for their bad habits: If Iran has driven out
its (presumably polluted) monarch and given itself over to a purification that demands even the interment of its beer bottles, then, by that
logic, what punishment and what purification would be sufficient for
America? The Ayatullah residing in some American consciences would
surely have to plow under not just the beer bottles, but an uncomfort-
ably large part of U.S. society itself.

The very idea of decadence, with all its fleshly titillations and 2
metaphysical phosphorescence, excites that kind of Spenglerian anxiety. A lot of Americans seem inclined to think of themselves as a
decadent people: such self-accusation may be the reverse side of the old
American self-congratulation. Americans contemplate some of the
more disgusting uses to which freedom of expression has been put; they

201

confront a physical violence and spiritual heedlessness that makes them wonder if the entire society is on a steep and terminal incline downward. They see around them what they call decadence. But is the U.S. decadent? Does the rich, evil word, with its little horripilations of pleasure and its gonging of the last dance, really have any relevant meaning?

Decadence is a wonderfully versatile idea—like a perfume that gives off different scents depending on a woman's body chemistry and heat. It arouses pleasure, disgust and bombast. And sometimes elaborate denial. The critic Richard Gilman recently published *Decadence* (Farrar, Straus & Giroux). His elegant treatise argues that the term is almost impossible to define, is constantly misinterpreted and misused, and quite possibly should be deleted from the language.

Gilman makes a persuasive, if somewhat pedantic, point. He argues that Americans overuse the word decadent, without knowing what they mean by it. They use it to describe a $50 bottle of Margaux, a three-hour soak in the tub, a 40-hour-a-week television habit, the crowds that tell the suicide to jump, a snort of cocaine. And yet Americans mean *something* by it. The notion of decadence is a vehicle that carries all kinds of strange and overripe cargo—but a confusing variety of meanings does not add up to meaninglessness. Decadence, like pornography (both have something of the same fragrance), may be hard to define, but most people think they know it when they see it.

They think it might cover, say, the Aspen, Colo., fan club that grew up two summers ago to celebrate Murderer Ted Bundy with, among other things, T shirts that read TED BUNDY IS A ONE-NIGHT STAND. Or the work of Photographer Helmut Newton, who likes to sell high-fashion clothes with lurid pictures of women posed as killers and victims, or trussed up in sadomasochistic paraphernalia; one of his shots shows a woman's head being forced into a toilet bowl. The school of S-M fashion photography may, of course, be merely a passing putrefaction.

People informally play a game in which they compile lists of the most decadent acts now in practice. For horrific sensationalism, they might start with the idea of the snuff film (pornography in which an actress performing sex is actually murdered on screen). In the same awful category, they might include Viennese Artist Rudolf Schwarzkogler, who decided to make a modernist artistic statement by amputating, inch by inch, his own penis, while a photographer recorded the process as a work of art.

The list would have to mention Keith Richards, a member of the Rolling Stones, who, by one account, in order to pass a blood test to enter the U.S. for concert tours, had a physician drain his own heroin-tainted blood from his body and replace it with transfusions from more sedate citizens. Some of the sadomasochistic and homosexual bars in

New York and San Francisco, with their publicly practiced urolagnia, buggery and excruciating complications thereof, would strike quite a few Americans as decadent.

In a less specialized realm, disco and punk songs like *Bad Girls* and *I Wanna Be Sedated* have a decadent ring. In fact, the entire phenomenon of disco has a certain loathsome glisten to it.   8

Extravagance has always been thought to have something to do with decadence. Some lists might mention Tiffany's $2,950 gold-ingot wristwatch, or a pair of $1,000 kidskin-and-gold shoes, or Harrods $1,900 dog collar, or Zsa Zsa Gabor's $150,000 Rolls-Royce with its leather, velvet and leopard interior. But be careful. Extravagance may actually be a sign of robustly vulgar good health. One can argue about such gestures as that of the 3rd century Roman Emperor Elagabalus, who once on a whim sent his slaves to collect 1,000 lbs. of cobwebs. They returned with 10,000 lbs. "From this," said Elagabalus, "one can understand how great is Rome." The Emperor would have enjoyed the Neiman Marcus catalogue, one of 20th century America's most fabulous menus of conspicuous consumption. The man who purchased His and Hers Learjets from the catalogue was helping to keep a lot of aircraft workers employed.   9

Decadence is a subjective word, a term of moral and psychological recoil. It expresses quite exactly those things that the speaker finds most awful, most repugnant, most dangerous and, as a Freudian might point out, most interesting. So a question arises: Are aberrant tastes decadent in themselves? Does the decadence consist in the fact that such tastes can now be openly practiced and even tolerated? Surely, tolerance is not decadence, unless it is a symptom of moral obliviousness.   10

Players in the game can pile up examples but still have difficulty arriving at any generality. Decadence, in one working definition, is pathology with social implications: it differs from individual sickness as pneumonia differs from plague. A decadent act must, it seems, possess meaning that transcends itself and spreads like an infection to others, or at least suggests a general condition of the society. Decadence (from the Latin *decadere*, "to fall down or away," hence decay) surely has something to do with death, with a communal *taedium vitae*, decadence is a collection of symptoms that might suggest a society exhausted and collapsing like a star as it degenerates toward the white dwarf stage, *"une race à sa dernière heure,"* as a French critic said.   11

Perhaps it is part of the famous narcissism of the '70s, but Americans forget how violent and depraved other cultures have been. There is something hilarious, in a grisly way, about George Augustus Selwyn, the late 18th century London society figure and algolagnic whose   12 morbid interest in human suffering sent him scurrying over to Paris whenever a good execution was scheduled. Americans may have displayed an unwholesome interest in the departure of Gary Gilmore two years ago, but that was nothing compared with the macabre fascinations, the public hangings, the *Schadenfreud* of other centuries. In the 17th century, Londoners sometimes spent their Sunday afternoons at Bedlam mocking the crippled and demented.

In Florence during Michelangelo's time, countless victims of stab- 13 bings by hit men were seen floating under bridges. In London during the Age of Enlightenment, gangs roamed the streets committing rape. Says Critic George Steiner: "Our sense of a lost civility and order comes from a very short period of exceptional calm—from the 1860s to 1914, or the interlude between the Civil War and World War I."

One of the problems with the concept of decadence is that it has 14 such a long moral shoreline, stretching from bleak and mountainously serious considerations of history to the shallow places where ideas evaporate 30 seconds after they splash. For all the range of its uses, decadence is a crude term. It houses fallacies. People think of decadence as the reason for the collapse of Rome, but the point is arguable. Rome at the height of its imperial power was as morally depraved as in its decline. Perhaps more so.

A second model is the metaphor of natural decay, the seasons of 15 human life, for example. Animals, people, have birth, growth, periods of vigor, then decline and death. Do societies obey that pattern? The idea of decadence, of course, implies exactly that. But it seems a risky metaphor. Historians like Arnold Toynbee, like the 14th century Berber Ibn-Khaldun and the 18th century Italian Giovanni Battista Vico, have constructed cyclical theories of civilizations that rise up in vigor, flourish, mature and then fall into decadence. Such theories may sometimes be too deterministic; they might well have failed, for example, to predict such a leap of civilization as the Renaissance. Ultimately, the process of decadence remains a mystery: Why has the tribe of Jews endured for so many centuries after the sophisticated culture of the Hittites disappeared?

Richard Gilman can be granted his central point: "that 'decadence' 16 is an unstable word and concept whose significations and weights continually change in response to shifts in morals, social, and cultural attitudes, and even technology." But the protean term is still tempting. It seems the one word that will do to point toward something moribund in a culture, the metastasis of despair that occurs when a society loses faith in its own future, when its energy wanes and dies. It would probably be more narrowly accurate to use words like corrupt or depraved to describe, say, punk rock, or murder in a gas line, but decadent is more popular because it contains a prophecy. To be decadent is to be not just corrupt, but *terminally* corrupt. "Decadence" speaks with the iron will of history and the punishment of the Lord. It is an accusation. "Woe to those who are at ease in Zion," wrote the prophet Amos, "and to those who feel secure on the mountain of Samaria. Woe to those who lie upon beds of ivory, who drink wine in bowls, and anoint themselves with the finest oils."

One could construct a kind of "worst-case scenario" to prove that   17
the U.S., with the rest of the West, has fallen into dangerous decline. The case might be argued thus: the nation's pattern is moral and social failure, embellished by hedonism. The work ethic is nearly as dead as the Weimar Republic. Bureaucracies keep cloning themselves. Resources vanish. Education fails to educate. The system of justice collapses into a parody of justice. An underclass is trapped, half out of sight, while an opulent traffic passes overhead. Religion gives way to narcissistic self-improvement cults.

There is more. Society fattens its children on junk food and then   18
permits them to be enlisted in pornographic films. The nation subdivides into a dozen drug cultures—the alcohol culture, the cocaine culture, the heroin culture, the Valium culture, the amphetamine culture, and combinations thereof. Legal abortions and the pervasive custom of contraception suggest a society so chary of its future that it has lost its will to perpetuate itself. Says British Author Malcolm Muggeridge: "What will make historians laugh at us is how we express our decadence in terms of freedom and humanism. Western society suffers from a largely unconscious collective death wish." Alexander Solzhenitsyn, who shares with Muggeridge an austere Christian mysticism, has been similarly appalled by Western materialism.

And yet, oddly, the U.S. probably seemed more decadent, or at   19
any rate, considerably more disturbed, eight or ten years ago than it does now. In the midst of the Viet Nam War, the ghetto riots, the assassinations, the orgasmic romanticism of the counterculture, the national rage was more on the surface. Says Milwaukee Sociologist Wayne Youngquist: "There is decadence in our society, but it is an ebb, not a rising tide. Our institutions are healing, the age of moral ambiguity and experimentation is in decline."

Americans must beware, however, of looking for decadence in the   20
wrong places. The things that can make the nation decay now are not necessarily what we think of when we say decadence: they are not Roman extravagances or Baudelaire's *fleurs du mal*, or Wilde's scented conceits. Nor, probably, do they have much to do with pornography, license or bizarre sexual practice. It is at least possible that Americans should see the symptoms of decadence in the last business quarter's alarming 3.8% decline in productivity, or in U.S. society's catastrophic dependence upon foreigners' oil, or in saturations of chemical pollu-

tion. It is such symptoms that betoken "a race which has reached its final hour."

But the word decadence, like an iridescent bubble, can be blown   21
too large; it will burst with too much inflation of significance. In any case, decadence is too much a word of simplification. The U.S. is too complicated, housing too many simultaneous realities, to be covered with one such concept. Subcultures of decadence exist, as they have in all societies. The amplifications of the press and television may make the decadence seem more sensational and pervasive than it really is. A sense of decay arises also from all of society's smoking frictions of rapid change, the anxiety caused by a sense of impermanence. The nation's creative forces, however, remain remarkably strong—in the sciences, for example, where achievements in physics, mathematics, biology and medicine rank beside anything so far accomplished on the planet. Before anyone tries to use too seriously the awful and thrilling word decadence, he ought to distinguish between the customary mess of life and the terminal wreckage of death.

For Discussion and Writing

1. How does Morrow define decadence? What are some problems with any definition of the term? By decadence does Morrow mean extravagance or tolerance of aberrant tastes?
2. Morrow poses the question: Is the U.S. decadent? What is his answer? How does he place decadence in an historical context?
3. In recent years there have been a number of controversies in the arts (Robert Maplethorpe's homoerotic photography, for instance), popular music (2 Live Crew) and entertainment (Andrew Dice Clay) that might be viewed as examples of decadence. Would Morrow be likely to change his opinion in light of these more recent examples? Why or why not?
4. Are you persuaded by Morrow's argument? Write your own critique of decadence in American life, or in the life of your age group. Define the term as clearly as you can, and cite concrete examples to support your interpretation.

Have We Abandoned Excellence?

LANCE MORROW

A new biography of Admiral Hyman Rickover records a Navy   1
captain's assessment: " 'Look around. Do you see excellence anywhere?
In medicine? In law? Religion? Anywhere? We have abandoned excellence . . . But Rickover was a genius who gave a generation of naval
officers the idea that excellence was the standard.' " Only the nuclear
submarines ran on time.

"Abandoned" seems a little strong to describe what we have done   2
to excellence. But of course a note of elegy always haunts discussions
of excellence and quality. It is human nature to imagine that our present
reality is squalid, diminished, an ignominious comedown from better
days when household appliances lasted and workers worked, and
manners were exquisite and marriages endured, and wars were just,
and honor mattered, and you could buy a decent tomato. The lament
for vanished standards is an old art form: besieged gentility cringes,
indignant and vulnerable, full of memories, before a present that behaves like Stanley Kowalski: crude, loud, upstart and stupid as a fist.

Americans seem especially wistful about excellence now. Stand-   3
ing waist-deep in a recession, after years of change that hurled the
cultural furniture around and turned much of it to junk, they are apt to
think longingly of excellence. They may watch a film like *Chariots of
Fire*, for example, with a nostalgic pang for the simplicity of its moral
lines, its portrait of excellence unambiguously pursued.

Is the Navy captain correct? Has a quality called Excellence gone   4
under like Atlantis in an inundation of the third-rate, a deluge of
plastics, junk food, bad movies, cheap goods and trashy thought? The
question has been asked since well before the decline of Athens; the
answer is generally yes—but wait. There is an enduring ecology of
excellence in the world. It is a good idea to remember Thomas Merton's
question: "How did it ever happen that, when the dregs of the world
had collected in Western Europe, when Goth and Frank and Norman
and Lombard had mingled with the rot of old Rome to form a patchwork of hybrid races, all of them notable for ferocity, hatred, stupidity,
craftiness, lust and brutality—how did it happen that, from all this,
there should come the Gregorian chant, monasteries and cathedrals, the

poems of Prudentius, the commentaries and histories of Bede ... St. Augustine's *City of God?*"

A couple of rules may apply to generalizations about excellence: 1) all recollections of past excellence should be discounted by at least 50%; memory has its tricks of perspective; 2) what might be called the Walt Whitman Rule: exuberant democratic energy usually finds its own standards and creates its own excellence, even though the keepers of the old standards may not like the new. A Big Mac may sometimes surpass the concoctions of Julia Child.

Of course, much that was once excellent has fallen into disrepair, or worse. The dollar, for example. New York City. American public education. Cars from Detroit. Standards of civility (which may not have been as civil in the past as we imagine). Public safety. But who said that any excellence is permanent?

Excellence demands standards. It does not usually flourish in the midst of rapid, hectic change. This century's sheer velocity has subverted the principle of excellence; a culture must be able to catch its breath.

In America and elsewhere in the industrial world, the idea of excellence acquired in the past 20 years a sinister and even vaguely fascistic reputation. It was the Best and the Brightest, after all, who brought us Viet Nam. For a long time, many of the world's young fell into a dreamy, vacuous inertia, a canned wisdom of the East persuading them—destructively—that mere being would suffice, was even superior to action. "*Let It Be,*" crooned Paul McCartney. Scientific excellence seemed apocalyptically suspect—the route to pollution and nuclear destruction. Striving became suspect. A leveling contempt for "elitism" helped to divert much of a generation from the ambition to be excellent.

The deepest American dilemma regarding excellence arises from the nation's very success. The U.S. has been an astonishing phenomenon—excellent among the nations of the world. But as the prophet Amos said, "Woe to them that are at ease in Zion." It is possible to have repose, or to have excellence, but only some decorative hereditary monarchs have managed to simulate both. Success has cost Americans something of their energetic desire. And those Americans not yet successful (the struggling, the underclass) are apt to aim at ease, not excellence: the confusion contaminates character and disables ambition.

The manic overstimulation of American culture also makes excellence rarer. The great intellectual flowering of New England in the 19th century (Hawthorne, Emerson, Melville, Thoreau, Longfellow, *et al.*) resulted in part from the very thinness of the New England atmosphere, an understimulation that made introspection a sort of cultural resource.

America today is so chaotically hyped, its air so thick with kinetic information and alarming images and television and drugs, that the steady gaze required for excellence is nearly impossible. The trendier victims retreat to sealed isolation tanks to float on salt water and try to calm down.

Yet excellence remains. The U.S. has won 140 Nobel Prizes since   11 World War II—although cuts in Government research grants will reduce the level of that particular excellence in the years to come. American medicine, biology and physics lead the world. American politicians (that least excellent breed) may be better educated, more honest and industrious—more excellent—than ever. Vermont maple syrup is excellent. American agriculture is excellent. Ted Hood's sails are excellent. American telephone service is excellent. American professional sports would be excellent if they were not so drenched in greed. Look abroad: the French language is excellent. Some would argue that the entire country of Switzerland is excellent (if somewhat savorless), from its unemployment rate (.3%) to its scenery to its national airline.

Americans have historically allowed themselves to become con-   12 fused by the fact that their practical excellence has been so profitable. But the meaning of excellence (serious excellence, not Big Macs) is essentially metaphysical. Excellent things are constantly destroyed, of course—bombed, defaced, or else misunderstood; a conquering army may some day bivouac in the Sistine Chapel and take idle target practice at the ceiling. But excellence is essentially invulnerable. It carries the prestige of the infinite with it, an ancestral resemblance to the ideal. It is ecstatic. For an irrevocable moment, it gives the mind what Melville called "top-gallant delight."

For Discussion and Writing

1. Morrow says that the word excellence, not unlike decadence in the previous essay, raises some problems in usage and meaning. What cautionary suggestions does he make to those who would indulge in "generalizations about excellence"?
2. As in his first essay, Morrow poses a rhetorical question: Has American excellence declined? What is his answer? What are some of the examples he cites as evidence of his conclusion?
3. What do you think Morrow means when he says, in the final paragraph, that "the meaning of excellence ... is essentially metaphysical," that "excellence is essentially invulnerable"?
4. Morrow claims that "the manic overstimulation of American culture also makes excellence rarer," that "the steady gaze required for excellence is nearly impossible" (10). Write an essay in which you consider the effects of mass or popular culture on high standards—in the arts,

education, even sport. Do the demands of filling the appetite of an always-hungry mass audience tend to water down quality? Where is excellence to be found today? As always, use examples and illustrations to back your assertions.

In the Land of Barry and the Pilots

LANCE MORROW

Two patients lie in the emergency room, beset by mysterious 1
pains. When the doctor arrives, one patient asks, "What's wrong with
me?" The other patient, who is an addict, pleads only, "Can you give
me something for the pain?" The two questions come from different
universes.

The U.S. has got into the habit of responding to its crises by 2
lurching into emergency rooms and pleading for the painkiller first.
Some important part of the American mind has gone over into a
territory of denial and evasion.

Once the avoidance begins to work, the patient cares less about 3
the diagnosis. Fear loses its power to instruct. Urgency vanishes before
magic. The country glides into a toxic subjectivity. The eyes glaze a little,
and clouds close over the glimpse of death. The problem will vanish,
the earth will get well. The mind billows off to locate better memories,
if it can (old glories, myths of its own innocence, old muscles, resources
long since squandered, wars won when the nation was young and
saved the world, when its virtue shone and sped by on tail fins).
Americans con themselves with nostalgias. Was it during the 1980s
under Ronald Reagan, the child of an alcoholic, that the addiction to
this dreaming got out of hand?

But the pain-killer wears off, the patient wakes. It is not morning 4
in America anymore but a somewhat frayed and bloodshot season.
American politics (shortsighted, vicious, stupid) plunges on. The government cannot pay its bills and goes on putting up the great-grand-
children as collateral. Congress and the President perform a dance of
breathtaking fecklessness over the federal budget.

This is the shape-shifting landscape of addict and alcoholic. The 5
two terms mean in essence the same thing: a powerless dependence
upon one drug or another, whether the chemical is legal or illegal. Here
boundaries blur and melt. "Responsible" adults—fathers, mothers,
bankers, Senators, solid citizens—become dangerous aliens. Their cars
fly across the median in the middle of the night. The high began as a
creamy indulgence and ends as a squalid necessity, a fix. The soul

begins to die. It passes over into realms of the surreal and savage, into moral blackout and passivity.

The rot in private minds eats away at public responsibility. Judges   6
in separate courtrooms the other day pronounced sentence on Marion Barry, the mayor of Washington (six months for possession of cocaine, the drug that is tearing his city apart) and on three Northwest Airlines pilots who, while drunk one morning last spring, flew a Boeing 727 with 91 passengers aboard from Fargo, N. Dak., to Minneapolis. Mayor Barry, still running the addict's street con, portrayed himself as the victim of racial prejudice and, worse, as a man who has recovered from his problem and mended his ways.

The mentality of addiction, of alcoholism, prevails in zones of   7
American life even when no drugs are involved. Americans are addicted to television, a true enslavement, a dreary mania. When diversion is all, real life vanishes. Americans are addicted to the consumption of energy, to profligate plastics and convenience power in all its fuming, humming expressions—cars, motorboats, air conditioners, home appliances. They are addicted to credit and debt, to mobility, to high speed. The American addictions tend to have this in common: a hope of painlessness.

But to live painlessly is to live powerlessly as well. Addictions,   8
chemical and otherwise, rob people of their abilities. The attention grows dull and scattershot. Curiosity dims. A motif of escape prevails— not adventurous escape, but a fade into drifting blankness or, conversely, into the sort of agitated irrelevance that rackets around, say, in political campaigns whose biggest issue is flag burning.

A people does not have to be literally drunk or drugged to be   9
self-deluding, grandiose, self-destructive, improvident and allergic to reality. A perverse style takes up residence in the mind, a sort of civic dybbuk. Things go out of control (the mayor; the captain in the cockpit; the national debt; the savings and loans, once prim as small-town librarians, that went as crazy as the gaudiest binger).

Every society has its obsessive traits. To name them is to trivialize   10
them, of course, to neutralize folly in cliché. Germans are addicted to order and scatology, the French to an empty elegance of language, the Italians to cynicism, the Irish to language and self-pity, the Slavs to romantic depression.

Fundamentalist Islam, addicted to its ruthless clarity under God,   11
condemns the Great Satan of the West, with its vices, its drugs and pornography, its demolished families and disastrous morals. Perhaps there is at work in the world some law of compensation enforcing the principle that greater material blessings, as in the West, bring on commensurate miseries (cirrhosis and gout and custody fights and homelessness).

In his diaries Jean Cocteau wrote, "Stupidity is always amazing, 12
no matter how used to it you become." Addictions are usually amazing
as well, and as mysterious as stupidity. The obsessive persists in the
folly over and over again, always believing that this time the result will
be different. In some sinister way, ignorance is becoming an American
addiction—part of a quest for painless life. Americans have come to
shoot ignorance like dope. Ignorance is, after all, one of the most
powerful anesthetics. Obliviousness pulses now with a willful, aggressive glow—a sort of active impatience, a passion to escape knowing.

Why this American addiction to the painless? The idea of the 13
nation's Manifest Destiny, of its ascendant virtue and inevitable success, was driven in the past by the professed ethic of hard work and
sacrifice. But somewhere the hardworking part of the formula got lost.

Did the American Dream all along mean nothing more than the 14
quest for painlessness? It is tragic if the dream has become a delusion,
a mirage that, as the doctor would say, is part of the sickness.

For Discussion and Writing

1. What is Morrow's essential claim about the American mind or character
   in this essay? What evidence does he cite to support his view?
2. Morrow describes American behavior with a metaphor—a nonliteral or
   figurative comparison. What is the central metaphor of "In the Land of
   Barry and the Pilots"?
3. Unlike his previous two essays, "In the Land" doesn't bother much with
   qualifications or balance. What do you think is the effect of Morrow's
   strident and even sweeping approach?
4. Write an angry condemnation of a tendency in contemporary life that
   you find damaging or otherwise self-destructive. Like Morrow, try your
   hand at using colorful, persuasive language—metaphor, connotative
   words, and a passionate tone.

Thinking and Writing about Chapter 15

1. Morrow addresses various themes in his three essays. Where do you see consistent ideas from one to the next? Where, if at all, does Morrow express contradictory or at least conflicting views?
2. Each of these pieces attempts to get at what might be called general or universal traits of American character. Is there a problem with such all-embracing generality, or are there specific qualities we can point to that accurately reflect the way the nation as a whole behaves?
3. Write your own consideration of the country's national character. Which virtues continue to shape our lives for the better? Which weaknesses do we find hard to shed? What do we seem most worried about? About what are we most proud? What recent problems and successes seem to define the national self at this moment in history?

PART THREE: Global Issues

16

War

$\mathbf{A}$ popular song lyric of the 1960s shouted, "War! What is it good for? Absolutely nothing!" It is a sentiment not unique to the anti-Vietnam War protests, but one that has been heard in one form or another from those who have opposed violent conflict. But its opposite has also been heard throughout history: the military drumbeat, the bugle call to take up arms. And the questions that war raises are, it seems, forever with us—making us uneasy, forcing our moral scrutiny, asking that we justify (however inconsistently) our actions.

Why do people fight wars? Because, as one author here says, they are inevitable? Because conflicts arise naturally between human communities? Because men are murderous beings with a primitive taste for blood and glory?

The writers here address each of these issues in their discussions of war. In "On War as a Permanent Condition," from September 1965, an anonymous author argues for war's inevitability. In "The Morality of War," from January 1967, an anonymous writer considers arguments for and against just wars against the backdrop of Vietnam. (Chapter 17 in this book addresses the Vietnam war in closer detail.) And in "The Warrior Culture," from October 1990 (before the onset of the Gulf War, which is treated in Chapter 18), Barbara Ehrenreich strongly condemns what she sees as a self-perpetuating male warrior ethic.

On War as a Permanent Condition

Five years ago a Norwegian statistician set a computer to work counting history's wars. The machine quickly, competently and a bit contemptuously announced that in 5,560 years of recorded human history there have been 14,531 wars, or, as the computer pointed out, 2.6135 a year. Of 185 generations of man's recorded experience, the machine noted with a touch of sarcasm, only ten have known unsullied peace. And even as he always has, man these days is fighting man.

In Kipling country, Indians and Pakistanis last week slammed away at one another with polyglot curses and American weapons. In South Viet Nam, sticks of paratroopers fell and bloomed from big-bellied U.S. Hercules transports in the grandest airdrop of the war. In Yemen, sun-blackened Arab guerrillas warily avoided Egyptian troops; in the Sudan, rebellious blacks kept up a tenacious hit-and-run pressure on Khartoum's troops. Befeathered Simbas in the Congo set ambushes for Colonel Mike Hoare's mercenary force. Turks and Greeks on Cyprus, Indonesians and Malays in the Malacca Straits, Portuguese and Angolans in West Africa, OAS troops and Dominicans in Santo Domingo—all kept their powder dry and their gunsights blackened.

Roughly speaking, ten wars are in progress throughout the world this week. They range from petty conflicts in which the strategic weapon is a poisoned arrow to major air raids in which jet B-52s bomb jungle hideaways. As a leading French strategist on the Quai d'Orsay puts it: "There is no longer such a thing as war and peace, just different levels of confrontation."

The Muscle-Bound Big Nations

Nuclear war, carried to holocaust, may yet scour the planet Earth; the "ultimate deterrent" may become, in Julian Huxley's phrase, the "ultimate detergent." But it is a valid interim observation that The Bomb seems to be keeping peace quite effectively among its possessors, bearing out Churchill's ironic comment that he "looked forward with great confidence to the potentiality of universal destruction." Illogically, the general feeling that nuclear war equals suicide or surrender

216

has induced a similar sentiment among some that any war is unthinkable. But a Pentagon count of conventional wars since 1945 adds up to 40, only a little fewer than history's average.

While the awful possibilities of their own strengths make the big 5 nations muscle-bound and the United Nations grows ever more helpless in preventing conflict, the small, non-nuclear countries have found limited wars to be a functional means of settling disputes. The very possession of doomsday weaponry by the U.S. and Russia has forestalled the main event, but lesser powers feel free to slug it out in dozens of other arenas.

There is, moreover, a larger supply of these small-bore combat- 6 ants. Since 1945 the nations of the world have almost doubled in number, from 68 to 127. Each new country has its own self-interest, its own power of decision and—thanks to the cold war and the resulting supplies of weapons and military training—its own armed forces. Alastair Buchan of London's Institute for Strategic Studies points out that "there are more military men acting as political leaders than at any time in the 20th century." He cites Pakistan's President Mohammed Ayub Khan, Burma's Ne Win, Thailand's Thanom Kittikachorn, Egypt's Gamal Abdel Nasser, Algeria's Houari Boumedienne, Saigon's Nguyen Cao Ky, France's Charles de Gaulle and such nonprofessional but militaristic figures as Cuba's Fidel Castro and Indonesia's Sukarno.

War thus needs continuous redefinition. Prussia's Karl von 7 Clausewitz (who died in 1831 of cholera) gave the modern starting point by defining war as the extension of state policy by other means. To him, victory was "the destruction of the enemy forces," but he held an equally warm regard for the limited objective. Defense was at least as strong a position as offense, and putting the enemy off stride as valuable as knocking him flat. To that extent, generals who could forestall defeat were as honorable as those who won famous victories.

Warfare since Clausewitz has grown more refined, and American 8 officials now look at it more in terms of intensiveness than offensiveness. General Harold K. Johnson, U.S. Army Chief of Staff, discerns three categories:

- HIGH-INTENSITY WAR uses the most modern military technology. Its 9 firepower is delivered largely by missiles, aircraft and missile-armed submarines. All of the knockout punch is thermonuclear and aimed by the most advanced intelligence and command techniques, undoubtedly including spy satellites and pushbuttons. It sounds like Armageddon, but Physicist Herman Kahn in his current Clausewitzian study, *On Escalation: Metaphors and Scenarios*, argues that high-intensity war has a rationale. He identifies 44 stages of escalation, ranging from

"Ostensible Crisis," in which no bridges are burned (Rung 1), through "Constrained Force-Reduction Salvo against weak links at the outbreak of a war" (Rung 35) to "Spasm or Insensate War" with "all buttons pressed." His point: controlled response is as possible with thermonuclear artillery as it was with the howitzers of yore.

- MID-INTENSITY WAR, a conventional-weapon conflict in which nei-   10
  ther total offense nor total victory is envisioned in planning, accepts policy limitations such as shunning air attacks against Hanoi in North Viet Nam. Korea and Viet Nam are the only postwar examples of mid-intensity war.

- LOW-INTENSITY WAR aims at establishing, maintaining or regaining   11
  control of land areas threatened by guerrillas, revolutionaries or conquerors. The U.S. might initiate a low-intensity war in a Latin American nation in order to preclude a Castroite takeover or to carry off a coup as it did in 1954 against Guatemala's Jacobo Arbenz. The Congolese rebellions of 1960–62 and 1964 were of low intensity, as were most of the Latin American and Middle Eastern conflicts of the past two decades. The battle between India and Pakistan over Kashmir has fluctuated between low intensity (as in such diversions as last spring's Rann of Kutch fighting) and mid-intensity (as in the current conflict, where neither side has weapons enough to carry the battle to total victory).

The Perfect Volley

The shift away from large-scale, high-intensity war marks a sig-   12
nificant turning point in the history of warfare, an atavism of arms that reverses a trend begun in 1793 with the French Revolution. Before then, war had been mostly a professional concern. The 10,000 Greeks who marched up-country with Xenophon were fighting for pay, not glory; early Rome practiced a limited conscription, but by the Augustan age (27 B.C.–14 A.D.), Rome's empire was firmly enough established to be secured by a tough army of 300,000 professionals. Apart from the mob-scene Crusades, the wars of medieval Europe were brief and relatively bloodless: Edward III had no more than 30,000 men at Crécy, and Henry V at Agincourt only 15,000.

From the mid-17th century to the end of the 18th, European   13
warfare grew less savage, more scientific. Gunpowder replaced cold steel; siege work and precision drill supplanted the wild charge. The key to victory lay in the "perfect volley" delivered at point-blank range by tautly disciplined infantrymen, as Wolfe demonstrated on the Plains

of Abraham. The key to defense lay in maneuver: French Marshal Comte Hermann Maurice de Saxe wrote, "I am sure that a clever general can wage war as long as he lives without being compelled to battle."

Mass war, precursor of this century's two world wars, began when [14] Napoleon instituted universal conscription. The generals of the 19th century also turned away from the minimal-loss thinking of their predecessors. "I desire nothing so much as a big battle," declared Bonaparte. U. S. Grant in the American Civil War concurred; indeed, only by the constant bloody pressure he put on the Army of Northern Virginia was the war won for the North. In World War I, Foch and Haig, Hindenburg and Ludendorff pressed the attack for four years—with the goal of lasting just 15 minutes longer than the enemy army.

With World War II and the arrival of the heavy bomber, that [15] strategy was broadened to include destruction of the enemy economy as well. And the atom bombs that the U.S. dropped on Hiroshima and Nagasaki proved the effectiveness of ending a war by wholesale destruction. In 1949 Russia acquired its own nuclear bombs, and the postwar peace that so many had believed would last forever now appeared threatened by the possibility of all-out nuclear war between the two giants. Any war at all, it was feared, must inevitably lead to a catastrophic blowup between the two great nuclear powers.

Then came Korea. Harry Truman's courageous decision to inter- [16] vene in 1950 showed not only that Communism could be contained without recourse to all-out nuclear war, but that a sizable, well-equipped conventional force was mandatory for any nation that would head off a Communist takeover. It was still the threat of massive retaliation that kept Stalin out of Western Europe, but it took American infantry and artillery, American ships and aircraft to secure the safety of South Korea. That same flexible mix, augmented by General Maxwell Taylor's Special Forces and clouds of helicopters, is now making the Viet Cong look like losers in South Viet Nam.

Thus has the interplay of weaponry and history left the U.S. [17] equipped for—and apparently in for—limited war. "The major powers will be drawn more and more into little wars," predicts the Quai d'Orsay strategist. "There will be a period of disequilibrium and tension for, say, the next 50 years." France's General Pierre Gallois contends that "Viet Nam is the beginning and not the end of America's great Asian adventure." The U.S. is in a sense fighting the same sort of wars that the British fought in the 19th century—peripheral battles at the end of thin red lines.

Viet Nam and many another of the era's conflicts represent Com- [18] munist aggressions under the umbrella of nuclear standoff: 23 of the 40 wars involved Communists. Of the remaining 17, eight were anticolonial struggles—ranging from the Indonesian rebellion against The Netherlands (1945–47) through Kenya's Mau Mau "emergency" (1952–53) and Algeria (1956–62) to the Angolan revolt, now five years old. Another six fall into the category of neighbor-against-neighbor, such as the Pakistani-Indian war in 1947–49 and its current revival or the Algerian-Moroccan border war of 1963.

There were three outright grabs, as when Red China captured 19 Tibet in 1950. Significantly, in only three cases have nuclear-armed nations indulged in high-handed power plays in the past 20 years: Britain and France in Suez (1956); Russia in Hungary the same year; the U.S. in Cuba (during 1961's Bay of Pigs debacle). Of the remaining confrontations, the only one that saw nuclear-armed nations opposing each other directly (rather than opposing a non-nuclear ally of a big power) was the Cuban Missile Quarantine of 1962.

"Sorry About That"

Pope John XXIII in his last encyclical rather wistfully held out 20 hope that *pacem in terris* is attainable without the shedding of blood. Yet "there are situations," argues Theologian Paul Tillich, "in which nothing short of war can defend the dignity of the person." Thus a nation may usually be defending national interests, but this purpose does not preclude defending moral interests as well.

The U.S. national interest came first, as Pentagon Planner Sey- 21 mour Deitchman points out, "in the use of the atom bomb, the Mexican war, the war with Spain over Cuba, the destruction of American Indian tribal society, failure to support the Hungarian rebellion. We were able to rationalize our moral problems, which were real and recognized, because the political and economic problems were greater and more urgent." Similarly, Kashmir is of national interest to Indians, who believe that its loss would put in jeopardy hundreds of other princely states and consequently imperil India's tenuous union itself. It is also of national interest to Moslem Pakistan that Kashmir (80% Moslem itself) be taken into the fold of political Islam.

But the limited wars that the U.S. is now fighting, and doubtless 22 will continue to fight for the next half-century or more, have a moral purpose too. In South Viet Nam, this purpose is to preserve freedom of choice for that country and others near it that the Communists might overwhelm. As Lyndon Johnson has time and time again explained, the U.S. seeks no territory, seeks no wider war.

No humane man can applaud the cruelties of war, yet no man of 23 dignity can shrink from war if he is to preserve his freedom. Indeed, wars often have the virtue of deciding issues more definitely than diplomacy. Israel exists today not because the Jews were capable negotiators but because they were courageous fighters against the Arabs.

India ignored its own sanctimonious praise of peace to seize Portuguese Goa and thus permanently removed that galling thorn from its side. By contrast, the feud between Turkish and Greek Cypriots still festers despite years of negotiations and may never be settled short of full-scale civil war.

War is, in sum, horrible but definitive, repellent but—pending realization of the dream of world order—inevitable. Soldiers in all wars usually manage to make some rueful appraisal of this human dilemma, and the G.I.s in South Viet Nam are no exception. Their catchall comment, endlessly applied to one another's hard-luck stories of great pain or minor difficulty, is a deadpan "Sorry about that." 24

For Discussion and Writing

1. How would you describe the author's attitude in this essay? Does he or she seem to view war as a tragic consequence of the human condition, a necessary evil, a glorious enterprise?
2. What are the three types of war this writer defines, and how does the shift away from one mark "a significant turning point in the history of warfare"?
3. What, in this author's view, justifies war? Do you agree?
4. In the closing remarks, the author concludes that war is inevitable. Write an essay in which you attack or defend this conclusion. Does accepting or expecting the inevitability of war become a self-fulfilling prophesy? Is there evidence to suggest that even limited conflict might be managed without resort to war?

The Morality of War

"**M**oralists are unhappy people," wrote Jacques Maritain. A 1
great many Americans are turning into unhappy moralists about the
war in Viet Nam. It is a new sensation. Americans are accustomed to
feeling right about the fights they get into. The majority probably still
feels right—but troubled. The President summed up the uneasy moral
choice in his State of the Union Address. "It is the melancholy law of
human societies," he said, quoting Thomas Jefferson, "to be compelled
sometimes to choose a great evil in order to ward off a greater evil." On
the other side, a chorus of clerics, academics and polemicists of every
tone proclaims that the U.S. position is evil, or at least morally questionable. When Cardinal Spellman exhorted American soldiers to hope and
fight for victory in Viet Nam, he was widely criticized by other churchmen, many of them Roman Catholics. William Sloane Coffin, chaplain
of Yale University, has said: "It may well be that, morally speaking, the
United States ship of state is today comparable to the *Titanic* just before
it hit the iceberg."

There are in the U.S. remarkably few Machiavellians who believe 2
that war is simply a matter of state, beyond questions of good or evil.
At the other extreme, there are also relatively few all-out pacifists. Most
critics concede that in certain conditions, war is morally justifiable—but
assert that this is not the case in Viet Nam. Why one war is justified but
not another is an immensely difficult question; the answer, tentative at
best, requires logic, precision and a measure of emotional detachment.
These qualities are largely missing in the Viet Nam debate. The tendency is to call anything there that is distasteful or tragic "immoral."
Yet the concept of a just or an unjust use of force involves complex
judgments of means and aims—an accounting of lives and deaths and
intentions—that go to the very heart of civilization.

Early Ground Rules

History was well along before it occurred to anybody that there 3
were two ways of looking at war. War was war—bloody, awful, sometimes glorious—and the normal way in which a nation established itself

222

in the days when Egypt, Babylonia, Assyria and Persia were harrying each other for territory and tribute. Aggression invariably had the sanction of a deity. The Israelites' takeover of the Canaanites was commanded by Jehovah himself. And wars were usually as total as soldiers with limited technology could make them.

War to the death only began to go out of style when the belliger- 4 ents recognized some kind of relationship, as in the case of the Greek city states, which tried to soften their deadly rivalry through diplomacy and mercy. But such temperateness was strictly limited to social equals; Aristotle, who is credited with inventing the term "a just war," could apply it to military action "against men, who, though intended by nature to be governed, will not submit." The Romans took over the idea of a just war as an instrument of efficient administration, and Cicero laid down some pragmatic ground rules. Only states could wage war, he insisted, and only soldiers could fight them—a useful device to preclude revolution. Before one state could attack another, hostilities had to be formally declared, leaving time for reply.

Biblical teaching brought a new note of individual responsibility 5 to war; the One God became the witness to every killing, the unerring judge of every motive. The basic Old Testament rules of warfare were laid down in *Deuteronomy*. Enemies within Israel were to be wiped out, and their cities razed, with the exception of the fruit trees. Cities outside Israel's borders were permitted to become tributaries. If they refused, the Bible permitted the killi·ʾg only of the men—the women and children had to be taken as slaves. The Jews were also prohibited from fighting on the Sabbath.

The early Christians extended the Sabbath ban against fighting to 6 every day of the week. A literal interpretation of the Sermon on the Mount obviously necessitated a pacifist position. Writing against the Christians some time between 170 and 180, the Roman philosopher Celsus made the point that "if all men were to do the same as you, there would be nothing to prevent the king from being left in utter solitude and desertion, and the forces of empire would fall into the hands of the wildest and most lawless barbarians." But Christians ceased to be pacifist when the Emperor Constantine turned Christianity from a fringe sect into the Establishment. It now behooved the church to defend the Christian empire, and St. Augustine, faced with the waves of barbarian invasions, built upon the codes of Aristotle, Plato and Cicero the Christian concept of the just war. First, he said, the motive must be just: "Those wars may be defined as just which avenge injuries" or repel aggression. A just war must be fought with Christian love for the enemy—the Sermon on the Mount was supposed to be followed as "an inward disposition." No one, wrote the saint, "is fit to inflict punishment save the one who has first overcome hate in his heart. The love of enemies admits of no dispensation, but love does not exclude wars of mercy waged by the good."

Old & New Crusades

St. Thomas Aquinas and others expanded Augustine's standards, and the list has been elaborated ever since. Modern criteria of a just war include 1) discrimination between killing soldiers and civilians; 2) reasonable possibility of victory; 3) "proportionality" between the amount of harm done by the war and the benefits hoped for.   7

Augustine's guidelines were hardly ever fully observed, but the concept of the just war persisted as a potent influence on European thought. The taking of a fellow Christian's life, even in legitimate warfare, was not viewed lightly in medieval times. In 1076, a council at Winchester decreed that any soldier in the Norman Conquest a decade earlier who had killed a man should do penance for a year; all archers were to do penance three times a day for 40 days. Eventually, the church achieved a remarkable palliation of mankind's bellicosity in the Peace of God, which limited the legitimate targets and areas of warfare, and the Truce of God, which prohibited fighting on Fridays, Sundays, and long periods around Christmas and Easter.   8

But such forbearance was for Christians only. The Crusades to liberate Jerusalem from the infidels amounted to a war of aggression launched by the church, with license for every kind of excess in the name of Christ. That the same body that could impose the Peace and Truce of God should be capable of rejoicing in a cargo of Saracen noses and thumbs or of filling the Temple of Solomon with blood has been the dark paradox of religious faith in every time and place. Just and holy wars are incompatible. The just war is predicated on awareness of human intemperateness, inadequacy and guilt; the holy war drowns all that in the joyous, irresponsible assumption of being an instrument of God's will. In this respect, Protestantism was no different from the Church of Rome. Luther and Calvin reworked Augustine's just-war doctrines, but the religious wars following the Reformation and periodic outbursts of heresy-hunting discarded the Sermon on the Mount for the text from Jeremiah: "Cursed be he that keepeth back his sword from blood."   9

In the 19th century, when humanism rather than Scripture undergirded much of man's morality, it seemed as though holy wars had become a thing of the past. But the new religion of nationalism was to demand its own crusades. Clergy blessed the guns on both sides as World War I broke out and quickly degenerated into frothing fanaticism. "Kill Germans!" cried the Bishop of London. "To kill them not for the sake of killing, but to save the world, to kill the good as well as the   10 bad, to kill the young men as well as the old . . . I look upon it as a war for purity." In the U.S. writes Yale Historian Roland H. Bainton, "Jesus was dressed in khaki and portrayed sighting down a gun barrel."

The reaction to the passion and the bloodletting of World War I [11] was a wave of idealistic pacifism. When World War II came 21 years later, the Allies went into it reluctantly, grimly and without elation, faced with an evil as obvious and inarguable as evil can ever be. Even scrupulous moralists agree that World War II was the closest thing to a just war in modern times. And yet, in retrospect, the means were horrifying. The saturation bombings of Hamburg, Dresden and Berlin were designed primarily to kill and demoralize civilians. The atomic bombing of Hiroshima and Nagasaki was justified as taking fewer Japanese and American lives than would have been lost in an invasion. But the fact remains that the bombing of Germany and Japan obliterated the discrimination of a just war between soldier and civilian. This led many Christian thinkers to decide that the concept of the just war was simply no longer applicable in modern times because a nuclear exchange would kill so much of the world's population that whatever good might be aimed for—freedom, for example—would itself be wiped out and rendered meaningless through nearly universal destruction.

The Chief Arguments

There is some limited dissent even from this almost universally [12] held view. According to Lateran University's Monsignor Ferdinando Lambrushchini, the destruction of military objectives with nuclear weapons might be morally more justifiable than the bombing of cities, with TNT. However, the moral condemnation of nuclear war is relatively obvious and easy. What is often overlooked is the fact that the very horror of using nuclear weapons may have inaugurated a new era in which limited, conventional wars are likelier than before. It is precisely in such limited conflicts that the old just-war principles seem pertinent again. Some churchmen deny this. Says the Rev. Paul Oestreicher of the British Council of Churches: "If the technical criteria of the just war are taken at face value, this is tantamount to pacifism, because no modern war conceivably measures up to them." Nevertheless, most of the moral objections advanced against the Viet Nam war are generally put in terms of the just-war principles, and they move quickly from moral abstraction to practical questions. Among the chief arguments:

Aggression or Civil War. A government's right to make war in [13] self-defense was reaffirmed by the Vatican Council in a statement that otherwise direly warned against the evil of total war. Some Viet Nam critics believe that the Korean War involved a legitimate case of self-

defense because the Communist attack occurred clearly across an established border line, and was carried out by an organized army;
besides, South Korea's defense was a U.N. action. In contrast, they
consider the Viet Nam conflict a civil war. This overlooks the fact that
there is such a thing as indirect aggression, and every realistic observer
knows that outside Communist help for the Viet Cong is a decisive
factor.

Civilian Casualties. Killing civilians for the purposes of terror and   14
demoralization is morally indefensible, all theologians and moral philosophers agree, violating the just-war principle of discrimination. The
conditions of warfare in which a factory can be as much of a military
installation as an airfield has created inevitable new hazards for non-
combatants. And Mao Tse-tung's dictim, "There is no profound difference between the farmer and the soldier," underlies the special
problems created by guerrilla warfare. The U.S. is not deliberately
trying to destroy and demoralize civilians; it is guerrilla tactics and
terror that attempt this. Writes Dr. Paul Ramsey, professor of Christian
ethics at Princeton: "If the guerrilla chooses to fight between, behind
and over peasants, women and children, is it he or the counter-guerrilla
who has enlarged the legitimate target and enlarged it so as to bring
unavoidable death and destruction upon a large number of innocent
people?"

The Possibility of Victory. Obviously, neither side in Viet Nam can   15
win, some critics argue, and thus to continue a painful war of attrition,
which is gradually destroying the whole country, is indefensible. It
violates the just-war principle that victory must be a reasonable possibility. Yet victory could mean various things, including an undramatic
fading-away of the Viet Cong or an internationally enforced compromise. Thus defined, victory may still be called remote or even unlikely,
but it is by no means impossible.

All these arguments eventually hinge on the question of propor-   16
tion: whether the toll in death and pain is proportionate to the possible
gains. The most vocal critics of U.S. policy answer no, but for various
reasons. Scarcely anyone argues that a favorable outcome in Viet Nam
is essential to American survival. On the other hand, few would agree
with the position at the opposite extreme—taken by U Thant, among
others—that Viet Nam is completely unimportant to U.S. interests.
Chicago Professor Hans Morgenthau, a strong critic of U.S. participation in Viet Nam, defines that what is moral is what is dictated by "the
national interest, rightly understood." The essence of the debate is
about a right understanding of the national interest.

The liberal Roman Catholic magazine *Commonweal* echoes a wide-   17
spread opinion when it admits that the outcome of the war will make
a difference but maintains that it cannot be "the decisive difference

needed to justify a war that will last longer than any America has ever fought, employ more U.S. troops than in Korea, cost more than all the aid we have ever given to developing nations . . . kill and maim far more Vietnamese than a Communist regime would have liquidated . . . The evil outweighs the good." The difficulty in this position is that it involves all kinds of intangible calculations, judgments and prophecies. Who can really balance the destruction of war against the slaughter of political enemies that would result from a Communist takeover? Who can really count future casualties in Viet Nam and weigh them against the casualties of another war that might have to be fought later in Thailand? These are agonizing questions, on which decent men can reach different conclusions. Even, says Professor Ramsey, if the conflict in South Viet Nam itself were to destroy "more values than there is hope of gaining, one must not forget that there are more values and securities and freedoms" to be reckoned with beyond Viet Nam—in Asia and elsewhere in the world.

Path of Love

This is acknowledged in principle by many of the critics, who [18] concede that one cannot rule out the need for violence in the fight for justice and who can even visualize hypothetical future wars or revolutions (for example in Latin America) against unjust or tyrannical regimes; yet they feel that this does not apply to Viet Nam. The evil represented by Communism simply is not as clear or overwhelming in the minds of most people today as was the evil of Nazism. Britain's Oestreicher allows that "tyranny is not peace" and believes that the use of violence against tyranny may be moral (for instance, the Hungarian uprising), but at the same time condemns the Vietnamese war as unjust. The Archbishop of Canterbury defends the U.S. right to be in Viet Nam because it is there "with the right motive, withstanding Communist aggression," but refuses to concede that any modern war can be just.

Such self-contradictory statements reflect the tortured attempts to [19] reconcile morality with the hard facts of history. It is a task for which modern Western man, and particularly the American, is ill prepared. The U.S., as the most powerful nation in the world, has never systematically thought out the legitimate uses and the inevitable limitations of power. The answer cannot lie either in mere swagger or in mere compassion. The age-old problem of reconciling love and justice is cogently analyzed by German Catholic Theologian Karl Rahner, who feels that "it is impossible to make our existence a paroxysm of nonviolence." The Christian "should always first opt for the path of love; yet as long as this world exists, a rational, hard, even violent striving for justice may well be the secular personification of love." Love, or even justice, may only be dimly discernible in the brutal landscape of Viet Nam—but that does not change the principle.

For Discussion and Writing

1. What is the central claim this author makes about the morality of war? When are wars just or unjust?
2. In recounting the history of warfare, this writer considers war as a function of the developing power of the Christian Church. How did Christianity, originally a pacifist religion, become involved in warfare? In what sense, according to this author, are "just" and "holy" wars incompatible?
3. Using the Vietnam War as an historical context or example, the author considers the general arguments against even so-called just wars. What are these, and what are the writer's responses to each?
4. Are you persuaded by the just war argument? Write an essay defending or attacking the notion that some wars are in fact just and moral, despite the horrible consequences they inevitably bring about. What is worth fighting for, in your view? Are there limits on the responses a nation should use when threatened, or should every conflict be entered with a "take no prisoners" attitude?

The Warrior Culture

BARBARA EHRENREICH

In what we like to think of as "primitive" warrior cultures, the passage to manhood requires the blooding of a spear, the taking of a scalp or head. Among the Masai of eastern Africa, the North American Plains Indians and dozens of other pretechnological peoples, a man could not marry until he had demonstrated his capacity to kill in battle. Leadership too in a warrior culture is typically contingent on military prowess and wrapped in the mystique of death. In the Solomon Islands a chief's importance could be reckoned by the number of skulls posted around his door, and it was the duty of the Aztec kings to nourish the gods with the hearts of human captives.

All warrior peoples have fought for the same high-sounding reasons: honor, glory or revenge. The nature of their real and perhaps not conscious motivations is a subject of much debate. Some anthropologists postulate a murderous instinct, almost unique among living species, in human males. Others discern a materialistic motive behind every fray: a need for slaves, grazing land or even human flesh to eat. Still others point to the similarities between war and other male pastimes—the hunt and outdoor sports—and suggest that it is boredom, ultimately, that stirs men to fight.

But in a warrior culture it hardly matters which motive is most basic. Aggressive behavior is rewarded whether or not it is innate to the human psyche. Shortages of resources are habitually taken as occasions for armed offensives, rather than for hard thought and innovation. And war, to a warrior people, is of course the highest adventure, the surest antidote to malaise, the endlessly repeated theme of legend, song, religious myth and personal quest for meaning. It is how men die and what they find to live for.

"You must understand that Americans are a warrior nation," Senator Daniel Patrick Moynihan told a group of Arab leaders in early September, one month into the Middle East crisis. He said this proudly, and he may, without thinking through the ugly implications, have told the truth. In many ways, in outlook and behavior the U.S. has begun to act like a primitive warrior culture.

We seem to believe that leadership is expressed, in no small part, 5
by a willingness to cause the deaths of others. After the U.S. invasion
of Panama, President Bush exulted that no one could call him "timid";
he was at last a "macho man." The press, in even more primal language,
hailed him for succeeding in an "initiation rite" by demonstrating his
"willingness to shed blood."

For lesser offices too we apply the standards of a warrior culture. 6
Female candidates are routinely advised to overcome the handicap of
their gender by talking "tough." Thus, for example, Dianne Feinstein
has embraced capital punishment, while Colorado senatorial candidate
Josie Heath has found it necessary to announce that although she is the
mother of an 18-year-old son, she is prepared to vote for war. Male
candidates in some of the fall contests are finding their military records
under scrutiny. No one expects them, as elected officials in a civilian
government, to pick up a spear or a sling and fight. But they must state,
at least, their willingness to have another human killed.

More tellingly, we are unnerved by peace and seem to find it 7
boring. When the cold war ended, we found no reason to celebrate.
Instead we heated up the "war on drugs." What should have been a
public-health campaign, focused on the persistent shame of poverty,
became a new occasion for martial rhetoric and muscle flexing. Months
later, when the Berlin Wall fell and communism collapsed throughout
Europe, we Americans did not dance in the streets. What we did,
according to the networks, was change the channel to avoid the news.
Nonviolent revolutions do not uplift us, and the loss of mortal enemies
only seems to leave us empty and bereft.

Our collective fantasies center on mayhem, cruelty and violent 8
death. Loving images of the human body—especially of bodies seeking
pleasure or expressing love—inspire us with the urge to censor. Our
preference is for warrior themes: the lone fighting man, bandoliers
across his naked chest, mowing down lesser men in gusts of automatic-
weapon fire. Only a real war seems to revive our interest in real events.
With the Iraqi crisis, the networks report, ratings for news shows rose
again—even higher than they were for Panama.

And as in any primitive warrior culture, our warrior élite takes 9
pride of place. Social crises multiply numbingly—homelessness, illiter-
acy, epidemic disease—and our leaders tell us solemnly that nothing
can be done. There is no money. We are poor, not rich, a debtor nation.
Meanwhile, nearly a third of the federal budget flows, even in moments
of peace, to the warriors and their weaponmakers. When those priorities are questioned, some new "crisis" dutifully arises to serve as
another occasion for armed and often unilateral intervention.

Now, with Operation Desert Shield, our leaders are reduced to 10
begging foreign powers for the means to support our warrior class. It

does not seem to occur to us that the other great northern powers—Japan, Germany, the Soviet Union—might not have found the stakes so high or the crisis quite so threatening. It has not penetrated our imagination that in a world where the powerful, industrialized nation-states are at last at peace, there might be other ways to face down a pint-size Third World warrior state than with massive force of arms. Nor have we begun to see what an anachronism we are in danger of becoming: a warrior nation in a world that pines for peace, a high-tech state with the values of a warrior band.

A leftist might blame "imperialism"; a right-winger would call   11
our problem "internationalism." But an anthropologist, taking the long view, might say this is just what warriors do. Intoxicated by their own drumbeats and war songs, fascinated by the glint of steel and the prospect of blood, they will go forth, time and again, to war.

For Discussion and Writing

1. Ehrenreich begins her essay with a number of illustrations from so-called primitive cultures—Masai tribesmen, Plains Indians, Solomon Islanders. What is the effect of such examples in setting the tone and attitude of her argument?
2. In what ways, according to Ehrenreich, has the U.S. begun "to act like a primitive warrior culture"? Do you find her evidence persuasive?
3. What is Ehrenreich's view of warrior culture? Is her opinion stated directly, or through more subtle or indirect means?
4. Ehrenreich implies without qualification that warrior culture is male culture—a man's world. Now that women have found a prominent place in the armed forces, do you agree? Write an essay in which you consider the question of gender and warfare. Is war just something that (male) warriors do, or is it a more universal characteristic of people, some of whom are women?

Thinking and Writing about Chapter 16

1. What would Ehrenreich say to the first author's claim that war is inevitable? What argument might she use to oppose such a position?
2. War as we think of it is a conflict between nations or peoples. Does war happen on a smaller scale as well? Consider some of the arguments made in these essays—that war is apparently inevitable, that it can be just, or that it is more or less an exclusively male pastime—and apply those ideas to lesser instances of war: gang conflict, political struggle, even violence between individuals or within families. Do descriptions of national or state wars hold at the other levels, or do they begin to break down? Is there a fundamental difference between conflict between individuals and that between nations or societies?
3. Write a personal reflection on what war means, or has meant, to your own life. You might want to consider friends or family who've been caught up in war, your own imaginary or real preparation for or involvement in armed conflict, or the general impact awareness of war has had on your daily life—whether it has affected your plans, your decisions, your view of morality or human nature.

17

The Vietnam Era

Certainly no period in recent American history was as difficult, and had such long-lasting effects, as the Vietnam era. The war between North and South Vietnam was more than a decade old before American involvement, but our own Vietnam problem began in the 1960s, with a vast increase of U.S. military forces in that country during the Kennedy and Johnson administrations. America had been in Vietnam for several years before social protests against the war started at home, but once they did begin, life in the United States changed radically. Scholars and historians of the period are still trying to sort out the various influences—the popular music culture, the increased availability of and interest in illegal drugs, and the campus and civic protests that led eventually to a national anti-war movement.

The Vietnam War and its aftermath—which, some would argue, continued at least until the War in the Persian Gulf in 1990–91—is far too complex an issue to be treated exhaustively in three brief essays. But the pieces here do give some sense of that period: of its beginning in the mid-sixties, when support was still fairly solid; of the anti-war protests that helped spawn a counter-culture; and of the plight of the ordinary soldier, the Vietnam veteran, whose fate continues to haunt many of the men and women who served in that faraway place.

The essays in this chapter span the history of the period. In "Viet Nam: The Right War at the Right Time," from May 1965, before the massive escalation, an anonymous writer presents the argument for U.S. involvement. In "Violent Protest: A Debased Language," from May 1970, shortly after the Kent State killings, an anonymous author laments the turn toward physical confrontation. And in "Bringing the Viet Nam Vets Home," Lance Morrow explains the veterans' plight and recommends a way to heal deep and lasting wounds.

Viet Nam: The Right War
at the Right Time

The Caribbean is closer to U.S. shores than the South China Sea, but despite the nearby uproar in the Dominican Republic, the crucial test of American policy and will is still taking place in Viet Nam.

By and large, U.S. public opinion seems strongly behind Lyndon Johnson's unyielding strategy of bombing the North and stepped-up ground action in the South. At the same time, an insistent—if by no means unanimous—chorus of criticism is heard, particularly on college campuses, from faculty as well as students. "Teach-ins," petitions and picketing get headlines. Most of the critics argue that the U.S. should stop the bombing and get out quickly, giving an odd combination of pragmatic and supposedly ethical reasons.

The pragmatic reasons add up to the notion that the U.S. either cannot win or need not win in order to safeguard its interests. The moral objections are often weakened by the fact that, while the critics condemn the use of force against North Viet Nam, they either condone or ignore it in other situations—such as Sukarno's guerrilla war against Malaysia, Red China's conquest of Tibet or, most important, the Viet Cong's own terror against South Vietnamese peasants.

Questions of Reality

Herewith a discussion of the six principal arguments.

- *The struggle in Viet Nam is a "civil war" and the U.S. has no right to interfere.* Certainly, there are elements of a civil war present. Many Viet Cong are not hard-line Communists but nationalistic and social revolutionaries whose aims include land reform and reunification. But as elsewhere, the local revolution has been captured by Communism. The Viet Cong have some autonomy, but they are trained, directed and supplied by North Viet Nam. In the Communist rebellions in Greece and Malaya, for example, almost identical arguments were heard; these were called civil wars in which the U.S. was supposedly backing reactionary regimes that lacked popular support and could not win. And yet in both cases, when outside Red help was shut off, the rebellions collapsed. Because the West has lately learned to live with Communist regimes that have been forced to cut back their export of revolution, it is sometimes forgotten that Communism still remains an international aggressive movement, that "infiltration" and "subversion" remain realities, not words to frighten children. No struggle in which Communism is involved is ever truly a civil war.

- *The South Vietnamese people don't care whether they live under Communism or not, as long as they get peace.* Obviously they desperately want peace, and they need more positive hopes than just anti-Communism to keep them going. But after a decade, South Viet Nam's army is still fighting, and sustaining casualties proportionately higher than U.S. casualties in two world wars. This is an amazing fact, recently heightened by the decline in government desertions, and in the increase in new recruitment.   6

- *The U.S. cannot fight for democracy by backing more or less undemocratic regimes in Saigon.* A democratic regime is hardly possible in a war-torn country without much democratic tradition. What the critics fail to admit is that even a bad non-Communist regime is usually subject to change, but once a Communist regime is established, it is virtually irreversible. Taking up the argument that the integrity of U.S. democracy at home depends on an end to the war, Columnist Max Lerner, himself a professor, recently replied: "No, it depends on not flinching from the reality principle, on maintaining clear goals without hypocrisy, and in showing that democracy has what it takes for survival against ruthless forces both at home and abroad."   7

- *"North Viet Nam's Ho Chi Minh might turn into the Tito of Asian Communism.* This is possible, but only if Red China changes its nationalist-expansionist direction. Tito's Yugoslavia is separated by 200 miles of Carpathian wilderness from Russia, while North Viet Nam has a common frontier with China. Moreover, the Chinese have traditionally pushed south. Ho, whose basic training and sympathies derive from the Soviet Union, is now 75; most of his rising lieutenants are pro-Peking. A Viet Nam united under Communist rule would, for the foreseeable future, remain a Peking satellite. It is absurd to suggest that after winning all of Viet Nam the Communists would then sit back and turn "mellow." Inevitably, they would seek domination of the whole area, and there is no sign that they would be resisted except in Thailand—and even here the Red pressure would be enormous.   8

- *U.S. escalation in Viet Nam is pushing Red China and Russia together.* 9
  Despite some parallel warlike noises from Moscow and Peking,
  there is little to support this belief. China seeks to control the
  Communist movement throughout the world, hopes to win that
  control by showing that "wars of liberation" pay off. Russia, on
  the other hand, is unwilling to give up the hard-won *détente* with
  the West, which permits Moscow greater concentration on internal development, in favor of the Chinese hard line. Should
  Mao prove his point by winning in South Viet Nam, Russia
  might well be forced into greater militancy.

- *Asia is not of vital importance to the U.S.* After all, so runs this 10
  argument, the U.S. is not omnipotent. Walter Lippmann contends that Asia is legitimately the sphere of Chinese influence,
  just as the Western Hemisphere is America's.* That contention is questionable. Since the early 19th century, the U.S. has
  grown to a major Pacific maritime power; to surrender the
  Pacific to China now makes no more sense than surrendering it
  to Imperial Japan would have in 1941. With Southeast Asia
  gone, the U.S. would rapidly approach a point where it might
  have no foothold in Asia from Okinawa to Australia. Beyond
  that, the argument cannot be sustained in the light of modern
  weaponry: geographic spheres of influence are simply not pertinent in an era of ICBMs. The Chinese themselves pay no
  attention to the theory, as is shown by their activities in Africa
  and Latin America.

Dangers of Inaction

The chief immediate demand of the critics is that the U.S. negoti- 11
ate. But such an argument leaves out of account the fact that the
Communists use negotiations only as a tactic to make further gains—
unless they are forced by superior power or self-interest to stick to their
bargains. They quickly broke the Geneva Agreement of 1954 and the
Laos Agreement of 1962 by refusing to withdraw Communist guerrilla
forces. Despite vague talk, no one has advanced even the outlines of an
international arrangement that could keep South Viet Nam secure from
Communism. Hanoi and Peking show no sign of considering any
international agreement except the kind of "neutralization" that would
put the Viet Cong in a position to capture power in Saigon.

---

*Irritated by the Lippmann argument, Pentagon officials made a study of his columns
during the Greek crisis of 1947–49 and concluded: "My God, Walter would have given
away Greece too!"

Obviously, after overcoming his early hesitation, Lyndon Johnson   12
will not allow the U.S. to be pushed out of Viet Nam. For if that were to
happen, Americans would only have to make another stand against
Asian Communism later, under worse conditions and in less tenable
locations. As Demosthenes said about expansionist Macedonia in the
4th century B.C.: "You will be wise to defend yourselves now, but if you
let the opportunity pass, you will not be able to act even if you want
to." Despite all its excruciating difficulties, the Vietnamese struggle is
absolutely inescapable for the U.S. in the mid-60s—and in that sense, it
is the right war in the right place at the right time.

For Discussion and Writing

1. Anti-war arguments, according to this author, take two forms: pragmatic and moral. What does he or she say about each?
2. Upon what kinds of political assumptions is this essay based? Have any
   of those general ideas been proved, in subsequent years, to have been
   mistaken? Which ones?
3. The argument for American intervention in Vietnam is stated here in its
   classic form: That a refusal to fight aggression now will only lead to a
   worse confrontation later. Has this argument been used in other, more
   recent, contexts? Is it any more or less persuasive now than it was then?
4. One of the anti-war arguments the author considers (7) is that the U.S.
   "cannot fight for democracy by backing more or less undemocratic
   regimes. . . ." As a general principle, should our policy be to support
   only democratic governments against aggression, or should we be
   willing to fight to prop up dictatorial or totalitarian governments that
   serve our larger interests? Write an argument for or against this proposition, including reasonable, logical justification for your view.

Violent Protest: A Debased Language

Words, like trees, bend with the prevailing winds. In the climate   1
of opinion of the past few years, the word dissent has undergone a
decided transformation. For most of U.S. history, it clearly meant
speech—the unorthodox opinion, the challenging idea. Then, during
the 1960s, civil rights protesters took to the streets to fight segregation,
and the word became associated with demonstrations as much as with
speech. As protests have continued to broaden and increase, dissent has
come to be used to describe and defend a wide variety of physical acts,
including violence toward property and even toward people.

The explanation many protesters offer for their switch from verbal   2
to physical dissent is that no one pays attention to words alone any
longer. However eloquent it has been, however imaginative its uses,
language has not succeeded in eliminating racial discrimination or
ending the war in Indochina. So the protesters have resorted to what
Social Psychologist Franklyn Haiman of Northwestern University calls
"body rhetoric"—sit-ins, lie-ins, marches—and more and more bodies
have started colliding. Such public confrontations are an expression of
gathering frustration over a society that no longer seems to respond to
more traditional forms of dissent.

Communication of Feeling

This argument contains a measure of truth. It is also true that in   3
many cases the massed forces of dissent—as at most of last week's
rallies mourning the Kent State four—have demonstrated a commend-
able restraint in not letting verbal protest build into violence. The fact
remains, however, that all too often these days dissent is a matter of
arson and rock throwing. The reason may be that protesters have
despaired of the efficacy of words before they have really mastered
them. It is significant that this generation of dissenters has failed to
produce a literature, or even a polemic that is likely to endure. On the
contrary, it has been persistently, even proudly, nonverbal. It has em-
phasized a communication of feeling rather than of words. The vocabulary of protest, often weighted down with an outmoded Marxism, is
relentlessly conventional and conformist. The same phrases—"up
against the wall," "get the pigs," "tell it like it is"—are endlessly

repeated, less for their intrinsic eloquence than for their emotive and symbolic value. And that sort of thing gets tiresome; to borrow from the jargon, it "turns people off." Even the most outrageous obscenities lose their impact when they are used ad nauseam.

There is often a disconcerting inexactness about today's rhetoric   4 of dissent. To denounce the Establishment in blanket terms makes little sense in a society composed of several establishments, each with its own ideology and set of mores—many of them surprisingly competitive. "Power to the people" is an admirable democratic slogan—except that, as used presently, what it really seems to mean is power to the leftist radicals who seek to control any revolution in America. It is verbal overkill to describe every mild demurral by whites against the most bluntly radical of black-militant demands as nothing but "racism." And the case for political dissent is weakened when almost any attempts, however peaceful, by college authorities to restore law and order on campus are automatically condemned by militant radicals as proof that the U.S. is a "fascist Amerika." Taken at face value, many protest slogans suggest that the dissenters have seriously misestimated U.S. society and its possibility for evolutionary change.

The ultimate debasement of language, of course, is violence. Ex-   5 cept for protesters who simply want to destroy—and there are more than a few—most dissenters turn to violence in a desperate effort to communicate their profound feelings of grievance. Yet surely this is too crude a way to get their message across. A bomb, for example, lacks specificity; its meaning is as scattered as its debris. Some people may interpret such an act as a signal to pay more attention to the protester and his cause; many more are likely to read into it a need to make life a lot tougher for the protester. Violence is, essentially, a confession of ultimate inarticulateness.

Throughout history, dissent has been more effectively expressed   6 by the word than by the weapon. The French Revolution was betrayed by the ruthless masters of the Terror who silenced all opposition with the guillotine. The enduring importance of the revolution lies, rather, in the principles enunciated on its behalf by the philosophers of the Enlightenment, who bequeathed the notion of human equality to the modern world. During its bleakest hours, the American Revolution was resuscitated not so much by brilliant military strategy as by brilliant words—those of Tom Paine in the "times that try men's souls." Even less persuasive and more recondite words can have an impact that dramatic acts do not. Wrote Lord Keynes: "Madmen in authority, who hear voices in the air, are distilling their frenzy from some academic scribbler of a few years back. I am sure that the power of vested interests is vastly exaggerated compared with the gradual encroachment of ideas."

Debasement of the language cannot be blamed on protesters 7
alone. The news media, the advertising agencies, the Government—
even President Nixon himself—have all helped flatten and attenuate
the English tongue. When radicals misuse language, they are only
applying the lesson they have been so well taught by their society. That
lesson has been reinforced by philosophers now in fashion—Marshall
McLuhan, for instance, who says that pictures are more important than
words and contemplates a society of inarticulate tribal emotions based
on instant sight and sound. Or Herbert Marcuse, who teaches that
protesting words are as empty as air in a technological society where
power is concentrated in a few hands. Such a contempt for language
makes people impatient with the orderly processes of thought. No
sooner is something glimpsed or considered than it is demanded. Not
only is dialogue destroyed, but so is rationality, when protesters insist
upon immediate capitulation to their "nonnegotiable demands." This
is what infants demand —and totalitarians.

Example of Agnew

Reactionary as the thought may seem, words are still as powerful 8
a force as ever, when they are cogently used. It was, after all, language
alone that catapulted Spiro Agnew from a political nonentity to a
national figure with an enthusiastic personal following. Agnew, to be
sure, can be accused of appealing to the raw emotions of the body politic
in his now-famous attacks on "effete snobs" and "tomentose exhibi-
tionists." On the other hand, a protester would have a hard time telling
the Vice President that mere speech is not capable of stirring people.
Unwittingly, he has shown his antagonists on the left that it can still be
done.

During a period of national turmoil and self-doubt, it is all the 9
more imperative for protesters to put down their rocks and find their
voices again. As a commentary on the Kent State tragedy, President
Nixon's remark that "when dissent turns to violence it invites tragedy"
is callously inadequate. His warning, however, carries the weight of
history: in a general unleashing of violence, dissent is the first casualty.
Today the nation is in considerable need of healing, as well as elevating,
language; often in the past that need has been filled by protesters whose
perspective on society matched their passionate commitment to its
improvement. Now is the time for dissenters to assert their own dignity
and maintain their tradition by upholding the ultimate value of the
word.

For Discussion and Writing

1. Why, according to this author, had dissent in the 1960s turned from verbal argument, unorthodox opinion, to physical confrontation? Does the writer think such a change is justified?
2. What are some of the flaws or faults this author finds with the protesters? In what sense is violent protest a "debased language"? Who does the author hold up, in contrast, as models of effective dissent?
3. Who else besides the protesters has helped to debase the language of dissent, and what specific consequences can such debasement lead to?
4. Violent protest did not begin and end with the Vietnam War. The Civil Rights movement, labor strife, gay rights protests, anti-abortion activism, militant environmentalism—all this and more has sometimes led to violence. Is violent protest ever justified, or is it always "a confession of ultimate inarticulateness"? Write an essay in which you consider the question of violence in dissent or civil disobedience.

Bringing the Viet Nam Vets Home

Lance Morrow

For a long time now, the chief ceremonial function of Memorial 1
Day has been simply to inform Americans that their summer has begun.
Of course, residual touches of drum-thumping Americana still cling to
the occasion—men in deep middle age parading up and down the
holiday, strutting the flag. It is a formal rite of remembering, but
remembering at a major distance. In their V.F.W. or American Legion
caps the old soldiers have long since made peace with their generation's
war. They have worn their memories of combat smooth with the retell-
ing. They have grown easy with what they did for their country as
young men; they won, and they are proud of it. The horrors that they
saw—or performed—so long ago in other countries have been effaced
by time, by the approval of history and of the nation they fought for.

The soldiers who fought America's latest and longest war, in Viet 2
Nam, do not participate very often in Memorial Day parades. The U.S.
has not developed a moral context for them yet, and no one parades
without a moral context. A nation does not fondly celebrate the memory
of its convulsions.

Viet Nam arrived in the American mind like some strange, violent 3
hallucination, just when the nation was most prosperous and ambitious, shooting spaceships at the moon. Sweet America cracked open
like a geode. The bizarre catastrophe of that war shattered so much in
American life (pride in country, faith in government, the idea of manhood and the worth of the dollar, to begin the list) that even now the
damage has not yet been properly assessed. When the country came to,
some time in the mid-'70s, it was stunned. In moral recoil from the
military failure and the huge, lurid futility of the excursion, Americans
did a humanly understandable thing: they suppressed the memory of
Viet Nam. They tried to recover from the wound by denying it.

But of course the veterans of Viet Nam were tangible evidence, the 4
breathing testimony, that it had all been humiliatingly real. Whether
walking straight or riding wheelchairs, whether prospering at their
work or glaring out at the rest of the nation from a daze of rage and
drugs and night sweats, they reminded America that the war had cost
and that it had hurt. For years, at least some part of every Viet Nam

veteran has inhabited a limbo of denial—the nation's or his own—often overcome by guilt and shame, and almost always by anger. Among other things, he has tended to think of himself as an awful sucker to have risked so much for so little. Most veterans (contrary to stereotype) have readjusted reasonably well to the civilian world. But many found that coming home was harder than fighting the war.

After World War I and World War II, the soldiers returned together   5 with their units; they had the long trip back in which to hear each other's confessions and apologies. And of course the piers in New York or San Francisco were crammed with waiting wives and children, the grateful nation craning to get a look at its boys, its heroes. During Viet Nam, in keeping with an almost sinister Government tendency to treat the war as an elaborate bureaucratic illusion, the military shipped people out alone and brought them back alone. The process caused surreal dislocations: one day in a firefight in I Corps, the next day standing on the American tarmac somewhere, as if nothing had happened. One veteran remembers the awful solitude of homecoming: "They let us off on the Oakland side of the Bay Bridge. I had to hitchhike to the San Francisco airport because of a transit strike." The Americans who fought in Viet Nam responded when their country asked them to give up their freedom and possibly their lives to do violence in the name of something the Government deemed right. Veteran Ron Kovic's painful book *Born on the Fourth of July* described how the image of John Wayne unreeling in the adolescent mind functioned as recruiting poster and subliminal role model. In any case, they went. But psychically at least, the country did not want them back.

Now that may be changing. A new attitude seems to be develop-   6 ing, in both Viet Nam veterans and the nation at large. Americans seem more disposed than at any time in the 13 years since the Tet offensive to admit that the Viet Nam veterans have borne too much of the moral burden for a war that went all wrong. If there is a burden to be carried, it should be assigned to the men who conceived and directed the war; or, more broadly, it should be shared—in the most profound explorations of which they are capable—by all Americans. Including those who went to Canada.

The denial has been peeling away slowly for several years. An odd   7 breakthrough occurred last January after the extravagantly emotional, almost giddy welcome home that America staged for the 52 hostages from Iran. The nation was an orgy of yellow ribbons and misting eyes. But then, a few days later, a countertheme surfaced. Viet Nam veterans watched the spectacle of welcome (the routes of motorcades lined with cheering, weeping Americans, the nation glued to its TV sets, the new President doing the hostages proud in the Rose Garden), and their years of bitterness boiled up to a choked cry: WHERE THE HELL IS MY PARADE? The nation, flushed from its somewhat too easy outpouring over the hostages, began acquiring the grace to admit that the Viet Nam veterans had a point.

Perhaps, too, enough history has passed to allow the country to   8
proceed to the next stage, to acknowledge the Viet Nam veterans without setting off a civil war or a national nervous breakdown. Fresh history has added a few new perspectives. Ronald Reagan, who last August described Viet Nam as a "noble cause," nonetheless proposed to eliminate $691 million in benefits for the Viet Nam veterans, including $30 million for the 91 valuable and even lifesaving storefront veterans' counseling centers around the country. Congress will probably save the counseling centers and some other benefits, and lobbying groups like the Viet Nam Veterans of America may find allies now among the voters who were not there before.

It is difficult to generalize about the Viet Nam veteran. The TV   9
scriptwriter's vision in the '70s pictured him as a damply sweating crazo-junkie who would erupt toward the end of the plot line and grease half of Southern California. A veteran named Glen Young took an elevator to a job interview recently and had a fellow passenger ask: "Are you one of the baby killers?"

A comprehensive group portrait of the veterans has become available   10
in the past few weeks. The Veterans Administration has published a five-volume study of Viet Nam veterans by the Center for Policy Research in New York City. Viet Nam veterans, the study concluded, have been paying a disproportionate social price for their experience. The war tore loose the wiring in many of their lives.

But it is a mistake to view all Viet Nam veterans as profoundly   11
troubled, as walking wounded. About half of the veterans, the study found, still carry disturbing, unsettling psychic baggage from Viet Nam. Even so, most cope pretty well. Americans may now be too quick to indulge in a "Lo, the Poor Vet" rhetoric. Dr. Arthur Egendorf, a Viet Nam veteran and a psychologist who was a principal author of the study, points out that those who pity Viet Nam veterans simply relegate them to the role of victim (which is not much help to the veterans). Liberals use their pity to help prove that the war was wrong. Some veterans, denied respect, make do with pity, and even trade on it. But that is sad.

Was the Viet Nam experience unique for those who fought it?   12
History would have to go on a manically inventive jag to top Viet Nam for wild, lethal ironies and stage effects—"a black looneytune," Writer Michael Herr called it in his Viet Nam masterpiece *Dispatches*. Indochina became the demented intersection of a bizarrely inventive killer

technology (all of those "daisy cutters" and carpet-laying B-52s and mad swarms of choppers and infra-red nightscopes) with a tunnel-digging peasantry in rubber-tire sandals: the amazing, night-dwelling Victor Charlie.

Still, Viet Nam was not unique in its effects upon the men who   13
fought there. From Odysseus onward, almost all soldiers have come back angry from war. And they have had problems. In Elizabethan England, a disbandment of armies automatically meant a major increase in the number of thieves and highwaymen preying on civilians. In fact, veterans are almost always treated badly after a war, even if the brass bands do turn out for a ceremonial welcome home. During the '20s, the windows of the nation's pawnshops were filled with soldiers' medals for heroism from the Great War. Catiline, Hitler and Mussolini constructed their sinister power bases upon the grievances of veterans.

The fact is that fighting a war, any war, is a grisly, shattering   14
business. Many men take years to recover from it; many never do. Curiously, societies almost always neglect their veterans for the first ten years after a war. Then the veterans get themselves organized into a political force (like the Grand Army of the Republic after the Civil War or the V.F.W. and American Legion after World War I) and politically extract the benefits and pensions that civilian gratitude or pity never got around to bestowing.

But Viet Nam was different from other American wars in one   15
crucial respect: the U.S. lost it. When a man soldiers on the winning side, the social contract of arms holds up; the young conscript is asked to endure all discomforts of the field, including death, but if he returns, the grateful nation (though it may soon grow indifferent) promises at least a banal ration of glory, a ceremonious welcome, the admiring opinion of his fellow citizens. Sometime between Tet and the last helicopter off the embassy roof in 1975, America threw away its social contract with the soldiers and left them to straggle back into the society as best they could. A lot of them have still not made it.

But Americans can renegotiate the contract, can extract lessons   16
and meaning from the disaster. They might begin by trying to help Viet Nam veterans restore their lives. Many veterans say that it is too late for rhetoric, too late for symbols such as the Viet Nam Veterans Memorial that will be built not far from the Lincoln Memorial next year. Such vets want concrete help: more assistance finding jobs, more time to use the G.I. Bill. They should get it. There is something notably irresponsible about a Government that dispatches its young to be chewed up in an obscure land and then does not know their names when it all goes bad. Among other things, that sort of disloyalty may make it difficult to recruit the young for future military enterprises.

But symbols and rhetoric are also incalculably important. The 17
hostages' return last January, with its powerful, complex effects, was all
ceremony and TV. Many veterans want chiefly to be thanked for what
they did, for doing as their nation asked. They crave an acknowledgment, a respect from their fellow Americans that they have never had
and may never get. The victor always gets respect, even if it is of a
shallow and predictable kind. The veterans of Viet Nam are entitled to
a deeper, different respect: the kind that goes to someone who has
endured deep anguish, even failure, and survived.

Viet Nam still chokes Americans. The nation will not recover from 18
it, or learn from all of that slaughter and guilt, until it acknowledges
that the men who fought the nation's first teen-age war (average age:
19.2 years) did not cook up that war themselves in a mischievous
moment. That was all of America out there. "It was a collective enterprise," says Dr. Egendorf, "and we were *all* damaged by it. A family
melodrama is still going on. Sometimes a psychologist cannot treat the
individual alone; he must see the whole family together."

America lost 56,480 men in Viet Nam, the last irreclaimable body 19
count. The nation also misplaced many thousands of men and women
who did make it home. To embrace them now may be a complicated,
belated and awkward exercise, but it should be done—done with a clear
historical eye, without pity or jingo or other illusions. It would mitigate
an injustice and might even improve the nation's collective mental
health. It would help to settle America's tedious quarrel with itself.
Americans should be able to repeat Robert Lowell's line in a calm
inward murmur: "My eyes have seen what my hand did."

For Discussion and Writing

1. According to Morrow, what are some of the reasons that Americans
   reacted differently to the return of the Vietnam veterans? What does
   Morrow say may have begun to change that attitude in 1981?
2. In what ways did Vietnam vets share the experiences of veterans of other
   wars? What was the crucial difference for the Vietnam vet?
3. What idea does Morrow propose to heal the wounds left by the war?
   Has his recommendation come true?
4. Morrow says that "it is a mistake to view all Viet Nam veterans as
   profoundly troubled, as walking wounded" (11). Based on your own
   experience of relatives or friends who may have served in Vietnam,
   write an essay about your sense of the veterans' plight. What picture of
   these men have you seen with your own eyes? If you do not have direct
   experience with Vietnam veterans, write about your sense of how the
   media (TV and movies, especially) portrays them.

Thinking and Writing about Chapter 17

1. What is your understanding of the Vietnam War and its aftermath? What does the war seem to stand for in your mind? To what extent does Vietnam continue to be an issue?
2. Do you view the student protests of the 1960s as an aberration—an unusual or even unique phenomenon—or do you think student activism is still alive and well on campus? What kind of issues provoke student protest today? Are students any more or less politically radical than they were a generation ago?
3. Write a reflective essay in which you consider how the Vietnam War may have influenced American life or culture. Are we more, or less, sympathetic to the military now? Has the treatment of Vietnam on film changed our attitude toward war? Have the protests and campus turmoil made it easier, or harder, for students to display public dissent? How has Vietnam affected our willingness to become involved in other foreign wars? How has Vietnam influenced our moral sense of ourselves as a nation?

18

The Persian Gulf War

If the Vietnam War was among the longest and most agonizing military and social battles in American history, the war in the Persian Gulf may have been one of the shortest. While American troups remained in the Middle East, afterward, one didn't hear much about them, except, perhaps, in "Doonesbury." As a media event, at least, the war, or "hyperwar," as it was later called, was over in a flash. It came and went with the swiftness of a Christmas vacation—and it left behind effects whose meaning it is still too early to determine.

Or is it? Some say the Gulf War ended the Vietnam Syndrome—the leftover guilt, the supposed fear of foreign involvement, the anti-military hostility. America is a winner again, our troups were justly viewed as heroes, our technology functioned beautifully, and the world has had a glimpse of a hypothetical "new order" based on United Nations action against aggressors.

Are things really different now? We'll have to wait and see. In the meantime, the essays in this chapter look at some of the basic issues raised by the Persian Gulf War—issues that may persist longer than many predict. In "The Case Against Going to War," from September 1990, Otto Freidrich argues against American participation. In "The Case for War," from November 1990, George J. Church take the opposing view. And in "A Moment for the Dead," from April 1991, Lance Morrow considers an aspect of our victory upon which few of us have cared to dwell.

The Case Against Going to War

OTTO FRIEDRICH

It is hard to remember a time when such influential American 1
opinion molders were so frantically demanding that the U.S. go to war,
and the sooner the better. "The ultimate goal now," writes A.M.
Rosenthal, columnist and former executive editor of the New York
Times, "has to be the elimination of the incurably murderous Baghdad
dictatorship by Western . . . economic and military reprisals." His fellow columnist at the *Times*, William Safire, even offers a game plan:
"Our declared-war strategy should be to (1) suppress Iraqi air defenses;
(2) take out war production at the 26 key targets; (3) launch a three-front
land war at the Turkish, Syrian and Kuwaiti borders . . . Our great
danger is delay." A *Wall Street Journal* editorial writer daydreams: "If
we take Baghdad and install a MacArthur regency, that is the opti-
mum."

Will such people never learn? The scenarios for war never do 2
justice to the real thing, which is far more horrific than pundits imagine.
A war against Iraq would not be like attacking Grenada or Panama. It
would almost certainly involve hundreds of thousands of people dying,
soldiers and civilians alike. Generals like to talk of "surgical strikes,"
but surgical strikes usually hit the wrong targets—like the misguided
air raid on Libya in 1986 that wrecked the French embassy and killed
Colonel Gaddafi's daughter.

Aside from all the bloodshed, wars waste vast quantities of 3
money—which this government hasn't got. Just preparing the intervention to protect allegedly threatened Saudi Arabia is costing about $46
million a day (and has just about killed all hope of a post-cold war peace
dividend). So far, the valiant resistance to higher oil prices has substantially increased the price of oil, and an actual war with Iraq would
undoubtedly increase it a great deal more. The impending recession
would deepen and spread around the world. So how is President Bush,
who can't even keep the budget deficit much under $150 billion (not to
mention the S&L disaster), going to pay for all that? More fund raising
among the Germans and Japanese?

President Bush has repeatedly declared that his goal is to over- 4
come Iraq by economic pressure, as authorized by the U.N., but the

bomb-Baghdad enthusiasts generally base their more aggressive arguments on two kinds of speculation. The first is that Americans like short battles but don't have the endurance for protracted conflicts (remember Vietnam). That may be true, but it seems a poor excuse for rushing into an attack on Iraq. More serious is the concern that Saddam Hussein might acquire nuclear weapons, a danger that the Israelis offered as the justification for their 1981 air raid on an Iraqi nuclear plant. It is worth emphasizing, though, that Iraq does not now have a nuclear weapon. Western intelligence agencies estimate that Saddam could build one in something like five years. A nuclear-armed Iraq is a scary possibility, but is it beyond the mind of man to try negotiating the creation of an internationally inspected nuclear-free zone throughout the Middle East? If so, and if the Israelis insist on their right to be the only nuclear power in the region, then they can probably be expected to deal unilaterally with any Iraqi attempt to join the nuclear club—with unforeseeable consequences. But all these speculations hardly justify a U.S. preemptive strike now.

It is not to be denied that Saddam is a brutal dictator, already   5
responsible for many deaths. But that does not make him either irrational or the incarnation of human evil. There are many people throughout the Arab world who regard him as a hero standing up to the imperialist West. And while Washington announces that the Iraq-Kuwait conflict should have been negotiated and that nothing justifies invading another country, we seem to have forgotten that President Bush sent 24,000 U.S. troops to invade Panama just eight months ago in violation of several treaties. Although Bush offered various legal pretexts for his very understandable wish to get rid of the loathsome General Noriega, the U.N. General Assembly condemned the U.S. aggression by a vote of 75 to 20 (with 39 abstentions). Moral preachings wear a little thin here. What country indeed has not used force in recent years to protect what it considered its interests? Britain in the Falklands? France in northern Africa? The Soviets in Afghanistan? Israel in Lebanon?

Though the conventional wisdom regards Iraq's seizure of Kuwait   6
as purely a demonstration of Saddam's wickedness, there are extenuating circumstances. Since the map of the Middle East was largely drawn by the European powers that had defeated the Ottoman Empire in World War I, the British arbitrarily created a kingdom of Iraq but maintained their separate protectorate over Kuwait. Iraq never accepted Kuwaiti sovereignty, even tried more than once to recapture the territory, but the main try was beaten back by the British. In the recent quarrel, Saddam accused Kuwait of stealing Iraqi oil by drilling at a slant into disputed oil fields. Kuwait's semisecret violation of OPEC production agreements also helped drive down the price of oil. This was fine for American motorists, but it deprived Iraq of badly needed

funds. Such conflicts have traditionally been regarded as fairly legitimate grounds for war—the U.S. acquired California in 1846 on thinner pretexts.

Saddam miscalculated in thinking the rest of the world would not   7
react so swiftly and vehemently against his seizure of Kuwait. But once he had made his move, all his supposedly heinous next moves seem perfectly understandable. If taking hostages would help fend off threatened U.S. air raids, why not? And to show they are not being harmed, why not exhibit them on TV? And so on.

Bush and Saddam have both made compromise difficult by stat-   8
ing their demands in the most extreme terms. Saddam not only annexes Kuwait but actually changes its name. Bush intimates that he may not be satisfied even by the restoration of the emirate to its opulent emirs. Both sides suggest that compromise is cowardly, not negotiable. It is obvious, however, that compromise is the only alternative to a disastrous war.

For Discussion and Writing

1. What are Friedrich's reasons for opposing a war against Iraq? What does he propose instead?
2. What does Friedrich say are the pro-war side's speculations, and what is his response to them?
3. From Iraq's perspective, what are the "extenuating circumstances" that help to explain, if not justify, Iraq's invasion of Kuwait?
4. Twenty-twenty hindsight, as the saying goes, is always perfect, and, in the aftermath of the war, Friedrich's argument now may seem less convincing. What are his strongest points? Is there any validity to his claim that compromise is better than a disastrous war? Whether you agree with him or not, write an essay in which you analyze Friedrich's anti-war position and seek to find his most persuasive ideas.

The Case for War

George J. Church

So Congress wants to reassert its constitutional prerogative to   1
decide whether or not the nation should go to war. About time. U.S.
Presidents have gone much too far toward claiming (or rather exercising without even bothering to claim) the power of Louis XIV to send a
whole nation into battle on his sole judgment, even whim. The makers
of the Constitution were determined never to give one man that power
in the new republic, and they were right. If the U.S. is to fight Iraq, it
should be by conscious decision of its elected representatives, reached
after full debate.

But that debate should not be dominated by the antiwar critics, as   2
the front and op-ed pages have been in the past few days. In a full-
fledged congressional debate, one may hope, the case for war will be
argued more forcefully and cogently than an oddly tongue-tied Bush
Administration has lately managed to do. And there *is* a compelling
case for war. Yes, even if one believes, as I do, that it will probably not
be won in a week or so by heavy bombing, but may turn into a long,
bloody and disruptive struggle with major casualties.

Oil is one reason, and to make (not concede) that point is by no   3
means to admit that we would be fighting for a few cents a gallon on
the price of gasoline or to maintain a fat, self-indulgent life-style. What
is at stake is the power to shut off the heat in millions of homes, freezing
the old and frail; to close down thousands of factories and utility plants,
causing mass unemployment and no little additional poverty. A price
run-up or supply restriction sharp enough could touch off a similar
worldwide recession—and an inflationary recession to boot. That
power cannot be put into the hands of a megalomaniac who can be
trusted to deal with anyone who might try to stop him by squeezing in
the most vulnerable spot. And if Saddam Hussein gets away with his
seizure of Kuwait, he will be master not only of the supplies from that
nation and his own Iraq, but also, through invasion or bullying, of the
oil pumped out of Saudi Arabia, the gulf sheikdoms and other states.
Of course, the U.S. should have acted long ago to lessen its dependence
on foreign oil. Of course, it should do everything it can in that direction
now. So what? For the immediate future, a reliable supply of oil at

affordable prices is vital to any modern economy. It just is, and the loftiest moral and ecological disapproval cannot change that brute fact.

But oil is not the only or even main cause for war, whatever the cynics say. Would the U.S. have fought to conquer the Middle Eastern oil fields if Saddam Hussein had peacefully persuaded Kuwait, Saudi Arabia et al. to restrict production enough to shoot the price up to $40 per bbl.? Get real. The central issue is aggression, and how—make that whether—it can be contained in the post-cold war world. And forget all the moaning about shedding blood to keep feudal autocracies in control of Kuwait and Saudi Arabia. One might well wish for more appealing victims and potential victims to champion. But if aggression is to be opposed only when the targets are kindly liberal democracies, the world is going to become a far more dangerous, savage and bloody place.

Comparisons of Saddam Hussein to Hitler may be overblown. The Iraqi dictator has not built a Middle Eastern Auschwitz—yet. But Saddam does seem to share one Hitlerian trait identified by British historian Alan Bullock: he is "consumed [by] the will to power in its crudest and purest form . . . power and domination for its own sake," to be expanded without limit. If Saddam is allowed to keep part of Kuwait—and make no mistake, that is what those advocating a "diplomatic solution" are hinting at—he will be back to take a bite out of another victim. Not right away, maybe, but after the U.S. troops have left Saudi Arabia and all has returned to a delusive quiet. If he meets resistance, he will use chemical, bacteriological and, one day, nuclear weapons. Millions may die.

Nor is Saddam the only leader who would redraw the map of the world by force—to rectify border disputes, reclaim "unredeemed" territory, seize a neighbor's natural resources. What lesson would these others draw from a failure to stop Saddam? Go ahead. The U.S. certainly will not stop you. Oh, it may shout and scream and bluster. But if it did not use force when a vital economic interest was threatened, when it had a clear moral justification and the support of a worldwide coalition, when would it? Letting Iraq's aggression stand is a recipe for a world of endless aggressions, of local and not-so-local wars, some possibly nuclear (India vs. Pakistan for a fourth round? Israel against the Arabs yet again?), and of bloody chaos from which the U.S. could not forever stand aloof.

But, says the antiwar faction, Saddam can be turned back without war, by persistence in the embargo. If only that were true! All too probably, those who make this argument are deluding themselves. Far more likely, if Iraq is still occupying Kuwait next Aug. 2, a year after the invasion, much of the world will conclude that Saddam has won. The embargo will begin leaking badly; nation after nation will start casting around for a diplomatic solution; Washington itself will be under growing pressure to bring G.I.s home from Saudi Arabia where they will have been "sitting around in the sand for a year accomplishing nothing." A formula will be found to let Iraq keep part of Kuwait. Curtains for any hope of a world in which aggression does not pay.

Maybe, just maybe, Saddam can be scared out of Kuwait by the threat of a war that would destroy his military machine and/or his life. But that would require something like an ultimatum, backed by a genuine readiness to fight, and Saddam might not believe it even then. So the U.S. has to prepare for war. Anyone with a shred of human feeling can say that only with a suppressed scream of fear and pain. The U.S. confronts a bitter, tragic, even ghastly necessity. But, this time, it is a necessity that there is no honorable way to avoid.

For Discussion and Writing

1. Church opens his case with a major qualification: that war may be the right choice, even though conflict might be long and bloody. By conceding the war's potential costs, what may Church gain with an anti-war audience?
2. What are Church's justifications for a pro-war stance? What is his argument against those who supported a trade embargo?
3. What is the underlying assumption of Church's argument? Is it stated explicitly in the essay? If so, where?
4. From all appearances, the war has justified Church's position. Has it? Write an essay in which you consider the war's effects—such as the environmental impact of the Kuwaiti oil fires, the death toll, the fact that Iraq's leader remained in power. Was the war worth the cost? Why or why not?

A Moment for the Dead

Lance Morrow

The Pentagon ordered 16,099 body bags to be shipped to the 1
Persian Gulf to bring home dead Americans. In the end, 15,773 of the
bags were not necessary.

The Iraqi army would have needed—what? One hundred thou- 2
sand body bags? More? No one knows or will ever know. No one has
counted the Iraqi corpses. Many of them were buried in the sand,
without ceremony; some have been taken care of by vultures.

That so few soldiers in the coalition died somehow seemed to 3
Americans a vindication. It was even a return of their shining self, of
Buffalo Bill, who (e.e. cummings wrote) could "ride a watersmooth-
silver stallion and break onetwothreefourfive pigeonsjustlikethat." The
unspoken text was this: the nation had recovered its immunity, its
divine favor, or anyway its gift for doing things right. The victory was
as satisfying as anything Americans have done together since landing
on the moon.

Would it be seemly to have a moment of silence for the Iraqi 4
corpses?

It is not inconsequential to kill 100,000 people. That much life 5
suddenly and violently extinguished must leave a ragged hole somewhere in the universe. One looks for special effects of a metaphysical
kind to attend so much death—the whoosh of all those souls departing.
But many of them died ingloriously, like road kill. Full of their disgrace,
facedown with the loot scattered around them. The conquered often die
ignominiously. The victors have not given them much thought.

Still, killing 100,000 people is a serious thing to do. It is not 6
equivalent to shooting a rabid dog, which is, down deep, what Americans feel the war was all about, exterminating a beast with rabies. All
those 100,000 men were not megalomaniacs, torturers and murderers.
They did not all commit atrocities in Kuwait. They were ordinary
people: peasants, truck drivers, students and so on. They had the love
of their families, the dignity of their lives and work. They cared as little
for politics, or less, than most people in the world. They were, precisely,
not Saddam Hussein. Which means, since Saddam was the coalition's
one true target in all of this, that those 100,000 corpses are, so to speak,

collateral damage. The famous smart bombs did not find the one man they were seeking.

The secret of much murder and evildoing is to dehumanize the victim, to make him alien, to make him Other, a different species. When we have done that, we have prepared ourselves to kill him, for to kill the Other, to kill a snake, a roach, a pest, a Jew, a scorpion, a black, a centipede, a Palestinian, a hyena, an Iraqi, a wild dog, an Israeli . . . it's O.K. **7**

If Saddam Hussein was a poisonous snake in the desert, and he had 1 million poisonous snakes arrayed around him, then it was good sense to drop bombs and kill 100,000 snakes and thus turn back the snake menace. **8**

But, of course, the 100,000 Iraqis were not snakes. **9**

To kill 100,000 people and to feel no pain at having done so may be dangerous to those who did the killing. It hints at an impaired humanity, a defect like a gate through which other deaths may enter, deaths no one had counted on. The unquiet dead have many ways of haunting—particularly in the Middle East, which has been accumulating the grievances of the dead for thousands of years. **10**

In any case, there is not, or there should not be, such a thing as killing without guilt—especially not mass killings without guilt. When people kill without remorse, we call them insane. We call them maniacs, serial murderers. **11**

Americans almost unconsciously regard the victory as a kind of moral cleansing: the right thing. But reality and horror have not been rescinded. All killing is unclean. It has upon it a stain that technology cannot annul or override. Americans are not omnipotent, not all virtuous, they should remind themselves, they do not bestride the world. Vainglory is one of the sillier postures: it invariably precedes the rude awakening. It is the sort of whooping glee that, in Daffy Duck cartoons, goeth before the fall. **12**

Did the dead Iraqis need to be killed? **13**

In the circumstances, yes. **14**

Having killed them, how do the victors feel? **15**

They feel great. **16**

In Texas lore, there is a defense for murder that goes like this: "He needed killing." Is there anything wrong with feeling great about killing 100,000 Iraqis who needed killing? **17**

There is nothing wrong with feeling relieved. It is not required, it is not human nature, to mourn the soldiers who were arrayed to kill you. Killing the Iraqis meant that Americans and their partners did not have to face them on the battlefield and maybe die. As it was, the Iraqis who were left in the field surrendered almost without a fight. **18**

Like some martial equivalent of the Reagan years, the victory in 19
the gulf makes Americans feel better about themselves. It was splendid
and necessary but also unreal—an action-adventure that, like most
movies, was divided into three chapters, with decisive turning points:
1) the Iraqi invasion and the buildup of coalition forces; 2) the onset of
the air war; and 3) the ground war and its denouement. The victory
came with such merciless ease that on the winners' side, the deeper
levels of experience (nobility, sacrifice, endurance and so on) were not
engaged. The victors now celebrate mostly their relief that they have
escaped what might have been. By the Fourth of July, the glorious
moment will seem a long time ago.

The prospects going into the war were horrifying: the fourth 20
largest army in the world, commanded by a thug whom we thought
cunning at the time and even invested with satanic powers. Saddam
was armed with chemical weapons and was working on the nuclear
kind. All those dark possibilities gave the coalition, in effect, a license
to kill. The killing was very well done. I hope it does not give us too
much pleasure.

For Discussion and Writing

1. Why does Morrow express sympathy for the 100,000 dead Iraqi soldiers? What is his view of the war?
2. Why does Morrow say that he hopes the killing "does not give us too much pleasure"? What may it mean for Americans that they "feel great" after the war, that we seem to feel no guilt in the war's aftermath?
3. Morrow uses strong connotative and figurative language to enhance his persuasive aim. Point out passages where his words are particularly striking, stirring, or powerful.
4. Chances are you saw at least some of the Gulf War coverage on television or read about it in the newspapers. Write an essay in which you address some of these questions: Is there any place for guilt, sorrow, a tragic sense of life, in our responses to this swift and overwhelming victory? Who should have our sympathy? Over what, if anything, should we feel guilt? Do we, should we, view the Iraqis as fellow humans, or, as Morrow says, as Other—snakes, wild dogs, vile pests? What are the consequences of dehumanizing the enemy?

Thinking and Writing about Chapter 18

1. Each of these writers takes a different view of the Gulf War. Compare and contrast their positions. Is there any common ground or shared belief among them?
2. What were your feelings, and those of your friends and family, before, during, and after the war? Did those attitudes remain consistent, or did they change over time?
3. Write a personal reflection or an argumentative essay in which you express your views on the Gulf War. What kind of assumptions about war in general do you bring to this conflict? Were there particulars that made this war somehow different or special? On what grounds do you justify or condemn our involvement in it?

19

Terrorism and Revolution

The history of societies is not only the history of battles between them. Upheavals from within are just as common, as nations transform themselves, throw off internal or external oppression, drive toward a revolutionary vision of the future. Not all revolutions succeed, of course, and some lead to even worse, more oppressive conditions. The French Revolution had its Reign of Terror, the Russian Revolution its bloody purges. And even the American Civil War, which was in its way a revolutionary struggle, caused catastrophic loss of life and brought with it a period of great social turmoil.

Yet the revolutionary impulse persists. In our own day we see it all around us—from Eastern Europe to China, from South Africa to the Middle East. And often, as in the past, revolutionary movements today can be associated with terrorism.

The essays in this chapter address three aspects of contemporary political upheaval. In "Islam Against the West?," from December 1979, Lance Morrow analyzes the historic context of Iran's Islamic revolution and Muslim-Western antipathy. In "Terror and Peace: the 'Root Cause' Fallacy," from September 1986, Charles Krauthammer argues against a particular view of revolutionary action. And in "Reflections on the Revolution in China," from June 1989, Krauthammer speculates on the battle between the will to freedom and its opposite.

Islam Against the West?

LANCE MORROW

Whenever they kindle a fire for war, Allah extinguishes it.
And they strive to create disorder in the earth, and Allah
loves not those who create disorder.

—The Koran

The West and the world of Islam sometimes resemble two differ-   1
ent centuries banging through the night on parallel courses. In full
raucous cultural panoply, they keep each other awake. They make each
other nervous. At times, as now, they veer together and collide: up and
down the processions, threats are exchanged, pack animals and zealots
bray, bales of ideological baggage spill onto the road. Embassies get
burned, hostages taken. Songs of revenge rise in the throat.

Are these collisions inevitable? The mutual misunderstandings of   2
the West and the Islamic world have a rich patina of history. Jews,
Christians and Muslims, all "People of the Book," draw much of their
faith from the same sources. Yet from the time of the Muslim conquests
and the Crusades, West and Islam have confronted each other by turns
in attitudes of incomprehension, greed, fanaticism, prurient interest,
fear and loathing. The drama has lost none of its historic tension in the
stagecraft of the Ayatullah Khomeini. "This is not a struggle between
the United States and Iran," he has told the faithful. "It is a struggle
between Islam and the infidel." At such moments, the Imam takes on
the wild and grainy aspect of a dire Mohammedan prophet by DeMille.

Khomeini may even wish to transcend Iranian nationalism and   3
export his fundamentalist Islamic revival. The prospect of such conta-
gious piety disturbs other Muslim leaders, the Saudi royal family, for
example. But it also raises apprehension and a certain amount of
bewilderment in the West. When Mahdist Saudi zealots took over the
mosque in Mecca last month, the Islamic world displayed a disconcerting readiness to believe Khomeini's incendiary report that the attack
had been the work of Zionists and U.S. imperialists. "The Americans
have done it again," many Muslims told themselves reflexively. Some

Americans have responded by asking with a truculent innocence: "What did we ever do to them?"

If the question is disingenuous, the answers are complex.   4

The U.S. never colonized Islamic countries, as, for example, Britain and France did. The U.S. has no large Islamic minority and thus, unlike the Soviet Union, has no record of bitter internal relations with Muslims. Besides (as some Muslim leaders know), Communism is far more inimical to Islam than capitalism. But in the past 30 years, the U.S. has been a chief participant in a cultural encounter that is in some ways even more traumatic to the world of Islam than colonialism: the full onslaught of secular, materialist modernization, 20th century civilization sweeping into the timeless Muslim villages. The vast apparatus of Western progress, a machine overwhelmingly vigorous, profoundly tempting and yet decadent by all the disciplines of the Prophet, has threatened Muslim identity.   5

Western science and technology have wounded the deep pride of Islam. The success of the unvirtuous, the infidel unfavored of Allah, is psychologically confusing. "Seen through Muslim eyes," writes Berkeley Historian Peter Brown, "the emergence of [the West] as the temporary master of the world remains an anomaly in the natural unfolding of the course of history." Muslims have recoiled from modernization in exact proportion to the force of its temptation for them. They have been attracted by secular materialism, have tried it in the guise of both capitalism and Marxism, but they have often been disappointed by it, have associated it with the colonial masters who introduced them to it. They have found it dangerously, almost radioactively, corrupt.   6

Some Muslims, of course, insist that Islam and modernization are perfectly compatible. Many Islamic countries supply the oil that is, for now, the indispensable ingredient of modernization, and they have tried to use their staggering and sudden wealth to buy the machines of progress without the devils that often inhabit them. Conservative Saudi leaders, for example, pursue a selective strategy regarding the technological riches of the West: they seek to modernize without the garish libertine free-for-all that Western secular individualism has promoted.   7

But for Muslims, the dilemma remains: if they are to develop economically, they must import Western technology. To master Western technology, they must send their young to be educated in the West. And that invariably means diluting their culture. Progress means better medicine and other mitigations of life's harshness, of course, but it also means the young women returning from Paris or Palo Alto in short skirts instead of *chadors*; it means 30% inflation, pollution, an open door to all the depressing vitality of the junk culture; it means the young leaving the villages and becoming infested with all kinds of Hefnerian tastes for hi-fis and forbidden pleasures. It is sometimes difficult for a   8

Westerner to understand that to a Muslim, the cultural dismantling of Islam, the governing apparatus of his life and civilization, is a tragedy that amounts to a form of annihilation.

The sort of Muslim fundamentalism evident in Iran or Muammar   9
Gaddafi's Libya may confirm a remark by Frantz Fanon, the philosopher of Third World uprisings: the native response to imperial domination is to fall back on what is authentic, what is resistant to modernization. The mosque becomes a symbolic safe haven.

Islam is not inherently or inevitably anti-Western, despite the   10
often bloody encounters of the past. Muslims have historically occupied a geographically vulnerable position, which may account for their militant touchiness. But the religion has become the vehicle for certain anti-Western, anti-American resentments and antipathies. In some ways, the specifically Islamic religious component is almost incidental: Islam is, as much as anything else, the repository for grievances, envies and hatreds that Third World have-nots harbor for the privileged of the globe. Islam gives cohesion to complaints about the injustices of the world. The Muslim tradition provides the language and symbolism to express a wide social message: it is not necessarily a religious phenomenon. It is not anti-Christian. In fact, Muslims really regard modern Westerners as a species of pagan. Ironically, some of the resentment has been aroused by the emergence of oil-rich classes within the Islamic countries themselves. With that wealth came a widening gap between rich and poor, a dangerous ambivalence of rising expectations and an anxiety that old ways might be endangered. The resentment of modernization is not anything so simply and piously self-abnegating as a wish to avoid luxury; it is also a bitterness at being forced to live adjacent to a wealth one cannot possess.

Iran embodies both the essence of the Islamic complaint against   11
the West and unique historical grievances of its own. By race (Aryan), language (Persian), religion (Shi'ite Muslim) and historical tradition (ancient Persia was conquered by Muslims in the 8th century), Iran is different from the rest of Middle Eastern Islam. It was never colonized, in the usual sense of the word, by the West. And yet the penetration of Western ideas was deeper in Iran than in some other parts of the Middle East and came to be seen in a considerably more sinister light.

While leaders in other Muslim states (Saudi Arabia and Libya, for   12
example) have moderated Western influences, the Shah embraced the West with (as it turned out) a heedless enthusiasm. He set up a secular state, destroying the classic and crucial unity in Islam between church and government. Under the Pahlavis, women were liberated from the traditional chador, permitted to vote and divorce their husbands. The Shah made the mistake of ignoring the mullahs (priests). The U.S., in turn, embraced him, and even had the CIA engineer a coup to restore

him to power in 1953. Corruption, dislocations of life and profoundly disorienting social change all accompanied his rule; so did political suppression and the tortures of SAVAK, his secret police. The U.S. was inextricably implicated in the career of this potentate—Ozymandias and Faust—and shared the people's judgment of him when it came.

Anti-Western, and specifically anti-American, sentiment in Iran is   13 therefore not surprising or irrational, whatever irrational forms it has taken. The deep social anger at the Shah and the U.S. that supported him has assumed an air of fanaticism in its Shi'ite expression. Shi'ites, who make up 10% of Islam, tend toward a passionate, activist religious life and flirtation with martyrdom (they have been known to commit suicide accidentally by bashing and mutilating themselves in mourning for their founder, Husain, the slaughtered grandson of the Prophet). Shi'ites also prefer charismatic leaders: they are forever parading the portrait of the Imam Khomeini.

The special ferocity and condensation of the will that are evident   14 in the Iranian revolution owe much to this tendency toward the cult of personality. (One ironic aspect is that Khomeini may not, strictly speaking, be a very good Muslim at all. He not only condoned the violation of Islam's protection of foreign emissaries, but also made inflammatory, groundless claims about the American responsibility for the Mecca attack. He has deliberately fomented violence, which the Koran forbids.)

The distinction between Sunnis and Shi'ites is, according to some   15 scholars of Islam, much greater than that between, say, Roman Catholics and Protestants. It is one of the most basic of many differences that make it not only inadvisable but impossible to generalize about Islam as if it were a single, coherent bloc. Just as the Communist world includes antagonists (U.S.S.R. and China, Viet Nam and Cambodia), the Islamic world is very much fragmented. Morocco and Algeria are fighting in the western Sahara. The Middle East is a psychodrama of the paranoiac fears entertained by Arabs for one another. North and South Yemen were at war earlier this year. Moderate Arab states like Saudi Arabia and Jordan fear a radical trend that might become uncontrollable. It is important to notice that for all the incendiary mobs that have eddied around American outposts in the past few weeks, none has ever got out of control of the governing authorities; when the government said stop, the rioting stopped. That suggests that the mobs might be viewed more as a form of demonstrative Muslim rhetoric (dangerous and expensive rhetoric, of course) rather than as any tidal force of history.

Furthermore, the world of Islam extends far beyond the Middle   16 East. The largest single concentration of Muslims in the world exists in

Indonesia, where there is virtually no Islamic outcry against the West or America. Says former Malaysian Premier Tunku Abdul Rahman: "It is a shame to think that Iran, one of the progressive Muslim countries, has, literally speaking, gone to the dogs."

One inexhaustible source of anti-Americanism in Muslims is U.S. 17 support of Israel and the question of a Palestinian homeland, issues that blend with the Third World prejudice against the privileged. But, says French Sociologist Jacques Berque, "any hopes or fears that the entire Muslim world will unite against the West amount to a romantic vision of pan-Islamism."

Muslims have aggressively sought the material wonders of the 18 West, yet are ambivalent in their souls. Berque locates the central dilemma of Islam: If Islam is ever to become an economic and political competitor of capitalism and Marxism, it must embrace a progress that may forever weaken its ethical and spiritual structures, just as other religions have been drained by the secularization of the Western world. So far, Islam has not proved itself a vehicle of social change, a program to confront the modern world.

Still, oil has convinced the Islamic world—or half—convinced it 19 of its worth and power. The presence of oil in the complicated psychology of anti-Westernism makes the volatility of the Islamic world especially perilous. It is an interesting point of Muslim psychology that the Arabs who grow unimaginably rich off Western payments for oil (and squander their petrodollars on Rodeo Drive in Beverly Hills, Calif., on Rolls-Royces and golden bathroom fixtures) have still in them enough desert asceticism to be contemptuous of the West's energy addictions. So here the old relation is reversed: the West is dependent on the East, and is learning something about the frustration that dependence brings.

In this encounter of East and West, the rage on either side has a 20 way of spiraling up in a murderous double helix: the anger of the Muslims may feed on itself, and the countering anger of the West may further ignite the anger of Islam. So great is the mutual incomprehension that international relations degenerate rapidly to the chaotic psychology of the mob. Although U.S. reactions have been, all things considered, remarkably mild, the Iranian crisis has legitimized among Americans a new stereotype of the demented Muslim. Says University of Wisconsin Historian Kemal H. Karpat: "Khomeini has done more harm to the Islamic image in one month than all the propaganda of the past 15 years."

It should be possible for Americans to preserve an intelligent 21 sympathy for the Islamic perspective without feeling vaguely guilt-stricken by the past. Anti-Americanism—the specific, sharper focus of anti-Westernism—is in some ways the Islamic world's excuse for its own failures, confusions and periodic collapses into incoherence. It is more convenient morally to blame the West than to gaze steadily at the Islamic dilemma, easier to devise revenge for the past than ideas for the future. Khomeini, with his absolutist pretensions and aggressive fantasies of *jihad* (holy war) against the West, demeans Islam; he gives it the aspect of a bizarre, dangerous but spiritually trivial cult. To the extent that Muslims support Khomeini, they share in the image of Islam that he has created.

For Discussion and Writing

1. According to Morrow, what is at the heart of the dispute between fundamental Muslims and the Western world? What dilemma do Muslims face in their relations with the West?
2. How does Iran embody the Islamic attitude toward the West? Which unique aspects of Iranian history support Iran's extreme view?
3. Why does Morrow say it is wrong to speak of the Islamic world as a single entity?
4. Since this essay appeared, the Iranian hostage crisis has ended, Khomeini has died and been replaced by a supposedly more moderate leader, and the Gulf War has occurred, bringing about the stationing of troups in Saudi Arabia and the cooperation of Islamic governments with the West. Write an essay in which you give your impressions of Islamic culture, and consider the future of its relations with the West in light of recent events.

Terror and Peace:
the "Root Cause" Fallacy

CHARLES KRAUTHAMMER

The idea of "root causes" has great political attraction. Some years ago in the U.S., it dominated debate on policy toward El Salvador. It was argued that the Administration's hopes for a military solution were futile because the real causes of the insurrection were poverty, misery and hunger.

Well, yes. Revolutions do need misery to feed on. (There are exceptions: Occasionally there are revolutions of the comfortable, as in the 1960s in the U.S. and France. Such facsimiles, however, are invariably short-lived and harmless.) But these conditions, while obviously a necessary cause of revolution, are not sufficient. If they were, there would be revolution everywhere and always, since, aside from in a few countries in very modern times, poverty is the common condition of mankind.

But revolution is neither ubiquitous nor permanent. We need, therefore, something beyond poverty and misery to explain why there is revolt in some places and not others. This takes us out of the realm of what is usually meant by root causes, to culture, history, revolutionary leadership, foreign sponsorship and other presumably contingent causes.

That some causes and not others are accorded the honorific "root" has consequences. The first is to confer some special legitimacy on one set of grievances and thus on the revolutionary action that is taken in its name.

A second consequence emerges from a peculiar property of root causes: on close examination they turn out to be, as a matter of practice or policy, insoluble. There is no conceivable American policy that will solve the problem of poverty in Central America. (Not that poverty can never be ameliorated. It can. But not by a simple act of political will. In the West, for example, the conquest of mass poverty was the product of two centuries of painful industrialization.) The term root tends to be assigned to the most intractable of conditions. Except in the mind of the revolutionary, that is. The idea of root causes is therefore an invitation to surrender—to the resistant reality of misery or to the revolutionary who alone offers the promise of instant redemption.

Thus the danger of the root cause idea. It is offered as an analytic   6
tool to understand an unpleasant reality: revolutionary violence. But whether intended or not, the logic of the root cause argument suggests one of two attitudes toward the unpleasantness: 1) despair, because root causes cannot be changed, or 2) moral ambivalence, because legitimacy necessarily accrues to those who fight with root cause on their side. One must not find oneself "on the wrong side of history."

That does not mean that revolutionary violence can never be   7
justified. It is hard to argue, for example, that South African blacks may not take up arms for their freedom. It means only that an appeal to root causes is not automatic justification. The Philippine Islands are replete with root causes as deep and difficult as any others in the world. Appeal to these causes, however, is not enough to justify either the ends (Communist) or the means (brutal and terroristic) of the New People's Army.

Three years ago, Senator Christopher Dodd delivered a nationally   8
televised speech on behalf of the Democratic Party opposing proposed aid to the government of El Salvador. "If Central America were not racked with poverty... hunger... injustice," argued Dodd, "there would be no revolution." That is the premise. And the conclusion? "Unless those oppressive conditions change"—Can they? Can the U.S. will them to?—"the region will continue to seethe with revolution." The choice? Either "to move with the tide of history" or "stand against it."

Today that argument is hardly heard anymore in the Central   9
American context. Something happened. The Salvadoran guerrillas are in retreat, and yet, mirabile dictu, root causes remain. The tides have changed, while poverty and misery endure. As for Nicaragua, those most habituated to the use of the root cause argument are *contra* opponents. They are hardly likely to invoke it to explain—i.e., legitimize—the *contra* cause.

One place where the root cause idea does survive is the Middle   10
East. The issue is terrorism, and the argument is familiar: Isn't the best way to fight terror to go after the root causes? Counterterrorism, embargoes, threats and, finally, air raids treat only symptoms. Band-Aids on a wound. (The metaphors mix.) Why not attack the root causes? In the context of the Middle East, that means "solving the Palestinian problem." Accommodation between Israel and the Palestinians. The way out of the nightmare. Jews and Arabs living together in historic Palestine. An end to war. Peace as the cure for terror.

It is an honorable dream. And it is based on a clear logic: since   11
much of the terrorism in the Middle East is committed either by Pales-

tinians or by others acting in their name, why not solve the terrorism problem by solving their problem?

Unfortunately—unfortunately for Palestinians, Israelis and as-   12
sorted innocents who wander into the crossfire—the logic fails. To understand why, one must start by asking, Who are the terrorists? The major sponsors of Middle East terror are Iran, Syria and Libya. And its major practitioners are Islamic fundamentalists, pro-Syrian nationalists and Palestinian extremists. These groups and states are distinguished not just by their choice of means but by the nature of their end. And their end is not peace with Israel. It is peace with no Israel.

The various terror groups have different versions of the end of   13
days, but none include a Jewish state. The *Achille Lauro* hijackers, for example, issued a communiqué in Cyprus saying they had planned to land at "Ashdod harbor in occupied Palestine." Ashdod is not in the West Bank or Gaza. It is within pre-1967 Israel. If you consider Ashdod "occupied," every inch of Israel is occupied.

For such people, the only peaceful solution to the Middle East   14
problem is a peace of the grave, a Zionist grave. Any settlement short of that will leave the terrorists unappeased. It will not solve the terrorists' problem. It thus does not solve the terrorism problem.

Indeed, it aggravates it. Any movement toward a negotiated peace   15
that permits any part of Palestine to remain occupied is considered a threat. Negotiations are thus a spur, not a deterrent, to terror. Whenever a "peace scare" breaks out, terrorism *increases*, as King Hussein of Jordan is well aware. During the time he was trying to arrange for joint Jordanian-Palestinian negotiations with Israel, his diplomats in Ankara, Bucharest and Madrid were assassinated. The talks are off now, and Jordanians abroad are enjoying a rare respite from attack.

Last July Prime Minister Peres of Israel flew to Morocco for peace   16
talks with King Hassan II, and before anyone knew the contents of the negotiations, Syria broke off diplomatic relations with Morocco and the P.L.O. declared it would oppose to the end *any* outcome. Some interested observers of this overture were candid and clear about the relationship between terrorism and peace, even a hint of peace: "Now," Royal Air Maroc stewards told a New York *Times* correspondent, "we will have to start worrying about hijackings and terrorist attacks."

The fundamental fact of the Middle East today is that those who   17
engage in terror do not want peace, and those who want peace are not engaged in terror. Those who make the slightest move to eliminate the vaunted root cause of terror—i.e., those who genuinely seek a compromise solution to the Israeli-Palestinian problem—get shot. The latest victim is the mayor of Nablus, whose crime was to take over responsi-

bility for fixing potholes. That was too much accommodation with the Zionist entity, as the rejectionists like to refer to Israel.

Issam Sartawi, the one P.L.O. leader who advocated exactly the 18 kind of solution Americans like to dream about, a Palestinian state living side by side with Israel, was also murdered, shot dead in Portugal in 1983. Not too many Palestinians have since risen to take up his cause. It is truer to say that terrorism is a root cause of the continuing Arab-Israeli conflict than vice versa.

Syria has little sympathy for *either* half of the peace envisioned in 19 the West. Syria not only rejects the existence of an Israeli state, it has little use for a Palestinian state. Syria and its favorite Lebanese terror group, the Syrian Socialist Nationalist Party, have a different vision. An Associated Press dispatch summarizes it nicely: "The secular SSNP seeks the merger of Lebanon, Syria, Jordan, pre-Israel Palestine, Iraq, Kuwait and Cyprus"—Cyprus!—"into a Greater Syria."

Abu Nidal, a Palestinian who was the author of last December's 20 Vienna and Rome airport massacres and may also be linked to the Karachi airport attack, concurs. "Syria for us is the mother country," he says. "For 2,000 years the Palestinians have not lived in an independent territory. Palestine of the future must be incorporated within Syrian territory."

Such people—and these are the people going around spraying 21 airliners and synagogues with bullets—will not retire even if Israel makes the most extreme concession and gives up the West Bank in favor of a Palestinian state. What Abu Nidal and Abu Abbas and indeed every Palestinian guerrilla group demand as a right is not a Hebron vineyard but downtown Tel Aviv. Even a radical West Bank solution will leave all of today's major terror groups and their sponsoring states aggrieved and in the field.

And even if peace were attainable, terrorism would outlive peace 22 for another reason: the Arab-Israeli dispute is not the sole—the root—cause of terror in the Middle East. There are at least two other fundamental causes of instability, war and murder. One is the anti-Western, antimodern, antisecularist movement that is sweeping the Islamic world and has already wholly captured Iran. As Daniel Moynihan has said of the United Nations, the anti-Zionist campaign there is but the leading edge of a larger anti-Western campaign. Israel, as the most vulnerable Western outpost, becomes the most convenient target. Israeli territory, however, turns out to be well guarded, and thus a dangerous and inconvenient target for terrorists to attack. So the imperialist demon is confronted at other, easier points: European planes, ships, discos—wherever Westerners, preferably Americans, preferably civilians, are to be found.

Anti-Western terrorism—from the seizure of American hostages   23
in Tehran to the blowing up of Western embassies in Kuwait to the
killing of American G.I.s in Germany—is not primarily concerned with
Israel. It is concerned with expelling an alien and corrupting West from
the Islamic world. The Ayatullah has had much to say on the subject.

The other great fuel for Middle East terrorism is also anti-Western,   24
but modern and secular, and is thus often at war with Islamic fundamentalism (sometimes quite literally, as in 1982 when President Assad
of Syria killed an estimated 30,000 of his own people in putting down
the Muslim Brotherhood revolt in Hama). Principally, however, this
form of terrorism is at war with the West or, more precisely, with
Western influence in the Middle East. This anti-Western strain is nationalist. The grievance is that after centuries of ascendancy, the Arab world
has in modern times been subordinated by the West, first by naked
colonialism, now by the more subtle devices of political, cultural and
economic neocolonialism. This complaint echoes "anti-imperialist"
sentiments felt in other parts of the Third World. And as with anti-
imperialism elsewhere, the issue is not Israel. Eradicate Israel and you
have not eradicated the grievance.

Nor the terrorism. Grievances, after all, need not result in terror.   25
Many groups have grievances. Occasionally, a few issue in terror. In the
Middle East, however, the resort to terror is ubiquitous. Think only of
the numberless atrocities of the Lebanese civil war, now twelve years
old. Revolutionary violence in the Middle East, whether Palestinian,
Islamic or pan-Arab in objective, routinely turns to terror as an extension of war by other means. First, because terrorism as an instrument
suits those who are otherwise not equipped to challenge superior
power in direct military confrontation. Terrorism thus becomes a kind
of appropriate technology for the warfare of the weak. But terrorism
must not only fit the struggle; it must fit the political culture. "To speak
of solving the problems of terrorism is an illusion," argues the West
German Middle East expert Helmut Hubel. "Over the past three centuries, terrorism has been regarded as a legitimate instrument of policy
and is part of Middle Eastern political culture."

The proof of this proposition is that in the Middle East terror is   26
not merely an instrument of the weak against the powerful Western
enemy. It is an endemic feature of local politics. In fact, most of the terror
practiced in the Middle East is not anti-Israel or even anti-West but
intra-Arab and intra-Muslim. It is a way for Syria to check Jordan, for
Iran to subvert Iraq (and vice versa), for Lebanese factions to deal with
one another, and for Libya to tame its enemies everywhere.

To see the Palestinian issue as the all-encompassing root cause of   27
terrorism is not just a misperception. It is a danger. To await the
messianic resolution of the Palestinian issue (messianic because the

terrorists reject any imaginable compromise) is to invite dangerous despair and passivity. It is to neglect those things that can be done to restrain terrorism by way of this-worldly means, such as political, economic and military pressure. The U.S. air raid on Libya was followed by months of relative quiet. With Karachi and Istanbul the respite is over. Perhaps a new wave of terror is about to begin. To expect that after 20 years of passivity, a single act of American retaliation should have put a permanent end to terrorism is absurd. Only the steady, unwavering application of all forms of pressure against terrorists and their more easily found sponsors will have any lasting effect.

There are men around who, in the name of some cause, take 28 machine guns onto airplanes and into synagogues and kill as many as they can. One of the overriding obligations of the age is to use every available means to hunt down today's machine gunners and deter tomorrow's. The pursuit of peace is also an obligation. But it is an entirely different enterprise.

For Discussion and Writing

1. In analyzing the notion of root causes of revolution, Krauthammer raises two logical objections. What are these?
2. According to Krauthammer, why does the root cause argument fail also when applied to the Middle East? Which two additional factors make an end to Middle Eastern terrorism unlikely?
3. If the root cause of terrorism cannot be solved, what does Krauthammer recommend?
4. Write an essay in which you consider the difficulties or inconsistencies in definitions of terrorism. Are some groups that use violence justified in their actions? Are there useful distinctions to be made between revolutionaries? When are terrorists "freedom fighters," and when are they merely thugs and gangsters?

Reflections on
the Revolution in China

CHARLES KRAUTHAMMER

Living as we are through the greatest global democratic awaken-   1
ing in history, it is hard not to feel the thrill Wordsworth felt when
contemplating the French Revolution ("Bliss was it in that dawn to be
alive/ But to be young was very heaven!"). Of course Wordsworth lived
to regret it. But there will be time for that later. Now is the time to thrill.

At the stunning uprising in China, of course. But it is only the   2
latest event in the democratic demarche, which began with the Philip-
pines and Korea and has now reached wondrous proportions.

In Lithuania the Soviet-installed, Communist-controlled, erst-   3
while puppet parliament votes for independence from the Soviet
Union.

In Hungary the two wings of the Communist Party are fighting   4
over whether upcoming multiparty elections mean the Communists
will be voted out of power in six years (the hard-line position) or sooner
(the moderate position).

Argentina is about to witness the first transition of power from   5
one popularly elected President to another since 1922, though, by
electing a Peronist, the Argentines have proved once again that democracy is a people's license to act stupidly.

In Chile a 15-year-old dictatorship holds a referendum on itself   6
and loses, proving once again that democracy is a people's license to
act enlightened.

Poland will not only hold free elections for the upper house of   7
parliament this month but, in a little noted provision of its pact with
Solidarity, will also have a popular election for President in six years.

With such goings-on, it's hard not to get gushy and to feel it a   8
privilege to have lived to witness such a dawn.

I admit to feeling a gush or two of Wordsworthian euphoria.   9
Though a drawing of Yuri Andropov graces my office wall (a warm
reminder of the good old days when The Enemy looked the part), I am
a cold warrior who does not mourn the passing of the great twilight
struggle. The cold war made thinking simpler in a "four legs good, two

legs bad" (the *Animal Farm* axiom) sort of way. But simpler doesn't mean better. There could be no happier outcome for the cold war than for us to win it and for old cold warriors to face the invigorating challenge of rethinking from the ground up what America's role in the world, if any, ought to be.

But some of the gushing is getting out of hand. The most common   10
bit of mush, endlessly repeated, whether the reporting is from China or the Soviet Union or Lithuania, is that once the genie of freedom is out of the bottle it can never be put back in. This is rank sentimentalism. The idea that somehow, if people have tasted freedom, the taste cannot be wrung out of them is a fallacy so large it is embarrassing just to hear it. Think only of this century. Russia tasted freedom in February 1917 and by October had lost it for 70 years. Weimar Germany tasted democracy for 14 years; it took Hitler and his storm troopers a few months to eradicate it. (Had Hitler not started World War II, the taste might to this day not have returned.) Hungarians let the genie out in 1956; five days and 5,000 tanks later, Khrushchev had stuffed it back in. Twenty-one years ago, the Czechs tasted freedom for an afternoon. Tell the Czechs that today's "Moscow Spring" is irreversible. Nothing is irreversible.

I admit that the genie cannot be put back in the bottle forever.   11
Oppression and extermination can repress the will to freedom for decades, sometimes generations, but inevitably it reappears. That is the lesson we learn from the earthquakes in China and the Soviet Union and Lithuania and Poland and Hungary.

The past decade has taught that the classical totalitarian theory of   12
the '40s and '50s was wrong. That theory, based on Stalin and Hitler as models, made the then quite reasonable assumption that modern totalitarianism, harnessed to high technology and mechanized power (Stalin was once called Genghis Khan with a telephone), had the capacity not only to suppress freedom but also to eradicate it. Classical theory postulated the brainwashed mind, utterly enslaved through terror and manipulation. It supposed the shattered society, its mediating structures and competing allegiances (family, church, union) destroyed, leaving an atomized individual enslaved to the all powerful state.

Not so. We learn that totalitarianism can terrorize individuals and   13
shatter civil society, but it cannot change human nature. The will to freedom can be suppressed, but inevitably it returns.

But to say that the will to freedom cannot be suppressed forever   14
is not to say that it cannot be suppressed for a very long time. And from the point of view of the individual with a finite life-span that is the same as forever. There are many Soviets who have lived and died in this century and never known freedom of any sort. Yes, the suppression of the Prague Spring did not forever abolish the Czech hunger for freedom. But it did crush the life of an entire generation.

No one knows where the Chinese revolution is leading. But the   15
notion that once a million people have marched in the streets, some
carrying effigies of the Statue of Liberty, things cannot be undone is
wishful thinking. History has provided a generous supply of Bona-
partes and Lenins. Maos too. This is not China's first revolution. And
even if this one does succeed, it will not be the last.

The will to freedom is, of course, a constant of human nature. But   16
so is the will to power. And power is intolerant of freedom. The drama
of today's revolution in China is the contest between the two. Neither
will is absolute. All victories are temporary.

Hail freedom! But precisely now that it is ascendant, do not   17
assume that it cannot be sent into long exile. Iran and Nicaragua and
Cuba are now the exception. But only a minute ago they were the rule.
They can be again.

For Discussion and Writing

1. While wanting to celebrate "the greatest global democratic awakening
   in history," Krauthammer qualifies his enthusiasm with some hard
   facts. Which historical evidence argues against the idea that democracy
   has won its final battle?
2. Despite setbacks in political freedom, does Krauthammer believe totalitarianism is ultimately doomed to failure? Why or why not?
3. Krauthammer's essay may be viewed as a warning to those who have
   lived to see a democratic revival. What does he caution them to think
   or do?
4. Krauthammer makes some basic assumptions about human nature in
   his discussion of the revolutionary democratic impulse. Do you agree
   that human beings everywhere have a natural desire to be free, or is
   democratic freedom something people can want only after more basic
   needs (food, clothing, shelter) are met? Write a reflective essay on the
   revolutionary impulse toward self-government, seeking to define it, to
   analyze its causes, and to give examples of the impulse in action.

Thinking and Writing about Chapter 19

1. Compare and contrast Morrow's and Krauthammer's views of possible peace or reconciliation among Western and Islamic viewpoints.
2. Krauthammer takes a fairly hard line in his views, and calls himself a "cold warrior." Do you agree, or disagree, with his general attitude? What do you think of his portrayal of the Israeli-Palestinian issue?
3. Throughout the world, nations are in upheaval, with budding or full-fledged revolutionary movements in South Africa, Eastern Europe, the Middle East, and parts of Asia and India. Where are the revolutionary impulses in the advanced industrial countries? Does America or Europe need a revolution? Are there smaller though important movements for political or social change afoot in those countries? Write an essay in which you analyze movement of social upheaval in your own back yard, or recommend that specific actions be undertaken.

20

Global Politics

Throughout modern history, people have had the sense that the world is shrinking—that what once seemed almost infinitely large was really not so big after all. In our own day, with the advent of satellite communications and that memorable photographic image of the earthrise taken from the Moon, the notion of the world as a small place has gained new force. On live TV we watch Scud missile attacks on Israel, interviews with Saudi princes, air raids on Baghdad. We talk about global environmental events, world-wide effects. And everybody everywhere seems to speak English.

One question that arises persistently is, What is America's role in this new global context? The Gulf War seemed to provide at least a partial answer: We were to be the coalition builders, the leaders of a claimed new world order. But what would our attitudes be toward those other cultures in the world, who maintained their identity despite American influence? What would be our military or political role when collation support was absent?

The essays in this chapter tackle some of the thorny issues that face us in the realm of global politics. In "Deep Down, We're All Alike, Right? Wrong," from August 1983, Charles Krauthammer dissects the notion that all the world's people's are essentially just like us. In "Going It Alone," from April 1986, Strobe Talbott defends the concept of American unilateral military action. And in "Welcome to the Global Village," from May 1989, Lance Morrow claims that communications technology has transformed global politics.

Deep Down, We're All Alike, Right? Wrong

CHARLES KRAUTHAMMER

"As is evident just from the look on his face," observes *The New Yorker* in a recent reflection on the Lincoln Memorial, "[Lincoln] would have liked to live out a long life surrounded by old friends and good food." Good food? *New Yorker* readers have an interest in successful soufflés, but it is hard to recall the most melancholy and spiritual of Presidents giving them much thought. *New Yorker* editors no doubt dream of living out their days grazing in gourmet pastures. But did Lincoln really long to retire to a table at Lutèce?

Solipsism is the belief that the whole world is me, and as Mathematician Martin Gardner points out, its authentic version is not to be found outside mental institutions. What is to be found outside the asylum is its philosophic cousin, the belief that the whole world is like me. This species of solipsism—plural solipsism, if you *like*—is far more common because it is far less lonely. Indeed, it yields a very congenial world populated exclusively by creatures of one's own likeness, a world in which Lincoln pines for his dinner with André or, more consequentially, where KGB chiefs and Iranian ayatullahs are, well, folks just like us.

The mirror-image fantasy is not as crazy as it seems. Fundamentally, it is a radical denial of the otherness of others. Or to put it another way, a blinding belief in "common humanity," in the triumph of human commonality over human differences. It is a creed rarely fully embraced (it has a disquieting affinity with martyrdom), but in a culture tired of such ancient distinctions as that between children and adults (in contemporary movies the kids are, if anything, wiser than their parents) or men and women ("I was a better man as a woman with a woman than I've ever been as a man with a woman," says Tootsie), it can acquire considerable force.

Its central axiom is that if one burrows deep enough beneath the Mao jacket, the *shapka* or the chador, one discovers that people everywhere are essentially the same. American Anthropologist Samantha Smith was invited to Moscow by Yuri Andropov for firsthand confirmation of just that proposition (a rare Soviet concession to the principle of on-site inspection). After a well-photographed sojourn during which she took in a children's festival at a Young Pioneer camp (but was spared the paramilitary training), she got the message: "They're just . . . almost . . . just like us," she announced at her last Moscow press conference. Her mother, who is no longer eleven but makes up for it in openmindedness, supplied the corollary: "They're just like us . . . they prefer to work at their jobs than to work at war."

That completes the syllogism. We all have "eyes, hands, organs, dimensions, senses, affections, passions." We are all "fed with the same food, hurt with the same weapons, subject to the same diseases, healed by the same means, warmed and cooled by the same winter and summer." It follows, does it not, that we must all want the same things? According to Harvard Cardiologist Bernard Lown, president of International Physicians for the Prevention of Nuclear War, that's not just Shakespeare, it's a scientific fact: "Our aim is to promote the simple medical insight," he writes, "that Russian and American hearts are indistinguishable, that both ache for peace and survival."

Such breathtaking non sequiturs (cardiological or otherwise) are characteristic of plural solipsism. For it is more than just another happy vision. It is meant to have practical consequences. If people everywhere, from Savannah to Sevastopol, share the same hopes and dreams and fears and love of children (and good food), they should get along. And if they don't, then there must be some misunderstanding, some misperception, some problem of communication. As one news report of the recent conference of Soviet and American peace activists in Minneapolis put it, "The issue of human rights sparked a heated discussion . . . and provided participants with a firsthand view of the obstacles to communication which so often characterize U.S.-Soviet relations." (The sadistic sheriff in *Cool Hand Luke* was more succinct: pointing to the rebellious prisoner he had just brutalized, he explained, "What we've got here is failure to communicate.") It is the broken-telephone theory of international conflict, and it suggests a solution: repair service by the expert "facilitator," the Harvard negotiations professor. Hence the vogue for peace academies, the mania for mediators, the belief that the world's conundrums would yield to the right intermediary, the right presidential envoy, the right socialist international delegation. Yet Iraq's Saddam Hussein and Iran's Ayatullah Khomeini, to take just two candidates for the Roger Fisher School of Conflict Resolution, have perfectly adequate phone service. They need only an operator to make the connection. Their problem is that they have very little to say to each other.

There are other consequences. If the whole world is like me, then certain conflicts become incomprehensible; the very notion of intractability becomes paradoxical. When the U.S. embassy in Tehran is taken over, Americans are bewildered. What does the Ayatullah want? The U.S. Government sends envoys to find out what token or signal or symbolic gesture might satisfy Iran. It is impossible to believe that the Ayatullah wants exactly what he says he wants: the head of the Shah. Things are not done that way any more in the West (even the Soviet bloc has now taken to pensioning off deposed leaders). It took a long time for Americans to get the message.

Other messages from exotic cultures are never received at all. The   8
more virulent pronouncements of Third World countries are dismissed as mere rhetoric. The more alien the sentiment, the less seriously it is taken. Diplomatic fiascoes follow, like Secretary Shultz's recent humiliation in Damascus. He persisted in going there despite the fact that President Assad had made it utterly plain that he rejected efforts by the U.S. (the "permanent enemy") to obtain withdrawal of Syrian forces from Lebanon. Or consider the chronic American frustration with Saudi Arabia. The Saudis consistently declare their refusal to accept the legitimacy of a Jewish state in the Middle East, a position so at variance with the Western view that it is simply discounted. Thus successive American Governments continue to count on Saudi support for U.S. peace plans, only to be rudely let down. When the Saudis finally make it unmistakably clear that they will support neither Camp David nor the Reagan plan nor the Lebanon accord, the U.S. reacts with consternation. It might have spared itself the surprise if it had not in the first place imagined that underneath those kaffiyehs are folks just like us, sharing our aims and views.

"The wise man shows his wisdom in separation, in gradation, and   9
his scale of creatures and of merits is as wide as nature," writes Emerson. "The foolish have no range in their scale, but suppose every man is as every other man." Ultimately to say that people all share the same hopes and fears, are all born and love and suffer and die alike, is to say very little. For it is after commonalities are accounted for that politics becomes necessary. It is only when values, ideologies, cultures and interests clash that politics even begins. At only the most trivial level can it be said that people want the same things. Take peace. The North Vietnamese want it, but apparently they wanted to conquer all of Indochina first. The Salvadoran right and left both want it, but only after making a desert of the other. The Reagan Administration wants it, but not if it has to pay for it with pieces of Central America.

And even if one admits universal ends, one still has said nothing   10
about means, about what people will risk, will permit, will commit in order to banish their (common) fears and pursue their (common) hopes. One would think that after the experience of this century the belief that a harmony must prevail between peoples who share a love of children

and small dogs would be considered evidence of a most grotesque historical amnesia.

From where does the idea of a world of likes come? In part from 11 a belief in universal brotherhood (a belief that is parodied, however, when one pretends that the ideal already exists). In part from a trendy ecological pantheism with its misty notions of the oneness of those sharing this lonely planet. In part from the Enlightenment belief in a universal human nature, a slippery modern creation that for all its universality manages in every age to take on a decidedly middle-class look. For the mirror-image fantasy derives above all from the coziness of middle-class life. The more settled and ordered one's life—and in particular one's communal life—the easier it becomes for one's imagination to fail. In Scarsdale, destitution and desperation, cruelty and zeal are the stuff of headlines, not life. Thus a single murder can create a sensation; in Beirut it is a statistic. When the comfortable encounter the unimaginable, the result is not only emotional but cognitive rejection. Brutality and fanaticism beyond one's ken must be made to remain there; thus, for example, when evidence mounts of biological warfare in faraway places, the most fanciful theories may be produced to banish the possibility.

To gloss over contradictory interests, incompatible ideologies and 12 opposing cultures as sources of conflict is more than antipolitical. It is dangerous. Those who have long held a mirror to the world and seen only themselves are apt to be shocked and panicked when the mirror is removed, as inevitably it must be. On the other hand, to accept the reality of otherness is not to be condemned to a war of all against all. We are not then compelled to see in others the focus of evil in the world. We are still enjoined to love our neighbor as ourselves; only it no longer becomes an exercise in narcissism.

But empathy that is more than self-love does not come easily. 13 Particularly not to a culture so fixed on its own image that it can look at Lincoln, gaunt and grave, and see a man ready to join the queue at the pâté counter at Zabar's.

For Discussion and Writing

1. Krauthammer uses a philosophical term, solipsism, to describe contemporary attitudes toward foreign cultures. What does solipsism mean, and what, according to Krauthammer, is its "central axiom"?
2. What kinds of political error or misjudgment can plural solipsism lead to? Why does Krauthammer say it is a nonsensical belief?
3. What does Krauthammer recommend in place of the mirror-image fantasy he attributes to American culture?

4. Media images of universal cultural harmony are common in advertising and fund raising. Krauthammer dismisses this as "ecological pantheism with its misty notions of the oneness of those sharing this lonely planet" (11). Do you agree, or disagree, with Krauthammer's view that people are finally very different, that "it is after commonalities are accounted for that politics becomes necessary"? Write an essay in which you consider this theme, either in America's global role, or as a general issue between people of diverse cultures.

Going It Alone

STROBE TALBOTT

The bombing attack against Libya is the most dramatic example   1
to date of an important theme in the foreign policy of the Reagan
Administration: a determination to use American military power
against enemies anywhere in the world, regardless of whether the U.S.
has the support of its allies. Being a superpower often means not having
to say either please or sorry.

Pundits and political scientists have a fancy, almost tongue-tying   2
bit of jargon for this tendency: global unilateralism. That phrase has
been bandied about by both admirers and critics of the Administration,
as well as by others who are ambivalent about official American attitudes and behavior.

Several other examples of global unilateralism look, in retrospect,   3
like dress rehearsals for this latest, most spectacular and most controversial military clash in the Reagan era. In 1981 the U.S. Navy made
quick work of Gaddafi's air force over the Gulf of Sidra, and late last
month the U.S. bloodied those waters again. There were also the 1983
invasion of Grenada and last year's interception of an Egyptian airliner
with the *Achille Lauro* hijackers aboard.

The new American penchant for going it alone is also apparent in   4
two more general commitments of the Administration: the so-called
Reagan Doctrine of support for anti-Communist guerrilla movements
and the Strategic Defense Initiative, or Star Wars.

The Reagan Doctrine holds that the U.S. should bypass nervous   5
and sometimes unreliable foreign friends in order to harass and, if
possible, overthrow Moscow's clients in the Third World. SDI, as originally conceived by Reagan in 1983, was a deus ex machina of global
unilateralism: a made-in-the-U.S.A. system for effectively disarming
the Soviet Union and any other foreign threat to the U.S. (including, in
a number of scenarios, a nuclear-armed Gaddafi or other Islamic fire-
brand).

These policies—whether quick-and-dirty one-shot actions such as   6
Sidra I, II and III or long-term strategies such as the Reagan Doctrine
and Star Wars—have evoked mixed reactions abroad. Denis Healey, the
British Labor Party's most prominent spokesman on foreign policy, has

continually protested global unilateralism in so many words. Last week Soviet Foreign Minister Eduard Shevardnadze, sensing a new buzz word in the Esperanto of Uncle Sam bashing, denounced the U.S. for "neo-globalism." At the same time, public remonstrations from the chancelleries of Europe and elsewhere have often been modulated with whispered encouragement to Washington to keep up the good work. The point about global unilateralism, however, is not whether others like it or not, but that the U.S. no longer cares quite so much one way or the other.

While the Reagan Administration has given global unilateralism   7 both doctrinal and operational standing that it did not have before, the phenomenon has been around for decades. After World War II, the U.S. found itself with global interests, global responsibilities and global reach. It also had in the Soviet Union an adversary of far-reaching ambitions and capabilities. Yet American alliances were, and remained, essentially regional. In the '50s and '60s, the U.S. worked hard to give its allies a sense that they were partners in the U.S.'s worldwide mission.

But the allies often balked, questioning the ends and means of   8 American policy in far-flung corners of the world and resisting participation in American missions. The West Europeans' ability to understand, and willingness to support, American exertions of force seemed inversely proportional to the distance of a trouble spot from the center of Europe. Even the Korean War, while fought under the flag of the United Nations and with the help of brave but largely token contingents from 15 other countries, was essentially an American (and, of course, South Korean) enterprise. The Viet Nam War was not just a losing exercise, it was an anguishingly, and disillusioningly, lonely one. Then in the late '70s and early '80s, the U.S. found itself at cross purposes with friends and allies over Iran and Nicaragua.

The battle against terrorism has been frustrating in a different way   9 and, in terms of the Atlantic Alliance, especially divisive. NATO is supposed to be based not just on shared geopolitical interests but on shared values as well. The trouble is that as in other, bigger wars, allied territory is often the battleground in the war of terrorism. That makes West Europeans less enthusiastic than Americans for shoot-'em-up methods and more inclined to subtlety if not accommodation. To large numbers of Americans, however, the apparent willingness of many West Europeans to tolerate Arab terrorism as a fact of life has made them seem not just parochial but pusillanimous.

Moreover, many Americans, particularly those on the resurgent   10 right, have long worried that while the U.S. was observing the niceties of bilateralism and multilateralism and all those other virtuous isms, the Soviet Union was very unilaterally getting away with murder around the world. It was time to play the Great Game by the same rules as the other superpower.

A number of conservative thinkers began to propound a radical 11 form of global unilateralism: since alliances and international bodies have become an impediment to the vigorous, assertive defense of the national interest, it is time for the U.S. to disregard if not jettison the U.N., NATO and the rest.

President Reagan has stopped well short of following that extreme 12 advice. He has an instinctive attachment to the vision not of Fortress America (that would be isolationism), but of Battleship America—or, more to the point last week, Aircraft Carrier America, steaming around the seven seas, flying the flag in friendly ports and, when provoked, launching air strikes against unfriendly ones. But he has tried to find a middle ground between global unilateralism and what might be called traditional internationalism. He has adopted a pattern of consulting allies in advance, welcoming their support if they offer it and trying to allay their misgivings if they object—but he is not going to make their backing a precondition for American action.

Whatever the merits of last week's attack, that essentially moder- 13 ate approach to the allies was in evidence. As Reagan put it in his Monday-night address to the nation, "I said that we would act with others if possible and alone if necessary." Such is the lot of a superpower.

For Discussion and Writing

1. What is Talbott's view of America's military role in the world? Does he limit that definition in any way?
2. What kinds of historical forces have contributed to America's tendency toward global unilateralism?
3. Many Americans have claimed over the years that the U.S. should not "police the world." Is U.S. willingness to confront enemies anywhere on earth a contradiction of the traditional American view? Why or why not?
4. In 1966, during the Vietnam War, former Secretary of State Dean Rusk said: "We cannot be indifferent to what happens anywhere on earth . . ." Write an essay in which you attack or defend Rusk's claim. How should the U.S. decide where and how to use its power? Should each involvement be determined separately, or are there certain general principles that should guide American military and foreign policy?

Welcome to the Global Village

LANCE MORROW

A new world has developed like a Polaroid photograph, a vivid,   1
surreal awakening.

The effect has been contradictory: a sense of sunlight and elegy at   2
the same time, of *glasnost* and claustrophobia.

Whenever the world's molecules reorganize themselves, of   3
course, someone announces a new reality—"All changed, changed
utterly: A terrible beauty is born," in W. B. Yeats' smitten lines about the
Irish rebellion of Easter 1916. Seventy-three years later, the Irish troubles
proceed, dreary, never beautiful—an eczema of violence in the margins.

But the world in the past few years has, in fact, profoundly   4
changed. In Tiananmen Square last week, many of the demonstrators'
signs were written in English. The students knew they were enacting a
planetary drama, that their words and images in that one place would
powder into electrons and then recombine on millions of little screens
in other places, other minds, around the world.

The planet has become an intricate convergence—of acid rains   5
and rain forests burning, of ideas and Reeboks and stock markets that
ripple through time zones, of satellite signals and worldwide television,
of advance-purchase airfares, fax machines, the miniaturization of the
universe by computer, of T shirts and mutual destinies.

The planetary circuits are wired: an integrated system, a   6
microchip floating in space. Wired for evils—for AIDS, for example, for
nuclear war, for terrorism. But also for entertainment, knowledge and
even (we live in hope) for higher possibilities like art, excellence,
intelligence and freedom. Justice has not gone planetary and never will.
But the village has indeed become global—Marshall McLuhan was
right. No island is an island anymore: the earth itself is decisively the
island now.

Travel and travel writing are enjoying a sort of brilliant late   7
afternoon, what photographers call the magic hour before sunset. But
the romantic sense of remoteness shrivels. Even the trash announces
that the planet is all interconnection, interpenetration, black spillage, a
maze of mutual implication, trajectories like the wrapped yarn of a
baseball.

A scene: blue plastic bags, bags by the thousands, struggle out of   8
the Red Sea onto the shores of Egypt.

The wind dries them, and then they inflate like lungs and rise on   9
the desert air. They come out of the sea like Portuguese men-of-war and
then, amphibious, as if in some Darwinian drama, sail off to litter
another of the earth's last emptinesses. Reverse Darwin, really: devolu-
tion, a flight of death forms.

Those who actually read Salman Rushdie's notorious best seller   10
The Satanic Verses may have absorbed Rushdie's brilliant perception of
what the planet has become: old cultures in sudden high-velocity
crisscross, a bewilderment of ethnic explosion and implosion simultaneously. The Ayatullah Khomeini's response to Rushdie is (whatever
else it is) an exquisite vindication of Rushdie's point. Khomeini's Iranian revolution was exactly a violent repudiation of the new world that
the Shah had sponsored. The struggle throughout the Middle East now
is, among other things, a collision between Islam and the temptations
and intrusions of the West. In the new world, everything disintegrates:
family, community, tradition, coherence itself. The old community peri-
shes in deference to a new community not yet born.

So the world is exactly Salman Rushdie's Indian characters pas-   11
sively seat-belted in their flight from Bombay to London, then blown
apart by a random, idiot bomb and soon seen pinwheeling down to a
soft landing off the English coast—the England where Kipling comes
home to roost and the empire will implode and intermingle.

A media tale: American television correspondent covering a unit   12
of government troops moving against a guerrilla post in El Salvador
keeps eyeing his watch and asking the commander when he will order
the attack. Distracted commander says, "Not yet, not yet." Correspondent finally explodes, "Goddammit, I've a bird [satellite feed to the
network] at 6 o'clock!" The leader, understanding perfectly, orders his
attack immediately.

The definition of conquest has changed. Japan has proved that   13
territory, sheer acreage, means nothing. The Soviet Union's geographi-
cal vastness has availed little in productivity.

The deepest change may be a planetary intuition that military war   14
is pointless. Except in atavistic places like the Middle East and Ireland,
conquering territory is a fruitless and counterproductive exercise. Why
conquer land? The Soviets have more trouble than they can manage
with their nationalities. The new world's battlegrounds are markets and
ideas. The Japanese and Germans, having learned their military lessons
the hard way, reentered the war by other means.

Cities like Cairo, Lagos, Nairobi, Mexico City are slouching to-   15
ward the new world in the darkest way. Life and death struggle with
one another: great birth rates, great death rates. This is the new world's

suffocation, of population, poverty, pollution. The country people crowd into the cities. Their continuities are broken, their communities, their village frameworks wrecked, with nothing to replace them.

In the new world, America has lost some of its radiant pride of   16
place. Japan has risen. Europe is organizing itself into a new collective power. The Soviet Union is struggling to escape the dustbin of history. Gorbachev, a magician of much élan, attempts to rescind the hoax of Communism without denouncing its idea. It is fascinating to watch a smart man trying to defend a premise that is beneath his intelligence.

What is the meaning of the new world? Like the older one, it goes   17
dark and then goes light. It flies through the air. It is perhaps too intimate to be heroic anymore. It is, on balance, better than the one before, because it is more conscious.

For Discussion and Writing

1. What sorts of influences have helped to bring about the Global Village?
2. What are the characteristics of the Global Village, as Morrow sees them? Are they all good?
3. With all its obvious problems, why does Morrow think that the new world is better than the old one?
4. Write an essay in which you support or oppose this claim: Despite the wiring of the world through satellites and instant global communications, most people live their lives on a regional or local scale, caught up in what's close at hand, generally unconcerned about the TV images of others far away.

Thinking and Writing about Chapter 20

1. Apply Krauthammer's notion of fundamental human and cultural differences to Morrow's idea of the Global Village, of "cultures in sudden high-velocity crisscross." Can you think of some recent examples brought about by global politics?

2. To what extent do you think that exposure to other peoples, other cultures, affects the possibilities of international conflict? With America's sudden and media-driven awareness of the Middle East, for example, have any bridges of understanding been built between our two cultures?

3. Do you see yourself as part of a world community, a world citizen, or is your identity still shaped by your own ethnic origins, local culture, or family? Write an essay in which you consider yourself as a member of the global community. What is the role of a world citizen? Is it even possible to think of oneself in such terms?

PART FOUR: Science and Technology

21

*Science
and Society*

Since the Scientific Revolution of the 17th century, Western societies have been vastly and ceaselessly transformed by scientific and technological knowledge. In medicine, transportation, communications, housing and sanitation, education, agriculture—in virtually every walk of life—the scientific method of inquiry has yielded new ways of looking at and living in the world. Much of this obvious material progress we take for granted, often asking of science, "What have you done for us lately?" Sometimes the answer isn't always a happy one, as we see how material progress has helped to pollute the environment, increase population pressures, and fill the world with goods of questionable necessity.

What is the relationship between science and society, and what should it be? Should it be a close partnership? Should science be judged by its usefulness alone? Does the scientific community have special and unique responsibilities?

The essays in this chapter investigate these and other central issues. In "Science: No Longer a Sacred Cow," from March 1977, Frank Trippett analyzes the public's attitude toward scientific progress. In "The Joy of Math, or Fermat's Revenge," Charles Krauthammer praises what he calls the beautiful uselessness of mathematics. And in "Science, Lies and The Ultimate Truth," Barbara Ehrenreich uses a recent controversy to condemn what she views as the increasing common practice of scientific deception.

Science: No Longer a Sacred Cow

Frank Trippett

> *The technologic euphoria which began about 1600 with*
> *Francis Bacon and was continued by the 19th century*
> *philosophers of the enlightenment achieved its most*
> *extreme expression among the 20th century futurologists,*
> *who took it for granted that the year 2000 would see the*
> *dawn of a technologic utopia.*
>
> —René Dubos, *Beast or Angel?*

America's euphoric awe of science began to ebb with the Pandoran gift to mankind of the atomic bomb. Yet the most extreme expression of the nation's continued reverence for science and technology—dramatized in the tendency to call products "wonders" (as in drugs) or "miracles" (as in fabrics) or "magic" (as in electronics)—awaited the moment that a human foot first touched the moon. That feat, the President of the U.S. assured his countrymen, was to be ranked as the greatest thing since—*Creation.* After that exaltation, there was only one way, by the law of psychological gravity, for Sci-Tech's prestige to go.

Sure enough, down it went. And in its place has risen a new public attitude that seems the antithesis of the former awe. That awe has given way to a new skepticism, the adulation to heckling. To the bewilderment of much of the scientific community, its past triumphs have been downgraded, and popular excitement over new achievements, like snapshots from Mars, seems to wane with the closing words of the evening news. Sci-Tech's promises for the future, far from being welcomed as harbingers of utopia, now seem too often to be threats. Fears that genetic tinkering might produce a Doomsday Bug, for example, bother many Americans, along with dread that the sst's sonic booms may add horrid racket to the hazards (auto fumes, fluorocarbons, strontium 90) that already burden the air.

Increasingly this new skepticism is spreading even among professionals in the world of Sci-Tech. Indeed, it could be heard conspicuously

290

last week as 4,200 members of the American Association for the Advancement of Science gathered in Denver for their annual brainstorming. Arthur Kantrowitz, head of Avco Everett Research Laboratory Inc. in Everett, Mass., came plugging, once again, for the creation of a "science court" that might help sort out "facts from values" in controversies that have been multiplying in the atmosphere of question and dispute. One of the speakers in Denver, Science Historian June Goodfield, a visiting professor at New York's Rockefeller University, welcomed public skepticism as a healthy development that is basically "a call for science to turn a human face toward society." The new spirit, said Goodfield, marks the end of "mutual myths" long held by society (about the scientist as hero) and science (about its freedom from obligation to society).

The new skepticism can be seen, as well as heard, in the emergence   4
of a fresh willingness to challenge the custodians of arcane technical knowledge on their own ground. It is most conspicuously embodied in the environmental crusade and the consumers' rebellion, but is also at play across a far wider field. It applies public light and political heat to Detroit's automotive engineers, who for generations had dispatched their products to an acquiescent public. It encompasses protests against the location of dams massively certified by science, opposition to the erection of nuclear power plants declared to be safe and sound, open disputes about the real values of scientifically approved medicines, and the increasing willingness of patients to sue physicians to make them account for mistakes in treatment. Sci-Tech, in a sense, has been demoted from its demigodhood. The public today rallies, in its untidy way, around the notion that Hans J. Morgenthau put into words in *Science: Servant or Master?*: "The scientist's monopoly of the answers to the questions of the future is a myth."

The fading of this mythology is the result of Americans' gradual   5
realization that science and technology's dreamy wonders sometimes turn out to be nightmarish blunders. Detergents that make dishes gleam may kill rivers. Dyes that prettify the food may cause cancer. Pills that make sex safe may dangerously complicate health. DDT, Cyclamates, thalidomide and estrogen are but a few of the mixed blessings that, all together, have taught the layman a singular lesson: the promising fruits of science and technology often come with hidden worms.

The public's anxiety, anger and skepticism have been reinforced   6
by the exposure of many remarkably human frailties within the halls of science. Biologist Barry Commoner's *Science and Survival*, documenting an erosion of scientific integrity and denouncing official secrecy and lying about nuclear fallout, came in 1966 as merely an early ripple in a wave of muckraking that has washed away the glowing image of the scientist as some kind of superman. Scientists now appear to be as

fallible as the politicians with whom they increasingly consort. In *Advice and Dissent: Scientists in the Political Arena,* two academic scientists, Physics Teacher Joel Primack of the University of California and Environmentalist Frank von Hippel of Princeton, present case histories documenting the tendency of many scientists to "look the other way" when the Government wants to lie about technical matters. A scholarly polemic by Lewis Mumford, *The Pentagon of Power,* scathes not the scientists but their intimacy with governmental powers. The identification is so complete that scientists, Mumford charges, have until lately "been criminally negligent in anticipating or even reporting what has actually been taking place."

Scientists themselves, like many of those at Denver, have been   7
increasingly questioning their own role. Protesting science's callous use of human guinea pigs for experimentation, Dr. Richard M. Restak, a Washington neurologist, decries the fact that the prestigious National Institutes of Health refused to establish a code governing such experiments until its sponsored researchers were found guilty of injecting live cancer cells into uninformed subjects. Writing on the Op-Ed page of the New York *Times,* Restak voiced "a creepy realization that when left to their own devices, biomedical scientists are capable of some rather nasty mischief indeed." Then he put a central, if often asked, question: "Do we need yet more horrors to bring home the truth that science is too important to be left to the scientists?"

America's current spirit of skepticism toward Sci-Tech is, above   8
all, the popular response to that question. The answer is a no so resounding that when it came, it was mistaken for a mortal war on science. So alarmed was Philip Handler, president of the National Academy of Sciences, that in 1972 he preached publicly on the urgent need to stave off the "crumbling of the scientific enterprise." Today, with that enterprise clearly waxing (federal funding for science this year: $24.7 billion, up 67% in eight years), Handler's excessive reaction may seem like that of a pampered sacred cow at the approach of a foot-and-mouth inspector. The fact is that the new skepticism, at bottom, is not antiscience at all. It is only at war with the once prevalent assumption that science and technology should be allowed utter freedom, with little or no accounting to those who have to live with the bad results as well as the good. If the layman on the street has discovered that science is fallible, that hardly makes him its permanent enemy. After all, everybody has forgiven Newton for thinking that the sun was populated.

So the new skepticism, in its present maturity, turns out to be   9
essentially political in its aspirations. Its successes include the very existence of the Environmental Protection Agency and, as a particular example, the EPA's recent action obliging the Ford Motor Co. to recall 54,000 cars to make sure that they meet emission standards. Skepticism

can be credited with last year's California referendum on nuclear power; the fact that the voters did not veto nuclear expansion misses the point, which is that an arcane subject hitherto considered the sole province of the scientist and engineer was submitted to ordinary citizens. And only a remarkably awakened citizenry could have inspired the self-criticism of the recent Senate committee report that chastised the Senate for laxness in overseeing the agencies that oversee the industries that are conduits of Sci-Tech.

Perhaps the most significant result so far of the new skepticism   10 might be called the Case of the Nonexistent Doomsday Bug. The scene: a session of the Cambridge, Mass., city council, with delegations from Harvard, M.I.T. and the National Institutes of Health in nervous attendance. The issue: Should Harvard and M.I.T. be permitted to go ahead with experiments in so-called recombinant DNA-experiments involving the implantation, in cells of a common bacterium, of alien DNA-borne genes? The crucial question: Do the risks of research that could engender a hypothetical Doomsday Bug—some new strain of bacteria that might find its invisible way into the bodies of the people—outweigh whatever knowledge might be gained?

There was a sobering question. Here is another, just as intriguing   11 and much easier to answer: How on earth did an issue like that wind up in the hands of a political body whose analytical resources are usually tested by questions of stop-light placement? Answer: three years ago, while contemplating the very first recombinant DNA experiments, many researchers themselves grew worried about the unfathomable risks. Instead of merely fretting among themselves, as scientists have usually done, they decided to make their fears public—and more. In a step unprecedented in the history of science, a group of them associated with the discoverer of DNA, James Watson, publicly asked colleagues around the world to suspend recombinant DNA experiments until the risks could be assessed and adequate safeguards established.

Without that, the public might never have heard of the risks—   12 until, perhaps, too late. Nor, last summer, would the Cambridge city council have got word that Harvard and M.I.T. were about to launch the controversial research. The council did hear, though. It thereupon put the experiments under a moratorium until the issue of risk could be studied by a committee of eight citizens—not a scientist among them. When the committee report emerged, it was greeted as a model of brevity, intelligence and balance. The upshot, approved by the council: the experiments could proceed, but only under safeguards a bit more strict than those recommended by the National Institutes of Health.

So the case was closed—but with surprisingly little attention to   13 the transcendent issue that had been settled. It was the issue of science's sovereignty, its traditional right to pursue research in the lab with neither guidance nor intervention from laymen. That sovereignty, in the Cambridge case, yielded to the public's claim to safety and well-being.

After that, the new skeptics are entitled to feel, so far so good. But 14 their very success has raised, in some minds, the question of how far society should go in exercising control over science. The answer must weigh the obvious danger that society might stifle or thwart the key profession on which it must rely for solutions to inescapably technical problems. One non-scientist at last week's A.A.A.S. convention—New York Lawyer George Ball, former Under Secretary of State—thinks that such a danger is already at hand. Ball sees the Cambridge council's monitoring of DNA experiments as an "ominous opening wedge" of a movement that might end up demanding "a bureaucratic preview of all scientific research to ascertain whether it meets some loosely defined test of social desirability."

Such an outcome would plainly be bad news for science and 15 society. But the good news, so far, is that nobody appears to be either demanding or expecting such a result. Even the most skeptical of the skeptics seem perfectly willing to let science go its way in the pursuit of knowledge. Still, if there is no sign that Americans fear what scientists may discover, there is also little expectation that any of their discoveries will provide answers to the enduring human mysteries that are impelling people these days on many a mystical and spiritual pilgrimage. All the new spirit of skepticism really asks is that science and society together take thoughtful stock when there seems a clear risk, as in the DNA experiments, that the pursuit of knowledge might damage, endanger or even exterminate human life. That seems little enough to ask.

For Discussion and Writing

1. What are the signs, according to Trippett, that an attitude of skepticism was replacing unquestioning reverence for science in the late 1970s? Does this same attitude exist in the 1990s?
2. What are some of the causes Trippett says have brought about this new view?
3. What does Trippett claim should be the reasonable result of the public's skeptical attitude?
4. As reflected by Trippett, the scare over DNA experimentation seems to have been exaggerated, with the huge industry of biotechnology having been spawned since the essay appeared. What kinds of worries about scientific inquiry bother the public today? Write an essay in which you express your sense of the thoughts, questions, fears, or desires people have about the role of science in their lives.

The Joy of Math, or Fermat's Revenge

CHARLES KRAUTHAMMER

For one brief shining moment, it appeared as if the 20th century 1
had justified itself. The era of world wars, atom bombs, toxic waste, AIDS,
Muzak and now, just to rub it in, a pending Bush-Dukakis race, had
redeemed itself, it seemed. It had brought forth a miracle. Fermat's last
theorem had been solved.

Fermat's last theorem is the world's most famous unsolved math- 2
ematical puzzle. It owes its fame to its age—it was born about five years
before Isaac Newton—and its simplicity. It consists of only one line. The
Greeks had shown that there are whole numbers for which $a^2 + b^2 = c^2$.
One solution for Pythagoras' theorem, for example, is $3^2 + 4^2 = 5^2$. Pierre
de Fermat conjectured that the Pythagorean equation doesn't work for
higher dimensions: for n greater than 2, $a^n + b^n = c^n$ is impossible. It won't
work for $n = 3$. (There are no integers for which $a^3 + b^3 = c^3$.) Nor,
theorized Fermat, for any higher power: for $n = 4$ or $n = 5$ and so on.

Then came the mischief. Fermat left the following marginal anno- 3
tation: "I have discovered a truly remarkable proof [of this theorem],
which this margin is too small to contain." And which for more than
three centuries the mind of man has been too dim to discern.

All these years mathematicians have given Fermat the benefit of 4
the doubt: the consensus was that the last theorem was probably true,
but that Fermat was mistaken in thinking or perverse in claiming that
he had proved it. Its legend grew as it defied 15 generations of the
world's greatest mathematical minds. It became the Holy Grail of
number theory. Then last month came news that a 38-year-old Japanese
assistant professor had found the solution. Between the banal and the
absurd that is the everyday, it seemed, something epic had happened.

Alas, it had not. Yoichi Miyaoka and his colleagues have been 5
checking, and found fundamental if subtle problems deep in his proof.
Miyaoka got a glimpse of the Grail, but no more. The disappointment
is keen—the 20th century stands unredeemed—but it is mixed with a
curious relief. "Next to a battle lost," wrote Wellington, "the greatest
misery is a battle gained." Easy for him to say. (He won.) Still, there is
wisdom in Wellington and comfort too. Solving Fermat would have

meant losing him. With Miyaoka's miss, Fermat—bemused, beguiling, daring posterity to best him—endures.

And mathematics gains. Miyaoka's assault on Fermat is a reminder, an enactment of the romance that is mathematics. Math has a bad name these days. In the popular mind, it has become either a syndrome (math anxiety is an affliction to be treated like fear of flying) or a mere skill. We think of a math whiz as someone who can do in his head what a calculator can do on silicon. But that is not math. That is accounting. Real math is not crunching numbers but contemplating them and the mystery of their connections. For Gauss, "higher arithmetic" was an "inexhaustible store of interesting truths" about the magical relationship between sovereign numbers. Real math is about whether Fermat was right.

Does it matter? It is the pride of political thought that ideas have consequences. Mathematics, to its glory, is ideas without consequences. "A mathematician," says Paul Erdös, one of its greatest living practitioners and one of the most eccentric, "is a machine for turning coffee into theorems." Mathematicians do not like to admit that, because when they do, their grant money dries up—it is hard to export theorems—and they are suspected of just playing around, which of course they are.

Politicians and journalists need to believe that everything ultimately has a use and an application. So when a solution for something like Fermat's last theorem is announced, one hears that the proof may have some benefit in the fields of, say, cryptography and computers. Mathematicians and their sympathizers, at a loss to justify their existence, will be heard to say, as a last resort, that doing mathematics is useful because "it sharpens the mind."

Sharpens the mind? For what? For figuring polling results or fathoming Fellini movies or fixing shuttle boosters? We have our means and ends reversed. What could be more important than divining the Absolute? "God made the integers," said a 19th century mathematician. "All the rest is the work of man." That work is mathematics, and that it should have to justify itself by its applications, as a tool for making the mundane or improving the ephemeral, is an affront not just to mathematics but to the creature that invented it.

What higher calling can there be than searching for useless and beautiful truths? Number theory is as beautiful and no more useless than mastery of the balance beam or the well-thrown forward pass. And our culture expends enormous sums on those exercises without asking what higher end they serve.

Moreover, of all such exercises, mathematics is the most sublime. It is the metaphysics of modern man. It operates very close to religion, which is why numerology is important to so many faiths and why a sense of the transcendent is so keenly developed in many mathematicians, even the most irreligious. Erdös, an agnostic, likes to speak of God's having a Book that contains the most elegant, most perfect mathematical proofs. Erdös' highest compliment, reports Paul Hoffman in the *Atlantic*, is that a proof is "straight from the Book." Says Erdös: "You don't have to believe in God, but you should believe in the Book."

In one of Borges' short stories, a celestial librarian spends his entire   12
life vainly searching for a similar volume, the divine "total book" that will explain the mystery of the universe. Then, realizing that such joy is destined not to be his, he expresses the touching hope that it may at least be someone else's: "I pray to the unknown Gods that a man—just one, even though it were thousands of years ago!—may have examined and read it. If honor and wisdom and happiness are not for me, let them be for others."

For a couple of days it seemed that honor and wisdom and   13
happiness were Miyaoka's. A mirage, it turns out. Yet someday Fermat's last theorem will be solved. You and I will not understand that perfect proof any more than we understand Miyaoka's version. Nonetheless, the thought that someone, somewhere, someday, will be allowed a look at Fermat's page in the Book is for me, for now, joy enough.

For Discussion and Writing

1. Krauthammer defines mathematics as "the metaphysics of modern man." What do you think he means? How would you describe his view of math?
2. How does Krauthammer justify his claim that mathematics need not have practical benefit to be important to mankind?
3. Do you agree that math is the enterprise of "searching for useless and beautiful truths"? If Krauthammer is correct, why is math so often seen as an essential part of one's education?
4. Write an essay in which you defend mathematics against those who see it as "useless." Can math be defined as useful in a way different from Krauthammer's? What are the many uses of math? As an alternate idea, write your own "Joy of . . ." essay about another of the sciences, such as biology, chemistry, physics, or computer science.

Science, Lies and The Ultimate Truth

Barbara Ehrenreich

If there is any specimen lower than a fornicating preacher, it must   1
be a shady scientist. The dissolute evangelist betrays his one revealed
Truth, but the scientist who rushes half-cocked into print or, worse yet,
falsifies the data subverts the whole idea of truth. Cold fusion in a
teacup? Or, as biologists (then at M.I.T.) David Baltimore and Thereza
Imanishi-Kari claimed in a controversial 1986 article that the National
Institutes of Health has now judged to be fraudulent, genes from one
mouse mysteriously "imitating" those from another? Sure, and parallel
lines might as well meet somewhere or apples leap back up onto trees.

Baltimore, the Nobel laureate and since 1990 president of Rocke-   2
feller University, has apologized, after a fashion, for his role in the
alleged fraud, and many feel that the matter should be left to rest. He
didn't, after all, falsify the data himself; he merely signed on as senior
scientist to Imanishi-Kari's now discredited findings. But when a young
postdoctoral fellow named Margot O'Toole tried to blow the whistle,
Baltimore pooh-poohed O'Toole's evidence and stood by while she lost
her job. Then, as the feds closed in, he launched a bold, misguided
defense of the sanctity of science.

What does one more lie matter anyway? Politicians "mispeak"   3
and are forgiven by their followers. Pop singers have been known to
dub in better voices. Literary deconstructionists say there's no truth
anyway, just ideologies and points of view. Lies, you might say, are the
great lubricant of our way of life. They sell products, flatter the powerful, appease the electorate and save vast sums from the IRS. Imanishi-
Kari's lie didn't even hurt anyone: no bridges fell, no patients died.

But science is different, and the difference does define a kind of   4
sanctity. Although we think of it as the most secular of human enterprises, there is a little-known spiritual side to science, with its own stern
ethical implications. Through research, we seek to know that ultimate
Other, which could be called Nature if the term didn't sound so tame
and beaten, or God if the word weren't loaded with so much human
hope and superstition. Think of it more neutrally as the nameless
Subject of so much that happens, like the It in "It is raining": something

298

"out there" and vastly different from ourselves, but not so alien that we cannot hope to know Its ways.

When I was a graduate student in biology—at Rockefeller, where Baltimore also earned his Ph.D.—I would have winced at all this metaphysics. The ethos of the acolyte was humility and patience. If the experiment didn't succeed, you did it again and then scratched your head and tried a new approach. There were mistakes, but mistakes could be corrected, which is why you reported exactly how you did things, step by step, so others could prove you right or wrong. There were even, sometimes, corners cut: a little rounding off, an anomalous finding overlooked.

But falsifying data lay outside our moral universe. The least you could do as a scientist was record exactly what you observed (in ink, in notebooks that never left the lab). The most you could do was arrange the experimental circumstances so as to entrap the elusive It and squeeze out some small confession: This is how the enzyme works, or the protein folds, or the gene makes known its message. But always, and no matter what, you let It do the talking. And when It spoke, which wasn't often, your reward, as one of my professors used to say, was "to wake up screaming in the night"—at the cunning of Its logic and the elegance of Its design.

This was the ideal, anyway. But Big Science costs big bucks and breeds a more mundane and calculating kind of outlook. It takes hundreds of thousands of dollars a year to run a modern biological laboratory, with its electron microscopes, ultracentrifuges, amino-acid analyzers, Ph.D.s and technicians. The big bucks tend to go to big shots, like Baltimore, whose machines and underlings must grind out "results" in massive volume. In the past two decades, as federal funding for basic research has ebbed, the pressure to produce has risen to dangerous levels. At the same time, the worldly rewards of success have expanded to included fat paychecks (from patents and sidelines in the biotech business) as well as power and celebrity status. And these are the circumstances that invite deception.

Imanishi-Kari succumbed, apparently, to the desire to make a name for herself and hence, no doubt, expand her capacity for honest research. But Baltimore is a more disturbing case. He already had the name, the resources and the power that younger scientists covet. What he forgot is that although humans may respect these things, the truth does not. What he lost sight of, in the smugness of success, is that truth is no respecter of hierarchy or fame. It can come out of the mouths of mere underlings, like the valiant O'Toole.

And if no one was physically hurt, still there was damage done. Scientists worldwide briefly believed the bogus "findings" and altered their views accordingly or wasted time trying to follow the false lead in their labs. Then there is the inevitable damage from the exposure of the lie: millions of people, reading of the scandal, must have felt their deepest cynicism confirmed. If a Nobel laureate in science could sink to the moral level of Milli Vanilli or a White House spin doctor, then maybe the deconstructionists are right and there is no truth anywhere, only self-interest masked as objective fact.

Baltimore should issue a fuller apology, accounting for his alleged   10
cover-up of the initial fraud. Then he should reflect for a week or two and consider stepping down from his position as president of Rockefeller University and de facto science statesman. Give him a modest lab to work in, maybe one in the old Rockefeller buildings where the microbe hunters toiled decades ago. I picture something with a river view, where it is impossible to forget that Manhattan is an island, that the earth is a planet, and that there is something out there much larger, and possibly even cleverer, than ourselves.

For Discussion and Writing

1. How is science different than other aspects of society, where, Ehrenreich claims, lies are "the great lubricant of our way of life"?
2. What is Big Science, and how has its influence helped to produce "circumstances that invite deception"?
3. What does Ehrenreich say are the consequences of dishonesty in science?
4. Ehrenreich refers to an It throughout her essay. What is It? What has it to do with her condemnation of scientific deception? Write an essay in which you consider science's relation to God or Nature (or invent your own term for "that ultimate Other"). Are there limits on what science can or should know?

Thinking and Writing about Chapter 21

1. Krauthammer implies that math can know ultimate truths about reality. What might Ehrenreich say to that idea? Do these two authors share any views about math and science?
2. Trippett recommends a close partnership between the scientific community and the larger society. Do you think such a partnership exists? Is Ehrenreich's Big Science (science working with government on expensive research projects) the answer?
3. What is your view of math and science? Write an essay in which you present your own sense of these sometimes difficult and challenging ways of thought. What can the sciences give us that no other disciplines can? What are their unique virtues? Where is science study most difficult, and why do you think that is? Has science provided you with moments of joy or pleasure?

22

Technology and the Future

If there is one defining aspect of modern life, it must be that we are surrounded by, and sometimes overwhelmed by, our inventions. Since the first attempts at tool-making in the primordial past, human beings have displayed a boundless capacity to create ever-more complex and specific technology—extensions of the human body, the human mind. For the most part, technology has developed to meet the needs of everyday life: transportation vehicles, power generation, weaponry, storage and refrigeration, time keeping, measurement, roads and bridges, housing and commercial architecture, communication, sight, entertainment, medical care.

But technology also seems to have its own imperative, an energy to keep going into an unknown and unseen future: space travel, artificial intelligence, miracle cures, life extension, nuclear waste, radiation-induced diseases, more garbage than we know what to do with. Where will technology take us? What new wonders or disappointments will it produce? Stay tuned.

The essays in this chapter consider several of the many fascinations of technology. In "The Futurists: Looking Toward A.D. 2000," from February 1966, an anonymous writer peers into what was then the technological distance, coming surprisingly close to the mark at times. In "The Mind in the Machine," from May 1982, Roger Rosenblatt speculates philosophically on the question of artificial intelligence. And in "Hoy! Hoy! Mushi-Mushi! Allo!," from January 1990, Lance Morrow writes a light-hearted meditation of the meanings of the telephone.

The Futurists:
Looking Toward A.D. 2000

The U.S. has always been a country in love with the future. 1
Americans have never quite shared the traditional notion that prying
into tomorrow is suspect if not downright dangerous—the sort of
feeling that made Dante consign soothsayers to the fourth chasm of the
Inferno. On the contrary, the U.S. readily accepted the fact that modern
science established progress as a faith and the future as an earthly Eden.
Yet recently, the American passion for the future has taken a new turn.
Leaving utopians and science-fiction writers far behind, a growing
number of professionals have made prophecy a serious and highly
organized enterprise.

They were forced into it by the fact that technology has advanced 2
more rapidly in the past 50 years than in the previous 5,000. Men in
business, government, education and science itself realize that they
must look at least two decades ahead just to keep abreast, must learn
to survive under totally different conditions. The new futurists, as they
sometimes call themselves, are well aware of past failures of vision.
Soon after World War II, top U.S. scientists dismissed and derided the
notion of an accurate intercontinental ballistic missile, and as late as
1956, Britain's Astronomer Royal called the prospect of space travel
"utter bilge." Relying on the atom's almost limitless energy, the
computer's almost limitless "intellect," the futurists predict an era of
almost limitless change. With remarkable confidence, and in considerable detail, they present a view of man not only in total control of his
environment but of his own brain and his own evolution.

New Skill & Time

The exploration of the future has become a sizable business. 3
General Electric has set up Tempo (Technical Management Planning
Organization) in Santa Barbara, where 200 physical scientists, sociologists, economists and engineers contemplate the future on a budget that
tops $7,000,000 a year. The armed forces have long been in the future
business. The Air Force, at Wright-Patterson A.F.B., conducts studies of
the whole problem of scientific prediction, also contributes $15 million
a year to Santa Monica's Rand Corp. to think—and not necessarily

about weapons systems. The nonprofit Hudson Institute investigates the possibilities of war and peace along with the future in general. At the University of Illinois, Dr. Charles Osgood is conducting a "computerized exploration of the year 2000," and the Southern Illinois University is providing money and facilities for Buckminster Fuller's World Resources Inventory. The American Academy of Arts and Sciences helps to support the Commission on the Year 2000, headed by Columbia Sociologist Daniel Bell. The Ford Foundation has allocated $1,400,000 this year to a group called Resources for the Future, also supports a Paris-based organization, headed by Veteran Futurist Bertrand de Jouvenel, whose studies are known as "Les Futuribles."

Forecasting is an art that still has few textbooks. Its basic tool is   4
extrapolation from yesterday and today. As John McHale, executive director of World Resources Inventory, puts it: "The future of the future is in the present." Some other methods seem fairly arcane. Defense Expert Herman Kahn, for instance, uses "scenario writing," in which various alternative future situations are dramatized. Some forecasters use computers to produce a symbolic "model" of particular social or economic structures—including whole industries or nations—and then simulate the interaction of variables. Rand uses the "Delphi" method, in which a wide range of experts are queried and re-queried for their forecasts, arriving finally at a near-consensus. Prognosticators concede that the timing and nature of pure inventions or basic breakthroughs— such as the achievement of atomic fission—are not predictable. In many cases, they must still rely on "imaginings."

In the recent flood of forecasts, what are the futurists saying? By   5
no means are all their predictions new, but taken together, they present a remarkable vision. Most convenient benchmark for that vision is the year 2000, a rounded and romantic date that is nearer than is generally realized—only 34 years away, it is nearly as close as the election of Franklin D. Roosevelt.

People & Weather

By A.D. 2000, the U.S. population will have risen to about 330   6
million, and nine out of ten Americans will be living in supercities or their suburbs. But cities, like industry, will tend to decentralize; with instant communications, it will no longer be necessary for business enterprises to cluster together. Futurist Marshall McLuhan even foresees the possibility that many people will stay at home, doing their work via countrywide telecommunication.

None of the forecasters seem to have any good solution for the   7
traffic problem, though they count on automated, and possibly underground, highways. McLuhan and others predict that both the wheel

and the highway will be obsolete, giving way to hovercraft that ride on air. Planes carrying 1,000 passengers and flying just under the speed of sound will of course be old hat. The new thing will be transport by ballistic rocket, capable of reaching any place on earth in 40 minutes. In Rand's Delphi study, 82 scientists agreed that a permanent lunar base will have been established long before A.D. 2000 and that men will have flown past Venus and landed on Mars.

That closer inner space, the ocean, will be even more radically 8
transformed. Rand experts visualize fish herded and raised in offshore pens as cattle are today. Huge fields of kelp and other kinds of seaweed will be tended by undersea "farmers"—frogmen who will live for months at a time in submerged bunkhouses. The protein-rich underseas crop will probably be ground up to produce a dull-tasting cereal that eventually, however, could be regenerated chemically to taste like anything from steak to bourbon. This will provide at least a partial answer to the doom-sayers who worry about the prospect of starvation for a burgeoning world population. Actually, the problem could be manageable before any frogman wets a foot; Oxford Agronomist Colin Clark calculates that if all the presently arable land were farmed as the Dutch do it, it could support a population of 28 billion. Even the gloomiest forecasts assume a world population of not more than twice the present size, or 6 billion by the year 2000.

One of the more dramatic changes will be climate control. Tempo 9
scientists estimate that the entire electrical energy needs of the U.S. could be supplied by a dozen nuclear generating stations spotted around the country, each with a capacity on the order of 60,000 mega-watts (*v.* 1,974 megawatts for Grand Coulee). If one such station were built on Mount Wilson above Los Angeles, the heat produced as a byproduct could be guided into the atmosphere, raising the inversion layer that hangs over Los Angeles to 19,000 feet, thus ridding the city of smog. A sea breeze could be drawn into the space beneath, bringing rain that would transform the high desert between Los Angeles and Las Vegas into a flowering land.

Medicine is in a similar state of exhilarated anticipation. Already 10
widely discussed today, artificial organs—hearts, lungs, stomachs—will be commonly available by the year 2000. An expected development in immunology will make possible the widespread transplanting of organs from either live donors or the recently dead.

The blind and the deaf will have new sight and new hearing. A 11
pocket radar will scan a blind man's surroundings, relay the informa-tion either through sounds or through vibrations. A comparable device will let the deaf "hear." Artificial arms and legs could be motorized and computerized, perhaps linked to the brain, so that the wearer will find his impulse translated into action. Medical men foresee fetuses grown

outside the uterus (in case women want to be spared the burdens of pregnancy) and human tissues grown to specifications. The Cleveland Clinic's Dr. Willem J. Kolff prophesies "artificial skin with all the appendages built in, such as ears and nose." How they would look is a cosmetic problem that the doctors dismiss with a shrug.

Nearly all experts agree that bacterial and viral diseases will have   12
been virtually wiped out. Probably arteriosclerotic heart disease will also have been eliminated. Cells have only a few secrets still hidden from probers, who are confident that before the year 2000 they will have found the secret that causes cancer. The most exciting, and to some the most frightening, prospect is the chemical and electrical treatment of the brain. Dr. David Krech, psychology professor at the University of California, believes that retarded infants will be diagnosed at birth, and chemical therapy will permit them to function as normal people. The memory loss accompanying senility will be eliminated.

In general, drug control of personality will be widely accepted   13
well before the year 2000. If a wife or husband seems to be unusually grouchy on a given evening, says Rand's Olaf Helmer, a spouse will be able to pop down to the corner drugstore, buy some anti-grouch pills, and slip them into the coffee. Or a lackadaisical person could be dosed into a sense of ambition. Electrical stimulus of brain areas has been shown to produce responses of fear, affection, laughter or sex arousal; such techniques, says Yale's Dr. José Delgado, "will certainly increase man's ability to influence the behavior of man." By the year 2000, a symbiotic link between the brain and a computer-memory may also be in the experimental stage.

An even more momentous prospect is offered by DNA, the compli-   14
cated molecule that contains the elements of heredity. Biologists think that before the century is out, they will have succeeded in changing the "information" contained in DNA. If so, it will become possible eventually to control the shape—or color—of men to come. Genetic "intervention" could improve learning capacity. Hudson Hoaglund, executive director of the Worcester Foundation for Experimental Biology, believes that thus "man will become the only animal that can direct his own evolution."

Some futurists are less sanguine; they worry not only about the   15
social problem of who would supervise this man-made evolution, but also about unforeseen side effects, such as genetic mutations. Medical optimism is also limited by the notion that there may be an increase of accidents and the general wear and tear of urbanization. Great population density will create the "encounter problem," the fact that the effect of any event, from an accident to a riot, may be multiplied beyond control when masses of people are involved. Even the most optimistic

experts see no real sign that they can learn enough about the process of aging to dramatically prolong life beyond 70 to 80 years average.

Food & Work

Some futurists like to make predictions about homey details of living. The kitchen, of course, will be automated. An A.D. 2000 housewife may well make out her menu for the week, put the necessary food into the proper storage spaces, and feed her program to a small computer. The experts at Stanford Research Institute visualize mechanical arms getting out the preselected food, cooking and serving it. Similarly programmed household robots would wash dishes, dispose of the garbage (onto a conveyer belt moving under the street), vacuum rugs, wash windows, cut the grass. Edward Fredkin, founder of Cambridge's Information International Inc., has already developed a computer-cum-mechanical-arm that can "see" a ball thrown its way and catch it. Soon, Fredkin expects his gadget to be able to play a mean game of pingpong.   16

As for shopping, the housewife should be able to switch on to the local supermarket on the video phone, examine grapefruit and price them, all without stirring from her living room. But among the futurists, fortunately, are skeptics, and they are sure that remote shopping, while entirely feasible, will flop—because women like to get out of the house, like to handle the merchandise, like to be able to change their minds. Not everything that is possible will happen—unless people want it. One thing they almost certainly will want is electronic "information retrieval": the contents of libraries and other forms of information or education will be stored in a computer and will be instantly obtainable at home by dialing a code.   17

In automated industry, not only manual workers, but also secretaries and most middle-level managers will have been replaced by computers. The remaining executives will be responsible for major decisions and long-range policy. Thus, society will seem idle, by present standards. According to one estimate, only 10% of the population will be working, and the rest will, in effect, have to be paid to be idle. This is not as radical a notion as it sounds. Even today, only 40% of the population works, not counting the labor performed by housewives or students. Already, says Tempo's John Fisher, "we are rationing work. By 1984, man will spend the first third of his life, or 25 years, getting an education, only the second one-third working, and the final third enjoying the fruits of his labor. There just won't be enough work to go around. Moonlighting will become as socially unacceptable as bigamy."   18

By 2000, the machines will be producing so much that everyone in the U.S. will, in effect, be independently wealthy. With Government   19 benefits, even nonworking families will have, by one estimate, an annual income of \$30,000–\$40,000 (in 1966 dollars). How to use leisure meaningfully will be a major problem, and Herman Kahn foresees a pleasure-oriented society full of "wholesome degeneracy."

There are some who gloomily expect a society run by a small 20 elected elite, presiding over a mindless multitude kept happy by drugs and circuses, much as in Huxley's *Brave New World*. But most futurists believe that work will still be the only way to gain responsibility and power.

Fear & Bliss

Social and political changes are far harder to forecast than techno- 21 logical ones. Futurists are earnestly considering all kinds of worries: the possible failure of underdeveloped countries to catch up with the dazzling future, the threat of war, the prospect of supergovernment. Today's "New Left" predicts the need for political movements to break up big organization. But the skeptics are plainly in the minority. Some futurists, like Buckminster Fuller, believe that amid general plenty, politics will simply fade away. Others predict that an increasingly homogenized world culture—it has been called "the culture bomb"— will increase international amity, although Rand's experts rate the probability of major war before the end of the century at 20%.

Certain prophets are in a positively millennial mood. Harvard's 22 Emmanuel Mesthene, executive director of a ten-year, \$5,000,000 program on Technology and Society commissioned by IBM, believes that for the first time since the golden age of Greece, Western man "has regained his nerve" and has come to believe, rightly, that he can accomplish anything. "My hunch," says Mesthene, "is that man may have finally expiated his original sin, and might now aspire to bliss."

This may be a rather naive form of *hubris*. But even the more 23 cautious futurists are caught up in a renewed sense of human freedom. "The function of prediction," says Columbia's Daniel Bell, "is not, as often stated, to aid social control, but to widen the spheres of moral choice." And Bertrand de Jouvenel has suggested that various types of future should be portrayed on TV, allowing the public to vote in a referendum on "the future of your choice." The chief message of the futurists is that man is not trapped in an absurd fate but that he can and must choose his destiny—a technological reassertion of free will.

For Discussion and Writing

1. What is the general prediction futurists made in the mid-1960s? How accurate has it turned out to be?

2. List the specific predictions this author attributes to the futurists. Which ones are accurate, or look as though they might be in our own future? Which ones have not come true, or are unlikely to?
3. Why do you think certain predictions of life in the year 2000 seem far-fetched even now, in the 1990s? What kinds of obstacles lie in the way of technological progress?
4. Write an essay in which you predict the future uses of technology, based on your current knowledge—or speculate about needed or unneeded future inventions or innovations. In which current directions is technology taking us? Where is it likely to produce benefit, or blight?

The Mind in the Machine

Roger Rosenblatt

The factory robot that crushed a man to death in Japan last year   1
did little to silence the talk that machines are a threat to human preeminence. That talk has been alive ever since people first discovered
that they could manufacture tools vastly superior to themselves; in
Samuel Butler's satire *Erewhon* (1872), the citizens establish a museum
of old machines in which they at once deposit and abandon their
mechanical inventions, which they believed would swallow up their
souls. When machines possess artificial intelligence, like computers, the
human fear of being overtaken seems both more urgent and more
complex. Science-fiction writers from Capek to Asimov have built
much of their genre around robots, androids, computers and their
kin—each fairly boring and predictable as characters, but all presenting
the same basic paradox: that they will eventually take command of the
world, and that a man can beat them every time.

This proposition is not as contradictory as it sounds, since, for one   2
thing, the fact that it takes real (*i.e.*, natural) intelligence to create the
artificial kind would seem to give humanity a perpetual edge; and, for
another, people are able to hold contraries in their heads simultaneously—a feat that is reassuring in itself, since it is one of the things
that distinguishes men from machines. Indeed, man tends to search out
such distinctions even as he endows his machines with increasing
sophistication, as if to make sure that his evolution is no slower than
that of his creations. Still, it is sometimes nerve-racking to read what
these boxes can do. Joseph Weizenbaum, of M.I.T., who has recently
come to criticize computer education for children as a context for "toy
problems," nonetheless got more than a toy gasp out of the public in
1968 when he unveiled his project ELIZA—an IBM 7094 programmed
by Weizenbaum to "practice" psychotherapy—and then published a
"conversation" between ELIZA and a real patient:

PATIENT: You are like my father in some ways.   3
ELIZA: What resemblance do you see?   4
PATIENT: You are not very aggressive, but I think you don't want   5
me to notice that.

310

ELIZA: What makes you think I am not very aggressive? 6
PATIENT: You don't argue with me. 7
ELIZA: Why do you think I don't argue with you? 8
PATIENT: You are afraid of me. 9
ELIZA: Does it please you to believe I am afraid of you? 10

The elements of parody notwithstanding, it is no joke to see a 11
machine become a man, especially in an era whose main (if somewhat
pro forma) worry centers on men becoming machines.

A great deal of intellectual effort is therefore spent these days— 12
mostly by the computer scientists themselves—trying to reassure everybody that, as smart as a machine can get, it can never be as intelligent
as its progenitor. In part, this effort is made in order to see that the
wizened, noncomputer generation—which often regards the younger
with the unbridled enthusiasm that the Chinese showed the Mongol
hordes—feels that it has a safe and legitimate place in modernity. In
part, the effort is made because the proposition is true: a computer
cannot possess the full range of human intelligence. Yet, in terms of
reconciling man and machine, this effort still misses the point. The
cultural value of computers does not lie in perceiving what they cannot
do, but what they can, and what, in turn, their capabilities show about
our own. In other words, a computer may not display the whole of
human intelligence, but that portion it can display could do a lot more
good for man's self-confidence than continuing reassurances that he is
in no immediate danger of death by robot.

Essentially, what one wants to know in sorting out this relation- 13
ship is the answers to two questions: Can computers think (a technical
problem)? And, should they think (a moral one)? In order to get at both,
it is first necessary to agree on what thinking itself is—what thought
means—and that is no quick step. Every period in history has had to
deal with at least two main definitions of thought, which mirror the
prevailing philosophies of that particular time and are usually in opposition. Moreover, these contending schools change from age to age. On
a philosophical level, thought cannot know itself because it cannot step
outside itself. Nor is it an activity that can be understood by what it
produces (art, science, dreams). To Freud the mind was a house; to Plato
a cave. These are fascinating, workable metaphors, but the fact is that
in each case an analogy had to be substituted for an equation.

At the same time, certain aspects of thinking can be identified 14
without encompassing the entire process. The ability to comprehend,
to conceptualize, to organize and reorganize, to manipulate, to adjust—
these are all parts of thought. So are the acts of pondering, rationalizing,
worrying, brooding, theorizing, contemplating, criticizing. One thinks
when one imagines, hopes, loves, doubts, fantasizes, vacillates, regrets.

To experience greed, pride, joy, spite, amusement, shame, suspicion, envy, grief—all these require thought; as do the decisions to take command, or umbrage; to feel loyalty or inhibitions; to ponder ethics, self-sacrifice, cowardice, ambition. So vast is the mind's business that even as one makes such a list, its inadequacy is self-evident—the recognition of inadequacy being but another part of an enormous and varied instrument.

The answer to the first question, then—Can a machine think?—is   15
yes and no. A computer can certainly do some of the above. It can (or will soon be able to) transmit and receive messages, "read" typescript, recognize voices, shapes and patterns, retain facts, send reminders, "talk" or mimic speech, adjust, correct, strategize, make decisions, translate languages. And, of course, it can calculate, that being its specialty. Yet there are hundreds of kinds of thinking that computers cannot come close to. And for those merely intent on regarding the relationship of man to machine as a head-to-artificial-head competition, this fact offers some solace—if not much progress.

For example, the Apollo moon shot in July 1969 relied on comput-   16
ers at practically every stage of the operation. Before taking off, the astronauts used computerized simulations of the flight. The spacecraft was guided by a computer, which stored information about the gravitational fields of the sun and moon, and calculated the craft's position, speed and altitude. This computer, which determined the engines to be fired, and when, and for how long, took part of its own information from another computer on the ground. As the Apollo neared the moon, a computer triggered the firing of a descent rocket, slowed the lunar module, and then signaled Neil Armstrong that he had five seconds to decide whether or not to go ahead with the landing. At 7,200 ft., a computer commanded the jets to tilt the craft almost upright so that Armstrong and Aldrin could take a close look at what the world had been seeking for centuries.

Would one say, then, that computers got men to the moon? Of   17
course not. A machine is merely a means. What got man to the moon was his desire to go there—desire being yet another of those elements that a computer cannot simulate or experience. It was far less interesting, for instance, that Archimedes believed he could move the earth with his lever than that he wanted to try it. Similarly, no machine could have propelled man to the moon had not the moon been in man in the first place.

Thus the second question—Should a machine think?—answers   18
itself. The question is not in fact the moral problem it at first appears, but purely a practical one. Yes, a machine should think as much as it can, because it can only think in limited terms. Hubert Dreyfus, a

philosophy professor at Berkeley, observes that "all aspects of human thought, including nonformal aspects like moods, sensory-motor skills and long-range self-interpretations, are so interrelated that one cannot substitute an abstractable web of explicit beliefs for the whole cloth of our concrete everyday practice." Marianne Moore saw the web her own way: "The mind is an enchanting thing,/ is an enchanted thing/ like the glaze on a/ katydid-wing/ subdivided by sun/ till the nettings are legion,/ Like Giesaking playing Scarlatti." In short, human intelligence is too intricate to be replicated. When a computer can smile at an enemy, cheat at cards and pray in church all in the same day, then, perhaps, man will know his like. Until then, no machine can touch us.

For the sake of argument, however, what if Dreyfus, Moore and common sense were all wrong? What if the mind with its legion nettings could in fact be replicated in steel and plastic, and all human befuddlements find their way onto a program—would the battle be lost? Hardly. The moon is always in the man. Even if it were possible to reduce people to box size and have them plonked down before themselves in all their powers, they would still want more. Whatever its source, there is a desire that outdesires desire; otherwise computers would not have come into being. As fast as the mind travels, it somehow manages to travel faster than itself, and people always know, or sense, what they do not know. No machine does that. A computer can *achieve* what it does not know (not knowing that $2 + 2 = 4$, it can find out), but it cannot yearn for the answer or even dimly suspect its existence. If people knew where such suspicions and yearnings came from, they might be able to lock them in silicon. But they do not know what they are; they merely know that they are—just as in the long run they only know that they exist, not what their existence is or what it means. The difference between us and any machine we create is that a machine is an answer, and we are a question.

But is there anything really startling in this? With all the shouting and sweating that go on about machines taking over the world, does anyone but a handful of zealots and hysterics seriously believe that the human mind is genuinely imperiled by devices of its own manufacture? In *Gödel, Escher, Bach* (1979), Douglas R. Hofstadter's dazzling book on minds and machines, a man is described—one Johann Martin Zacharias Dase (1824–61)—who was employed by governments because he could do mathematical feats like multiplying two 100-digit numbers in his head, and could calculate at a glance how many sheep were in a field, for example, or how many words in a sentence, up to about 30. (Most people can do this up to about six.) Were Mr. Dase living today, would he be thought a computer? Are computers thought of as men? This is a kind of cultural game people play, a false alarm, a ghost story recited to put one's mind at rest.

The trouble is that "at rest" is a poor place to be in this situation,   21
because such a position encourages no understanding of what these
machines can do for life beyond the tricks they perform. Alfred North
Whitehead said that "civilization advances by extending the number of
important operations which we can perform without thinking about
them." In that sense, computers have advanced civilization. But thinking about the computer, as a cultural event or instrument, has so far not
advanced civilization one whit. Instead, one hears humanists either
fretting about the probability that before the end of the century computers will be able to beat all the world's chess masters, or consoling
themselves that a computer cannot be Mozart—the response to the first
being, "So what?" and to the second, "Who ever thought so?" The thing
to recognize about the computer is not how powerful it is or will
become, but that its power is finite. So is that of the mind. The finitudes
in both cases are not the same, but the fact that they are comparable may
be the most useful news that man's self-evaluation has received in 200
years.

For too long now, generations have been bedeviled with the idea,   22
formally called romanticism, that human knowledge has no limits, that
man can become either God or Satan, depending on his inclinations.
The rider to this proposition is that some human minds are more
limitless than others, and wherever that notion finds its most eager
receptacles, one starts out with Byron and winds up in Dachau. To be
fair, that is not all of romanticism, but it is the worst of it, and the worst
has done the world a good deal of damage. For the 18th century, man
was man-size. For the 19th and 20th, his size has been boundless, which
has meant that he has had little sense of his own proportion in relation
to everything else—resulting either in exaggerated self-pity or in self-
exaltation—and practically no stable appreciation of his own worth.

Now, suddenly, comes a machine that says in effect: This is the   23
size of man insofar as that size may be measured by this machine. It is
not the whole size of man, but it is a definable percentage. Other
machines show you how fast you can move and how much you can lift.
This one shows you how well you can think, in certain areas. It will do
as much as you would have it do, so it will demonstrate the extent of
your capabilities. But since it can only go as far as you wish it to go, it
will also demonstrate the strength of your volition.

Both these functions are statements of limitation. A machine that   24
tells you how much you can know likewise implies how much you
cannot. To learn what one can know is important, but to learn what one
cannot know is essential to one's well-being. This offers a sense of
proportion, and so is thoroughly antiromantic. Yet it is not cold 18th
century rationalistic either. The computer simply provides a way of

drawing a line between the knowable and the unknowable, between the moon and the moon in man, and it is on that line where people may be able to see their actual size.

Whether the world will look any better for such self-recognition 25 is anybody's guess. The mind, being an enchanted thing, has surprised itself too often to suggest that any discovery about itself will improve economies or governments, much less human nature. On face value, however, the cultural effects of these machines are promising. Every so often in history man makes what he needs. In one sense he made the computer because he needed to think faster. In another, he may have needed to define himself more clearly; he may have sensed a need for intellectual humility. If he needed intellectual humility at this particular time, it may be a sign that he was about to get out of hand again, and so these contraptions, of which he pretends to be so fearful, may in fact be his self-concocted saving grace. The mind is both crafty and mysterious enough to work that way.

For Discussion and Writing

1. According to Rosenblatt, what is the cultural value of computers? Why does the claim that "a computer cannot possess the full range of human intelligence" miss the point in terms of reconciling man and his machines?
2. What are the two questions Rosenblatt places at the heart of his essay, and what is his answer to each? How does his definition of thinking play a role in his responses?
3. What useful or educational effect may computers have on humankind's conception of itself and its capabilities?
4. Rosenblatt's essay reassures us that future computer intelligence should not be a cause for worry. Write an essay attacking or defending his general proposition. In what ways may the computerization of life lead to less delightful results? What, if anything, worries you about computer technology, artificial intelligence, or the uses to which computers can be put?

Hoy! Hoy! Mushi-Mushi! Allo!

LANCE MORROW

When Mel Brooks' 2,000-Year-Old Man was asked to name the 1
greatest invention in the history of the world, he answered without
hesitation: "Saran Wrap." A nice try, but wrong. The greatest invention
in the history of the world was—is—the telephone.

The telephone is a commonplace item on a much-wired planet. 2
The idea of being able to throw your voice around the world and in a
few seconds hit precisely the ear you wanted among all the globe's 10
billion ears has lost its capacity to surprise. But the telephone has
strange powers. The sudden little Ice Age that descended upon AT&T
last week may have given some Americans, in an almost subliminal
way, a dose of the metaphysical spooks.

One hundred fourteen years ago, Bell's instrument began the 3
electronization of the earth. The telephone system has amounted to the
first step toward global mental telepathy. The telephone and its elaborations (computer modems, fax machines and so on) have endowed the
planet with another dimension altogether: a dissolution of distance, a
warping of time, a fusion of the micro (individual mind) and macro (the
world). Charles de Gaulle declined to have a telephone, undoubtedly
because he had already fused micro and macro—*Le monde, c'est moi.*

With the telephone, reality began to dematerialize and go magic, 4
disintegrating here to recombine over there. Information began riding
around the world on electricity. The abrupt disconnection of such a
familiar yet mysterious faculty, the telephone, must be profoundly
unsettling—like a glimpse of a dead world, a premonition of absolute
cold.

The telephone is one of those miracles one can discuss in terms 5
either sacred or profane. (The same is true of babies.) The phone is of
course a mere home appliance and business tool, and by the standards
of the 21st century, a primitive one. To bring electronic mysticism to the
telephone may seem something like illustrating the wonders of flight
by discussing pigeons.

If you think of the telephone purely as a secular voice thrower, it 6
arrives in the mind at its most irritating. For example, no one has yet
devised a pleasant way for a telephone to come to life. The ring is a

sudden intrusion, a drill in the ear. Pavlov's dog hears and picks the damned thing up. The Satanic bleats from some new phones are the equivalent of sound lasers. *Don't hurt me again,* says the dog. *I'll talk.* Perhaps the phone that looks like a duck decoy and quacks instead of ring will breed new species—phones that bark or baaa or moo or, maybe, sound like distant summer thunder.

But the ring cannot be subtle. Its mission is disruption. The phone   7 is the instrument we were issued for a march into the age of discontinuity. The telephone call is a breaking-and-entering that we invite by having telephones in the first place. Someone unbidden barges in and for an instant or an hour usurps the ears and upsets the mind's prior arrangements. Life proceeds in particles, not waves. The author Cyril Connolly wrote lugubriously about the sheer intimacy of intrusion that a telephone can manage. "Complete physical union between two people is the rarest sensation which life can provide—and yet not quite real, for it stops when the telephone rings."

Something about telephones is obscurely comic, related to some   8 manic vaudeville. In your fist you clutch to the ear an object that looks ignominiously like the shining plastic cousin of a shoe. Designers have produced more streamlined models, but an essential ungainliness is inescapable. It results partly from the pressing of technology against anatomy. The technosmooth circuitry is pushed bizarrely against the old Darwinian skull. The talker's being comes unfocused from the visual immediate room and refocuses—through the ear!—elsewhere. The Here communes with There through sudden activations of breath, vocal cords, jawbone, tongue, lips, eyes, emotions. Through the thing held to the ear, we hear voices from another world. We would be amazed by this spectacle if we were not so used to it.

In 1886 a poet named Benjamin Franklin Taylor caught both the   9 metaphysics and unintentionally, the comedy when he wrote this rhapsody to the phone: "The far is near. Our feeblest whispers fly/ Where cannon falter, thunders faint and die./ Your little song the telephone can float/ As free of fetters as a bluebird's note."

Alexander Graham Bell thought the telephone should properly be   10 answered by saying, "Hoy! Hoy!"—an odd term from the Middle English that became the sailor's "ahoy!" and reflected Bell's sense that those speaking on early telephones were meeting like ships on a lonely and vast electronic sea. The world has now grown electronically dense, densest of all perhaps among the Japanese, who answer the phone with a crowded, tender, almost cuddling, quick-whispered *mushi-mushi.* The Russians say *slushaiyu* (I'm listening). The hipper Russians say *allo.* Italians say *pronto* (ready). The Chinese say *wei, wei* (with a pause between the words, unlike the Japanese *mushi-mushi*). *Wei, wei* is meaningless, except as a formula to answer the phone.

Why is the telephone the greatest invention in the history of the   11
world? Forget its existential oppressions (the disruptions, the discontinuities of mind, or, if you want to look for trouble, the horrifying
thought of the sheer obliterating noise that would be made if all the
telephone conversations of the earth at a given moment were audible
at once). All of that is nattering. The telephone, with the fluidities of
information that it has enabled, has proved to be a promiscuously,
irrepressibly democratic force, a kinetic object with the mysterious
purity to change the world. The telephone, like the authority to kill,
might have been legally restricted to kings and dictators. But it is in a
way the ideal instrument of freedom—inclusive, unjudging, versatile,
electronic but old-fashioned (here so long no one really fears it). The
telephone, like democracy, is infinitely tolerant of stupidity; it is a
virtual medium of stupidity, a four-lane highway of the greedy and false
and brainless. But it is (unless tampered with) a faithful channel of
words from mouth to distant ear, mind to mind, and that is, absolutely
and exactly, the meaning of freedom.

For Discussion and Writing

1. What effects does Morrow say the telephone has had upon life?
2. Morrow defines what he sees as essential characteristics of the telephone as a modern invention. What are some of these?
3. According to Morrow, why is the telephone the greatest invention in the
   world? Are there serious reasons to agree?
4. Write your own philosophical speculation about the nature of the
   telephone—or another piece of contemporary technology, such as the
   Walkman, the TV remote control device, the VCR, the personal computer, and so on—looking at its essential features, its impact on people
   and behavior, its meaning.

Thinking and Writing about Chapter 22

1. Compare and contrast these authors' views of technology. Which of them seems most unquestioning in his or her support?
2. To what extent do you think technological development still is viewed as the cure for our ills? Is there a kind of religious worship of technological innovation? What might be some examples of such adoration? What kinds of problems can technology not solve? Do those issues receive as much attention as do the technological ones?
3. What is the place of technology in human life? Is it a source of endless progress and betterment? Is it a mixed blessing? A blight on a more natural and less manic or destructive way of life? Write an essay expressing your honest feeling about technology's virtues or faults, the emphasis it receives, the way it either dominates, or serves, the human race.

23

Nature and the Environment

The first Earth Day was in spring 1970, a generation ago, and clearly the environmental movement, and the public's overall awareness of environmental issues, has grown much since then. But has it made a difference? Statistics show that it has. Air pollution in our major cities, while not eliminated, is down from earlier levels. Many of the nation's lakes and waterways have been saved, protected, even resurrected from the dead. Environmental legislation at federal, state and local levels puts obstacles in the path of those who would treat the earth as a garbage can.

But the battle is far from over. The vital ozone layer in our atmosphere is in worse condition than formerly thought. The oceans are getting dirtier by the day. Groundwater pollution from toxic chemicals has become a threat to millions of households across the country. Chemical and nuclear waste continue to plague efforts at their disposal, and landfill sites are filling up and dwindling. Industry continues to produce products—disposable diapers, plastic bottles, packaging materials, and thousands of other items—that will never be anything but unusable junk. The earth's forests are disappearing. Man-made catastrophic events—such as massive oil spills and fires—occur with dispiriting regularity. And the greenhouse effect, the warming of the earth due to heat-blocking air pollution in the upper atmosphere, continues unabated.

The essays in this chapter give us a glimpse at one of the world's most complex and persistent problems. In "The Age of Effluence," from May 1968, an anonymous writer outlines the ecological crises that began today's environmental movement. In "Forest of Dreams," from

February 1990, Lance Morrow praises a Bush Administration proposal to create a Earth Corps, an organized forestry and conservation enterprise. And in "Down with the God Squad," from November 1990, Ted Gup argues against those (also serving under president Bush) who are trying to limit the Endangered Species Act.

The Age of Effluence

What ever happened to America the Beautiful? While quite a bit 1
of it is still visible, the recurring question reflects rising and spreading
frustration over the nation's increasingly dirty air, filthy streets and
malodorous rivers—the relentless degradations of a once virgin continent. This man-made pollution is bad enough in itself, but it reflects
something even worse: a dangerous illusion that technological man can
build bigger and bigger industrial societies with little regard for the iron
laws of nature.

The problem is much bigger than the U.S. The whole industrial- 2
ized world is getting polluted, and emerging nations are unlikely to
slow their own development in the interest of clearer air and cleaner
water. The fantastic effluence of affluence is overwhelming natural
decay—the vital process that balances life in the natural world. All
living things produce toxic wastes, including their own corpses. But
whereas nature efficiently decays—and thus reuses—the wastes of
other creatures, man alone produces huge quantities of synthetic materials that almost totally resist natural decay. And more and more such
waste is poisonous to man's fellow creatures, to say nothing of himself.

Man has tended to ignore the fact that he is utterly dependent on 3
the biosphere: a vast web of interacting processes and organisms that
form the rhythmic cycles and food chains in which one part of the living
environment feeds on another. The biosphere is no immutable feature
of the earth. Roughly 400 million years ago, terrestrial life consisted of
some primitive organisms that consumed oxygen as fast as green plants
manufactured it. Only by some primeval accident were the greedy
organisms buried in sedimentary rock (as the source of crude oil, for
example), thus permitting the atmosphere to become enriched to a
life-sustaining mix of 20% oxygen, plus nitrogen, argon, carbon dioxide
and water vapor. With miraculous precision, the mix was then maintained by plants, animals and bacteria, which used and returned the
gases at equal rates. About 70% of the earth's oxygen is thus produced
by ocean phytoplankton: passively floating plants. All this modulated
temperatures, curbed floods and nurtured man a mere 1,000,000 or so
years ago.

To primitive man, nature was so harsh and powerful that he 4
deeply respected and even worshiped it. He did the environment very
little damage. But technological man, master of the atom and soon the

322

moon, is so aware of his strength that he is unaware of his weakness—the fact that his pressure on nature may provoke revenge. Although sensational cries of impending doom have overstated the case, modern man has reached the stage where he must recognize that real dangers exist. Indeed, many scholars of the biosphere are now seriously concerned that human pollution may trigger some ecological disaster.

Consuming Nothing

For one thing, the impact of human pollutants on nature can be vastly amplified by food chains, the serial process by which weak creatures are typically eaten by stronger ones in ascending order. The most closely studied example is the effect of pesticides, which have sharply improved farm crops but also caused spectacular kills of fish and wildlife. In the Canadian province of New Brunswick, for example, the application of only one-half pound of DDT per acre of forest to control the spruce budworm has twice wiped out almost an entire year's production of young salmon in the Miramichi River. In this process, rain washes the DDT off the ground and into the plankton of lakes and streams. Fish eat the DDT-tainted plankton; the pesticide becomes concentrated in their bodies, and the original dose ultimately reaches multifold strength in fish-eating birds, which then often die or stop reproducing. DDT is almost certainly to blame for the alarming decrease in New England's once flourishing peregrine falcons, northern red-shouldered hawks and black-crowned night herons.

In the polluting sense, man is the dirtiest animal, and he must learn that he can no longer afford to vent smoke casually into the sky and sewage into rivers as he did in an earlier day, when vast reserves of pure air and water easily diluted the pollutants. The earth is basically a closed system with a waste-disposal process that clearly has limits. The winds that ventilate earth are only six miles high; toxic garbage can kill the tiny organisms that normally clean rivers. Today, industrial America is straining the limits.

One massively important factor is that the U.S. consumer actually consumes nothing; he merely uses things, and though he burns, buries, grinds or flushes his wastes, the material survives in some form, and technology adds to its longevity. The tin can used to rust away; now comes the' immortal aluminum can, which may outlast the Pyramids. Each year, the U.S. produces 48 billion cans, plus 28 billion long-lived bottles and jars. Paced by hardy plastic containers, the average American's annual output of 1,600 lbs. of solid waste is rising by more than 4% a year. Disposal already costs $3 billion a year.

All this effluence is infinitely multiplied in big cities—and 70% of Americans live on only 10% of the country's total land area. Every day,

New York City dumps 200 million gallons of raw sewage into the Hudson River. Each square mile of Manhattan produces 375,000 lbs. of waste a day; the capital cost of incinerating that 1-sq.-mi.-output is $1.87 million, and 30% of the residue drifts in the air as fly ash until it settles on the citizens.

The sheer bulk of big cities slows the cleansing winds; at the same time, rising city heat helps to create thermal inversions (warm air above cold) that can trap smog for days—a crisis that in 1963 killed 400 New Yorkers. Cars complete the deadly picture. While U.S. chimneys belch 100,000 tons of sulfur dioxide every day, 90 million motor vehicles add 230,000 tons of carbon monoxide (52% of smog) and other lethal gases, which then form ozone and peroxyacetyl nitrate that kill or stunt many plants, ranging from orchids to oranges. Tetraethyl lead in auto exhausts affects human nerves, increasing irritability and decreasing normal brain function. Like any metal poison, lead is fatal if enough is ingested. In the auto's 70-year history, the average American's lead content has risen an estimated 125-fold, to near maximum tolerance levels. Arctic glaciers now contain wind-wafted lead.

Air, Water & the Sewer

By the year 2000, an estimated 90% of Americans will live in urban areas and drive perhaps twice as many cars as they do now. The hope is that Detroit will have long since designed exhaust-free electric or steam motors. Another hope is nuclear power to generate electricity in place of smoggy "fossil fuels" (oil, coal), but even with 50% nuclear power, U.S. energy needs will so increase by 2000 that fossil-fuel use may quadruple. Moreover, nuclear plants emit pollution: not only radioactive wastes, which must be buried, but also extremely hot water that has to go somewhere and can become a serious threat to marine life.

Industry already devours water on a vast scale—600,000 gal. to make one ton of synthetic rubber, for example—and the resultant hot water releases the dissolved oxygen in rivers and lakes. This kills the oxygen-dependent bacteria that degrade sewage. Meanwhile, the country's ever-mounting sewage is causing other oxygen-robbing processes. By 1980, these burdens may well dangerously deplete the oxygen in all 22 U.S. river basins. The first massive warning is what happened to Lake Erie, where overwhelming sewage from Detroit and other cities cut the oxygen content of most of the lake's center to zero, turning a once magnificently productive inland sea into a sink where life is catastrophically diminished. With state and federal aid, the cities that turned Erie's tributaries into open sewers are now taking steps to police the pollution, and if all goes well, Erie may be restored to reasonable life in five or ten years.

But the problem goes on. Though one-third of U.S. sewage sys-   12
tems are below health standards, improving them may also kill lakes. The problem is that treated sewage contains nitrate and phosphate, fertilizing substances widely used in agriculture that make things worse in overfertilized lakes. Though nitrate is normally harmless in the body, intestinal bacteria can turn it into nitrite, a compound that hinders hemoglobin from transporting oxygen to the tissues, causing labored breathing and even suffocation.

The Systems Approach

It seems undeniable that some disaster may be lurking in all this,   13
but laymen hardly know which scientist to believe. As a result of fossil-fuel burning, for example, carbon dioxide in the atmosphere has risen about 14% since 1860. According to Ecologist Lamont C. Cole, man is thus reducing the rate of oxygen regeneration, and Cole envisions a crisis in which the amount of oxygen on earth might disastrously decline. Other scientists fret that rising carbon dioxide will prevent heat from escaping into space. They foresee a hotter earth that could melt the polar icecaps, raise oceans as much as 400 ft., and drown many cities. Still other scientists forecast a colder earth (the recent trend) because man is blocking sunlight with ever more dust, smog and jet contrails. The cold promises more rain and hail, even a possible cut in world food. Whatever the theories may be, it is an established fact that three poisons now flood the landscapes: smog, pesticides, nuclear fallout.

Finding effective antidotes will take a lot more alertness to ecolog-   14
ical consequences. What cities sorely need is a systems approach to pollution: a computer analysis of everything that a total environment— greater Los Angeles, for example—is taking in and giving out via air, land, water. Only then can cities make cost-benefit choices and balance the system. Equally vital are economic incentives, such as taxing specific pollutants so that factories stop using them. Since local governments may be loath to levy effluence charges, fearing loss of industry, the obvious need is regional cooperation, such as interstate river-basin authorities to enforce scientific water use. Germany's Ruhr River is ably governed this way. A shining U.S. example is the eight-state Ohio River Valley Water Sanitation Commission, which persuaded 3,000 cities and industries to spend $1 billion divesting 99% of their effluent to sewage plants.

Similar "air shed" action is starting between some smog-bound   15
states and is considered preferable to federally imposed air standards,

which might not fit local climate conditions. Still, far greater federal action—especially money—is urgently needed to help cities build all kinds of waste-treating facilities. In fact, the Secretary of the Interior really ought to be the Secretary of the Environment. To unify federal leadership, he might well be given charge of the maze of rival federal agencies that now absurdly nibble only at their own slice of the pollution mess.

One of the prime goals in attacking pollution ought to be a vast shrinkage of the human impact on other creatures. The war on insects, for example, might actually go a lot better without chemical pesticides that kill the pests' natural enemies, such as birds. One of the best strategies is to nurture the enemies so they can attack the pests; more insect-resistant crops can also be developed. Florida eliminated the screw-worm fly not by spraying but by sterilizing hordes of the male flies, then liberating them to produce infertile eggs. A still newer method is the use of sex attractants to lure male insects into traps and thus to their death.

Above all, man should strive to parallel natural decay by recycl- 16 ing—reusing as much as possible. Resalvaging already keeps 80% of all mined copper in circulation. But U.S. city incinerators now destroy about 3,000,000 metric tons of other valuable metals a year; magnetic extractors could save the metal and reduce incineration by 10%. The packaging industry could do a profound service by switching to materials that rot—fast. The perfect container for mankind is the edible ice-cream cone. How about a beer container that is something like a pretzel? Or the soft-drink bottle that, when placed in the refrigerator, turns into a kind of tasty artificial ice? Soft drinks could also come in frozen form, as popsicles with edible sticks.

To cut air pollution, a Japanese process can be used to convert fly 17 ash into cinder blocks. Since the market is too small for commercial success, public subsidies would make sense; recovering waste at the source is almost always cheaper than cleanup later. There are some real prospects of profit in reconstituting other waste. Take sulfur, for example, which is in short supply around the world. While 26 million tons are mined a year, smokestacks belch 28 million tons of wasted sulfur dioxide, which could easily be trapped in the stack and converted to sulfuric acid or even fertilizer. Standard Oil of California is already profitably recovering the refinery sulfur waste that pollutes streams.

To reduce smog over cities, one of the most visible and worst forms 18 of pollution, smog-causing power plants might be eliminated from densely populated areas. Why not generate electricity at the fuel source—distant oil or coal fields—and then wire it to cities? On the other hand, industrialization must not be taken to distant places that can be better used for other purposes. Industrializing Appalachia, for example, would smogify a naturally hazy region that settlers aptly named the Smokies. The right business for Appalachia is recreation; federal money could spur a really sizable tourist industry.

Sometimes pollution can even help recreation. In flat northeastern Illinois, for instance, the handsomest recreation area will soon be Du Page County's fast-rising 118-ft. hill and 65-acre lake—artfully built on garbage fill. One form of pollution could even enhance—rather than spoil—water sports. Much of the nation's coastline is too cold for swimming; if marine life can be protected, why not use nuclear plant heat to warm the water? Or even create underwater national parks for scuba campers? 19

In Harmony with Nature

Ideally, every city should be a closed loop, like a space capsule in which astronauts reconstitute even their own waste. This concept is at the base of the federally aided "Experimental City" being planned by Geophysicist Athelstan Spilhaus, president of Philadelphia's Franklin Institute, who dreams of solving the pollution problem by dispersing millions of Americans into brand-new cities limited to perhaps 250,000 people on 2,500 acres of now vacant land. The pilot city, to be built by a quasi-public corporation, will try everything from reusable buildings to underground factories and horizontal elevators to eliminate air-burning cars and buses. The goal is a completely recycled, noise-free, pure-air city surrounded by as many as 40,000 acres of insulating open countryside. "We need urban dispersal," says Spilhaus, "not urban renewal." 20

In the search for solutions, there is no point in attempting to take nature back to its pristine purity. The approach must look forward. There is no question that just as technology has polluted the country, it can also depollute it. The real question is whether enough citizens want action. The biggest need is for ordinary people to learn something about ecology, a humbling as well as fascinating way of viewing reality that ought to get more attention in schools and colleges. The trouble with modern man is that he tends to yawn at the news that pesticides are threatening remote penguins or pelicans; perhaps he could do with some of the humility toward animals that St. Francis tried to graft onto Christianity. The false assumption that nature exists only to serve man is at the root of an ecological crisis that ranges from the lowly litterbug to the lunacy of nuclear proliferation. At this hour, man's only choice is to live in harmony with nature, not conquer it. 21

For Discussion and Writing

1. The writer of this essay lists several primary causes of environmental pollution. What are they?
2. Which specific recommendations does this author suggest to fight pollution? Which of these has been implemented in the years since the essay appeared?
3. According to this writer, what is the false assumption that helps to cause the world-wide pollution problem? What does he or she recommend instead? Has that proposal been heeded?
4. Based on your own experience, write an informative essay detailing an environmental problem and what is being done about it. You might focus your attention on specific issues in your hometown or state, something about which you can speak with authority. Some questions to consider: How did the problem arise? When were its effects first noticed, and what where they? Did the problem worsen? What kinds of actions were taken, and by whom, in response? What's the current situation? What's the prognosis for the future?

Forest of Dreams

LANCE MORROW

With the names of trees you can make a fine pagan bouquet of words: hornbeam, ginkgo, quickbeam, oak, white willow, tamarind, Lombardy poplar, false cypress, elder, laburnum, larch, baobab, black gum, rowan, hazel, whitebeam, tree of heaven, ash . . . 1

At one time trees were sacred. Gods inhabited them and took their forms. Trees were druidic. They rose out of the earth, gesticulating, tossing their hair. They were the tenderest life-form: cooling, sheltering, calming, enigmatic. Or else they might harbor terrors: beasts and devils in the dark forest. They were, in either case, magic. Still are, of course, although they have also evolved into mere lumber. 2

The spiritual descendants of those who worshiped trees may sentimentalize them now as some green sermon. Ronald Reagan did not. Once during the 1980 campaign, in a nuke-the-wimps frame of mind, Reagan claimed that no matter what environmentalists say, trees are a source of deadly pollution. On the campaign plane later, Reagan's press secretary James Brady sighted forests below and shouted, "Killer trees! Killer trees!" It seems that Reagan was confusing nitrous oxide with deadlier oxides of nitrogen. Never mind. 3

The Republican President in the White House now may not poeticize trees—he takes a certain pride in not poeticizing anything—but he does have a fine secular appreciation of what trees do. They hold the earth and scrub the air. Chop them down, and the world becomes a moonscape in a greenhouse. Egypt's eastern desert is a cautionary text: each tree in the sparse landscape is under the protection of a Bedouin family. Sometimes the people build a wall around each tree to guard the leaves from goats. 4

George Bush, who said he wanted to be an environmental President, is making trees a kind of fetish of his Administration. In his budget submitted last week, Bush allotted $175 million to plant 1 billion trees this year. By the year 2000 there should be 10 billion new trees that eventually should absorb 13 million tons of carbon dioxide a year, or 5% of the nation's annual emissions of the gas. 5

The news is that a larger environmental ambition is in harness. John Kennedy launched the Peace Corps. There may be some symmetry 6 in the fact that a man in the Bush White House has hatched the idea for something called the Earth Corps, which will try to enact the spirit of the last line of Kennedy's Inaugural Address in 1961: "Here on earth God's work must truly be our own."

The Earth Corps is the inspiration of James Pinkerton, the 31-year-old Deputy Assistant to the President for Policy Planning. Pinkerton did not begin by thinking about trees, but rather about the wreckage of America's inner cities and the prospects that face young black males. Looking for an approach to the problem, he considered the way that the Army, at its best, trains people—teaches them discipline, teamwork and such values as courage, honor, strength, loyalty, pride. The experience, when all goes well, can transform lives. The welfare system institutionalizes an abject status quo and produces generations of angry, mired victims.

Pinkerton made a triangular connection among these points: the unused energy and gifts of young blacks, the real needs of the environment, and the motivating focus of some parts of military life. Pinkerton wanted to remove the Earth Corps from direct Government (and therefore congressional/political) control and from the sort of bureaucratic and ideological overelaboration that came with the Great Society. Unlike Franklin Roosevelt's Civilian Conservation Corps, which was run by the U.S. Army, the Earth Corps is to be not a Government agency but a nonprofit corporation funded by private donations and perhaps eventually some Government grants. Its director and chief executive officer is John Wheeler, 45, an intense, effective idealist who graduated from West Point in 1966, served in Viet Nam, took degrees from Harvard Business School and Yale Law School and among other things headed the foundation that got the Viet Nam Veterans Memorial installed on the Mall in Washington.

With a grant of $300,000 in seed money from the Annie E. Casey Foundation and office space near the White House donated by lawyer Allan Fox, Wheeler is developing plans to establish an Earth Corps Academy, probably in Virginia, by next year. The corps will recruit 500 cadets for a two-year tour of service that will start with three months of forestry, academic and environmental training at the academy. The recruits will be young men—and women—ages 16 to 21, with preference given to attracting the poor. Recruits will have to pass a qualifying examination and must be drug free. Their main work will be reforesting the nation, starting with some 1.3 million acres of South Carolina that were torn apart by Hurricane Hugo. Eventually, Wheeler hopes, the corps will attract 4,000 recruits a year. By encouraging local and state conservation corps as well, the Earth Corps may be able to double Bush's 10 billion trees by the year 2000.

Cadets will wear uniforms with the Earth Corps insignia (the 10
earth seen from space and the words TRUTH, DUTY, ONE EARTH). They will
receive food, shelter and the minimum wage, a portion to be set aside
in savings. When a cadet leaves the corps, he will have technical skills
and environmental training. The corps will work to find him a job or a
path to higher education.

Pinkerton and Wheeler are concerned that the military image 11
might deter recruits. It is the military esprit they want, not military
coercion or rigidity. Wheeler is also steering 10,000 miles clear of the
welfare mentality. The corps will not be remedial, not mandatory, not a
punishment, not an entitlement, not cushy and not trivial. Excellence
and dignity are words that recur in Wheeler's conversation. Cadets will
do hard, necessary work—reforestation, fire fighting, fire prevention,
wetland protection, cleaning up oil spills and protecting habitats for
endangered species.

The Earth Corps is still a seedling. But it is a daring idea. From the 12
first landfall, the logic of the American enterprise was the ax, clearing
the way west through wilderness. That was a way to make a civilization, as Brazil is now making a civilization by burning itself down. The
idea of the Earth Corps draws a line that circles back to the sacred.

For Discussion and Writing

1. Morrow uses a poetic strategy to set up the tone and stance of his essay.
   How do the tree names and qualities he lists at the opening contrast
   with the last word in paragraph 2? What effect do you think Morrow is
   aiming for?
2. What is the Earth Corps, and upon what long-standing institution is it
   to be modeled? What are the Corps' projected goals?
3. In what way is the idea of the Earth Corps a return "to the sacred"?
4. Based on Morrow's information, what is your general response to
   Pinkerton's proposal? What about the specifics—for example, that the
   recruits are to be young black men and women, that they must be drug
   free, that they'll be paid the minimum wage with a portion saved for
   them automatically? Write an essay in which you critique the Earth
   Corps idea, analyze potential strengths and weaknesses, and perhaps
   make your own friendly amendments to the proposal.

Down with the God Squad

TED GUP

Imagine revising *Genesis.* In the new version Noah stands on the 1
gangplank to the ark, reviewing the species of the world pair by pair,
deciding on a purely economic basis which creatures to save and which
to consign to the deepening waters. He turns away the pests, the
serpents and other species he deems useless to man or too costly to take
along. If such a vision strains the imagination, consider the call by some
Bush Administration officials to amend the Endangered Species Act.
Their aim is to expand greatly the powers of a committee of political
appointees that already can exempt species from the protection of the
act when man's economic interests so dictate. The committee is commonly known as the "God Squad," not for its collective wisdom but
because the decisions it may render were once left to an even higher
authority.

Noah's directive was to preserve all species. Modern man has no 2
such option. Some species are already doomed, the incidental victims
of logging, mining, dams and the fragmentation of their habitats.
Almost daily we face another agonizing conflict between ecology and
economics. In the Pacific Northwest loggers' jobs are pitted against the
need to save ancient forests, the habitat of spotted owls. In the South-
west a $582 million water project is delayed because it threatens the
squawfish. In Arizona a $200 million observatory was held up on behalf
of some 150 rare Mount Graham red squirrels. Are all these species
worth saving? And who among us is fit to make such decisions?

The preservation of species is a task involving a volatile mix of 3
biology, politics, economics and morality. For 17 years the Endangered
Species Act has provided a "911" distress line for life forms teetering on
the edge. But its species-by-species approach does little to avert conflict.
Man cannot manage nature through a series of ad hoc rescue attempts,
ignoring the underlying causes for the loss of biodiversity. The answer
is not to dilute the Endangered Species Act but to better anticipate the
consequences of human activity, focusing on entire ecosystems rather
than on single species. By the time a creature joins the endangered list
it may be too late, the genetic stock impoverished, its habitat destroyed.

Species preservation depends upon political resolve. Costs of conservation can be stunning, appearing all the more so when weighed against the abstract value of a species. Increasingly, biologists intent on saving a species are heard to cite either its usefulness to man or the dangers to man attendant upon its loss. Thus the tropical rain forests are said to hold medicinal, agricultural and scientific wealth. This kind of argument, credible as it may be, reflects scientists' perceptions that only appeals to man's self-interest will generate public support for conservation. But anthropocentric arguments legitimatize the notion that species must justify their right to exist by proving their utility to man. That leaves the vast majority of species defenseless and debases the fundamental reason for preserving them—their intrinsic worth.

Precisely what makes the Endangered Species Act unique is that it views the world not through man's eyes but from the high ground of the Creation. It sets no test for survival and respects the meek as it does the mighty. The humpback whale and the black rhinoceros enjoy no greater protection than the noonday snail and the lakeside daisy. Recently an inch-long unpigmented eyeless shrimp found in a sinkhole near Gainesville, Fla., joined the ranks of the imperiled. In shielding the humblest species, the act expresses its highest reverence for diversity, and has evolved into an almost sacred covenant defining the nation's relationship with nature.

In recent months, Agriculture Secretary Clayton Yeutter Jr., Interior Secretary Manuel Lujan and some in Congress have suggested amending the law and letting the God Squad make the toughest calls. That would be the effective demise of the act. The Senate last week defeated a measure that would have empowered the God Squad to settle the dispute over timbering the ancient forests. But the broader question remains. Ruling on a species' fate has eternal consequences. A political appointee's vision dims beyond the next election. Matters of such gravity ought to reflect society's broadest interests. Biologists, environmentalists, theologians, historians and, yes, representatives of industry have a claim to participate in such decisions. Some in this Administration and its predecessor have criticized the Endangered Species Act and shown a willingness to subordinate biological evidence to political expediency. Such was the case with the spotted owl and the Mount Graham squirrel.

Today species are vanishing on a grand scale. There are 1,116 imperiled species on the list, an additional 3,600 candidate species behind them. Some will die out waiting to be listed. These numbers are only a pale reflection of a wider problem. In tropical rain forests, loss of habitat is pushing at least 20,000 species a year into extinction, according to Harvard entomologist Edward O. Wilson. If the U.S. is to influence policy overseas, it will be by dint of example, not rhetoric. Wealthy nations must check their own appetites before asking far greater sacrifices of poorer nations.

A relative newcomer on earth, man knows little about the species   8
with whom he shares the landscape. Fewer than 1.4 million of earth's tens of millions of species have been named, much less examined for their part in making the planet more hospitable. How then do we measure each loss or know when we have severed a vital link with nature? Observes noted paleontologist Stephen Jay Gould: "It would be a very bleak world with cockroaches and dogs and not much else." The final blessing of the Endangered Species Act is that it preserves the elements that stir man's sense of wonder. That benefit alone is too precious for the God Squad to barter away.

For Discussion and Writing

1. What is the "God Squad"? What is its aim? What does Gup want us to think about this group?
2. According to Gup, what is wrong with the argument that species should be saved because of their usefulness to human beings?
3. How is the Endangered Species Act an attempt to combat the God Squad attitude? Is there a religious or ethical assumption in Gup's argument? If so, what is it?
4. Gup says that the political conflict here is between ecology and economics. What is your view of the issue? Has Gup persuaded you that economics should never displace environmental protection? Write an essay attacking or defending his essential claim that species preservation must not be bartered for economic gain.

Thinking and Writing about Chapter 23

1. All three essays here are clearly in favor of environmental responsibility. Are there any arguments to be made for a looser or less concerned attitude toward the earth's ecology? What is the common view of those who seem unconcerned about, or actively engaged in, environmental harm?
2. To what extent do religious ideas enter into these three writers' treatment of environmental issues? Which of the essays make explicit references to religious themes or matters of faith?
3. Of the many suggestions contained in these essays, one, in the final paragraph of "The Age of Effluence," applies directly to students: "The biggest need is for ordinary people to learn something about ecology, a humbling as well as fascinating way of viewing reality that ought to get more attention in schools and colleges." To what extent has your education included such learning? Have you been raised to be environmentally concerned and responsible? Write an essay in which you reflect upon your own attitudes toward nature and the environment, analyze the sources of those views, and explain how they influence your behavior toward the natural world.

PART FIVE: Values and Beliefs

24

Myth and Religion

America was born of an apparent contradiction: created in the Age of Reason by men of faith. The conflicts between reason and belief, science and God, church and state, continue, often quite heatedly, into our own day. Religious zealotry has always played an important role in national politics. Conflicts between scientific and religious views of the world, many of them echoes of the infamous Scopes trial of 1925, have plagued our schools. Our leaders bemoan our loss of moral fiber, the breakdown of the family, while television evangelism flourishes, drive-in churches pop up throughout California, and city councils argue about Christmas decorations that portray religious images.

What do we really believe in? It depends who you talk to. If freedom of religion was a founding tenet of America, it has spawned a vast array of variations on that theme, from traditional forms of belief, to creative blends of religion and secular philosophies, to private and highly specialized personal mythologies.

The essays in this chapter address three major issues of faith. In "The Need for New Myths," from January 1972, Gerald Clarke profiles mythologist Joseph Campbell before he was widely known, using the opportunity to discuss the role of myth in daily life. In "In the Beginning: God and Science," from February 1979, Lance Morrow looks at the traditional conflict between science and religion, and how it may be moderating with new theories of the cosmos. And in "Defenders of the Faith," from November 1984, Roger Rosenblatt tackles the church-and-state debate, finding in recent political murders a reason to maintain traditional separation.

The Need for New Myths

GERALD CLARKE

The latest incarnation of Oedipus, the continued romance of Beauty and the Beast, stands this afternoon on the corner of 42nd Street and Fifth Avenue, waiting for the traffic light to change.

—Joseph Campbell

That statement, fanciful as it sounds, is simply a short-hand way of saying that everyone is a creature of myth, that the ancient legends and tales of the race are still the master keys to the human psyche. The science-minded Victorians who sneered at myths as superstitious twaddle were guilty of a kind of scientific superstition themselves: the belief that reason could explain all human motives. Aided by psychoanalysis, anthropology and three-quarters of a century of archaeological discovery modern scholarship has replaced the Victorians' sneers with respect and even awe. Mythology, its partisans are now claiming, tells as much about humanity—its deepest fears, sorrows, joys and hopes—as dreams tell about an individual. "Myths are public dreams," says Joseph Campbell, who is probably the world's leading expert on mythology. "Dreams are private myths. Myths are vehicles of communication between the conscious and the unconscious, just as dreams are."

The trouble is, Campbell asserts, that this communication has broken down in the modern Western world. The old myths are no longer operative, and effective new myths have not risen to replace them. As a result, he maintains, the West is going through an agony of reorientation matched only by a period during the 4th millennium B.C., when the Sumerians first conceived the concept of a mathematically ordered cosmos and thus changed utterly man's concept of the universe around him.

Campbell's words carry extraordinary weight, not only among scholars but among a wide range of other people who find his search down mythological pathways relevant to their lives today. A professor of literature at Sarah Lawrence College in Bronxville, N.Y., Campbell has written and edited some 20-odd books on mythology. They include a massive four-volume work entitled *The Masks of God; The Flight of the Wild Gander* and the book for which he is most famous, *Hero With a Thousand Faces,* a brilliant examination, through ancient hero myths, of man's eternal struggle for identity. *Hero,* which has had sales of more than 110,000 copies, an impressive figure for a scholarly book, has become a bestseller on campus. After 37 years of teaching in relative obscurity, Campbell, at 67, has now become a well-known and respected figure in academe.

What is a myth? In Campbell's academic jargon, it is a dreamlike 4 "symbol that evokes and directs psychological energy." A vivid story or legend, it is but one part of a larger fabric of myths that, taken together, form a mythology that expresses a culture's attitude toward life, death and the universe around it. The Greek myth of Prometheus, the Titan who stole fire from Olympus and gave it to man, thus symbolizes the race's aspirations, even when they conflict with the powers of nature. The almost contemporary Hebrew myth of the trials of Job, on the other hand, symbolizes man's submission to a power above nature, even when that power seems cruel and unjust. The two myths are, in effect, picture stories that tell the philosophies of two totally divergent cultures. The Greek stresses man's heroic striving for human values and civilization; the Hebrew emphasizes, rather, man's humble spiritual surrender to God's will. Abraham's willingness to sacrifice Isaac is the supreme symbol of this attitude.

Though not true in a literal sense, a myth is not what it is considered to be in everyday speech—a fantasy or a misstatement. It is rather a veiled explanation of the truth. The transformation from fact to myth is endlessly fascinating. The battle of Achilles and Hector, for example, is symbolic, but there was a Trojan War in which great heroes fought. The psychological duel between Faust and the Devil is a philosophical and psychological metaphor, but Georg Faust, a German magician who was born about 1480, did live and did make claims to superhuman power, including the ability to restore the lost works of Plato and Aristotle and to repeat the miracles of Christ. Yet it was not until poets like Christopher Marlowe and Goethe took up the legend that Faust became famous—and mythic. The Faust story appealed to Marlowe and to Goethe because the times in which they lived, eras in which faith and reason were in basic conflict, called for such a symbolic struggle.

What should a mythology do? In Campbell's view, a "properly 6 operating" mythology has four important functions:

• To begin with, through its rites and imagery it wakens and 7 maintains in the individual a sense of awe, gratitude and even rapture, rather than fear, in relation to the mystery both of the universe and of man's own existence within it.

- Secondly, a mythology offers man a comprehensive, under- 8 standable image of the world around him, roughly in accord with the best scientific knowledge of the time. In symbolic form, it tells him what his universe looks like and where he belongs in it.

- The third function of a living mythology is to support the social 9 order through rites and rituals that will impress and mold the young. In India, for example, the basic myth is that of an impersonal power, Brahma, that embodies the universe. The laws of caste are regarded as inherent features of this universe and are accepted and obeyed from childhood. Cruel as this may seem to Westerners, the myth of caste does give Indian society a stability it might otherwise lack and does make life bearable to the impoverished low castes.

- The fourth and, in Campbell's view, the most important func- 10 tion of mythology, is to guide the individual, stage by stage, through the inevitable psychological crises of a useful life: from the childhood condition of dependency through the traumas of adolescence and the trials of adulthood to, finally, the deathbed.

The churches and synagogues still provide mythological guid- 11 ance for many, Campbell argues; for many others, however, this guidance fails. The result is that, where once religion served, many have turned to psychoanalysis or encounter groups. "All ages before ours believed in gods in some form or other," wrote Carl Jung, whose theories of the collective unconscious have most profoundly influenced Campbell's thinking. "Heaven has become empty space to us, a fair memory of things that once were. But our heart glows, and secret unrest gnaws at the roots of our being." In search of something that they can hold on to, many people in the West, particularly the young, are either returning to Christian fundamentalism through the Jesus Revolution or turning to the religions of the East, chiefly Buddhism and Hinduism. "The swamis are coming from India, and they're taking away the flock," says Campbell. "They're speaking of religion as dealing with the interior life and not about dogmatic formulae and ritual requirements."

For the vast majority, Campbell believes, the West's general lack 12 of spiritual authority has been a disaster. Forty years in the study of eternal symbols have made Campbell a conservative of a rather dark hue. Though he is optimistic about the long range, he finds the present bleak indeed. "We have seen what has happened to primitive communities unsettled by the white man's civilization," he observes. "With their old taboos discredited, they immediately go to pieces, disintegrate, and become resorts of vice and disease. Today the same thing is happening to us."

Many Oriental and primitive societies even today have working   13
mythologies, and Communist countries have at least the basis of a mythology in Marxism. The Marxist dream of the withering away of the state, after which each man will give according to his abilities and receive according to his needs, echoes numerous religious beliefs of a paradise on earth or a Second Coming. The Chinese Communists have, in addition, the myth of the "Long March" in the '30s and the subsequent sanctuary of Mao Tse-tung and his followers in the caves of Yenan. The events were real enough, but for this generation of Chinese, and probably for generations to come, they will have much the same deep mythological significance that the Trojan War had for the Greeks.

In the West there have been desperate attempts to provide at least   14
fragments of a modern mythology. Churchill brilliantly re-created the myth of St. George and the dragon during World War II: the picture of little Britain, a citadel of justice, besieged by the evil Nazi hordes. The situation, of course, was much as he painted it—Britain was besieged and Hitler was evil—but a Neville Chamberlain would not have been able, as Churchill was, to light up his people with the basic themes of their culture. Charles de Gaulle, both as wartime leader and President of the Fifth Republic, quite consciously resurrected the ghost of Joan of Arc. "To my mind," he wrote, "France cannot be France without greatness." The founders of Israel similarly evoked, and still evoke, mythic images of the Bible's chosen people to enable Israelis to survive in their hostile environment.

Often, such attempts add up merely to rhetoric or incantation.   15
John Kennedy sought to revive the American myth that the U.S. was a country with a messianic mission. "Now the trumpet summons us again," he said in his Inaugural Address, "to a struggle against the common enemies of man: tyranny, poverty, disease and war itself." A post-Viet Nam U.S. can no longer quite believe in such an American mission. And Martin Luther King Jr. worked to provide the nation's blacks with a myth of their own. "I've been to the mountaintop and I've looked over, and I've seen the promised land," King said the night before he was killed, echoing the Bible's story of Moses on Mount Sinai.

For centuries Americans were emboldened by the myth of the   16
endless frontier, the notion that a new life could always be started out West, whether the West was Ohio or California. That version outlasted the frontier itself, but no one believes in it today. Campbell hopes that

the landings on the moon will reinvigorate that mythic tradition. Only a handful of people can go to the moon, and no one would want to stake out his 160 acres there, but the excitement of the journey itself is infectious, a reenactment on the TV screen of Prometheus' stealing fire from the gods. Beyond that, Campbell believes, there is an even more durable myth: the "American Dream." That is the idea, grounded in fact, that a man is judged on his own ability rather than on his family or his place in society. "This pessimistic optimist thinks that that myth still works," he says. "The fact that Nixon was a poor boy and was yet elected President is a good example."

In the final analysis, however, it is wrong in Campbell's view to   17
ask for one grand mythology that will guide people today. Instead there must be many different mythologies for many different kinds of people. "There is no general mythology today," Campbell says, "nor can there ever be again. Our lives are too greatly various in their backgrounds, aims and possibilities for any single order of symbols to work effectively on us all." The new myths must be internalized and individual, and each man must find them for himself. Some, in fact, are following mythological paths today, unconsciously and without design. The hippie who leaves society and goes off to a commune, for example, is being guided by a mythological map of withdrawal and adventure laid down by Christ in the desert, the Buddha at Bodh-Gaya, and Mohammed in his cave of meditation at Mount Hira.

The man in search of an ideal could at least begin, Campbell   18
thinks, by searching through the myths of antiquity, religion and modern literature. For the elite who can read and understand them, T.S. Eliot, James Joyce, Thomas Mann, among modern writers and poets, and Pablo Picasso and Paul Klee, among modern artists, have updated the ancient mythological motifs. Campbell and the other mythologists are, in a sense, providing the workbooks for the poets—the modern Daedaluses in turtlenecks. "It doesn't matter to me whether my guiding angel is for a time named Vishnu, Shiva, Jesus, or the Buddha," Campbell says. "If you're not distracted by names or the color of hair, the same message is there, variously turned. In the multitude of myths and legends that have been preserved to us—both in our own Western arts and literatures, synagogues and churches, and in the rites and teachings of those Oriental and primitive heritages now becoming known to us—we may still find guidance."

The mythologists are not providing myths, but they are indicating   19
that something is missing without them. They are telling modern man that he has not outgrown mythology and will never outgrow it so long as he has hopes and fears beyond the other animals.

For Discussion and Writing

1. According to Clarke, how does Campbell define mythology, and what is its place in the modern world?
2. What does Campbell say are the main functions of mythology? Without such mythological support, according to Campbell, what happens to society?
3. Our own day, Campbell says, calls for a new kind of mythology. What is this? Why do modern human beings still need myths to guide them?
4. To what extent do mythic ideas or stories guide your life? Some examples: the American Dream of individual achievement; the hero's quest for adventure, social value, self-understanding; the artist's or scientist's desire to discover and create; the individual's need to be a meaningful part of family, community, or cosmos. Write a reflective essay in which you define the guiding principles of your life, analyse their mythological qualities, and explain how they help you to live.

In the Beginning: God and Science

LANCE MORROW

Sometime after the Enlightenment, science and religion came to 1
a gentleman's agreement. Science was for the real world: machines,
manufactured things, medicines, guns, moon rockets. Religion was for
everything else, the immeasurable: morals, sacraments, poetry, insan-
ity, death and some residual forms of politics and statesmanship. Religion became, in both senses of the word, immaterial. Science and
religion were apples and oranges. So the pact said: render unto apples
the things that are Caesar's, and unto oranges the things that are God's.
Just as the Maya kept two calendars, one profane and one priestly, so
Western science and religion fell into two different conceptions of the
universe, two different vocabularies.

This hostile distinction between religion and science has softened 2
in the last third of the 20th century. Both religion and science have
become self-consciously aware of their excesses, even of their capacity
for evil. Now they find themselves jostled into a strange metaphysical
intimacy. Perhaps the most extraordinary sign of that intimacy is what
appears to be an agreement between religion and science about certain
facts concerning the creation of the universe. It is the equivalent of the
Montagues and Capulets collaborating on a baby shower.

According to the Book of Genesis, the universe began in a single, 3
flashing act of creation; the divine intellect willed all into being, *ex nihilo*.
It is not surprising that scientists have generally stayed clear of the
question of ultimate authorship, of the final "uncaused cause." In years
past, in fact, they held to the Aristotelian idea of a universe that was
"ungenerated and indestructible," with an infinite past and an infinite
future. This was known as the Steady State theory.

That absolute expanse might be difficult, even unbearable, to 4
contemplate, like an infinite snow field of time, but the conception at
least carried with it the serenity of the eternal. In recent decades,
however, the Steady State model of the universe has yielded in the
scientific mind to an even more difficult idea, full of cosmic violence.
Most astronomers now accept the theory that the universe had an
instant of creation, that it came to be in a vast fireball explosion 15 or 20
billion years ago. The shrapnel created by that explosion is still flying

outward from the focus of the blast. One of the fragments is the galaxy we call the Milky Way—one of whose hundreds of billions of stars is the earth's sun, with its tiny orbiting grains of planets. The so-called Big Bang theory makes some astronomers acutely uncomfortable, even while it ignites in many religious minds a small thrill of confirmation. Reason: the Big Bang theory sounds very much like the story that the Old Testament has been telling all along.

Science arrived at the Big Bang theory through its admirably 5 painstaking and ideologically disinterested process of hypothesis and verification—and, sometimes, happy accident. In 1913, Astronomer Vesto Melvin Slipher of the Lowell Observatory in Flagstaff, Ariz., discovered galaxies that were receding from the earth at extraordinarily high speeds, up to 2 million m.p.h. In 1929, the American astronomer Edwin Hubble developed Slipher's findings to formulate his law of an expanding universe, which presupposes a single primordial explosion. Meantime, Albert Einstein, without benefit of observation, concocted his general theory of relativity, which overthrew Newton and contained in its apparatus the idea of the expanding universe. The Steady State idea still held many astronomers, however, until 1965, when two scientists at Bell Telephone Laboratories, Amo Penzias and Robert Wilson, using sophisticated electronic equipment, picked up the noise made by background radiation coming from all parts of the sky. What they were hearing, as it turned out, were the reverberations left over from the first explosion, the hissing echoes of creation. In the past dozen years, most astronomers have come around to operating on the assumption that there was indeed a big bang.

The Big Bang theory has subversive possibilities. At any rate, in a 6 century of Einstein's relativity, of Heisenberg's uncertainty principle (the very act of observing nature disturbs and alters it), of the enigmatic black holes ("Of the God who was painted as a glittering eye, there is nothing now left but a black socket," wrote the German Romantic Jean Paul), science is not the cool Palladian temple of rationality that it was in the Enlightenment. It begins to seem more like Prospero's island as experienced by Caliban. Some astronomers even talk of leftover starlight from a future universe, its time flowing in the opposite direction from ours. A silicon-chip agnosticism can be shaken by many puzzles besides the creation. Almost as mysterious are the circumstances that led, billions of years ago, to the creation of the first molecule that could reproduce itself. That step made possible the development of all the forms of life that spread over the earth. Why did it occur just then?

A religious enthusiasm for the apparent convergence of science 7 and theology in the Big Bang cosmology is understandable. Since the Enlightenment, the scriptural versions of creation or of other "events," like the fall of man or the miracles of Jesus Christ, have suffered the condescension of science; they were regarded as mere myth, superstition. Now the faithful are tempted to believe that science has performed a laborious validation of at least one biblical "myth": that of creation.

But has any such confirmation occurred? Robert Jastrow, director 8 of NASA's Goddard Institute for Space Studies, has published a small and curious book called *God and the Astronomers*, in which he suggests that the Bible was right after all, and that people of his own kind, scientists and agnostics, by his description, now find themselves confounded. Jastrow blows phantom kisses like neutrinos across the chasm between science and religion, seeming almost wistful to make a connection. Biblical fundamentalists may be happier with Jastrow's books than are his fellow scientists. He writes operatically: "For the scientist who has lived by his faith in the power of reason, the story ends like a bad dream. He has scaled the mountains of ignorance; he is about to conquer the highest peak; as he pulls himself over the final rock, he is greeted by a band of theologians who have been sitting there for centuries."

Isaac Asimov, the prodigious popularizer of science, reacts hotly 9 to the Jastrow book. "Science and religion proceed by different methods," he says. "Science works by persuasive reason. Outside of science, the method is intuitional, which is not very persuasive. In science, it is possible to say we were wrong, based on data." Science is provisional; it progresses from one hypothesis to another, always testing, rejecting the ideas that do not work, that are contradicted by new evidence. "Faith," said St. Augustine, "is to believe, on the word of God, what we do not see." Faith defies proof; science demands it. If new information should require modification of the Big Bang theory, that modification could be accomplished without the entire temple of knowledge collapsing. Observes Harvard University Historian-Astronomer Owen Gingerich: "*Genesis* is not a book of science. It is accidental if some things agree in detail. I believe the heavens declare the glory of God only to people who've made a religious commitment."

A number of theologians concur that the apparent convergence of 10 religious and scientific versions of the creation is a coincidence from which no profound meaning can be extracted. "If the last evidence for God occurred 20 billion years ago," asks Methodist W. Paul Jones of Missouri's St. Paul School of Theology, "do we not at best have the palest of deisms?" Jesuit Philosopher Bernard Lonergan goes further: "Science has nothing to say about creation, because that's going outside the empirical. The whole idea of empirical science is that you have data. Theologians have no data on God." There comes a point, somewhere short of God, at which all computers have no data either. With the Big Bang theory, says Jastrow, "science has proved that the world came into being as a result of forces that seem forever beyond the power of scientific description. This bothers science because it clashes with scientific religion—the religion of cause and effect, the belief that every effect has a cause. Now we find that the biggest effect of all, the birth of the universe, violates this article of faith."

Some scientists matter-of-factly dismiss the problem of creation. 11 Says Harvey Tananbaum, an X-ray astronomer at the Harvard-Smithsonian Astrophysical Laboratory: "That first instant of creation is not relevant as long as we do not have the laws to begin to understand it. It is a question for philosophers and religionists, not for scientists." Adds Geoffrey Burbidge, director of Kitt Peak National Observatory: "Principles and concepts cannot be measured. A question like 'Who imposed the order?' is metaphysical." Still, virtually everyone—both scientists and laymen—is taken by the sheer unthinkable opacity of the creation and what preceded it. Says Jastrow: "The question of what came before the Big Bang is the most interesting question of all."

One immense problem is that the primordial fireball destroyed all 12 the evidence; the temperature of the universe in the first seconds of its existence was many trillion degrees. The blast obliterated all that went before. The universe was shrouded in a dense fog of radiation, which only cleared after 1 million years, leaving the transparent spangled space we see in the night sky now. The first million years are as concealed from us as God's face. There are many forms of knowing: science, experience, intuition, faith. Science proceeds on the theory that there is method in all mysteries, and that it is discoverable. It obeys, reasonably, what is called the "first law of wingwalking": "Never leave hold of what you've got until you've got hold of something else." Faith, by definition, is a leap. It must await its verification in another world.

If it has done nothing else, however, the new coincidence of 13 scientific and theological versions of creation seems to have opened up a conversation that has been neglected for centuries. Roman Catholic Theologian Hans Küng detects the beginning of a new period, which he calls "pro-existence," of mutual assistance between theologians and natural scientists. People capable of genetic engineering and nuclear fission obviously require all the spiritual and ethical guidance they can get. As for theologians, the interchange between physics and metaphysics will inevitably enlarge their ideas and give them a more complex grounding in the physically observed universe. The theory of the Big Bang is surely not the last idea of creation that will be conceived; it does suggest that there remain immense territories of mystery that both the theologian and the scientist should approach with becoming awe.

For Discussion and Writing

1. According to Morrow, what has been the hostile distinction between science and religion since the 18th century?
2. What is the Big Bang theory, and how does it differ from the Steady State view of the universe? Why is the Big Bang seen as having similarities to the Old Testament creation story?
3. Not all scientists agree that religion and science have met in common understanding. What, according to Isaac Asimov, are religion and science's fundamental differences? As he defines them, can such distinctions ever be eliminated?
4. There has been much controversy in recent years about the conflicting claims of religion and science, not the least of which has been what each view says about human evolution. Write an essay in which you reflect upon the nature of science and religion, and try to determine whether these worldviews must remain forever separate. It is best for them to keep their distance, acting as different but equally valuable ways of describing reality? Can science and religion agree on some common ground? Is each ultimately a different form of a single human attempt to understand the world?

Defenders of the Faith

ROGER ROSENBLATT

Conquer your passions and you conquer the whole world.

—Hindu proverb

Whatsoever is not of faith is sin.

—St. Paul, Romans 14: 23

Two murders reported in a single week, seeming to have little   1
connection with each other and less connection with us. Last week
India's Prime Minister Indira Gandhi was shot to death by her Sikh
guards, while in Poland the body of the pro-Solidarity priest Jerzy
Popieluszko was recovered from a reservoir. It was not known whether
the suspected assailants were working for the Polish government, by
eliminating a troublemaker, or against it, by creating problems for the
relatively softline Premier Wojciech Jaruzelski. Either way, both killings
involved clashes between the faithful and the state. In one instance, a
religion struck at a government; in the other, politics struck at religion.
For many of us, the events might have occurred in another galaxy. Yet
all summer long, America has been arguing the issue of church and
state, of the proper relationship of religion and politics. Suddenly, two
object lessons or one lesson divided in two.

However different their tactics, the Polish priest and the Sikh   2
assassins would both be considered defenders of the faith. Popieluszko
preached against an oppressive government, and the Sikhs lashed out
at a leader who they feared was out to destroy them. What generated
both acts of protest was not any popular consensus or parliamentary
vote but the deep-seated belief that the protesters were doing the work
of God. Such a belief propels all acts of faith, which grow out of a special
state of mind. Faith is belief without reason. Fundamentally, religions
oppose rational processes, perhaps on the theory that a God who could
be approached by mere rational thought would not be worth reaching.
"Reason is the greatest enemy that faith has," said Martin Luther. "It

349

never comes to the aid of spiritual things, but . . . struggles against the divine Word, treating with contempt all that emanates from God."

This way of thinking accounts for all that is beautiful in religion. 3 It builds cathedrals, paints Madonnas, lends credence to miracles, sings hymns, offers communion with the suffering, fills the coffers of charities, proffers salvation to the soul and brings the world to its knees. It also sets heretics on fire, promotes ignorance, inflames bigotry, encourages superstition, erases history, invades nations, and slaughters the opposition. (The playful Huguenots buried Roman Catholics up to their necks so as to use their heads for ninepins.) Underlying all such activities are the adoration of mystery and the desire for submission: God works in mysterious ways, and lead thou me on. The basic premise of religion is both wondrous and antilogical: God is unknowable, and he provides clear and specific errands for his flock.

Governments, which can behave quite as terribly as religions and 4 occasionally as beautifully, are built and run on exactly opposite bases. Governments depend wholly on rational processes. Not only do they strive to manage and contain a rationally ordered society; they seek to persuade people that it makes sense for them to be governed the way they are—this despite the fact that certain governments may behave irrationally or may manipulate rationality for brutal ends. When religions and governments clash, therefore, it is a collision not simply of institutions but of entirely different ways of apprehending experience. If a priest adopted the thinking of a Prime Minister, the faith would go out of his calling. If a Prime Minister adopted the thinking of a priest, laws would be made in heaven.

All this connects with the American debate on church *vs.* state in 5 a fundamental way. Those who would like to see religion exert more control over government claim that the founding fathers wanted it that way. They are nearly right. People like Franklin, Washington, Jefferson and Madison sought to separate church and state so that no one sectarian God would ever bestride the land. Yet the founders wanted God somewhere in the picture, as a guide to national moral conduct. Thus arose the God of our civil religion. You've seen him. Big fellow. Flexible but no pushover. Spencer Tracy could have played him. His good book is the Constitution, his psalms were written by Walt Whitman, fairminded citizens constitute his clergy.

What the founders did not want, however, was a country run on 6 the bases of religion. America was born of the Age of Reason, so named not because people were more reasonable in the middle of the 18th century than at other times but because they set reason as the standard of human aspiration. "What reason weaves, by passion is undone," wrote Alexander Pope. Alexander Hamilton agreed, though warily: "Men are rather reasoning than reasonable animals, for the most part governed by the impulse of passion." It was one thing for individuals to be governed by emotions and another to assign such governance to a new country. Keeping church and state apart was a way of separating reason and passion, or reason and faith, another check and balance.

This is easier proposed than carried out, but it is worth the effort, since the premises of church and state are not merely opposed but actively antagonistic. Faith implies the refusal to accept any laws but God's. How can a government that relies on the perpetuation of its authority be compatible with an institution that takes dictates from invisible powers? Prime Minister Gandhi's soldiers fired on the Sikhs for acts of civil disorder. The Sikhs killed Mrs. Gandhi for an act of desecration.   7

In short, church and state are natural enemies, not because one is superior to the other (can reason be proved superior to faith, or vice versa?), but because they make antipodal and competing claims on the mind. Frequently the mind is torn between such claims, as Geraldine Ferraro indicated when she stated her public and private views on abortion. Still, the essential antagonism lies not in issues but in premises, which suggests that no matter how many grounds of agreement church and state may find, the basic conflict will remain unresolvable. When the 3rd century theologian Tertullian said that Athens can never agree with Jerusalem, this is what he meant.   8

Those who would like 'o foist church on state may be advised to look east this week. Two deaths in places as different as Poland and India were brought about by a hostility that goes as deep as anything in our experience. When Adam bit into the apple, he moved from the world of faith to that of reason, and so was expelled by a God who decreed that two such different modes of thought could not possibly live in the same garden. What God has put asunder, let no man join together.   9

For Discussion and Writing

1. According to Rosenblatt, what is the fundamental distinction between religion and government?
2. Roseblatt levels some fairly harsh criticism at religion in general. Of what does he accuse it? Do you agree?
3. What does Rosenblatt say were the Founding Fathers' intentions with respect to separation of church and state? From what context did those intentions arise?
4. Rosenblatt claims that the premises of church and state are "actively antagonistic," that church and state are natural enemies. Write an essay

in which you attack or defend this view. Some questions to consider: Are there good reasons to lessen the separation between church and state in the U.S.? What is lost or gained if governments become vehicles of religious belief? Are all governments non-religious? Can we learn anything from those that are not?

Thinking and Writing about Chapter 24

1. Compare the views of faith and reason offered in these essays. Where do the writers agree or differ?

2. In your view, are there fundamental or irreconcilable differences between faith, religion, or myth, on the one hand, and science and reason, on the other? Can faith or myth be reasonable or at least logically consistent? Can confidence in reason and scientific inquiry be a matter of faith or belief?

3. People take nothing more seriously than their beliefs, whether those be mythological, religious, scientific, or political. Write an essay in which you set forth your articles of faith—the basic beliefs that you accept without further question. Do you believe in God, the human spirit, nature, scientific progress? What are these things, and what do they mean to you?

25

Honesty

Some years ago, there was a spate of television quiz shows based on the notion that lying can be a form of entertainment. In one game, "To Tell the Truth," contestants tried to convince panelists by lying about their real identities. It was good clean fun. The show was a huge hit for years. What does it say about the American character, or human nature, that lying is so commonplace, and that we often find it amusing? Should humans be called "the lying animal," since deception seems to be one of their special abilities?

At the same time, though, we're all raised with the value that "honesty is the best policy," that good people don't lie, cheat, steal— even when all around them others are doing so, and getting away with it. The individual's place at the center of this conflict is one of the toughest tests any of us faces. How will we be and behave? Are we to be honest, even when that may seem foolish or idealistic, or are we to give in to the pressures and temptations of everyday crimes—shaving the truth, cheating a little here and there, taking what does not belong to us because we want it and probably won't get caught? And what happens to our communities and nations when all these little transgressions start to add up?

The essays in this chapter consider the often difficult problem of personal honesty. In "Larceny in Everyday Life," from September 1966, an anonymous writer analyzes the evidence that America is becoming "a nation of smalltime chiselers." In "The Busting of American Trust," from October 1980, Frank Trippett looks at what happens when duplicity becomes an epidemic. And in "Kidnapping the Brainchildren," from December 1990, Lance Morrow uses a discussion of plagiarism to consider more basic aspects of human character.

Larceny in Everyday Life

I t was just an ordinary day. Mom was at the store, taking back a   1
party dress she swore she had never once put on (it was only slightly
stained with lipstick). Sister, browsing in the Teen Scene department,
was staring with fascination at a pair of earrings she might just forget
to pay for, if no one was going to be looking too hard. Sonny was in
school, doing pretty well on a math test by dint of some judicious
copying from a friend's paper. And Dad was busy at the office, adding
a few fictitious lunches to his expense account and wondering about
the feasibility of his company's renting another suite in Miami to be
written off as a business expense.

While this is hardly a picture of the typical American family, it   2
does represent a pressing moral problem that has been largely obscured
by the more dramatic issues of war, sex and civil rights. The problem is
the erosion of Everyman's conscience about how he conducts his everyday life in less spectacular areas. A nation's ethical climate is made up
of small, half-automatic decisions taken by ordinary people in response
to life's daily bumps and urgings. That climate in the U.S. today seems
far from salubrious.

Some of the alarmists who see every act of dishonesty as a symp-   3
tom of general corruption make the mistake of judging people by
utopian rather than human standards. A spark of larceny leaps in
everyone, and the scene would be dull without it. Nor is the evidence
about dishonesty clear-cut.

Everybody is supposedly eager to cheat the Government on his   4
tax return. That impression is reinforced by the occasionally epic search
of U.S. business for tax loopholes—which may be ethically debatable
but are, by definition, not illegal. In fact, the American is a model
taxpayer, and was so even before Internal Revenue installed its formi-
dable, automated data-processing system known as "the Machine."
The Government last year indicted fewer than 2,000 out of 102.5 million
taxpayers for fraud. Even the most pessimistic estimate of unreported
income—$26 billion a year—suggests that more than 95% of all income
was reported.

Second only to taxes, credit is seen as an area of everyday fraud.   5
Initially, America's burgeoning credit-card business suffered considerable damage from high livers who could buy now but not pay later. The
magic inherent in those little plastic rectangles hypnotized many into

355

becoming adventurers—such as the man whose idea of the good life was to bed down in a variety of hospitals on stolen Blue Cross cards. But such abuses are now insignificant—thanks to more responsible screening of applicants and automated accounting techniques—even though credit keeps expanding. In department-store charge accounts, the default rate is only 1% or 2%. The U.S. lives in a credit economy that is essentially based on trust and responsibility.

With all this conceded, there is still plenty of evidence to support those who fear that America is becoming a nation of smalltime chiselers.   6

Boosters & Snitchers

Shoplifting, for instance, is dramatically on the rise, and the value of the average item taken from supermarkets has risen from $1.11 in 1961 to $3.06 in 1965. Most shoplifters, whether professionals ("boosters") or amateurs ("snitchers"), are women, perhaps because the female form and the clothes that cover it best lend themselves to secreting a variety of boodle. Pros use such props as "Jane Russell bras" and "booster bloomers"; sometimes a roomy coat is fitted out with interior hooks that can turn a little old lady into an ambulatory notions counter. Many an obviously pregnant shopper has been delivered as soon as she got home—of anything and everything except a baby. "Booster boxes," apparently well-wrapped packages equipped with hinged flaps, are standard equipment for both amateurs and professionals. Some of the devices get to be pretty specialized; pizza boxes are ideal for boosting or snitching phonograph records. On Madison Avenue, naturally, stealing acquires tone; Abercrombie & Fitch reports that its shoplifters use booster boxes made from attaché cases.   7

Store owners are striking back. Small items, such as razor blades and lipsticks, are kept near the cashier and made as large as possible by encasing them in plastic bubbles and affixing them to cards. Large convex mirrors are scattered about as much for their deterrent effect as for surveillance. One ingenious piece of psychological warfare is the "spook" technique: a supermarket customer suspected of slipping something into her pocket is confronted by the manager, who silently and significantly drops an identical item into her shopping cart. The shocked snitcher is frequently so embarrassed that she returns both items before leaving the store. A favorite object of snitching is the shopping cart itself; hundreds of thousands disappear each year to become baby carriages, barbecues and laundry baskets.   8

By current estimates, one out of every 52 supermarket customers is secreting at least one item that will not be paid for. Somebody will pay, though—the 51 honest customers to whom the cost of America's $2 billion–$3 billion annual shoplifting loss is passed along in higher   9 prices, together with the cost of the security guards, preventive devices and legal prosecution of those who are caught.

A variant of shoplifting that is plaguing department stores is   10 refund chiseling. Perhaps the refunder merely preys on a store's concern for customer good will to wear a dress once, then take it back, pretending to herself that her intentions were honest all along. On the rise, though, is the practice of picking up something and bringing it up to the counter as yesterday's purchase being returned. Stores that normally require a sales slip will often waive the rule for a flustered lady who perhaps produces the "wrong" slip, legitimately acquired with a lesser purchase.

Finger Bowls & Bibles

Business and industry lose uncounted millions to the depreda-   11 tions of employees—from the clerk who pre-empts stamps and stationery to the truckdriver who knocks off work with a truckload of company products for his own private enterprise. There is the classic case of the aircraft company on the West Coast, which one evening instructed its workers as they left the factory to assemble in the yard. The management intended to take a group photograph, but the workers assumed that there was going to be some kind of inspection, and the ground was suddenly littered with hastily abandoned tools and equipment.

Such petty thefts are growing, and so are big-time dippings into   12 tills. Last year an estimated $1 billion was embezzled from U.S. business.

Stealing from one's employer is often hardly considered stealing   13 at all. According to Harvard Sociology Professor Chad Gordon, people either justify it by such unconscious mechanisms as "The company has it coming" and "They owe it to me" (because they didn't give me a raise), or cheaters neutralize their dishonesty by saying "Everybody does it." People play down their peculations, says Gordon, with attitudes like 'It's the right of every good union man to take home so many power tools a year.' They feel as if it's owed to them in the same way that academics feel that publishers owe them free books or top executives feel the company owes them a country club."

Bigness—and the impersonality that goes with it—is an invitation   14 to the everyday dishonesty of upright citizens. Who knows this better than the telephone company? Legend has it that the first pay phone, installed in Hartford, Conn., in 1889, was loaded with slugs on its first day's operation. Since then, human ingenuity has been taxed to find new ways of robbing public phones, ranging from stuffing the coin slots with paper to tampering with the wires that control the coin release.

Another popular device is to use the phone to transmit signals without paying; this is done by letting the phone ring a certain number of times or by making incompleted person-to-person calls to one's own home according to a prearranged code. Hotels are traditional victims. New York's Americana lost 38,000 demitasse spoons, 18,000 towels, 355 silver coffee pots, 15,000 finger bowls and 100 Bibles during its first ten months of operation. Ski resorts have had so much pilferage of equipment in recent winters that they have taken to putting plainclothesmen in ski clothes and searching outbound buses.

The big insurance companies are considered fairest of fair game.   15
A flash flood can turn into a windfall for the average suburban chiseler; old cracks in the foundations, bucklings in walls or walks—all kinds of ancient damage—are claimed for the wind and water of the moment. A crumpled fender can be padded into a complete overhaul for the family car with the aid of the friendly garage mechanic ("Don't worry, I do it for all my customers"). Then there are lucrative medical claims. The increasing occurrence of whiplash—the jolting of the neck by rear-end collision, which is attended by a galaxy of vague and often prolonged symptoms—has proved a boon to the insured and a bane to the insurers. Companies can only wince and add the cost of cheating to their rates. It comes to a sizable sum; the claims bureau of the American Insurance Association estimates that 75% of all claims are dishonest in some respect and amount to an overpayment of more than $350 million a year.

Cheating in Class

The child is father to the man. Beyond question, student attitudes   16
toward cheating have deteriorated. "You used to catch them, and they'd feel guilty," says a Brooklyn high school teacher. "I'd rip up their papers and give them a talking to in private. I don't do that any more. I just rip up the paper and walk away. I'm afraid to lecture them. If I did, they'd think I'm out of the dinosaur age."

The proportion of students who cheat is a tricky statistic to arrive   17
at. In a recent survey made for the National Broadcasting Co., 65% of the national adult average said that they had cheated in school at one time or another. Perhaps because they are more honest, 75% of the clergy and 78% of the teachers sampled confessed to having cheated. A study by William J. Bowers at Columbia University's Bureau of Applied Social Research put the figure at 50% to 60%. But however many of them do it, students tend to regard cheating almost as an open option, like whether or not to wear a necktie. Many even seem uncertain about what constitutes cheating in the first place. Dr. Malcolm Klein, a social-psychology lecturer at the University of Southern California, says that

in a survey he worked on in Boston, a majority of students "thought there was nothing at all wrong with answering 'Present' for another student, submitting as one's own a paper written by another student in a past year, or submitting the same paper to more than one class."

Most student cheaters stick to the time-honored devices—notes 18 on facial tissue, watch crystals and various accessible portions of the anatomy—though electronics have been pressed into service by the gadget-minded, who use radio transmitters to beam information to tiny receivers disguised as hearing aids. One company has introduced a battery-operated PockeTutor to fit into the breast pocket, in which a note-crammed tape can be rolled behind a transparent window by means of a switch on the student's wristwatch.

Yet in a few schools and colleges, there is practically no cheating 19 at all. Perhaps the most famous of these is the University of Virginia, where an honor system was first established in 1842. Virginia is old-fashioned enough for the old ideal of "gentleman" to be given some meaning. A code of honor, says Dean Hardy Dillard of the Law School, "demands not that an individual be good, but that he be unambiguously strong—a quality generally known as character. The man who lies, cheats or steals is fundamentally weak." It may, in other words, be morally wrong to gamble but completely honorable. The dishonest thing is to cheat.

At Virginia, all examinations are unsupervised. If one student 20 suspects another of cheating or otherwise acting dishonorable, he is bound by his loyalty to the school to investigate the matter secretly and speedily and, if still convinced of the other's guilt, accuse him to his face; if no convincing explanation is forthcoming, he must demand that the other student leave the university within 24 hours. The accused can do so—and no one else will ever know why—or he can appeal to an eleven-man student committee. The enduring success of the honor system is attested to by the Virginia National Bank, which claims that its branch in Charlottesville, which is heavily populated by University of Virginia alumni, has the lowest incidence of bad checks of its 32 branches.

At Haverford College, examinations are not only unproctored, but 21 students can take most of them whenever they want during a nine-day period. This requires the maintenance of a tightly buttoned lip in the presence of those who have not yet taken the exam; conscientious students have been known to turn themselves in (and be disciplined) for leaving an exam muttering, "Boy, that was a stinker!" within earshot of a fellow student in the same course.

The honor system requires too many special conditions of consen- 22 sus and tradition to be widely workable, especially given today's huge student bodies. The alternative is to have strict rules and stringent supervision. And this, according to the findings of Bowers' Columbia study, leads to more cheating. It's like the difference between a supermarket and a neighborhood delicatessen, says one undergraduate. "When you were a kid, did you steal from one of these big supermarkets? A lot of people do, but nobody steals from the deli because you know the guy depends on you not to."

Personal dishonesty is excused or at least explained by a great   23
many arguments. Many Americans, particularly the young, blame hypocrisy in the society at large. Says Poet Kenneth Rexroth: "The kids pick up a paper and read some editorial condemning the Free Speech movement, and then turn the page and find an entertainment section that looks like the wallpaper in a Hungarian whorehouse."

From Guilt to Shame

There is much cynicism about everything from TV commercials   24
and pressagentry to politicians with ghostwriters, the implication being that this is the modern way of doing things. A lot of blame is also put on the high pressure of modern life, on the drive for success at all costs, on the decline of old ethical restraints. As long ago as two decades, Anthropologist Ruth Benedict observed that the U.S. was changing from a "guilt culture," in which people's consciences restrained them, to a "shame culture," in which the main deterrent was fear of getting caught.

All this may be true enough, or at least half true, but such assump-   25
tions are usually accompanied by the nostalgic and false notion that the past was better, more straightforward, more honest. The fact is that in freewheeling 19th-century America, high-level fraud was far more spectacular than today, when business, trade and politics must function under rigid controls and searching publicity. What has increased is the opportunity for the pettier kinds of cheating, largely because of the growth of communities and of population. In the urbanizing world in which crossroads are turning into shopping centers, towns into cities, and cities into megalopolises, nobody knows his neighbor's name—or feels responsible to him. The impersonality of the supermarket, the super-university, the super-corporation gives the individual a guilt-proof out: "After all, I'm not hurting anybody in particular."

Yet whatever the rationalizations, most people, if pressed, will   26
face up to and admit their own missteps. There are no accurate measurements, but this is suggested by many factors, from opinion surveys to the behavior of defendants in court. It is a hopeful sign, because perhaps the worst part of dishonesty is being dishonest with oneself. As Groucho Marx said: "There's one way to find out if a man is honest—ask him. If he says Yes, you know he's crooked." Americans

on the whole do not seem to overrate their dishonesty—or their honesty, either.

For Discussion and Writing

1. What is the essential worry or fear this author analyzes? What are some examples that support the essay's position?
2. What does the author cite as main or contributing factors to the problem of everyday dishonesty?
3. What are some of the excuses dishonest people give for their behavior? Are these, or others, legitimate reasons for dishonesty?
4. Write an essay expressing your sense of everyday ethics. In your experience, are people generally honest? If not, how serious a problem is it? Have you been tempted by dishonesty in any form—stealing, lying, just getting away with something? Does such behavior erode character, make it easier to repeat? Can it be justified by the excuse that "everybody does it"? Do the moral arguments against dishonesty outweigh its sometimes practical benefits?

The Busting of American Trust

FRANK TRIPPETT

"Trust is a social good to be protected just as much as the air we   1
breathe or the water we drink." So argues Sissela Bok, a lecturer on
medical ethics at Harvard Medical School, in her book *Lying*. Most
Americans would readily agree. Yet Americans are finding it ever more
risky to trust the world about them. Duplicity crops up so often and so
widely that there are moments when it seems that old-fashioned honesty is going out of style.

That is certainly not the case. Most Americans are dependable and   2
forthright—most of the time. Enough people fall short of square dealing, however, to have left Americans a keen hunger for someone to
trust. While political lying may have entered an "era of mass production," as Critic Robert Adams says in *Bad Mouth*, the problem of deception goes far beyond politics. Many people in academia, in science, in
engineering, in medicine, in law, in the crafts—all have been caught in
the act of exercising the scruples of a fly-by-night lightning-rod salesman. Skulduggery turns up so often in the commercial world that the
best graduate schools of business train students to cope with deceptive
practices. Americans as a whole so stretch the truth in preparing their
tax returns that the Internal Revenue Service claims that it cost the U.S.
Treasury at least $18 billion last year. An obscure copy editor at the New
York *Herald Tribune* coined the phrase Credibility Gap 15 years ago to
jazz up a headline over a story about L.B.J.'s Washington. Today Credibility Gap appears to span the continent.

Honesty, as Diogenes would caution, has never been the strong   3
suit of the human species. Mandatory oath taking in legal proceedings
was not invented out of faith in the natural probity of witnesses.
Everybody fibs, alas. It is also true that every epoch has its roster of
villains, its quota of predatory deceit. Yet today the roster seems far
longer than usual, and most observers agree that the quota of duplicity—from artful dodging to elaborate fraud—is growing intolerably
large.

Why? In addition to the ever present greed and the lust for special   4
advantage, there are a number of reasons for increased deception. The
general relaxation of moral codes is doubtless one. Another is the

steadily growing pressure for personal achievement in an increasingly competitive world. The incentive to cheat is heightened by the fact that society is more and more an aggregate of strangers dealing impersonally with each other. Finally, there is the snowballing impression that everybody must be cheating.

That accumulating impression, though false, is what takes such a 5 toll of social faith. The abuse of trust has become so commonplace that one must wonder whether society's very capacity to believe is not being gradually undermined. It has taken a drubbing in recent decades. Watergate yesterday, Abscam today. In between, the people's credulity has been hounded by far more than the usual con games and rackets. The pathetic fact is that Americans seem to be resorting more and more to preying, with methodical duplicity, on other Americans.

Only the young could be unaware of a change in the tone of many 6 ordinary business dealings in the country. Twenty years ago the householder who called a repairman tended to assume, more often than not, that the job would be fairly estimated and honestly carried out. Today Americans are far more likely to feel uneasy when they find it necessary to deal with crafts of all sorts —home improvement companies, television repairmen, appliance mechanics. Investigations of automobile repair shops have turned up such widespread hanky-panky that some car owners half expect to be ripped off when their vehicle needs fixing. Consumer complaint bureaus spend a good deal of their energy handling complaints about price gouging and false representation. The wish to avoid being victims, as well as the wish to save, has turned many Americans into do-it-yourselfers.

Duplicitous practices have also been staining the nation's most 7 prestigious realms. Athletes at several Pacific-10 Conference universities turn out to have been the beneficiaries of a wide-spread traffic in bogus credits and forged transcripts, sometimes with the connivance of academic administrators. Surgeons have been caught prescribing needless operations and letting medical equipment salesmen suture incisions; one salesman even assisted in a hip joint replacement. Lawyers and doctors have turned up operating auto accident rackets to bilk insurance companies. Engineers have been found out faking X-ray inspections of joints in the Alaska oil pipeline. Enough—though there is much more.

Duplicity racks up innumerable specific victims, to be sure, but 8 the more enduring results are not as easy to spot. The concentrated lying imposed on victims of brainwashing can eventually cause a mind, as Philosopher Hannah Arendt put it, to refuse "to believe in the truth of anything, no matter how well it may be established." Americans clearly have not reacted to widespread deceptions in that pathological way. Even if disenchanted, they have so far tended to become more mulish and skeptical as voters, more diligent as consumers and more strenuous as activists. They have, for example, persuaded Congress and state legislatures to pass a large collection of truth-in-almost-everything laws to ward off duplicity in such activities as lending, labeling and advertising.

Still, some ill effect has been achieved when a nation becomes 9 obsessed with and doubtful about the credibility of just about everybody and everything. One thing that has become more constant than corruption, says Robert O'Brien, a Massachusetts Consumers Council executive, is "the expectation of corruption." Such deepening doubt can be seen as both cause and effect in the every-man-for-himself spirit that has tended to show itself since the early 1970s—at great cost to the spirit of community.

Americans in the best of times must cope with a world designed 10 to confuse the powers of belief and disbelief. Theirs is a huckstering, show-bizzy world jangling with hype, hullabaloo and hooey, bull, baloney and bamboozlement. The supersell of some advertising and the fantasies that stutter forth from TV are enough to keep credulousness off balance.

Today's sheer quantity of disinformation suggests that the people 11 best equipped to cope with contemporary life might be the Dobu Islanders of Melanesia: they habitually practice deceit on everybody and exult in the craft of treachery. Anthropologist Ruth Benedict, who chronicled the ways of the Dobu tribe in *Patterns of Culture,* noted that, in their eyes, a "good" and "successful" man was one "who has cheated another of his place." The U.S. is far from living by any such absurd, upside-down ethic. Yet, in the light of today's trends, it can do no harm to ponder the price society pays for the incessant abuse of trust.

For Discussion and Writing

1. Trippett cites several reasons for increased deception in American life. What are these?
2. What are some of the examples of duplicity Trippett lists for the 1980s? What new ones would you add from your own experience?
3. According to Trippett, what are duplicity's effects on individuals and society?
4. Anthropologist Ruth Benedict is cited in both this and the previous essay. In "Larceny in Everyday Life," the author mentions Benedict's idea that we are changing from a "guilt" to a "shame" culture. Write an essay in which you consider this issue. Do you think there is a widespread belief that dishonesty is only wrong if you get caught? Are there strong pressures on people to abandon honesty as foolish, and, like the Dobu Islanders, adopt cheating as their moral standard?

Kidnapping the Brainchildren

LANCE MORROW

A story that haunts me: 1

The book critic for a newspaper plagiarized an old essay of mine. 2
Someone sent the thing to me. There on the page, under another man's
name, my words had taken up a new life—clause upon clause, whole
paragraphs transplanted. My phrases ambled along dressed in the same
meanings. The language gesticulated as before. It argued and whistled
and waved to friends. It acted very much at home. My sentences had
gone over into a parallel universe, which was another writer's work.
The words mocked me across the distance, like an ex-wife who shows
up years later looking much the same but married to a gangster. The
thoughts were mine, all right. But they were tricked up as another man's
inner life, a stranger's.

Coming upon my own words, now alienated, I was amused, 3
amazed, flattered, outraged, spooked—and in a moment, simply
pained: I learned that after the article was published, the plagiarist had
been found out, by someone else, not me, and had committed suicide.

I do not know what to make of his death, or of my bizarre and 4
passive implication in it: the man died of the words that he stole from
me, or he died of shame. Or something more complex; I cannot say.
Maybe he killed himself for other reasons entirely. But his death has a
sad phosphorescence in my mind.

Strange:.we know that plagiarism may be fatal to reputation. But 5
it is seldom so savage that it actually kills the writer. Plagiarism is
usually too squalid and minor to take a part in tragedy; maybe that was
the suicide's true shame, the grubbiness. Plagiarism proclaims no ma-
jestic flaw of character but a trait, pathetic, that makes you turn aside
in embarrassment. It belongs to the same rundown neighborhood as
obscene phone calls or shoplifting.

That is why it is hard to make sense of the information that Martin 6
Luther King Jr. was guilty of plagiarism a number of times in the course
of his academic career. How could it be that King, with his extraordinary
moral intelligence, the man who sought the transformation of the
American soul at the level of its deepest wrong (race), could commit
that trashy offense, not once but many times?

Character is unexpected mystery. King wrote his doctoral disser- 7
tation about the theologians Henry Nelson Wieman and Paul Tillich
and plagiarized passages from an earlier student's dissertation. Tillich,
one of the great theologians of the 20th century, also had secrets,
including a taste for pornography and many women not his wife.

I believe in the Moping Dog doctrine. Ralph Waldo Emerson 8
wrote about the inconsistencies of human behavior: "It seems as if
heaven had sent its insane angels into our world as to an asylum, and
here they will break out in their native music and utter at intervals the
words they have heard in heaven; then the mad fit returns and they
mope and wallow like dogs."

Part of the mystery is that King had no need to plagiarize. He dealt 9
himself a gratuitous wound. And what he lifted from others, or failed
to attribute, tended to be pedestrian—a moping prose.

Plagiarism at least proclaims that some written words are valuable 10
enough to steal. If the language is magnificent, the sin is comprehensi-
ble: the plagiarist could not resist. But what if the borrowed stuff is a
flat, lifeless mess—the road kill of passing ideas? In that case there is
less risk, but surely no joy at all. (Does the plagiarist ever feel joy?) Safer
to steal the duller stones. None but the dreariest specialists will remember them or sift for them in the muck.

The Commandments warn against stealing, against bearing false 11
witness, against coveting. *Plagiarius* is kidnapper in Latin. The plagiarist snatches the writer's brainchildren, pieces of his soul. Plagiarism
gives off a shabby metaphysic. Delaware's Senator Joseph Biden, during the 1988 presidential primaries, expanded the conceptual frontier
by appropriating not just the language of British Labour Party leader
Neil Kinnock but also of his poignant Welsh coal-mining ancestors.
Biden transplanted the mythic forebears to northeastern Pennsylvania.
He conjured them coming up out of the mines to play football. "They
read poetry and wrote poetry and taught me how to sing verse." A
fascinating avenue: the romantic plagiarist reinvented himself and his
heritage entirely. He jumped out of his own skin and evicted his
ancestors from theirs as well.

Why plagiarize? Out of some clammy hope for fame, for a grade, 12
for a forlorn fix of approbation. Out of dread of a deadline, or out of
sheer neurotic compulsion. Plagiarism is a specialized mystery. Or the
mystery may be writing itself. Many people cannot manage it. They
borrow. Or they call up a term-paper service.

The only charming plagiarism belongs to the young. 13
Schoolchildren shovel information out of an encyclopedia. Gradually
they complicate the burglary, taking from two or three reference books
instead of one. The mind (still on the wrong side of the law) then
deviously begins to intermingle passages, reshuffle sentences, disguise

raw chunks from the Britannica, find synonyms, reshape information until it becomes something like the student's own. A writer, as Saul Bellow has said, "is a reader moved to emulation." Knowledge transforms theft. An autonomous mind emerges from the sloughed skin of the plagiarist.

There is a certain symmetry of the childish in the King case. 14 Something childish in King's student mind was still copying out of encyclopedias, just as something immature in his sexual development had him going obsessively after women. And something childish in every mind rejects imperfection in heroes. King's greatness came from somewhere else entirely, a deeper part of the forest. No character is flawless, and if it were flawless, that would be its flaw. Everything in nature, Emerson wrote, is cracked.

For Discussion and Writing

1. Morrow's stance is, unlike most of the essays in this book, directly personal, at least at the start. What is the effect of his opening anecdote about the newspaperman's suicide?
2. In what way, according to Morrow, is plagiarism a kind of kidnapping? In what way is it mysterious? In what way childish?
3. Explain what Morrow mean's by Emerson's "Moping Dog doctrine" (8), and by his notion that everything in nature "is cracked" (14).
4. Morrow asks the question, Why plagiarize? Write an essay in which you speculate about various answers. Do some students steal the words and ideas of others because they don't know how to avoid doing so? Do they steal out of laziness, or fear that their own ideas won't measure up? Out of grade competition? How frequent a problem is it? Have you ever plagiarized?

Thinking and Writing about Chapter 25

1. The first essay expresses the fear that America is becoming "a nation of smalltime chiselers." The second essay claims that most Americans are trustworthy. Which is it? Has everyday honesty and trust declined, or are we generally the same as we always have been: "dependable and forthright"?
2. What are the common fears, and examples of those worries, that these writers express? How do the examples differ among the essays?
3. One important focus in these essays is student cheating. Write an essay in which you express your views on that issue. How widespread is it? What forms of cheating seem most common? Have you ever cheated? How did it make you feel? Have you seen others do it? What should or can be done about student dishonesty?

26

Wealth,
Status
and Snobbery

"Strike it rich! Play Lotto and win a million! You too can be one of the lucky ones!" How would you like to take up residence on Easy Street, receiving six-figure monthly checks, driving $30,000-dollar European sports cars, basking in luxury on the French Rivera with a bottle of the world's most exquisite champagne? Sounds nice, doesn't it. It's everybody's dream, right?

Maybe more than we think. While pundits are telling us that the 1990s will see a turn away from the greed and materialism of the previous decade, it remains to be seen whether the turn will be only a slight swerve in the long road of American dreaming about wealth, money, "financial security," and material well-being. For those ideas are nothing new in the national mind—they've been there from the beginning, when explorers saw in the North American wilderness vast resources to harvest and sell. The American dream, in one of its varieties at least, is the classic rags-to-riches story, and it's still with us—an almost unconscious drive to accumulate and consume, to be as rich in things and the symbols of social standing as it is within our power to be.

In this chapter, three writers focus on the hunger for wealth and status. In "The Sad Truth About Big Spenders" from December 1980, Roger Rosenblatt reflects on the role of conspicuous consumption in our lives. In "Hard Times for the Status-Minded," from December 1981, Frank Trippett looks at how status-seeking has become "a gaudy muddle." And in "A Good Snob Nowadays Is Hard to Find," from September 1983, Lance Morrow offers an extended definition of snobbery, and a glimpse at the decade to come.

The Sad Truth About Big Spenders

ROGER ROSENBLATT

The face of luxury (a dizzy little thing) seems to pop up at the 1
oddest times. In our own odd times, for example, there are very few
signs of a world in the chips. Yet, on a given street on a given day,
Rolls-Royces idle bumper to splendid bumper; the air is soaked in *Bal
à Versailles;* diamonds go like Tic Tacs. From now to Christmas *The New
Yorker* will be heaving with ads for crystal yaks and other lavish doo-
dads in "limited editions," for which one assumes there must be buyers.
Saks Fifth Avenue, which advertises itself as all the things we are, has
recently decided that we are a 14-karat gold charge plate ($750). Of
course such stuff is not for the multitudes. But you would think that the
multitudes might get rather sore at the spectacle of the luxuriating few.
Occasionally they do. Today in Italy and West Germany, the rich are
growing shy about strutting their stuff in public. On the whole, however, they are about as reticent as Bette Midler. On the whole, too,
nobody resents the flaunting.

For luxury exists quite comfortably on two incompatible planes 2
of thought. The higher plane is moral. On it luxury is heartily condemned, as indeed it has been heartily condemned throughout history.
"Ye cannot serve God and mammon," it says plainly in *Matthew.* Cato
offered a practical note. "Beware of luxury," he told the Romans. "You
have conquered the province of Phasis, but never eat any pheasants."
And that has been the general line on the subject, spliced here and there
with a quibble on what actually constitutes a luxury (Voltaire holding
that it is anything above a necessity), or a rare defense: "Give us the
luxuries of life and we will dispense with its necessities" (John Lathrop
Motley). Still, history's high livers have been accused of every imaginable sin: active, cardinal, political, cosmic, original.

Since that is so, it ought to follow that the world's big spenders 3
would constantly be shrinking from the public's stony stare, like devils
in the sunshine. That they do not shrink, that instead they swell and
shimmer, may be yet another sign of our essential depravity. For all its
sermons to the contrary, the world loves a big spender. We cannot help
ourselves. We may be stripped of all our possessions, out in the cold,

370

down to our last charge plate (not one from Saks), and standing last in a breadline that accepts only cash. But let a Silver Shadow come humming along, and our hollow faces will suddenly be laved in an involuntary beatific glow, like the Ancient Mariner just before the bird dropped. Why?

If such things were to be explained rationally, several possible   4
answers come to mind: 1) luxury redistributes wealth; 2) luxury is a sign of national strength; 3) individual big spending redounds to the well-being of the masses. Unfortunately, none of these explanations pertains. The general reason the world loves big spenders is fascination—not just for what they buy, but also for who they are, what they want of life. If the rich are different from you and me, it is not because they have more money, but rather because their money has enabled them to live in an apparently perfect tense: the hypothetical fantastical. To most people the question "What if . . . ?" is mere hazy speculation. To the luxuriating rich, "What if" is a lever, the foretaste of a fact. It works the same way for artists as well, but the dreams of the rich fall something short of art.

So David Bowie, the rock star, outfitted his Lincoln Continental   5
with a television, paintings and plants hanging from the roof. And a Saudi sheik recently bought a jet that he furnished with a $40,000 mink bedspread and 24-karat gold shower fixtures. Such stuff is child's play compared with oldtime big spenders like the Maharajah of Gwalior, whose model electric train ran on 250 feet of silver tracks between the kitchen and the banquet hall. But it is *all* child's play: Hugh Hefner's flying rabbit no less than the royal yacht *Britannia*, with space for a Rolls below decks. There seems a special need on the part of big spenders to locate treasures within treasures, thus ensuring the possibility of continuous surprise and delight. When little Willie Hearst asked his mother to buy him the Louvre, he may have foreseen whole hours of contentment.

The curious thing about a "What if" state of mind is that it ought   6
to provide lives of exquisite variety. In fact, it seems to lead to the most limited choices. There have been exceptions to be sure—the Chinese Emperor Qin Shihuang, who built 270 fully equipped palaces, each a replica of one that had belonged to a defeated king or warlord; and the Roman Emperor Elagabalus, who once had slaves bring him 10,000 pounds of cobwebs because it seemed like a good idea. Among the more gallant big spenders was the 8th century caliph Harun al-Rashid, who, in order to reduce the homesickness of a Greek slave girl he was fond of, built her an exact replica of her home town, and populated it with thousands of his own subjects. Among the more picturesque was Gerald, Lord Berners, who installed a piano in his Rolls and invited a horse to tea.

Unhappily, such ingenuity is a thing of the past—except for the   7
oil-well-off Arabs who, no matter what sniffy Westerners may think of
their taste, have at least restored adventure to money. A London Arab
has redone his Regency bedroom in polyurethane clouds and stars that
twinkle. He shows a sweet imagination, if not a wild one. For the most
part, however, the rich follow disappointingly uniform patterns of
spending.

First they buy a house, a very big house, or two or ten. These days   8
it is a hardship even for the wealthy to build a mansion from the ground
up, but they may always acquire one ready-made. Jerry Buss, owner of
the Los Angeles Lakers and Los Angeles Kings, has recently bought the
legendary Pickfair (Will he rename it Bussfare?). It has 22 rooms, which
sounds a lot for a bachelor, but big spenders always enjoy an abundance
of rooms, even when those rooms have no particular functions.

It is as if the rooms were chambers of the heart, and the houses   9
their owners objectified. Each room not only has a mood (blue, red) but
also is one; and the rooms that are rarely or never entered are like
secrets. The great old houses are less like gothic castles than gothic
novels, laced with crooked passages and sudden stairs that add control-
lable menace to ensurable surprise. More child's play still. Even the
temporary homes of the rich, the so-called luxury hotels, are homes
with a difference. The brand-new Palace Hotel in mid-Manhattan plans
a library that will contain 4,000 fake-fronted books, thus creating what
has to be the largest fake-fronted book collection in the country.

After houses come gardens. A big house is one way to establish   10
Paradise, but a garden, historically, is a more appropriate place to start.
The childish "What if" that envisions a mansion is not nearly so
ambitious as one that seeks to transplant cypresses from one soil to
another (as Hearst did in San Simeon) or to display the rarest species.
(After seeing Lionel Rothschild's Japanese garden in London, the Japanese Ambassador was said to remark: "We have nothing like this in
Japan.") Versailles, the model of gardening for so many big spenders,
must have had Eden as its model, as a place at once disciplined and
open-ended. That is the way the rich would have nature: apparently
free yet under the thumb. They would have their animals the same way,
which is why they are often attended by clawless panthers and gaga-
looking bears.

First houses, then gardens, then animals, then man. The rich   11
cannot create man, but they can toss a party for him. No passage in *The
Great Gatsby* is more strangely moving than the list of party guests; the
silly, nursery-rhyme names—Clarence Endive, Edgar Beaver, the
Catlips—roll out like streamers. Yet Gatsby's parties were restrained
compared with, say, the $200,000 "picnic" that T.C. and Phyllis Morrow

of Houston threw last December for 1,000 friends, including Farrah Fawcett and John Travolta (who did not show), which featured a "country disco band." The emphasis of such fiestas is on the collecting of people, who if they cannot be owned outright may at least be rented.

But what do these versions of *Genesis* come to? After the big house   12 and the big garden and the big animals, parties and people, what do most of the world's big spenders announce? That they are bored. *Bored.* The gods created men because they were bored, said Kierkegaard, so evidently the rich do likewise. They start out shimmying with hope and wind up hung over, believing with Baudelaire that the world will end by being swallowed up in an immense yawn. Their gardens are Candide's, not Eden's. Ever present at the creation, they find it wanting, and ask for sympathy in their autobiographies.

Does the world comply? Absolutely. For all their crackpot self-   13 indulgences, the big spenders ought to be razzed off the earth. Instead, the world takes them to its heart, which brings us back to the why. Perhaps because we find them sad, the way a huge child can be sad—frightening because of its unnatural size, but essentially sad nonetheless. It is not that the rich are any sadder than the rest of us, of course, but that they are so surprised at finding themselves sad at all. It is not that they are any more bored than the rest of us, either, but that they go to so much trouble to avoid being so.

Then too there is the possibility that our hearts go out to these   14 people because they suffer on our behalf. Most of us merely dream nonsense, but the rich have to live it; and while we rarely endure the consequences of our fantasies, they do so relentlessly. Allan Carr, the co-producer of *Grease,* reflecting on his Malibu dream house and his Beverly Hills mansion with its copper-walled disco chamber, exulted, "This is my fantasy . . . I'm dreaming all this." Then he added that he would kill anyone who awakened him. Who would think of doing that? Thanks to the Allan Carrs, all our harebrained desires are realized by proxy, like hiring a mercenary to fight in a war.

Yet perhaps the most endearing virtue of big spenders is that they   15 are wonderfully entertaining. There is nothing like them. If a conga line could be made up extending from Qin Shihuang and Elagabalus, through Hearst, the sheiks and Allan Carr, we would need no Broadway shows. It is not just their polyurethane clouds and disco chambers; it is their hilarious innocence, their religious concentration on themselves. What's more, they rarely know how entertaining they are. Nero, for example, when he entered his Golden House with its statue of himself, 120 feet high, and its private lake, observed: "At last I am beginning to live like a human being." Who but a real trouper could have come up with a line like that?

For Discussion and Writing

1. Rosenblatt says that people have decidedly mixed feelings about luxury and those who can afford it. What are the two sides of this inconsistent attitude?
2. What is one of the primary attractions of "the luxuriating rich" in the public mind? In what ways are wealthy spending patterns uniformly unimaginative?
3. What is "sad" about the rich? Is Rosenblatt serious when he says that the rich "suffer on our behalf"? What is the "endearing virtue" of the wealthy?
4. Is luxurious wealth a positive thing for society—"a sign of national strength," a model for the middle-class and poor to emulate, a way of rewarding effort and achievement? Write an essay in which you reflect on the meaning of material riches—what it says about us, what good or ill it does, whether even those who claim to oppose wealth would succumb to its seductions if they could.

Hard Times for the Status-Minded

FRANK TRIPPETT

He may never have been a Galileo of the social firmament, but as a journalist Vance Packard is clear-eyed enough to have seen, before anybody else, that the post-World War II U.S. had got caught up in a compulsive competition for status. The proof came in *The Status Seekers* (1959), a dissection of those Americans who, as the author put it, were "continually straining to surround themselves with visible evidence of the superior rank they are claiming." Since that happened to include just about the entire U.S. population, the great status game, once focused, provoked a great many fears that it would damage the egalitarian ideal and hasten the evolution of sharp class lines. What none of the fearful saw was that, given the services of mass production and sustained prosperity, universal chasing after prestige would engender such a gorgeous and gaudy muddle of status symbols as to reduce the game to farce—which it has now plainly become. 1

Status in its diverse forms still exists, no doubt, and many an American is still out there grabbing after some of it. What makes the spectacle ridiculous now is that, except in rare cases, people who have latched onto some status cannot be sure of how to flash the news to the world, and people who are watching cannot be sure who is dramatizing what sort of status with what symbol. Order Gucci loafers and you only risk winding up shod the same way as the boy who delivers them. A Cadillac today signifies nothing about the owner except that he might well pull in at the next Burger King. Incontrovertibly, any game has been seriously maimed when you can no longer tell who is winning or losing. The status game had surely begun to turn absurd as soon as the man in the gray flannel suit began turning up in denim and sneakers— with no loss of prestige. The absurdity had clearly become utter by the year now ending: it was the year in which the President of the U.S. had to resort to the jelly bean for a symbol that set him apart from other folks. 2

The present symbolic muddle is enough to make one nostalgic for the good old days when everybody imagined that he could peg a person's status with only a few facts about the subject's clothes, schooling, job, neighborhood and car. The days when everybody enjoyed the 3 habit of looking at all the artifacts of civilized existence as though they were primarily badges of rank. The days when elitist Middle Americans casually sneered at fellow citizens who lived in suburban split-level houses—which only a Rockefeller could afford today. Inflation is just one of the things that undermined the great status chase. The prior years of sustained prosperity contributed to the same end—giving people of middling status possession of most of the fashions and products (luxury gadgetry, stereos, color TV sets) that only the well-heeled could afford formerly. Then, too, the cultural conniptions of the 1960s and '70s helped subvert the rules of the status game; hell-raising youth provided adult Americans with (besides headaches) liberating proof that it is possible to have a good time while disdaining conventional symbols.

So many of the game's players, as well as its symbols, have   4 changed. Many Americans have lost interest in status showing off, as is handily deduced from a *Wall Street Journal* headline of this very season: MOST BOSSES SHUN SYMBOLS OF STATUS. Other Americans have taken to picking their symbols to reflect values other than social rank. In *The New Elite*, out this year, David Lebedoff reports that professional and artistic Americans have begun shrugging aside the traditional symbols of economic rank. Says Lebedoff: "They can't afford them, so they downplay them. A mink coat at a faculty party is a disaster." Another social critic, John Brooks, suggests (in *Showing Off in America; From Conspicuous Consumption to Parody Display,* published last summer) that people are undermining the traditional status competition by mocking it. Says Brooks, for instance, of those who sport so-called high-tech decor in their homes: "They flaunt commercial and industrial objects to prove that they don't have to be serious about such matters."

The confusion of the U.S. status race has been abetted by, among   5 all else, the widespread adulteration of the very idea of the status symbol. The phrase has long since been stretched into an all-purpose label that gets promiscuously stuck on things that symbolize not status but mere fashion and faddishness. Even those graffiti-stamped T shirts that have had such a long, hot run of popularity have been called status symbols. Nonsense. If such garments symbolize status, it is surely the entire spectrum of status, high and low; the same can be said for those ubiquitous sports shirts with little alligators on the chest.

Careless use of the phrase tells just how frequently the meaning   6 of status is overlooked by ostensible status auditors. Status is not merely rank, but rank within a hierarchy of esteem or prestige. The accouterments of style and fashion do not always or even usually amount to symbols of status. A privately owned yacht still symbolizes high financial status, but Sperry Top Siders—now worn by landlubbers of all varieties—no longer symbolize the status of yachtsman as they once did. Initialed handbags of the Louis Vuitton sort signaled uppering status in the days when people spoke of "going abroad"; now such bags have been so replicated that they represent little but the exhaustion of pop imagery. A VW Rabbit driven by a rich man dramatizes not status but conservation chic, in the same way that the now popular pickup truck, in the hands of suburbanites, is a symbol not of rank but of utilitarian chic. Some observers speak of solar heating panels as the new status symbols, but these devices do not dramatize social standing nearly as much as a philosophic (and economic) attitude. Those beepers that summon people to unseen telephones? Years ago, when they were rare, beepers emanated some prestige, but today, in profusion, they signal little but duty.

The status show, old style, still trudges on, to be sure, but it is most   7
noticeable nowadays among the rich and most amusing to notice in Washington, which displays in concentration the social mode that reflects the country's ascendant mood. Says Diana McClellan, who closely monitors the status chase as the Washington *Post* gossip columnist: "There's more of a polarization now between the really rich and everybody else. These people are plastered with rubies and things to the point where you don't think you've got a chance. How can you hope to top $700,000 worth of Bulgari jewels around somebody's neck? You don't—you give up and go with plastic Scottie dogs or something."

Status, as notion or fact, is inseparable from the human condition.   8
Given the nature of the U.S. as an open society cherishing the premise that anybody is free to rise, a good deal of status chasing was inescapable from the outset. If the chase had indeed rigidified the lines of class in the society, the symbols of status could only have become ever more clear. Reflecting upon that fact, one contemplates the present symbolic (and hierarchical) muddle with a light heart.

For Discussion and Writing

1. According to Trippett, why has the status game become ridiculous, a farce?
2. How has status-seeking changed from what Trippett calls "the good old days"?
3. What influences have helped to change the way status symbols are viewed today?
4. Write an essay about the status symbols of your generation. What are they now? How have they changed? What do they actually stand for? How seriously do their owners take them? What are status seekers willing to give up, or pay, to acquire such symbols?

A Good Snob
Nowadays Is Hard to Find

LANCE MORROW

It was not the Bach on the harpsichord that offended, or his way with celestial navigation, or the servants, or the phone calls from Ronald Reagan. No: his worst affront seemed to be the custom chopped-and-stretched chauffeur-driven Cadillac with the partition and the special back-seat temperature control. It was not even the fact that William F Buckley Jr. rides around in such a car, like a Mafia don in his land yacht, that gave some reviewers eczema. It was the way that he wrote about it, with such a blithe air of entitlement. No right-wing intellectual on the go, Buckley seemed to suggest, should be asked to function without this minimal convenience, for God's sake.

Buckley's new book, *Overdrive*, a journal of a few days in his ridiculously overachieving life, is a funny and charming exercise. Some critics who object to Buckley's politics, however, were outraged by his life-style, or more accurately by the obvious pleasure with which he described it. It is all right to live that way, but one should have the grace to conceal it, or at least to sound a little guilty about it; Buckley luxuriates in his amenities a bit too much, and one hears in his prose the happy sigh of a man sinking into a hot bath. So his enemies try to dismiss him as Marie Antoinette in a pimpmobile. They portray him as, among other things, a terrible, terminal snob.

To make the accusation is to misunderstand both William F. Buckley Jr. and the nature of snobbery. Buckley is an expansive character who is almost indiscriminately democratic in the range of his friends and interests. He glows with intimidating self-assurance. The true snob sometimes has an air of pugnacious, overbearing self-satisfaction, but it is usually mere front. The snob is frequently a grand porch with no mansion attached, a Potemkin affair. The essence of snobbery is not real self-assurance but its opposite, a deep apprehension that the jungles of vulgarity are too close, that they will creep up and reclaim the soul and drag it back down into its native squalor, back to the Velveeta and the doubleknits. So the breed dresses for dinner and crooks pinkies and drinks Perrier with lime and practices sneering at all the encroaching

378

riffraff that are really its own terrors of inadequacy. Snobbery is a grasping after little dignities, little validations and reassurances. It is a way of swanking up the self, of giving it some swag and flounce and ormolu. It is a way of asserting what one is not (not like *them*), what one is better than.

There was a period during the '60s and early '70s when snobbery 4 of the classic sort seemed, superficially, at least, in some danger of disappearing into the denim egalitarianism of the time. It never could, of course. It just changed form; and the Revolution, while it lasted, enforced its own snobberies, its own political and even psychic pretensions. Today, snobbery is back in more familiar channels. A generation of high-gloss magazines (*Connoisseur, Architectural Digest, House and Garden,* for example) flourishes by telling Americans what the right look is. The American ideal of the Common Man seems to have got lost somewhere; the Jacksonian theme was overwhelmed by the postwar good life and all the dreamy addictions of the best brand names. The citizen came to be defined not so much by his political party as by his consumer preferences. It might be instructive to compare the style of the White House under Ronald Reagan with that of, say, Harry Truman. One imagines the snorting contempt with which Truman would have regarded the $1,000 cowboy boots and the Adolfo gowns.

Washington, in fact, is a hotbed of snobbery. It is an essentially 5 brainless city that runs, in the shallowest way, on power and influence and office. Access to power is the magic—access to the President, or access to the people who have access to the President, or access to lunch at the White House mess, or to Ed Meese across a crowded room, or to those chunky little cuff links with the presidential seal. But Washington is like other cities: the snobs reveal themselves by the clothes they wear and the clubs they join and the schools they send their children to and the company they keep and the houses they buy and the caterers they call.

The English, who have flirted with Beatles music and the leveling 6 principle, have returned to their ancient heritage of snobbism. They worship their ancestors and buy *The Official Sloane Ranger Handbook* and dream of country houses and old money. They have a look, both wistful and satirical, at the Duke of Bedford's *Book of Snobs,* with its indispensable advice: "A tiara is never worn in a hotel, only at parties arranged in private houses or when royal ladies are present." They think longingly of the right public school, the right regiment, the right club (Whites, if possible, or Boodles, or Pratt's, if you must). They dread the fatal slip, the moment when they might, for example, eat asparagus with knife and fork: *Use your fingers, idiot!*

It is probably more difficult to be a snob now than it once was. The 7 logistical base is gone. If Buckley were one, he would have to be considered one of the last of the great Renaissance snobs, a generalist capable of insufferable expertise on everything from Spanish wines to spinnakers. But the making of such a handsomely knowledgeable, or even pseudo-knowledgeable, character requires family money and leisure of a kind not often available in the late 20th century. "A child's education," Oliver Wendell Holmes once remarked, "should begin at least one hundred years before he was born." It does not take quite that much marination to make a great snob, since the secret of snobbery is mere plausibility, the appearance of knowledge and breeding. Still, in a busy world it is difficult to find the time and resources to give the laminations and high gloss, the old patina, that used to be the mark of great snobbery.

The true snob is a complex character. He is not merely a status 8 seeker in Vance Packard's sense of the term, or a simple show-off. (Still, touches of artful swank are essential—the polo mallet cast casually onto the back seat of the car, or the real, working buttonholes on jacket sleeves that betray the Savile Row suit.) The authentic snob shows it by his attitude toward his superiors and his inferiors. Gazing upward, he apes and fawns and aspires to a gentility that is not native to him; looking down, he snubs and sniffs and sneers at those who don't share his pretensions.

Snobbery has traditionally been founded on 1) birth; 2) knowl- 9 edge or pseudo knowledge, or merely self-assured ignorance, all of them amounting to the same thing in snob terms; 3) access to power, status, celebrity; 4) circumstances, such as the place one lives or even the things one does not do, such as watch television.

Anyone who thinks that birth and heritage are an immutable 10 circumstance should send away to one of the genealogy services that will, for a fee, supply one's family tree and family crest. It is astonishing to learn from these services that most of America, back in the mists, springs from ancient royalty.

Snobbery today tends to be fragmented. The snobbery based on 11 knowledge is particularly socialized. A person who is otherwise completely unpretending and unimpressive may do some reading and become, for example, a wine snob; he will swirl and sniff and smell the cork and send bottles back and otherwise make himself obnoxious on that one subject. Another person may take up, say, chocolate, and be able to discourse absurdly for an hour or two on the merits of Krön over Godiva. This kind of snobbery based upon a narrow but thorough trove of expertise is a bit depressing, because it reduces one of the great forms, snobbery, to the status of a mere hobby.

A larger, more interesting kind of snobbery based on knowledge 12 is language snobbery. The tribe of such snobs seems to be increasing, even as they slog through solecisms and wail eloquently that the numbers of those who understand the English language are vanishing like the Mayas or Hittites. Droves of purists can be seen shuddering on every street corner when the word hopefully is misused. Their chairman of the board is NBC-TV's Edwin Newman, their chief executive officer the New York *Times's* William Safire. One author, the late Jean Stafford, had a sign on her back door threatening "humiliation" to anyone who misused hopefully in her house.

The snobbery of residence and place persists, although the price   13
of housing makes it more complicated to bring off. Years ago, a Boston banker moved his family two blocks over on Beacon Hill, in the wrong direction from Louisburg Square. Mrs. Mark Anthony De Wolfe Howe, trying to be polite, remarked, "Oh yes, people are beginning to live there now, aren't they?"

Today, snobberies of residence and place can sometimes be   14
achieved by the familiar flip into reverse snobbery. By the process of gentrification, certain snobs can pioneer in new territories (sections of Brooklyn, for example) and achieve a certain cachet of simultaneous egalitarianism and chic. Then too, there is what might be called the ostentatious plainstyle. In West Texas, for example, extremely wealthy ranchers, their oil wells serenely pumping dollars out of the range day and night, sometimes live in willfully ordinary ranch houses and get around in pickups.

Being a snob of any kind is sometimes more difficult now. In a   15
society of high discretionary capital and instantaneous communications, the snob and recherché effects tend to be copied and even mass-produced with stunning speed. For generations, much of America's old money walked around wearing beat-up crew-neck sweaters that had been around from St. Mark's or New Haven; the khakis were always a little too short, ending just at the ankles, and there were Top-Siders without socks. And so on. Then this came to be known as the Preppie Look, and every upstart from the suburbs was marching around looking as if he were home from Princeton for the weekend. So how were the real aristocrats to proclaim themselves? By going punk? Slam-dancing at the Harvard Club? As soon as one finds something to be snobbish about, everyone else has got hold of it, and so the central charm of snobbery, the feeling of being something special, vanishes.

The very nature of capitalism militates against a stable snobbery: 16
the capitalist seeks the widest possible market; quality chases the dollars of the mob, but when the mob buys en masse, the illusion of quality, of specialness, vanishes. With metaphysical complexity, the makers of Lacoste shirts have understood this, and are making Lacoste shirts that have no alligator on them, a spectacular instance of self-supersession. In one stroke, Lacoste has taken snobbery into another dimension.

Snobbery is always preposterous but also sometimes useful. "The 17
use of forks at table," observes the English writer Jasper Griffin,
"seemed to our Tudor ancestors the height of affectation, and the first
to follow that Italian custom doubtless did so, in large part, to impress
their neighbors with their sophistication. Evolution itself is a process of
rising above one's origins and one's station." The writer Sébastien
Chamfort located what is surely the ultimate snob, a nameless French
gentleman: "A fanatical social climber, observing that all round the
Palace of Versailles it stank of urine, told his tenants and servants to
come and make water round his château."

For Discussion and Writing

1. How does Morrow define the nature of snobbery? According to him,
   why is William F. Buckley not a snob?
2. Why is it harder to be a snob nowadays? In what way is the snob "a
   complex character"?
3. Morrow mentions several recent types of snobbery. What are these?
4. Write an essay offering your extended definition of snobbery, citing
   examples from your own knowledge and experience, perhaps dividing
   the subject into types or categories, or analyzing how fads and fashions
   in snobbery rise and fall.

Thinking and Writing about Chapter 26

1. Are materialism, status-seeking, and snobbery the same thing? What do they have in common? How are they distinct from one another?
2. In what ways is your generation materialistic, status-conscious, or snobbish? What are the emblems of coolness, self-assurance, social standing? Are they material things, personal attitudes, family backgrounds, skills (such as athletics or music)?
3. All three essays explore the theme of "keeping up with the Joneses"— trying to stay even with, or ahead of, whatever is the current trend in consumption, status, snobbish affectation. Write an essay exploring the pressures you feel to behave, dress, speak, think, or consume in ways that identify you as either in synch with or against certain trends. To what extent do you try to avoid any such influences, charting your own course instead?

27

The
Work Ethic

In the 1980s, it seemed, work and the working life moved to center stage in American culture. A list of movie titles—"Nine to Five," "Risky Business," "Broadcast News," "Wall Street," "Working Girl"—gives some sense of how work played a prominent role in the popular imagination. The news was filled with stories about glamorous jobs, huge salaries, of fortunes made through enterprise and persistent effort, and styles of business attire came to dominate fashion. The terms workaholic and burnout seemed to be on everyone's lips. The Roaring Eighties, even with its many excesses, was a decade at least partly devoted to an old-fashioned American idea—that hard work is meaningful and rewarding, not only in material gain but in personal satisfaction.

But the U.S., like most societies, is hardly consistent in its views, and cycles of concern about the value and meaning of work seem to rise and fall with some regularly. In the late 1960s and early 1970s, for instance, so-called counter-cultural values seemed to hold sway, and being laid back and natural was the order of the day. People wore cowboy boots and blue jeans, not Gucci loafers and pinstripes. In the 1990s, the work ethic is again under revision, with working women asking for more family time and men taking early retirement while they're still alive to enjoy it.

In this chapter, three essays consider attitudes toward the work ethic in American life. In "Is the Work Ethic Going Out of Style?," from October 1972, Donald M. Morrison sees a radical change in working values. In "What Is the Point of Working?," from May 1981, Lance Morrow poses a similar question at the start of a new decade. And in "The Anguish of the Jobless," from January 1982, Frank Trippett considers another side of the work ethic: unemployment.

384

Is the Work Ethic Going Out of Style?

Donald M. Morrison

In the pantheon of virtues that made the U.S. great, none stands 1
higher than the work ethic. As Richard Nixon defined it in a nationwide
radio address: "The work ethic holds that labor is good in itself; that a
man or woman at work not only makes a contribution to his fellow man
but becomes a better person by virtue of the act of working." Lately the
President has so often mentioned the work ethic—and so often suggested that it may be endangered—that its veneration and preservation
have become something of a campaign issue. The President warns
ominously: "We are faced with a choice between the work ethic that
built this nation's character—and the new welfare ethic that could cause
the American character to weaken."

In Nixon's implied demonology, the man who stands for "the 2
welfare ethic" is George McGovern. Candidate McGovern briefly proposed that, as a substitute for some existing federal assistance programs, the Government give a $1,000 grant to every man, woman and
child in the land, whether working or not. Yet McGovern, every bit as
compulsive a worker as Nixon, is solidly in favor of the work ethic,
saying "I have very little patience with people who somehow feel that
it is of no consequence if they do not work." He contends that most
people share his dedication to toil, and will work if only given the
opportunity.

But will they? Or is the work ethic really in trouble? 3

There are signs aplenty that the ethic is being challenged, and not 4
just by welfare recipients. In offices and factories, many Americans
appear to reject the notion that "labor is good in itself." More and more
executives retire while still in their 50s, dropping out of jobs in favor of
a life of ease. People who work often take every opportunity to escape.
In auto plants, for example, absenteeism has doubled since the early
1960s, to 5% of the work force; on Mondays and Fridays it commonly
climbs to 15%. In nearly every industry, employees are increasingly
refusing overtime work; union leaders explain that their members now
value leisure time more than time-and-a-half.

Beyond that, an increasing number of Americans see no virtue in 5
holding jobs that they consider menial or unpleasant. More and more

reject such work—even if they can get no other jobs. Though unemployment is a high 5.5% of the labor force, shortages of taxi drivers, domestic servants, auto mechanics and plumbers exist in many places.

Young adults are particularly choosy: many have little interest in   6
the grinding routine of the assembly line or in automated clerical tasks like operating an addressing machine or processing a payroll. The nation's 22.5 million workers under 30, nursed on television and still showing their Spock marks, may in fact be too educated, too expectant and too anti-authoritarian for many of the jobs that the economy offers them. Affluence, the new rise in hedonism, and the antimaterialistic notions expressed in Charles Reich's *The Greening of America* have turned many young people against their parents' dedication to work for the sake of success.

More than the youth are uneasy. A Gallup poll of workers of all   7
ages last year showed that 19% were displeased with their jobs, up from 13% in 1969. Observes Psychiatrist Robert Coles: "Working people with whom I have talked make quite clear the ways they feel cornered, trapped, lonely, pushed around at work and confused by a sense of meaninglessness."

These developments should not come as too much of a surprise,   8
considering that only fairly recently in human development has man— or woman—had anything but contempt for work. The Greeks, who relied on slaves for their work, thought that there was more honor in leisure—by which they meant a life of contemplation—than in toil. As Aristotle put it: "All paid employments absorb and degrade the mind." Christianity finally bestowed a measure of dignity on work. Slaves and freemen are all one in Christ Jesus, said St. Paul, adding: "If any one will not work, let him not eat." For the medieval monks, work was a glorification of God; the followers of St. Benedict, the father of Western monasticism, set the tone in their rule: "*Laborare est orare*"—to work is to pray. During the Reformation, John Calvin asserted that hard-earned material success was a sign of God's predestining grace, thus solidifying the religious significance of work. Around Calvin's time, a new, commerce-enriched middle class rose. Its members challenged the aristocracy's view that leisure was an end in itself and that society was best organized hierarchically. In its place they planted business values, sanctifying the pursuit of wealth through work.

The Puritans were Calvinists, and they brought the work ethic to   9
America. They punished idleness as a serious misdemeanor. They filled their children's ears with copybook maxims about the devil finding work for idle hands and God helping those who help themselves. Successive waves of immigrants took those lessons to heart, and they aimed for what they thought was the ultimate success open to them— middle-class status. They almost deified Horatio Alger's fictional he-

roes, like Ragged Dick, who struggled up to the middle class by dint of hard work.

During the Great Depression, the work ethic flourished because people faced destitution unless they could find something productive to do. World War II intensified the work ethic under the banner of patriotism. While the boys were on the battlefront, the folks on the home front serenaded Rosie the Riveter; a long day's work was a contribution to the national defense. In sum, the American work ethic is rooted in Puritan piety, immigrant ambition and the success ethic: it has been strengthened by Depression trauma and wartime patriotism.   10

Not much remains of that proud heritage. Today, in a time of the decline of organized churches, work has lost most of its religious significance. Horatio Alger is camp. Only a minority of workers remember the Depression. Welfare and unemployment benefits have reduced the absolute necessity of working, or at least made idleness less unpleasant.   11

Automation has given many people the ethic-eroding impression that work may some day be eliminated, that machines will eventually take over society's chores. Says John Kenneth Galbraith: "The greatest prospect we face is to eliminate toil as a required economic institution."   12

Do all these changes and challenges mean that Americans have lost the work ethic? There is considerable evidence that they have not. After all, more than 90% of all men in the country between the ages of 20 and 54 are either employed or actively seeking work—about the same percentage as 25 years ago. Over the past two decades, the percentage of married women who work has risen from 25% to 42%. Hard-driving executives drive as hard as they ever did. Even welfare recipients embrace the work ethic. In a recent study of 4,000 recipients and non-recipients by Social Psychologist Leonard Goodwin, those on welfare said that given a chance, they were just as willing to work as those not on welfare.   13

Despite signs to the contrary, young people retain a strong commitment to work. A survey of college students conducted by the Daniel Yankelovich organization showed that 79% believe that commitment to a career is essential, 75% believe that collecting welfare is immoral for a person who can work, and only 30% would welcome less emphasis in the U.S. on hard work.   14

What is happening is that the work ethic is undergoing a radical transformation. Workers, particularly younger ones, are taking work *more* seriously, not less. Many may have abandoned the success ethic of their elders, but they still believe in work. Young and old are willing to invest more effort in their work, but are demanding a bigger payoff in satisfaction. The University of Michigan Survey Research Center asked 1,533 working people to rank various aspects of work in order of   15 importance. "Good pay" came in a distant fifth, behind "interesting work," "enough help and equipment to get the job done" "enough information to do the job," and "enough authority to do the job."

Indeed in labor contract negotiations expected to begin early next   16
summer, the United Auto Workers intend to make a major point of its demand for increased participation by workers in decision-making within plants. "People look at life in different ways than they used to," says Douglas Fraser, a U.A.W. vice president. "Maybe we ought to stop talking about the work ethic and start talking about the life ethic."

The trouble is that this new humanistic, holistic outlook on life is   17
at odds with the content of many jobs today. Most white collar work involves elemental, mind-numbing clerical operations. Factory work is usually dull and repetitive, and too often dirty, noisy, demeaning and dangerous as well. It is a national scandal that last year on-the-job accidents killed 14,200 U.S. workers. In most auto assembly plants, a worker must even get permission from his foreman before he can go to the bathroom. The four-day week offers no real prospect for humanizing work; doing a boring, job for four days instead of five is still an empty experience. Charles Reich says: "No person with a strongly developed aesthetic sense, a love of nature, a passion for music, a desire for reflection, or a strongly marked independence could possibly be happy in a factory or white collar job."

A few enlightened employers have concluded that work, not   18
workers, must change. Says Robert Ford, personnel director at American Telephone & Telegraph: "We have run out of dumb people to handle those dumb jobs. So we have to rethink what we're doing." In restructuring work, corporate experimenters have hit on a number of productive and promising ideas. Among them:

Give workers a totality of tasks. In compiling its telephone books,   19
Indiana Bell used to divide 17 separate operations among a staff of women. The company gradually changed, giving each worker her own directory and making her responsible for all 17 tasks, from scheduling to proofreading. Results: work force turnover dropped, and errors, absenteeism and overtime declined.

Break up the assembly line. A potentially revolutionary attempt at   20
change is under way in the Swedish auto industry. Volvo and Saab are taking a number of operations off the assembly line. Some brakes and other sub-assemblies are put together by teams of workers; each performs several operations instead of a single repetitive task. In the U.S., Chrysler has used the work team to set up a conventional engine-assembly line; two foremen were given complete freedom to design the

line, hand-pick team members and use whatever tools and equipment they wanted.

Permit employees to organize their own work. Polaroid lets its scien- 21
tists pursue their own projects and order their own materials without
checking with a supervisor; film assembly workers are allowed to run
their machines at the pace they think best. A T & T eased supervision
of its shareholder correspondents and let them send out letters to
complainants over their own signatures, without review by higher-ups.
Absenteeism decreased and turnover was practically eliminated. Syn-
tex Corp. allowed two groups of its salesmen to set their own work
standards and quotas; sales increased 116% and 20% respectively over
groups of salesmen who were not given that freedom.

Let workers see the end product of their efforts. Chrysler has sent 22
employees from supply plants to assembly plants so they can see where
their parts fit into the finished product. The company has also put
assembly-line workers into inspection jobs for one-week stints. Said one
welder: "I see metal damage, missing welds and framing fits that I never
would have noticed before."

Let workers set their own hours. In West Germany, some 3,500 firms 23
have adopted "sliding time." In one form of the plan, company doors
are open from 7 a.m. until 7 p.m., and factory or office workers can come
in any time they like, provided that they are around for "core time,"
from 10 a.m. to 3 p.m., and they put in a 40-hour week. Productivity is
up, staff turnover is down, and absenteeism has fallen as much as 20%.

Treat workers like mature, responsible adults. A few firms are at- 24
tempting to give workers more status and responsibility. In its Topeka,
Kans., plant, for example, General Foods has eliminated reserved park-
ing spaces for executives, banished time clocks, made office size dependent not on rank but on need, abandoned the posting of in-plant
behavior rules and put the same carpeting in workers' locker rooms as
in executives' offices.

The work ethic is alive, though it is not wholly well. It is being 25
changed and reshaped by the new desires and demands of the people.
"The potential of the work ethic as a positive force in American industry
is extremely great," says Professor Wickham Skinner of the Harvard
Business School. "We simply have to remove the roadblocks stopping
individuals from gaining satisfaction on the job. The work ethic is just
waiting to be refound."

In the new ethic, people will still work to live, but fewer will live 26 only to work. As Albert Camus put it: "Without work all life goes rotten. But when work is soulless, life stifles and dies." It will be a long while, if ever, before men figure out ways to make the work of, say, a punch-press operator or a file clerk soul-enriching. While waiting for that millennium—which may require entirely new forms of work—bosses who expect loyalty from their employees should try to satisfy their demands for more freedom, more feeling of participation and personal responsibility, and more sense of accomplishment on the job.

For Discussion and Writing

1. What is the work ethic as Morrison defines it? Is the work ethic in decline, as some claim?
2. From what historical sources did the work ethic arise? In what sense, according to Morrison, is that ethic undergoing "a radical transformation"?
3. What are the proposed workplace changes (as of 1972) that promise better conditions and more satisfied employees? Which of these recommendations have become at least part of contemporary working life?
4. Based on your own knowledge and experience, what have recent attitudes been toward the work ethic? Write an essay in which you try to define today's common understanding of work's meaning or significance, and its place in people's lives.

What Is the Point of Working?

LANCE MORROW

When God foreclosed on Eden, he condemned Adam and Eve   1
to go to work. Work has never recovered from that humiliation. From
the beginning, the Lord's word said that work was something bad: a
punishment, the great stone of mortality and toil laid upon a human
spirit that might otherwise soar in the infinite, weightless playfulness
of grace.

A perfectly understandable prejudice against work has prevailed   2
ever since. Most work in the life of the world has been hard, but since
it was grindingly inevitable, it hardly seemed worth complaining about
very much. Work was simply the business of life, as matter-of-fact as
sex and breathing. In recent years, however, the ancient discontent has
grown elaborately articulate. The worker's usual old bitching has gone
to college. Grim tribes of sociologists have reported back from office
and factory that most workers find their labor mechanical, boring,
imprisoning, stultifying, repetitive, dreary, heartbreaking. In his 1972
book *Working*, Studs Terkel began: "This book, being about work, is, by
its very nature, about violence—to the spirit as well as to the body." The
historical horrors of industrialization (child labor, Dickensian squalor,
the dark satanic mills) translate into the 20th century's robotic
busywork on the line, tightening the same damned screw on the
Camaro's fire-wall assembly, going nuts to the banging, jangling Chap-
linesque whirr of modern materialism in labor, bringing forth issue,
disgorging itself upon the market.

The lamentations about how awful work is prompt an answering   3
wail from the management side of the chasm: nobody wants to work
any more. As American productivity, once the exuberant engine of
national wealth, has dipped to an embarrassingly uncompetitive low,
Americans have shaken their heads: the country's old work ethic is
dead. About the only good words for it now emanate from Ronald
Reagan and certain beer commercials. Those ads are splendidly mythic
playlets, romantic idealizations of men in groups who blast through
mountains or pour plumingly molten steel in factories, the work all grit
and grin. Then they retire to flip around iced cans of sacramental beer
and debrief one another in a warm sundown glow of accomplishment.

391

As for Reagan, in his presidential campaign he enshrined work in his rhetorical "community of values," along with family, neighborhood, peace and freedom. He won by a landslide.

Has the American work ethic really expired? Is some old native   4
eagerness to level wilderness and dig and build and invent now collapsing toward a decadence of dope, narcissism, income transfers and aerobic self-actualization?

The idea of work—work as an ethic, an abstraction—arrived   5
rather late in the history of toil. Whatever edifying and pietistic things may have been said about work over the centuries (Kahlil Gibran called work "love made visible," and the Benedictines say, "To work is to pray"), humankind has always tried to avoid it whenever possible. The philosophical swells of ancient Greece thought work was degrading; they kept an underclass to see to the laundry and other details of basic social maintenance. That prejudice against work persisted down the centuries in other aristocracies. It is supposed, however, to be inherently un-American. Edward Kennedy likes to tell the story of how, during his first campaign for the Senate, his opponent said scornfully in a debate: "This man has never worked a day in his life!" Kennedy says that the next morning as he was shaking hands at a factory gate, one worker leaned toward him and confided, "You ain't missed a goddamned thing."

The Protestant work ethic, which sanctified work and turned it   6
into vocation, arrived only a few centuries ago in the formulations of Martin Luther and John Calvin. In that scheme, the worker collaborates with God to do the work of the universe, the great design. One scholar, Leland Ryken of Illinois' Wheaton College, has pointed out that American politicians and corporate leaders who preach about the work ethic do not understand the Puritans' original, crucial linkage between human labor and God's will.

During the 19th century industrialization of America, the idea of   7
work's inherent virtue may have seemed temporarily implausible to generations who labored in the mines and mills and sweatshops. The century's huge machinery of production punished and stunned those who ran it.

And yet for generations of immigrants, work was ultimately   8
availing; the numb toil of an illiterate grandfather got the father a foothold and a high school education, and the son wound up in college or even law school. A woman who died in the Triangle Shirtwaist Co. fire in lower Manhattan had a niece who made it to the halcyon Bronx, and another generation on, the family went to Westchester County. So for millions of Americans, as they labored through the complexities of

generations, work worked, and the immigrant work ethic came at last to merge with the Protestant work ethic.

The motive of work was all. To work for mere survival is desper-   9
ate. To work for a better life for one's children and grandchildren lends the labor a fierce dignity. That dignity, an unconquerably hopeful energy and aspiration—driving, persisting like a life force—is the American quality that many find missing now.

The work ethic is not dead, but it is weaker now. The psychology   10
of work is much changed in America. The acute, painful memory of the Great Depression used to enforce a disciplined and occasionally docile approach to work—in much the way that older citizens in the Soviet Union do not complain about scarce food and overpopulated apartments, because they remember how much more horrible everything was during the war. But the generation of the Depression is retiring and dying off, and today's younger workers, though sometimes laid off and kicked around by recessions and inflation, still do not keep in dark storage that residual apocalyptic memory of Hoovervilles and the Dust Bowl and banks capsizing.

Today elaborate financial cushions—unemployment insurance,   11
union benefits, welfare payments, food stamps and so on—have made it less catastrophic to be out of a job for a while. Work is still a profoundly respectable thing in America. Most Americans suffer a sense of loss, of diminution, even of worthlessness, if they are thrown out on the street. But the blow seldom carries the life-and-death implications it once had, the sense of personal ruin. Besides, the wild and notorious behavior of the economy takes a certain amount of personal shame out of joblessness; if Ford closes down a plant in New Jersey and throws 3,700 workers into the unemployment lines, the guilt falls less on individuals than on Japanese imports or American car design or an extortionate OPEC.

Because today's workers are better educated than those in the   12
past, their expectations are higher. Many younger Americans have rearranged their ideas about what they want to get out of life. While their fathers and grandfathers and great-grandfathers concentrated hard upon plow and drill press and pressure gauge and tort, some younger workers now ask previously unimaginable questions about the point of knocking themselves out. For the first time in the history of the world, masses of people in industrially advanced countries no longer have to focus their minds upon work as the central concern of their existence.

In the formulation of Psychologist Abraham Maslow, work func-   13
tions in a hierarchy of needs: first, work provides food and shelter, basic

human maintenance. After that, it can address the need for security and then for friendship and "belongingness." Next, the demands of the ego arise, the need for respect. Finally, men and women assert a larger desire for "self-actualization." That seems a harmless and even worthy enterprise but sometimes degenerates into self-infatuation, a vaporously selfish discontent that dead-ends in isolation, the empty face that gazes back from the mirror.

Of course in patchwork, pluralistic America, different classes and   14
ethnic groups are perched at different stages in the work hierarchy. The immigrants—legal and illegal—who still flock densely to America are fighting for the foothold that the jogging tribes of self-actualizers achieved three generations ago. The zealously ambitious Koreans who run New York City's best vegetable markets, or boat people trying to open a restaurant, or chicanos who struggle to start a small business in the *barrio* are still years away from est and the Sierra Club. Working women, to the extent that they are new at it, now form a powerful source of ambition and energy. Feminism—and financial need—have made them, in effect, a sophisticated-immigrant wave upon the economy.

Having to work to stay alive, to build a future, gives one's exer-   15
tions a tough moral simplicity. The point of work in that case is so obvious that it need not be discussed. But apart from the sheer necessity of sustaining life, is there some inherent worth in work? Carlyle believed that "all work, even cotton spinning, is noble; work is alone noble." Was he right?

It is seigneurial cant to romanticize work that is truly detestable   16
and destructive to workers. But misery and drudgery are always comparative. Despite the sometimes nostalgic haze around their images, the preindustrial peasant and the 19th century American farmer did brutish work far harder than the assembly line. The untouchable who sweeps excrement in the streets of Bombay would react with blank incomprehension to the malaise of some $17-an-hour workers on a Chrysler assembly line. The Indian, after all, has passed from "alienation" into a degradation that is almost mystical. In Nicaragua, the average 19-year-old peasant has worked longer and harder than most Americans of middle age. Americans prone to restlessness about the spiritual disappointments of work should consult unemployed young men and women in their own ghettos: they know with painful clarity the importance of the personal dignity that a job brings.

Americans often fall into fallacies of misplaced sympathy. Psy-   17
chologist Maslow, for example, once wrote that he found it difficult "to conceive of feeling proud of myself, self-loving and self-respecting, if I were working, for example, in some chewing-gum factory . . ." Well, two weeks ago, Warner-Lambert announced that it would close down

its gum-manufacturing American Chicle factory in Long Island City, N.Y.; the workers who had spent years there making Dentyne and Chiclets were distraught. "It's a beautiful place to work," one feeder-catcher-packer of chewing gum said sadly. "It's just like home." There is a peculiar elitist arrogance in those who discourse on the brutalizations of work simply because they cannot imagine themselves performing the job. Certainly workers often feel abstracted out, reduced sometimes to dreary robotic functions. But almost everyone commands endlessly subtle systems of adaptation; people can make the work their own and even cherish it against all academic expectations. Such adaptations are often more important than the famous but theoretical alienation from the process and product of labor.

Work is still the complicated and crucial core of most lives, the occupation melded inseparably to the identity; Freud said that the successful psyche is one capable of love and of work. Work is the most thorough and profound organizing principle in American life. If mobility has weakened old blood ties, our coworkers often form our new family, our tribe, our social world; we become almost citizens of our companies, living under the protection of salaries, pensions and health insurance. Sociologist Robert Schrank believes that people like jobs mainly because they need other people; they need to gossip with them, hang out with them, to schmooze. Says Schrank: "The workplace performs the function of community."   18

Unless it is dishonest or destructive—the labor of a pimp or a hit man, say—all work is intrinsically honorable in ways that are rarely understood as they once were. Only the fortunate toil in ways that express them directly. There is a Renaissance splendor in Leonardo's effusion: "The works that the eye orders the hands to make are infinite." But most of us labor closer to the ground. Even there, all work expresses the laborer in a deeper sense: all life must be worked at, protected, planted, replanted, fashioned, cooked for, coaxed, diapered, formed, sustained. Work is the way that we tend the world, the way that people connect. It is the most vigorous, vivid sign of life—in individuals and in civilizations.   19

For Discussion and Writing

1. Why was the work ethic an article of faith for most Americans during the 19th century? According to Morrow, what was the motive of the work ethic then?
2. How does psychologist Abraham Maslow's hierarchy of needs help us to better understand the work ethic in America? What are some limits of Maslow's approach?

3. Morrow closes with a metaphorical interpretation of work—not just one's boring job, but something much more encompassing. What does he mean in his final sentences? Do you agree with him?
4. What is your philosophy of work? How important is meaningful work in your life? For you, what is that work? Have you found it yet, or are you still looking? Write a reflective essay in which you address this issue.

The Anguish of the Jobless

Frank Trippett

The new unemployment rate: 8.9%. Everyone who hears that 1
percentage will know it is fraught with troublesome forebodings. Yet
the modern habit of mistaking statistics for reality makes it easy to
overlook the fact that the rate stands for an indigestibly large number
of individuals—9.5 million. Each point in the unemployment rate also
represents, as the President explained last month, roughly $19 billion
in potential but lost federal revenues, plus some $6 billion in financial
assistance that the Government disburses to the jobless. Such statistical
elaborations usefully suggest the vast scope of unemployment and its
staggering cost in both forfeited wealth and rescue efforts. Yet it is
essential to remember that statistics tell nothing whatever about the
reality of joblessness.

That reality is always personal and almost always lashed with a 2
confusion of difficult emotions. Indeed, the psychological cost of joblessness is more hurtful to many victims than the strain of making
financial ends meet. A few individuals, true enough, are so oddly
disposed that they can take unemployment with upbeat nonchalance,
making a lark of it or seizing the opportunity to switch careers. Still,
Americans more typically take a cruel psychic bruising when they lose
a job (never mind the cause). And if joblessness goes on for long, men
and women of all ages, occupations and economic classes tend to suffer
a sharp loss of self-esteem, a diminished sense of identity, a certain
murkiness of purpose, a sense of estrangement from their friends—a
sort of feeling of exile from wherever they feel they really belong.

The loss of a job remains, by definition, an economic event. Nat- 3
urally, it is the economic aspect of the world of the jobless that has
become most familiar to the public: the struggle to pay the rent and keep
food on the table, the suspenseful search for new work. The intangible
atmosphere of the jobless world is less familiar only because it is
ordinarily more private, often downright obscure. The most obvious
personal wounds of joblessness are often easy to spot, as in the language
of Ronald Poindexter, 34, a Washington bricklayer out of work for six
months: "I feel sick." But the profound wrench of unemployment is not
often disclosed as plainly as in the reflection of Connie Cerrito, 52, of

New York City, who last July lost the cosmetics factory position she had held for 35 years. Says Cerrito: "My job was my whole life. That's all I did. It's unbearable now. Staying home is terrible. I can't go on like this."

Common among the jobless is a sense of being condemned to   4
uselessness in a world that worships the useful. Out-of-work people who do not develop such feelings on their own are apt to be given them when they visit the unemployment office: there the applicant is more often treated like an alien culprit in need of interrogation than an unlucky citizen in need of assistance. Says a young writer who was among the anonymous hundreds that Harry Maurer taped for the oral history *Not Working:* "I always get the feeling that the people at the unemployment office think I'm a bum or something." Says another of Maurer's subjects, a welder, of the unemployment rites: "You get a feeling of rejection. Especially the feeling that they're better than you."

The worst jolt of joblessness may be that first notice of it—the   5
firing, the layoff, the company closure. That event, whatever its form, typically arouses feelings like grief, as though a loved one had died, according to experts like Industrial Psychologist Joseph Fabricatore of Los Angeles. The victim, says Fabricatore, passes through stages of disbelief ("This can't be happening"), shock, numbness, rage. The elemental severity of such a reaction tells a great deal about the invisible desolation that is possible—and commonplace—in the world of the jobless. The bruising can show up in feelings of worthlessness. Rage, sadly, often crops up in the form of destructive behavior—wife beating, child abuse, neglect of friends, drunkenness—that increases predictably among the jobless. (In a study of the social effects of unemployment over a 34-year period, Sociologist M. Harvey Brenner of Johns Hopkins University in Baltimore found that a 1% increase in the national unemployment rate was associated with a 4.1% increase in the suicide rate and increases of 3.4% in admissions to state mental hospitals, 4% in state prison admissions and 5.7% in the homicide rate.)

Surprisingly, or so it seems at first glance, most of the emotional   6
beating that the jobless take is self-administered condemnation. Says a former publishing company worker in her 30s, who was one of Maurer's subjects: "I was persuaded that I must be not only as bad as the company must have thought I was to fire me, but much worse than that. Probably the world's worst. Probably I didn't deserve to live. It doesn't simply take away your self-confidence. It destroys you." Elliot Liebow, chief of the Federal Government's Center for Work and Mental Health, says that the very nub of the lost-job syndrome is the victim's feeling of being cut off from personal and social power. The sense of powerlessness is compounded by all but universal self-blame, says Liebow, adding: "One very destructive thing is the enormous difficulty people have in seeing themselves as victims of the system. They always

blame themselves, and it doesn't matter if you're talking about a plant shutdown or a government layoff."

It is not surprising, only ironic, that the unemployed should take 7 such an uncharitable view of their own ordeal. Actually, they have merely carried into joblessness, and applied to themselves, the attitudes inculcated in them by workaday society. The American view of joblessness has never been overly sympathetic. Pioneer America flaunted its punitive sentiment in a vulgar aphorism: "Root, hog, or die!" While that position has been softened a bit (witness unemployment benefits that have ranged from $9 billion to $19 billion annually in the past few years) in the face of the fact that most of today's idleness is involuntary, the nation has not relinquished its basic view of work as sacred and work-lessness as sin. Proof that the old creed persists lies in the self-chastising of the unemployed.

Such social convictions cannot be changed by preaching. Yet it is 8 fitting, considering the frequent bleakness of the world of the jobless, to mourn the nation's way of casually accepting increased unemployment as an unavoidable trade-off cost in the effort to achieve monetary stability and defeat inflation. Newspaper Columnist Russell Baker had the notion of that trade-off in mind a few years back when he wrote: "It is obvious that umemployment is an honorable form of service to the nation." The pity is that he spoke more truth than humor.

For Discussion and Writing

1. Trippett claims that joblessness tends to produce certain clear-cut effects. What are they?
2. What sorts of emotions do most unemployed people experience?
3. Trippett talks about "the old creed" that idleness is sinful. How does this idea effect the unemployed? How does it connect with the general notion of the work ethic?
4. Write a personal essay detailing your experience with one or more of these ideas: Losing a job, being unemployed, searching for a job, failing to be hired for a job you wanted, or being hired for a job. How did you feel in any of these situations? How did your feelings change from one situation to another? To what extent did, or does, employment help shape your identity, your sense of self-worth, your attitude toward life?

Thinking and Writing about Chapter 27

1. Nine years after Morrison's essay, Morrow asks virtually the same question. Is his answer different? If so, how?
2. Compare these authors' views of the work ethic. If the ethic is changing, or declining, why is unemployment accompanied by such anguish?
3. Write an essay in which you consider the role of the work ethic, job hunting, career prospects, and so on, in your generation. Is your view of work different or unique in any way? Are the conditions of the economy or workplace factors in your situation? Do you view your commitment to work as a moral value?

28

Mortality

Perhaps few images, few ideas, are as imprinted as strongly on the human psyche as are those of our own mortal limits. Death is the formative principle of human awareness, the source of our greatest fears, the essential ingredient of religious faith, the one human characteristic that may define us better than any other. Not that we die—all living creatures die—but that we know that we do.

As the authors here indicate, views of death change, and sometimes seem mutually exclusive or contradictory. In our own day, for instance, we see gastly forms of carnage all around—caused by natural disasters, wars, human cruelty, fate—yet we think it entertaining to watch movies where teenagers are eviscerated by lunatics, or romantic characters come back after death to resolve love affairs, solve crimes, or otherwise continue having a hand in the land of the living. Do we really know what we think about death?

The essays in this chapter confront some of the ways we view our own mortality, that of others, and our place in a community of mortals. In "On Death as a Constant Companion," from November 1965, an anonymous writer looks at the modern predicament of death. In "Do You Feel the Deaths of Strangers?," from December 1984, Roger Rosenblatt defines the qualities of sympathy he thinks are missing from life. And in "The Start of a Plague Mentality," from September 1985, Lance Morrow tackles what was then the new problem of AIDS, wondering what it will lead to.

On Death as a Constant Companion

Life is too short. Perhaps no single force has worked so power-   1
fully on man as his knowledge that he must surely die. The whole civilizations have been built in death's dominion: the Egyptians turned their
land into a vast necropolis, and the Aztecs conquered Mexico not for
booty but for human sacrifices to blunt the lethal appetites of their
man-eating gods. Trying to cope with the dreadful and perplexing fact
of death, man has erected great intellectual edifices; philosophers as far
apart as Socrates and (2,300 years after him) Karl Jaspers have held that
the essence of philosophy is preparation for death. Others have sought
to exorcise death with magic. Or with reason. "When I am, death is not,"
said Epicurus. "When death is, I am not. Therefore we can never have
anything to do with death." The vanquishing of death was
Christianity's great enterprise. "O death, where is thy sting? O grave,
where is thy victory?" cried the apostle Paul.

But Atropos with her shears, Time with his scythe, the Pale Horse   2
and Rider of the Apocalypse, the grinning skeleton at the revels of
Everyman—and the God of Judgment—have maintained their power
on earth, to frighten man and elate him, to drive him to noble works
and to dreadful deeds.

Today, throughout the Western world and especially in America,   3
man's attitude toward the mystery of death is making a break with
human tradition. Medically, death seems to be constantly receding, and
some scientists think seriously about an almost indefinite life span for
man (the late Norbert Wiener, for one, was horrified at the prospect of
the overcrowded world this might bring about). Socially, the rites of
death and mourning, except at those rare times when whole nations
hear the muffled drums for a Churchill or a Kennedy, are growing more
impersonal and grudging. Religiously, the promise of immortality has
become dim and uncertain. Much of the fear and mystery that once
attended death has been dispelled—but so has much of the meaning.

The "Management" of Dying

Instead of incorporating his mortality into his total view of what   4
he is and how he should live, instead of confronting his finitude with
all the resources of myth and hope and wonderment that are his
heritage, modern man seems to be doing his best to dismiss death as an

unfortunate incident. Carl Jung warned against abandoning the traditional view of death "as the fulfillment of life's meaning and its goal in the truest sense, instead of a mere meaningless cessation." Psychologist Rollo May feels that the repression of death "is what makes modern life banal, empty and vapid. We run away from death by making a cult of automatic progress, or by making it impersonal. Many people think they are facing death when they are really sidestepping it with the old eat-drink-and-be-merry-for-tomorrow-you-die—middle-aged men and women who want to love everybody, go every place, do everything and hear everything before the end comes. It's like the advertising slogan, 'If I've only one life . . . let me live it as a blonde.' "

Half a century ago, the death of mothers in childbirth was com- 5
monplace, as was the death of infants. Happily, both are a rarity today. California Sociologist Robert Fulton estimates that the average American family can go for 20 years without encountering death, which is more than ever confined to old people. And the old people are more than ever out of the way, many of them in playpen "Sunset Villages." Their absence, and the universality of the hospital, means that dying is done offstage; gone are the hushed house, the doctor's visits, the solemn faces, the deathbed scenes that put death in life's perspective. Children of the TV generation are such strangers to natural death that on hearing that Grandfather is dead, they have been known to ask: "Who shot him?"

Physicians today write papers about the problems involved in 6
"the management of death" and debate how to handle (in that most hideous of jargon phrases) the "terminal case." There can only be gratitude for the elimination of suffering—but "management of death" raises difficult questions.

One frequent problem is whether a patient "should be told." There 7
is much medical opposition to telling him—mostly for good and sufficient reasons. But there may be other reasons not so good. Some psychiatrists have noticed that doctors tend to have a high degree of thanatophobia (fear of death). To them death is the enemy and its victory a personal defeat from which they naturally turn away. In addition, indications are that many doctors had above-average anxiety about death in their childhood, and Dr. Herman Feifel, psychologist at the Los Angeles Veterans Clinic, speculates that this is why they became doctors in the first place.

Patients often make it clear that they do not want to know the 8
truth. Yet in a study of attitudes among the dying, Dr. Feifel found the patients eager to talk about the subject that was being so carefully avoided by physician, family and friends. Once the old liturgies asked God's protection from a sudden death; today it is expected that people hope to die suddenly. And they do. In automobiles and airplanes,

through war or crime, death comes ever more abruptly, ever more violently. And after middle age, it comes suddenly through heart attack or stroke. There is hardly time to put one's life in order, in the ancient phrase, and to prepare for the end. In many a modern dying, there is no moment of death at all. Without realizing the momentous thing that is happening to them, patients are eased into the long, final coma. No matter how humane and sensible, this does raise the question of when and whether it is proper to "deprive a person of his death."

One doctor who devotes full time to giving people their death is 9 Britain's Cicely Saunders of London's St. Joseph's Hospice, which cares almost exclusively for the incurably ill. The effort at St. Joseph's is to let each patient know he is dying and help him to live as thoroughly as possible during his last weeks or days. "This is the time in their lives when they can be emotionally and psychologically most mature," says Dr. Saunders. "You remember when Pope John said, 'My bags are packed. I am ready to leave.' We are helping patients to pack their bags—each in his own individual way and making his own choices."

Not every traveler would or could face this journey in this way. 10 But it represents a compassionate frankness that has perhaps become too rare.

The Decline of Mourning

A decade ago, Anthropologist Geoffrey Gorer wrote a much re- 11 printed article on "the pornography of death." Gorer's point, also made by German Theologian Helmuth Thielicke, is that death is coming to have the same position in modern life and literature that sex had in Victorian times. Some support for the theory is provided by the current movie *The Loved One*, which turns death into a slapstick dirty joke.

Is grief going underground? People want briefer funeral services, 12 says Dr. Quentin Hand, an ordained Methodist who teaches at the theological school of Georgia's Emory University. "No one wants a eulogy any more—they often ask me not to even mention Mother or Father." Even those much scolded death-deniers, the undertakers, seem to sense that something is missing. Dean Robert Lehr of the Gupton Jones College of Mortuary Science in Dallas says that whereas students used to study only embalming, they now go in heavily for "grief psychology and grief counseling." Explains Lehr: "There are only 16 quarter hours in embalming now and 76 in other areas. We're in a transition period."

The outward signs of mourning—veils and widow's weeds, black 13 hat- and armbands, crape-hung doorways—are going the way of the hearse pulled by plumed horses. There is almost no social censure against remarrying a few months after bereavement in what one psychiatrist calls "the Elizabeth Taylorish way" (referring to her statement six months after Husband Mike Todd was killed in a plane crash: "Mike is dead now, and I am alive"). Many psychologists who have no quarrel with the life-must-continue attitude are dubious about the decline in expression of grief. Psychology Professor Harry W. Martin of Texas Southwestern Medical School deplores the "slick, smooth operation of easing the corpse out, but saying no to weeping and wailing and expressing grief and loneliness. What effect does this have on us psychologically? It may mean that we have to mourn covertly, by subterfuge—perhaps in various degrees of depression, perhaps in mad flights of activity, perhaps in booze." In his latest book, *Death, Grief and Mourning*, Anthropologist Gorer warns that abandonment of the traditional forms of mourning results in "callousness, irrational preoccupation with and fear of death, and vandalism."

Whether or not such conclusions are justified, the take-it-in-stride 14 attitude can make things difficult. Gorer cites his brother's widow, a New Englander, whose emotional reticence, combined with that of her British friends, led her to eschew any outward signs of mourning. As a result, "she let herself be, almost literally, eaten up with grief, sinking into a deep and long-lasting depression." Many a widow invited to a party "to take her mind off things" has embarrassed herself and her hostess by a flood of tears at the height of the festivities. On occasion, Gorer himself "refused invitations to cocktail parties, explaining that I was mourning; people responded to this statement with shocked embarrassment, as if I had voiced some appalling obscenity."

Funerals seem ever harder to get to in a high-pressure, computer- 15 ized way of life. But the social repression of grief goes against the experience of the human race. Mourning is one of the traditional "rites of passage" through which families and tribes can rid themselves of their dead and return to normal living. Negro funeral parades, Greek *klama* (ritual weeping), Irish wakes—each in their own way fulfill this function. Orthodox Jewish families are supposed to "sit *shivah*"; for seven days after the burial they stay home, wearing some symbol of a "shredded garment," such as a piece of torn cloth, and keeping an unkempt appearance. Friends bring food as a symbol of the inability of the bereaved to concern themselves with practical affairs. For eleven months sons are enjoined to say the prayers for the dead in the synagogue twice a day.

By no means all observers agree that the decline of such demand- 16 ing customs is a bad thing. The old rituals, while a comfort and release for some, could be a burden to others. And grief expressed in private can be more meaningful than the external forms. London Psychiatrist Dr. David Stafford-Clark thinks that the new attitude toward death should be considered in the context of "the way the whole structure of life has changed since World War II, particularly the very different attitude toward the future which has arisen. It is a much more expectant attitude—an uncertain one, but not necessarily a more negative one."

The Fading of Immortality

In quantitative terms, the 20th century seems more death-ridden   17
than any other. Yet mass death is strangely impersonal; an 18th century hanging at Tyburn probably had more immediate impact on the watching crowd than the almost incomprehensible statistics of modern war and calculated terror have today. In the last century, Byron, Shelley, Keats and a whole generation of young poets haunted by romanticism and tuberculosis could be "half in love with easeful Death," wooing it as they would woo a woman. Even before World War I, German Poet Rainer Maria Rilke could still yearn for "the great death" for which a man prepares himself, rather than the "little" death for which he is unprepared.

In today's literature there are few "great deaths." Tolstoy, Thomas   18
Mann, Conrad gave death a tragic dimension. Hemingway was among the last to try; his heroes died stoically, with style, like matadors. Nowadays, death tends to be presented as a banal accident in an indifferent universe. Much of the Theater of the Absurd ridicules both death and modern man's inability to cope with it. In Ionesco's *Amédée, or How to Get Rid of It*, the plot concerns a corpse that grows and grows until it floats away in the shape of a balloon—a balloon, that is, on the way to nowhere.

"If there is no immortality, I shall hurl myself into the sea," wrote   19
Tennyson. Bismarck was calmer. "Without the hope of an afterlife," he said, "this life is not even worth the effort of getting dressed in the morning." Freud called the belief that death is the door to a better life "the oldest, strongest and most insistent wish of mankind." But now death is steadily becoming more of a wall and less of a door.

For prehistoric man, everything he saw probably seemed alive;   20
death was the unthinkable anomaly. The situation is reversed in a scientifically oriented world; amid dead matter, life seems an unaccountable, brief flash in the interstellar dark. Not that this has destroyed the power of faith to confront death. Beyond the doubts of its own "demythologers," and on a plane of thought beyond either denial or confirmation by science, Christianity still offers the hope of eternal life. Theologians are debating whether this means immortality in the sense of the survival of the soul, or resurrection, in the sense of a new creation. Either concept is totally different from the endless treadmill of reincarnation visualized by the Eastern religions; the Christian view of eternity

is not merely endless time, and it need not involve the old physical concept of heaven and hell. It does involve the survival of some essence of self, and an encounter with God. "Life after death," said Theologian Karl Barth, should not be regarded like a butterfly—he might have said a balloon—that "flutters away above the grave and is preserved somewhere. Resurrection means not the continuation of life, but life's completion. The Christian hope is the conquest of death, not a flight into the Beyond."

The Fear of Nothingness

Admittedly, this hope so stated is more abstract than the fading 21
pictures of sky-born glory, of hallelujah choruses and thrones of waiting loved ones. "People today could be described as more realistic about death," says one psychiatrist. "But inside I think they are more afraid. Those old religious assurances that there would be a gathering-in some day have largely been discarded, and I see examples all the time of neuroses caused by the fear of death," Harvard Theologian Krister Stendahl agrees. "Socrates," he points out, "died in good cheer and in control, unlike the agony of Jesus with his deep human cry of desertion and loneliness. Americans tend to behave as Socrates did. But there is more of what Jesus stands for lurking in our unconsciousness."

Alone with his elemental fear of death, modern man is especially 22
troubled by the prospect of a meaningless death and a meaningless life—the bleak offering of existentialism. "There is but one truly serious philosophical problem," wrote Albert Camus, "and that is suicide." In other words, why stay alive in a meaningless universe? The existentialist replies that man must live for the sake of living, for the things he is free to accomplish. But despite volumes of argumentation, existentialism never seems quite able to justify this conviction on the brink of a death that is only a trap door to nothingness.

There are surrogate forms of immortality: the continuity of history, 23
the permanence of art, the biological force of sex. These can serve well enough to give life a purpose and a sense of fulfillment. But they cannot outwit death, and they are hardly satisfactory substitutes for the still persistent human hope that what happens here in threescore years and ten is not the whole story.

"*Timor Mortis conturbat me*," wrote the 15th century Scottish poet 24
William Dunbar, and he continued:
Since for the Death remedy is none, 25
Best is it that we for Death dispone. 26
That groan may be shared by all men. And perhaps it should be, 27
as should the Christian admonition to be ready to die at all times—counsel more applicable than ever in a day of sudden deaths. For it is

only in daring to accept his death as a companion that a man may really possess his life.

For Discussion and Writing

1. According to this author, what has been humankind's traditional view of death? How is that attitude changing today?
2. What are some of the hallmarks of this different view of the meaning of death? What is the predicament of modern men and women when they lose belief in immortality?
3. How does accepting death as a companion enhance one's ability to possess life?
4. Write an essay in which you describe contemporary attitudes toward death as you see them. Following this author's examples, you might consider health care and medicine, rituals of acceptance and mourning, belief or nonbelief in forms of immortality, carelessness or even death-wish behavior. With which views are you most comfortable?

Do You Feel the Deaths of Strangers?

ROGER ROSENBLATT

"**A**ny man's death diminishes me." It has always sounded   1
excessive. John Donne expressed that thought more than 350 years ago
in a world without mass communications, where a person's death was
signaled by a church bell. "It tolls for thee," he said. Does it really? Logic
would suggest that an individual's death would not diminish but rather
enhance everybody's life, since the more who die off, the more space
and materials there will be for those who remain. Before his conversion,
Uncle Scrooge preferred to let the poor die "and decrease the surplus
population." Scrooge may not have had God on his side, but his
arithmetic was impeccable.

Are Donne's words merely a "right" thing to say, then, a slice of   2
holy claptrap dished out at the Christmas season? What does it mean
to believe that any man's death diminishes me? In what sense, diminishes? And even if one wholeheartedly accepted Donne's idea, what
then? What use could one possibly make of so complete an act of
sympathy, particularly when apprised of the deaths of total strangers?

Assume that at the basic minimum the process of diminishing   3
requires a state of grief. Is it really possible to grieve for *any* person's
death? A year ago in Lebanon, a fanatic drove a truck bomb into the
Marine compound at Beirut International Airport, killing 241. We responded to those deaths, all right; Americans grieving for Americans.
The truck driver also died in the explosion. Any grief left over for him?
What about all the Lebanese who have been dropping in the streets for
a decade? Feel those deaths, do we? We say yes sincerely, but we only
mean that we experience brief pangs of pity and sadness, especially if
television shows death close enough to allow us to make identifications
with the sufferers.

Last week in a place most Americans never heard of, more than   4
2,500 residents of Bhopal, India, were killed by leaking toxic gas. How
deeply did we really feel that news? Numbers are always tossed up first
in such events, but almost as a diversion; there seems a false need to
know exactly how many died, how many were hospitalized; reports
supersede reports. When the count is finally declared accurate, it is as
if one were mourning a quantity rather than people, since the counting

409

exercise is a way of establishing objective significance in the world. Still, we wept at the pictures, for a day or two.

Just as we wept or shook our heads sorrowfully for the citizens of   6
Mexico City who were caught in the gas explosion and fire several weeks ago. Just as we have been weeping for the starving Ethiopians for several weeks in a row. There we could provide more than tears. There was money to send; one could do that.

But Donne seemed to be advocating a response that is deeper and   7
more consistent: Any man's death makes me smaller, less than I was before I learned of that death, because the world is a map of interconnections. As the world decreases in size, so must each of its parts. Donne's math works too. Since the entire world suffers a numerical loss at an individual's death, then one must feel connected to the entire world to feel the subtraction equally.

The equation gets more complicated. Donne liked to think that   8
everyone represented a world within himself. When anyone died, a planet died; messages of condolence should be flashed across the galaxy. All this intricate imagery simply provided a hard shell for soft feelings. In *The Third Man*, Harry Lime peered down from the top of a Ferris wheel at the dotlike people below, and asked who would really care if one of those dots were to stop moving. Donne saw the dots as close relatives.

For most people the difficulty may lie not in giving dollars or a   9
moment's sympathy to a distant tragedy but in feeling a part of the world in the first place. Show me an Ethiopian mother holding her skin-sore baby—belly ballooned, limbs like an insect's—and my eyes will spill tears. Naturally. What do you take me for? But ask that I see the Ethiopian mother when she is off the screen, in the caves of my mind when I am about my business . . . ah, well. Donne's thesis was that human sympathy ought not to be what we dust off occasionally but what we display all the time. Thus would we weep not only for death at a distance but for the sufferers who are closer at hand, for the family down the street whose plight goes unnoticed and untelevised—for all those in fact whom we might actually help.

Thus, too, would we be prepared for history's surprises, so that   9
when the species goes berserk and comes up with a Hitler or a Pol Pot, we would not turn our backs on those in danger. In his book *Language and Silence*, George Steiner was perplexed to consider how the torture-murders committed at Treblinka could be occurring at precisely the same time that people in New York were making love or going to the movies. Were there two kinds of time in the world, Steiner wondered—"good times" and "inhuman time"? The matter was troubling and confusing: "This notion of different orders of time simultaneous but in

no effective analogy or communication may be necessary to the rest of us, who were not there, who lived as if on another planet. That, surely, is the point: to discover the relations between those done to death and those alive then, and the relations of both to us."

But it may not be enough to establish a relationship between those done to death and the survivors. It may be necessary to make a connection with all those who die, under any circumstances—any man's death, at any time—in order to keep one's capacity for sympathy vigilant. There may not be two kinds of time in the world, but there seem to be two kinds of sympathy: one that weeps and disappears, and one that never leaves the watch. Sympathy, unlike pity, must have some application to the future. If we do not feel deeply the deaths we are powerless to prevent, how would we be alert to the deaths we might put an end to?   10

Of course, this is asking a lot of you and me, who are, after all, pretty good people, who recognize despair when we see it and even respond generously when appeals are made. Especially in this season. We are very good in this season. And how realistic was Donne's idea, given human indifference and lapses of memory? Yet at times the world can feel as small as Donne's. If nothing else, we have vulnerability to share. A reporter walking about Bhopal last week remarked how on some streets people were living normally, while adjacent streets were strewn with bodies. Everything depended on where the wind was blowing.   11

For Discussion and Writing

1. Rosenblatt tries here to get at a difficult and complex idea. In your own words, what is the author's essential point about the deaths of strangers?

2. Throughout the essay, Rosenblatt refers to English poet John Donne. What is Donne's idea of human sympathy?

3. Following Donne, Rosenblatt proposes that there may be "two kinds of sympathy" in the world. What are these, and which does he clearly advocate?

4. Do you feel the deaths of strangers? To what extent do you agree with Rosenblatt's position? Can any human being feel as much as the author suggests? Write an essay in response to Rosenblatt's appeal for us to expand our horizons of sympathy. You might offer your own definition of sympathy, and look at examples of sympathy in action.

The Start of a Plague Mentality

LANCE MORROW

An epidemic of yellow fever struck Philadelphia in August 1793.   1
Eyes glazed, flesh yellowed, minds went delirious. People died, not
individually, here and there, but in clusters, in alarming patterns. A
plague mentality set in. Friends recoiled from one another. If they met
by chance, they did not shake hands but nodded distantly and hurried
on. The very air felt diseased. People dodged to the windward of those
they passed. They sealed themselves in their houses. The deaths went
on, great ugly scythings. Many adopted a policy of savage self-preser-
vation, all sentiment heaved overboard like ballast. Husbands deserted
stricken wives, parents abandoned children. The corpses of even the
wealthy were carted off unattended, to be shoveled under without
ceremony or prayer. One-tenth of the population died before cold
weather came in the fall and killed the mosquitoes.

The plague mentality is something like the siege mentality, only   2
more paranoid. In a siege, the enemy waits outside the walls. In a plague
or epidemic, he lives intimately within. Death drifts through human
blood or saliva. It commutes by bugbite or kiss or who knows what. It
travels in mysterious ways, and everything, everyone, becomes suspect: a toilet seat, a child's cut, an act of love. Life slips into science
fiction. People begin acting like characters in the first reel of *The Invasion
of the Body Snatchers.* They peer intently at one another as if to detect the
telltale change, the secret lesion, the sign that someone has crossed over,
is not himself anymore, but one of *them,* alien and lethal. In the plague
mentality, one belongs either to the kingdom of life or to the kingdom
of death. So the state of mind glints with a certain fanaticism. It is said
that when children saw the telltale sign during the Black Death in the
14th century, they sang "Ring around a rosie!" That meant they saw a
ring on the skin around a red spot that marked the onset of the Black
Death. "A pocket full of posies" meant the flowers one carried to mask
the ambient stench. The ditty ended in apocalypse: "All fall down." The
Black Death eventually took off half the population of Europe.

During the American Civil War, more soldiers died of typhoid   3
than died in battle. The epidemic of Spanish influenza in 1918-19 killed
more than 500,000 Americans. Before the Salk vaccine, nearly 600,000

412

Americans were infected by poliomyelitis, and 10% of them died. The polio epidemic caused memorable summers of trauma, during which swimming pools and shopping centers across the U.S. were closed.

In the past four years, some 6,000 people have died of AIDS in the   4
U.S. From a statistical point of view, AIDS is not a major plague. Still, one begins to detect a plague mentality regarding the disease and those who carry it. Paradoxically, homosexuals are both victims of the plague mentality and themselves perpetrators of it. Because 73% of those who have AIDS are homosexuals, the general populace tends to look with suspicion on all homosexuals. Because the virus is transmitted by homosexual intercourse, homosexuals themselves bring to their intimate lives a desperate wariness and paranoia.

The mentality was most evident last week in other quarters,   5
among the mothers of New York schoolchildren, for example. A plague mentality results from ignorance and fear, but not in the way that is usually meant. When medicine is ignorant about a lethal disease, then the only intelligent approach, by mothers or anyone else, is to be fearful and intensely cautious. But, like a plague itself, a plague mentality seems an anachronism in the elaborately doctored postindustrial U.S. The discussion in recent years has gone in the other direction: Has medicine got so good that it is keeping people alive past their natural time? At a moment when rock fans of the First World undertake to cure a biblical scourge like the Ethiopian famine with 24 hours of music bounced off a satellite, AIDS, implacable and thus far incurable, comes as a shock. It arrives like a cannibal at the picnic and calmly starts eating the children.

Cancer used to be the most dreaded word to be uttered in a   6
doctor's office. But cancer no longer means a virtual sentence of death. AIDS does. AIDS therefore sounds with a peculiar and absolute resonance in our minds. It catches echoes of the voice of God and of nuclear doom. AIDS carries significances that go beyond the numbers of those afflicted.

In many minds, AIDS is a kind of validation of Judeo-Christian   7
morality. The virus is a terrible swift sword in the hand of God, a punishment for transgressions against his order. Thus the disease partakes, so to speak, of the prestige of the infinite. AIDS becomes a dramatically targeted refinement of the doctrine that all disease is a form of God's retribution upon fallen and sinful man. "Sickness is in fact the whip of God for the sins of many," said Cotton Mather. AIDS renews in many minds, sometimes in an almost unconscious way, questions of the problem of sin: Is there sin? Against whom? Against what? Is sex sometimes a sin? Why? And what kind of sex? And so on.

The psychological reaction to AIDS, apart from the real fears it   8
engenders, represents a collision between the ordered world of religious faith—God presiding, Commandments in force—and a universe

that appears indifferent to the Decalogue or the strictures of St. Paul, one in which a disease like AIDS, a "syndrome," is as morally indifferent as a hurricane: an event of nature. Beyond that argument, which itself now seems ancient, it is probable that in most minds a vague dread of the disease is accompanied by a sympathy for those afflicted. Sympathy, alas, is usually directly proportional to one's distance from the problem, and the sentiment will recede if the virus spreads and the sympathetic become the threatened.

In a way, AIDS suits the style of the late 20th century. In possibly   9
overheated fears, it becomes a death-dealing absolute loose in the world. Westerners for some years have consolidated their dreads, reposing them (if that is the word) in the Bomb, in the one overriding horror of nuclear holocaust. A fat and prosperous West is lounging next door to its great kaboom. It is both smug and edgy at the same time. Now comes another agent of doomsday, this one actually killing people and doubling the number of its victims every ten months as if to reverse the logic of Thomas Malthus. The prospect of nuclear holocaust may be terrible, but the mind takes certain perverse psychological comforts from it. It has not happened, for one thing. And if it does happen, it will be over in a flash. AIDS is much slower and smaller, and may not add up ultimately to a world-historical monster. But the bug has ambitions, and is already proceeding with its arithmetic. Meantime, science, which dreamed up the totalitarian nuke, now labors desperately to eradicate its sinister young friend.

For Discussion and Writing

1. What is the plague mentality, as Morrow defines it? Does he judge that view?
2. In what sense does AIDS suit "the style of the late 20th century"?
3. Writing in 1985, Morrow reflects current knowledge about AIDS. How has our awareness of or attitudes toward the disease changed or developed in the years since this essay appeared? For instance, is AIDS still widely viewed as a punishment of homosexuals? Has Morrow's general prediction of a plague mentality come to pass?
4. AIDS may be the acid test of human sympathy, as we learn about contaminated blood and infected organ transplants, and are treated by doctors and dentists wearing latex gloves and plastic shields. How has awareness of this disease affected your attitudes toward others, your views on your own human nature, or even your sense of mortality? Write an essay expressing your serious thoughts and concerns about the AIDS crisis, how it affects people now, and what it may mean for society in the future.

Thinking and Writing about Chapter 28

1. Both Morrow and Rosenblatt speak of sympathy for the dead or dying. How does Morrow's prediction of sympathy for AIDS victims differ from Rosenblatt's appeal for more active and vigilant sympathy?
2. What have been you experiences with the deaths of others—friends, relatives, loved ones? How have these concrete encounters with death helped to form your thoughts about and your responses to it?
3. Write a reflective essay in which you confront your feelings about mortality. Is it something very real to you, or a vague abstraction? In what ways does, or should, awareness of one's mortality influence character, behavior, conduct toward others, or personal values? Does death have meaning, with or without belief in life beyond death?

PART FOUR: For Further Reading

29

Assorted Issues and Ideas

Since they began, in 1965, *Time* essays have scanned the social landscape, covering an enormous variety of topics, and any attempt to gather a representative selection must by necessity omit much that is valuable. This chapter includes several excellent additional pieces that address contemporary problems.

From June 1980, "Guarding the Door," by Lance Morrow, takes a hard look at the issue of immigration policy. "The Individual Is Sovereign," by Otto Friedrich, from July 1986, argues in strong support of the right of privacy. Michael Kinsley's July 1989 essay "The New Politics of Abortion" analyzes the consequences of an impending Supreme Court reversal of the *Roe* v. *Wade* decision. In "Our Health-Care Disgrace," from December 1990, Barbara Ehrenreich blames the private insurance industry for the health-care mess. Pico Iyer's "Are Men Really So Bad?," from April 1991, questions the portrayal of men in current film and fiction. And in "Evil," a June 1991 cover-story essay, Lance Morrow speculates on one of our most challenging philosophical and moral problems.

Guarding the Door

LANCE MORROW

Their journey repeats the classic American immigrant sagas. To   1
escape the old country (the ration line, the future foreclosed, the totalitarian rant), they climb aboard overcrowded boats and go pitching out
across the water to a different life. When they glimpse the new land,
they throng to the rails; they peer toward the dock with that vulnerable
immigrant look of yearning that everyone carries in memory, like a
cracked photograph: the faces at Ellis Island, the Golden Door—or at
least the servants' entrance—to the new world and all its redemptions.

The drama, now replayed by thousands of Cubans in their 110-   2
mile trek across the Straits of Florida, can still raise a glow of patriotic
nostalgia in Americans. It is "a nation of immigrants," after all, as John
Kennedy wrote 100 years after his Irish great-grandfather left County
Wexford to become a cooper in Boston. But today Americans are having
trouble rising to the occasion. Drifting into a recession whose depths
they cannot yet judge, skittish about plant closings and lost jobs, about
oil prices and taxes that already seem too high for Government services
that provide too little, Americans are less disposed to invite more
strangers into the house. The beds are all taken, they say. The basement
is jammed with illegal aliens—as many as 12 million, by some counts,
with thousands more daily piling across the borders.

Ku Klux Klansmen have paraded around Florida lately, dispens-   3
ing their old nativist bile and giving a bad name to an argument
(AMERICA FOR AMERICANS, the picket signs say) that has more thoughtful
and respectable proponents. The *New Republic's* columnist, TRB, a voice
of intelligent liberalism, writes with some truculence: "Sooner or later,
America must face reality. It is going to be painful . . . The trouble is that
huddled masses need jobs. The American frontier (worse luck) is gone."
The American ideal of endless hospitality and refuge presupposed
perpetually expanding resources. Now, says the argument, an emerging order of scarcity mandates self-interest, selectivity, limitation, ex-
clusion. No more the profligate America with arms open in
Whitmanesque embrace, ready to issue a shovel to anyone strong
enough and willing to dig.

Actually, Congress posted very picky bouncers at the Golden 4
Door in 1921, when it began the quota system. But official strictures on
immigration have become a kind of charade. The flow of illegal immigrants persists, merely inconvenienced by the understaffed Immigration and Naturalization Service and the Border Patrol. And the U.S. has
often made massive exceptions to the law in order to admit refugees—
36,000 from Hungary after the 1956 uprising, for example, and 872,000
from Cuba since the Castro revolution. Future upheavals will undoubtedly produce massive new exceptions. A new law, the Refugee Act of
1980, attempts to bring some order to immigration, but it is not much
help in resolving the questions of fairness, humanity, precedent and
priority that the new mass Cuban migration raises.

The most basic matter of American fairness, of who is entitled to 5
what, was brought up with a theatrical appropriateness by the black
riots in Miami, the capital of Cuban America. The heavy infusion of
Spanish-speaking Latins into southern Florida has been one factor in
making blacks there (citizens with deep and painful roots in the American past) feel even more intensely wronged than blacks elsewhere in
the nation. Latins argue that the Cubans (450,000 in Dade County alone)
have accelerated business development, brought fresh blood and vigor
to the area, and thus more jobs. That is true. In fact, the entire logic of
immigration rests upon the fact that immigrants are almost always an
asset, a new presence, a little bit frightened and often culturally ingenious. But the Latin renaissance has left blacks in an unhappy third
place in the community. Often they cannot get jobs if they do not speak
Spanish; they feel, therefore, doubly estranged. Their question presents
an almost unanswerable grievance: Why does America welcome
strangers and mistreat its own?

Whites as well object that newcomers overtax the housing (the 6
vacancy rate in Dade County is less than 1%), the overburdened schools
and other public services. Beyond the matter of fairness to American
blacks and other minorities, the new Cuban infusion raises questions
about what is fair to other refugees and immigrants. Millions of people
around the world want to get into America; they pay the nation the
compliment of a sometimes desperate yearning to settle here. There are
now 9 million foreigners applying and only a small percentage of them
will get the chance to enter the U.S. legally.

Those who wish to pull up the gangplank should probably re- 7
member that arguments eerily similar to their own have been offered
almost since the beginning of the nation. In 1797 a Congressman declared that while liberal immigration policies were fine for a country
new and unsettled, the U.S. was now mature and fully populated and
so the gates must close to newcomers. In the depression of 1873,

workers rioted in some cities over the immigrants who were stealing their jobs from them. Americans, so idealistically generous and expansive in their official mythology, have generally greeted foreigners with fear and loathing. A New York newspaper editorial in the late 19th century commented on the Italian influx: "The bars are down. The dam is washed away. The sewer is choked. The scum of immigration is viscerating upon our shores." Franklin Roosevelt held rigidly to his immigrant quotas all through the '30s, when Europe's Jews were desperately seeking refuge from Hitler. The American failure to welcome Europe's Jews may have encouraged Hitler.

By comparison, the reception for the new Cubans has been fairly hospitable. The Carter Administration, after committing its customary sins of oversteering, veering in the process from one side of the issue to the other, is now trying to strike a workable, intelligent balance that will honor both the practical dilemma (the Cubans are here in the U.S., and it would be barbaric to try to ship them back) and the necessary precedents and principles (quota systems must be honored, American jobs must be protected, and the country cannot possibly take everyone who wants to come). 8

The U.S. cannot be sealed off like a medieval fortress at sundown. The Cubans who have come to the U.S. should be made welcome; but the U.S. must seek ways to discourage further outpourings. The old promiscuous invitation of the land of the free must be muted somewhat. That is an idea that Americans as well as potential immigrants may find painful to accept: a nation that has always cherished a self-congratulatory illusion that it could be all things to all who appeared at the front door must now have the character to make the sort of serious choices that might leave America seeming as vulnerable and diminished and woefully crass as the rest of the world. There are rational, realistic lines to be drawn—and promises inside the house that need to be redeemed. 9

"The Individual Is Sovereign"

OTTO FRIEDRICH

Not everyone will agree with this, but for the sake of argument 1
let us stipulate that homosexuality and other variant forms of sex are
distasteful and should generally be discouraged. Let us also stipulate
that the kind of pornography that flourishes in most cities is also
distasteful and to be discouraged. Now even if this were all true—and
a majority of Americans think it is—does it mean that the forces of law
and government should proclaim such sexual activities illegal and
threaten all offenders with prison terms? More generally, does it mean
that the permissiveness of the past 20 years has finally gone too far,
particularly in its blatant public displays, and that the government has
a moral duty to call a halt? That certainly seems to be the implication
of the Supreme Court's ruling on a Georgia sodomy case two weeks ago
and of the Meese commission's report on pornography last week. If so,
these are very questionable judgments on a very complex problem.

Granted that the government has a right to interfere if anyone is 2
being injured or coerced, the history of official efforts to regulate sex is
a long and fairly unhappy one. Both sides invoked it in the sodomy
case. "Condemnation of those practices is firmly rooted in Judeo-
Christian moral and ethical standards," said Chief Justice Burger in
concurring with Justice White's majority opinion. "Homosexual sodomy was a capital crime under Roman law ..." The same line of
argument could presumably be made to support slavery, and Justice
Blackmun's dissent offered a spirited rebuke from Oliver Wendell
Holmes Jr.: "It is revolting to have no better reason for a rule of law than
that it was laid down in the time of Henry IV. It is still more revolting
if the grounds upon which it was laid down have vanished."

Customs do change. Babylonian law decreed drowning as the 3
proper punishment for a woman accused of adultery, but if she floated
after being forced to jump into a sacred river, she was judged innocent.
In the Middle Ages, someone who had sexual relations with a Jew could
be punished by burial alive; adulterers were flogged through the streets,
prostitutes had their noses slit, and men were burned alive for having
sex with dogs, goats, cows, even geese.

In the Enlightenment of the 18th century, the Austrian Empress　4
Maria Theresa appointed a troop of spies known as Commissioners of
Chastity to enforce her prim views. Said the irrepressible Giacomo
Casanova: "They carried off to prison, at all hours of the day and from
all the streets of Vienna, poor girls whom they found alone, who in most
cases went out only to earn an honest living." Sodomy was long
considered a capital offense, and the Marquis de Sade was sentenced to
death for engaging in it. Hitler threw homosexuals into concentration
camps. In recent years the resurgence of Islamic law means that adulterers face flogging in countries like Iran, Saudi Arabia, Pakistan. And
down through the centuries, despite all the decrees, people have gone
right on, of course, enjoying sex as best they could.

Perhaps the most persuasive case against government intrusion　5
into most areas of private morality was made by John Stuart Mill in his
1859 essay, *On Liberty:* "The only purpose for which power can be
rightly exercised over any member of a civilized community, against
his will, is to prevent harm to others. His own good, either physical or
moral, is not a sufficient warrant . . . Over himself, over his own mind
and body, the individual is sovereign." The framers of the U.S. Constitution seem to have had similar views in mind when they declared in
the Ninth Amendment that "the enumeration in the Constitution of
certain rights shall not be construed to deny or disparage others retained by the people." This, plus the 14th Amendment's due-process
clause, was the basis for the Georgian's plea in the sodomy case.

For more than a half-century, the Supreme Court has been pro-　6
claiming and broadening a constitutional right to privacy, which Justice
Brandeis described in 1928 as "the right to be let alone—the most
comprehensive of rights, and the right most valued by civilized man."
Justice Douglas reasserted that idea in a landmark 1965 decision striking down a law forbidding married couples to use contraceptives
(*Griswold vs. Connecticut*). Said he: "The First Amendment has a penum-
bra where privacy is protected from governmental intrusion."

Implicit in all these controversies over sexual privacy has been the　7
admirable social goal of protecting and supporting the family. The
traditional religious taboos probably once had a similar goal. Government lawmakers simply followed that tradition (Burger's "Judeo-
Christian moral and ethical standards") when they tried to ban lewd
movies or lewd whatever, and the Justices did much the same, even in
their Georgia sodomy ruling.

This tradition ignored the changes brought by birth control, and　8
the fact that most sexual activity has very little to do with procreation.
But it seems to have been a convenient justification for government
action—or inaction. Though the Georgia homosexual was never pros-
ecuted, he challenged the convenient tradition itself by claiming that

the constitutional right to privacy applied to him as well as to anyone else. There had, after all, been no children involved, no victim of any kind, no coercion, no public misbehavior. In such circumstances, doesn't a free citizen have a right to do as he pleases? One can sense a certain irritation over such a "gay rights" claim in the brusque rejection by Justice White. It is, said White, "at best, facetious."

Supporters of gay rights quite naturally criticize the court's decision, but there is a more fundamental point in Justice Blackmun's dissent. "A necessary corollary of giving individuals freedom to choose how to conduct their lives is acceptance of the fact that different individuals will make different choices," he wrote. "It is precisely because the issue raised by this case touches the heart of what makes individuals what they are that we should be especially sensitive to the rights of those whose choices upset the majority." In this, Blackmun was echoing a famous argument by Holmes: "If there is any principle of the Constitution that more imperatively calls for attachment than any other it is the principle of free thought—not free thought for those who agree with us but freedom for the thought that we hate." 9

In some senses, sex is also an idea, subject to all the competing influences of love and hostility, of persuasion and rejection, of enthusiasm and anxiety, of conformity and ridicule. It generally ends in conditions of privacy; and the right to privacy, "the right to be let alone," includes a rule that says, Uncle Sam, and all other uninvited guests, please keep out. 10

The New Politics of Abortion

MICHAEL KINSLEY

Who said politicians are power hungry? American politicians 1
are greeting the happy news that they are free once again to exercise
their democratic prerogatives on the subject of abortion with a reserve
bordering on clinical depression. "It's terrible to have this issue back
again," New York Assembly Speaker Mel Miller told the New York
Times. Others gloomily predict "a mess" and "havoc."

The disaster facing America's state legislators, and potentially its 2
national legislators, is that they may have to address an issue of public
policy on which many of their constituents have strong and irreconcilable opinions. This they hate to do and are skilled at avoiding, even
though it is what they are paid for. They would far rather pass laws
against burning the flag. But there is no Gramm-Rudman-style automatic chopping machinery that can resolve the abortion issue. Nor can
abortion be finessed by handing it over to a commission of distinguished experts (although this ploy will undoubtedly be tried).

The politicians have the Supreme Court to thank for the fact that 3
the abortion issue is now a nightmarish gauntlet that has to be run
between two ravening mobs. Not because of last week's *Webster* decision, which opened the door (at least partway) to legislation restricting
a woman's right to abortion, but because of the famous *Roe v. Wade*
decision of 16 years ago, creating that virtually absolute, constitutional
abortion right, which *Webster* partially overturned.

Before *Roe*, abortion was slowly being legalized, state by state, 4
under varying rules, amid moderate controversy. *Roe* told abortion
supporters and opponents alike that it was all or nothing at all, a
Manichaean battle in which compromise was impossible. A generation
of social-issue conservatives was politicized and mobilized. As a result,
today's Republican Party officially endorses a human-life amendment
that would not merely return the abortion issue to the states but would
constitutionally ban abortion except to save the mother's life.

Meanwhile, many believers in a woman's right to control her own 5
body have become absolutists as well, hooked on the Constitution.
They fear that any breach in the constitutional barrier—that is, any role
for the democratic process in settling the abortion issue—will condemn

424

women to mass death by coat hanger. In April hundreds of thousands marched on Washington in a quixotic attempt to influence the very branch of Government whose independence from public pressure they count on to protect them from the mob on the other side.

You can argue it either way about who will win the coming   6 legislative battles over abortion and what effect those battles will have on politics at large. My bet is that the repeal of *Roe* (especially if it is completed by the court next year, as seems likely) will awaken and politicize social-issue liberals the way *Roe* itself energized conservatives 16 years ago. From 1973 until recently, abortion mattered a lot more to the antis than to the pros; that is already starting to change. The new politics of abortion will also put many Republican politicians in the sort of bind Democrats have been in more often in recent years: trapped between the demands of a vocal interest group at the core of their party and the preferences of the moderate voters whose support they need. They cannot abandon the human-life amendment without hell to pay. Now that it matters, they cannot continue to trumpet this extreme position without at least heck to pay. It will be an albatross around their necks. Already it is a pleasure to watch Rudolph Giuliani, a Republican candidate for mayor of New York City, squirm.

In the end, America's abortion policy could end up roughly where   7 it is now: abortion available more or less on demand for the first three months (when more than 90% of today's abortions take place anyway), available only for certain weighty reasons in mid-pregnancy and generally unavailable for the last few weeks. But we would arrive at that sensible arrangement without all the embarrassing intellectual paraphernalia of "trimesters" and "viability" that came out of Justice Blackmun's futile effort, in the *Roe* decision, to derive a necessary compromise between moral absolutes from first principles. There are no first principles, constitutional or otherwise, that can settle the abortion question once and for all; only politics can do that.

A political compromise could deal with subsidiary issues, such as   8 clinic standards and parental-notification requirements, on their own merits, whereas they have until now usually been cynical attempts to sneak around *Roe's* absolute constitutional ban. On the one side issue pro-choicers have generally lost—government funding of abortions for poor women—they might even find the opposition more accommodating once the general issue is open for debate and compromise. Right-to-life absolutists will find themselves isolated. Appeals to fairness, not to mention more cynical arguments regarding the cost to society of poor women having unwanted babies, will be more likely to succeed when banning government-paid abortions is no longer virtually the only restriction available to those who think unrestricted abortion is wrong.

For a decade and a half, the abortion issue has made extremists   9
and hypocrites of us all—pro-choicers enshrining trimesters in the
Constitution, pro-lifers using an ostensible concern for the mother's
health to restrict the mother's freedom of choice. Now we can start
being honest again. And with the Supreme Court out of the picture, we
can have the arduous but exhilarating democratic experience of deciding an important issue for ourselves.

Our Health-Care Disgrace

Barbara Ehrenreich

National health insurance is an idea whose time has come . . . 1
and gone . . . and come again, sounding a little more querulous with
each return, like any good intention that has been put off much too long.
It was once, way back in the 1930s, a brisk, young, up-and-coming idea.
By the late '60s, when Richard Nixon first declared a health-care "crisis," it was already beginning to sound a little middle-aged and weary.
Today, with the health-care situation moving rapidly beyond crisis to
near catastrophe, the age-old and obvious solution has the tone of a
desperate whine: Why can't we have national health insurance—like
just about everybody else in the civilized world, *please*?

Health-care costs have nearly doubled since 1980, to become the 2
leading cause of personal and small-business bankruptcy. Collectively
we spend $600 billion a year on medical care, or 11% of GNP—a higher
percentage than any other nation devotes to health. But the U.S. health
system may be one of the few instances of social pathology that truly
deserve to be compared to cancer. It grows uncontrollably—in terms of
dollars—but seems to become more dysfunctional with every meta-
static leap.

For a thumbnail index of failure, consider the number of people 3
left out in the cold. Despite per capita medical expenditures that dwarf
those of socialized systems, 37 million Americans have no health insurance at all. For the uninsured and the underinsured—who amount to
28% of the population—a diagnostic work-up can mean a missed car
payment; a child's sore throat, an empty dinner table.

Even among those fortunate enough to be insured, the leading 4
side effect of illness is often financial doom. Consider the elderly, whose
federally sponsored insurance program, Medicare, inspires so much
drooling and sharpening of knives at budget time. Even with Medicare,
older Americans are forced to spend more than 15% of their income for
medical care annually. And since nursing-home care is virtually uncovered, the elderly are pushed to degrading extremes—like divorcing a
beloved spouse—in order to qualify for help through a long-term
debilitating illness. Or, as more than one public figure has suggested,
they can shuffle off prematurely to their reward.

We can't go on like this. Our infant-mortality rate is higher than   5
Singapore's; our life expectancy is lower than Cubans'. As many as 50%
of inner-city infants and toddlers go unimmunized. In the face of AIDS,
our first major epidemic since polio, we are nearly helpless. Our city
hospitals are overflowing with victims of tuberculosis, poverty, AIDS, old
age and exposure. Our rural areas don't have this problem; they have
fewer and fewer hospitals or, increasingly, less medical personnel of any
kind.

But everyone knows that the system is broken beyond repair.   6
According to the *New England Journal of Medicine*, 3 out of 4 Americans
favor a government-financed national health-care program. The AFL-CIO
is campaigning vigorously for national health care, and Big Business,
terrified by the skyrocketing cost of employee health benefits, seems
ready to go along. Even in the medical profession—the ancient redoubt
of free-enterprise traditionalists—a majority now favor national health
insurance.

So what stands in the way? There's still the American Medical   7
Association, of course, which has yet to catch up to its physician
constituency. But the interest group that arguably has the most to lose
is the health-insurance industry, which spends more than $1 million a
year to forestall any thoroughgoing government action. And why not?
The insurance industry already enjoys a richly rewarding, gruesomely
parasitic relationship to the public health domain. In broad schematic
outline, it goes like this:

For decades the private insurers have fanned the crisis by blithely   8
reimbursing the fees of greedy practitioners and expansionary hospitals. Then, as costs rise, the private insurers seek to shed the poorest and
the sickest customers, who get priced out or summarily dropped. For
some companies, a serious and costly illness is a good enough reason
to cancel a policy. Others refuse to insure anybody who *might* be gay
and hence, actuarially speaking, might get AIDS.

So over the years, government has moved in to pick up the rejects: 9
first the elderly, then the extremely poor. Since the rejects are of course
the most expensive to insure, Government is soon faced with a budget
nightmare. Draconian cost-control measures follow. But because government can only attempt to control the costs of its own programs, the
providers of care simply shift *their* costs onto the bills of privately
insured patients. Faced with ever rising costs, the private insurers
become more determined to shed the poorest and the sickest . . . and so
the cycle goes.

The technical term for this kind of arrangement is lemon social-   10
ism: the private sector gets the profitable share of the market, and the
public sector gets what's left. The problem with this particular lemon
is that it tends to sour us on the possibility of real reform. Even those

who crave a national program covering everyone are wont to throw up their hands in despair: Nothing works! It's so complex! Maybe in 100 years!

It's time to cut the life-support system leading to the hungry maw   11
of the insurance industry. The insurance companies can't have it both ways: they can't refuse to insure the poor, the old and the sick while simultaneously campaigning to prevent a government program to cover everyone alike. The very meaning of insurance is risk sharing—the well throwing in their lot with the sick, the young with the old, the affluent with the down-and-out. If private enterprise won't do the job, then let private enterprise get out of the way.

With the largest-ever consensus behind it, national health care's   12
time is surely here at last. Otherwise, let us bow our heads together and recite the old Episcopal prayer: "We have left undone those things which we ought to have done . . . and there is no health in us."

Are Men Really So Bad?

Pico Iyer

Everyone knows, more than they would like perhaps, about the   1
nature, the publishing history and the unspeakable horrors of Bret
Easton Ellis' new novel, *American Psycho*. However broadly it seeks to
indict, in indelible, blood-red ink, the excesses and depravities of the
degenerate '80s, the book has certainly raised a threshold of taste, or
psychic pain, much higher than most readers would like (much as the
smash movie *The Silence of the Lambs* exposes even toddlers to a level of
psychological violence that would have been unthinkable—or at least
less powerful—some years ago). A protagonist who eats, tortures and
dismembers victims is clearly assaulting all that we hold sacred. And it
is painfully easy to see the damage such a book can do to the way in
which men see, and therefore treat, women.

But what of the way the book treats men, and affects our notion   2
of them? Insofar as Ellis has deliberately created a monstrous deformity,
it is nonetheless striking that the monster is male, and preys mostly on
women; and insofar as he intends a closer identification with his creation, the author himself is implicated in the guilt. In either case, the
culprit is a male, and the novel is unlikely to endear the unfairer sex to
a nation that is already all too conscious of the harm men can do.

Ellis' plot line is, of course, true to criminal statistics, and to our   3
intuitive sense that terrible physical violence is all too often perpetrated
by men on women. But it is very much to be hoped that the outrage
would be no less if Ellis' monster had been a woman, or more of its
victims men (the offense, in other words, lies not in the object of the
sentences but in the sentences themselves).

Consider, for example, another just published novel, by another   4
highly touted young writer, which, if it gets less exposure than Ellis',
will probably win more praise: *Two Girls, Fat and Thin*, by Mary
Gaitskill. And consider for a moment how the novel looks at men. The
first of the eponymous girls is repeatedly—and graphically—abused
sexually by her father (who, when not molesting her, pushes her down
the stairs and calls her "an argument for abortion"): the other girl is
abused, also graphically, at the age of five by a male friend of her
father's. The boys at the local high school are "murderously aggressive"

and have "monstrous voices": the nicest of them is blessed with "a morbidly cruel personality" and "seemed happiest when torturing small animals by himself."

The thin girl's first lover is a boy with "cruel lips" who plays a 5 rapist in the school play and more or less carries that role over to real life: her most attractive lover is "an abusive mental case" whose eyes "glitter with the adrenal malice of a sex criminal." Everywhere one looks there are repulsive men, "fat creatures mostly, baked pink and bearded, their self-satisfaction and arrogance expressed in their wide, saggy-bottomed hips." Meanwhile, in the background, we see a constant procession of "abusive lovers," porn collectors and groping, "gloating" lechers. The only faintly appealing male in 304 pages—his name is Knight—ran away from home "to escape an alcoholic father" and gently betrays his fiancé. Small wonder, then, that at novel's end, one girl concludes that most men are "really awful" and the other rails against "the chemical and hormonal forces that goad that sex to kill, rape and commit crimes of horrific sadism." The men in Gaitskill's first book are, if anything, even worse.

All this is fair enough, perhaps, and true to the way life may seem 6 to many contemporary young women. It could be said that women do not fare much better in Gaitskill's world, and that this view of men reflects in part the distorted vision of two neurotic girls (though if so, Gaitskill suggests, that is because of the ill treatment they have suffered at the hands of men). It could even be argued that this is how women apprehend a world largely fashioned by the likes of Bret Easton Ellis. Yet to say this is to draw dangerously close to the case for *American Psycho:* by revealing disgusting attitudes, it reveals its disgust for such attitudes. And just imagine, for a moment, that the pronouns were reversed, and that every woman in a long and serious novel was treated as oppressive: Would there not be an uproar? And is Gaitskill's form of emotional violence really much better than the more viscerally appalling kind?

None of this, of course, is to deny or defend the abuse of women 7 in much male fiction: nor is it to make the perverse point that a man mistreating women is simply giving a bad name to men. It is, rather, to suggest that sometimes, for whatever reasons, the violence flows in the other direction too, and in ways no less insidious for being less conspicuous. Meryl Streep and others have rightly complained that all the best roles in movies go to men, but a medium that takes Schwarzenegger and Stallone as its heroes is not being so kind to men either. The two hottest box-office movies not so long ago—*The Silence of the Lambs* and *Sleeping with the Enemy*—both portrayed men as psychopaths and bullies taking out their sicknesses on plucky, intelligent women; such critical favorites as *GoodFellas* and the *Godfather* trilogy merely replace monsters with mobsters. If Hollywood still too often treats women as bimbos and hookers, it is apt to see men as homicidal maniacs; the sad truth of it may be that all of us—in pop culture's imagination—are diminished as often as uplifted.

Again, this is not to exonerate Ellis: it is only to say that the interaction of the sexes, like everything else, can only be demeaned if it is caricatured as a contest of black against white. And in our justifiable sensitivity to certain kinds of violence, we may blind ourselves to others. As it is, students are being taught in school that "patriarchal" is the worst kind of insult, and misogynists must be sought out everywhere. But what is the term for misogyny in reverse? It sometimes seems that we would rectify a long history of violence against women by simply engaging in violence against everyone: equal-opportunity abuse. And that we would seek to replace one kind of double standard with another. Might it not be better to try to raise our vision of both parties?

8

Evil

LANCE MORROW

I think there should be a Dark Willard. 1

In the network's studio in New York City, Dark Willard would 2
recite the morning's evil report. The map of the world behind him
would be a multicolored Mercator projection. Some parts of the earth,
where the overnight good prevailed, would glow with a bright transparency. But much of the map would be speckled and blotched. Over
Third World and First World, over cities and plains and miserable
islands would be smudges of evil, ragged blights, storm systems of
massacre or famine, murders, black snows. Here and there, a genocide,
a true abyss.

"*Homo homini lupus,*" Dark Willard would remark. "That's Latin, 3
guys. Man is a wolf to man."

Dark Willard would report the natural evils—the outrages done 4
by God and nature (the cyclone in Bangladesh, an earthquake, the
deaths by cancer). He would add up the moral evils—the horrors
accomplished overnight by man and woman. Anything new among the
suffering Kurds? Among the Central American death squads? New
hackings in South Africa? Updating on the father who set fire to his
eight-year-old son? Or on those boys accused of shotgunning their
parents in Beverly Hills to speed their inheritance of a $14 million
estate? An anniversary: two years already since Tiananmen Square.

The only depravity uncharted might be cannibalism, a last frontier 5
that fastidious man has mostly declined to explore. Evil is a different
sort of gourmet.

The oil fires over Kuwait would be evil made visible and billow- 6
ing. The evil turns the very air black and greasy. It suffocates and blots
out the sun.

The war in the gulf had an aspect of the high-tech medieval. What 7
Beelzebubs flew buzzing through the sky on the tips of Scuds and smart
bombs, making mischief and brimstone? Each side demonized the
other, as in every war: *Gott mit Uns.* Saddam Hussein had George Bush
down as the Evil One. George Bush had Saddam down as Hitler. In most
of the West, Hitler is the 20th century's term for Great Satan. After the

war, quick and obliterating, Hussein hardly seems worthy of the name of evil anymore.

Is there more evil now, or less evil, than there was five year ago, or five centuries?   8

The past couple of years has brought a windfall of improvements   9 in the world: the collapse of communism; the dismantling of apartheid; the end of the cold war and the nuclear menace, at least in its apocalyptic Big Power form. State violence (in the style of Hitler, Stalin, Ceausescu) seemed to be skulking off in disrepute. Francis Fukuyama, a former U.S. State Department policy planner, even proclaimed "the end of history." The West and democratic pluralism seemed to have triumphed: satellites and computers and communications and global business dissolved the old monoliths in much of the world. Humankind could take satisfaction in all that progress and even think for a moment, without cynicism, of Lucretius' lovely line: "So, little by little, time brings out each several thing into view, and reason raises it up into the shores of light." But much of the world has grown simultaneously darker.

Each era gets its suitable evils. The end of the 20th century is   10 sorting out different styles of malignity. Evil has been changing its priorities, its targets, its cast of characters.

The first question to be asked, of course, is this: Does evil exist? I   11 know a man who thinks it does not. I know another man who spent a year of his childhood in Auschwitz. I would like to have the two of them talk together for an afternoon, and see which one comes away persuaded by the other.

The man who does not believe in the existence of evil knows all   12 about the horrors of the world. He knows that humanity is often vicious, violent, corrupt, atrocious. And that nature's cruelties and caprices are beyond rational accounting: Bangladesh does not deserve the curse that seems to hover over it. But the man thinks that to describe all that as evil gives evil too much power, too much status, that it confers on what is merely rotten and tragic the prestige of the absolute. You must not allow lower instincts and mere calamities to get dressed up as a big idea and come to the table with their betters and smoke cigars. Keep the metaphysics manageable: much of what passes for evil (life in Beirut, for example) may be just a nightmare of accidents. Or sheer stupidity, that sovereign, unacknowledged force in the universe.

The man's deeper, unstated thought is that acknowledging evil   13 implies that Satan is coequal with God. Better not to open that door. It leads into the old Manichaean heresy: the world as battleground between the divine and the diabolical, the outcome very much in doubt: "*La prima luce*," Dante's light of creation, the brilliant ignition of God, against the satanic negation, the candle snuffer. Those uncomfortable with the idea of evil mean this: You don't say that the shadow has the same stature as the light. If you speak of the Dark Lord, of the "dark side of Sinai," do you foolishly empower darkness?

Or, for that matter (as an atheist or agnostic would have it), do such terms heedlessly empower the idea of God? God after all, does not enjoy universal diplomatic recognition.   14

Is it possible that evil is a problem that is more intelligently addressed outside the religious context of God and Satan? Perhaps. For some, that takes the drama out of the discussion and dims it down to a paler shade of Unitarianism. Evil, in whatever intellectual framework, is by definition a monster. It has a strange coercive force: a temptation, a mystery, a horrible charm. Shakespeare understood that perfectly when he created Iago in his secular and motiveless malignity.   15

. . .

In 1939, as World War II began, Albert Camus wrote in his note-book: "The reign of beasts has begun." In the past year or two, the reign of beasts seemed to end, in some places anyway: brilliant days, miraculous remissions. But as Jung thought, different people inhabit different centuries. There are many centuries still loose in the world today, banging against one another. The war in the gulf was in part a collision of different centuries and the cultural assumptions that those centuries carry with them. Camus's beasts are still wandering around in the desert and in the sometimes fierce nationalisms reawakening in the Soviet Union. They are alive and vicious in blood feuds from Northern Ireland to Sri Lanka.   16

Saddam Hussein raised atavistic questions about evil. But the West has grown preoccupied by newer forms—greed, terrorism, drugs, AIDS, crime, child abuse, global pollution, oil spills, acid rain. The fear of nuclear holocaust, which not long ago was the nightmare at the center of the imagination, has receded with amazing speed.   17

It is touching in this era, and rather strange, that nature even at its most destructive, has clean hands. Humankind does not. For centuries nature's potential for evil, its overpowering menace, made it an enemy to be subdued. Today, at least in the developed world, nature is the vulnerable innocent. The human is the enemy.   18

New forms of evil raise new moral questions. Who is to blame for them? Are they natural evils—that is, acts of God and therefore his responsibility, or acts of the blind universe and therefore no one's? Or are they moral evils, acts that men and women must answer for?   19

. . .

Padrica Caine Hill, former bank teller, Washington mother and wife, dresses her three children one morning, makes breakfast for them,   20 smokes some crack cocaine and lets the kids watch cartoons. Then with a clothesline she strangles eight-year-old Kristine and four-year-old Eric Jr. She tries to strangle two-year-old Jennifer, but leaves the girl still breathing softly on the floor. When the police come, Padrica Hill says she loves her children. Why did she kill them? "I don't know," she answers in apparently genuine bewilderment. "I hadn't planned on it."

Who or what is responsible? The woman herself? She did smoke   21
the crack, but presumably the effect she anticipated was a euphoric high, not the death of her children. The drug arrived like Visigoths in her brain and destroyed the civilization there, including the most powerful of human instincts, her mother love. The crack itself? The dealer who sold the crack? The others in the trade—kingpins and mules who brought the cocaine up from South America encased in condoms that they had swallowed? The peasants in Colombia who grew the coca plants in the first place?

The widening stain of responsibility for evil on a constricting   22
planet changes moral contexts. Microevil, the murder of an individual child, becomes part of the macroorganism: all the evils breathe the same air, they have the same circulatory system. They pass through the arteries of the world, from the peasant's coca plant in Colombia to the mother's brain in Washington, thence to her fingers and the clothesline that kills the children in the middle of morning cartoons.

· · ·

Many writers have said that one of evil's higher accomplishments   23
has been to convince people that it does not exist. Ivan Karamazov's bitter diabology was a bit different: "If the devil doesn't exist, but man has created him, he has created him in his own image and likeness." In a nightmare, Ivan meets the devil, a character of oddly shabby gentility, who mentions how cold it was in space, from which he lately came, traveling in only an evening suit and open waistcoat. The devil speaks of the game of village girls who persuade someone to lick a frosted ax, to which of course the tongue sticks. The devil wonders idly, "What would become of an ax in space?" It would orbit there, "and the astronomers would calculate the rising and setting of the ax." Dostoyevsky's devil was prescient, speaking a century before bright metal began to fly up off the earth and circle round it. There is something spookily splendid about evil as an ax in space.

You must ask what evil would be if it did exist. What does the   24
word evil mean when people use it?

Evil means, first of all, a mystery, the *mysterium iniquitatis*. We   25
cannot know evil systematically or scientifically. It is brutal or elusive, by turns vivid and vague, horrible and subtle. We can know it poetically,

symbolically, historically, emotionally. We can know it by its works. But evil is sly and bizarre. Hitler was a vegetarian. The Marquis de Sade opposed capital punishment.

Evil is easier than good. Creativity is harder than destructiveness. Dictators have leisure time for movies in their private screening rooms. When Hitler was at Berchtesgaden, he loved to see the neighborhood children and give them ice cream and cake. Saddam Hussein patted little Stuart Lockwood's head with avuncular menace and asked if he was getting enough cornflakes and milk. Stalin for years conducted the Soviet Union's business at rambling, sinister, alcoholic dinner parties that began at 10 and ended at dawn. All his ministers attended, marinating in Vodka and terror. Sometimes one of them would be taken away at first light by the NKVD, and never seen again.

Evil is the Bad elevated to the status of the inexplicable. To understand is to forgive. Evil sometimes means the thing we cannot understand, and cannot forgive. The Steinberg case in New York City, in which a lawyer battered his six-year-old foster daughter Lisa to death, is an example. Ivan Karamazov speaks of a Russian nobleman who had his hounds tear an eight-year-old boy to pieces in front of the boy's mother because he threw a stone at one of the dogs. Karamazov asks the bitter question that is at the heart of the mystery of evil, "What have children to do with it, tell me, please?"

. . .

Evil is anyone outside the tribe. Evil works by dehumanizing the Other. A perverse, efficient logic: identifying others as evil justifies all further evil against them. A man may kill a snake without compunction. The snake is an evil thing, has evil designs, is a different order of being. Thus: an "Aryan" could kill a Jew, could make an elaborate bureaucratic program of killing Jews. Thus: white men could come in the middle of the night in Mississippi and drag a black man out and hang him.

Getting people to think in categories is one of the techniques of evil. Marxist-Leninist zealots thought of "the bourgeoisie," a category, a class, not the human beings, and it is easy to exterminate a category, a class, a race, an alien tribe. Mao's zealots in the Cultural Revolution, a vividly brainless evil, destroyed China's intellectual classes for a generation.

Pol Pot's Khmer Rouge sent to the killing fields all who spoke French or wore glasses or had soft hands. The Khmer Rouge aimed to cancel all previous history and begin at Year Zero. Utopia, this century has learned the hard way, usually bears a resemblance to hell. An evil chemistry turns the dream of salvation into damnation.

Evil is the Bad hardened into the absolute. Good and evil contend in every mind. Evil comes into its own when it crosses a line and commits itself and hardens its heart, when it becomes merciless, relentless.

William James said, "Evil is a disease." But it can be an atrocious liberation, like the cap flying off a volcano. The mind bursts forth to explore the black possibilities. Vietnam taught many Americans about evil. Hasan i Sabbah, founder of a warrior cult of Ismailis in the 11th century in Persia, gave this instruction: "Nothing is true, everything is permitted." It is a modern thought that both charmed and horrified William Burroughs, the novelist and drug addict who like many in the 20th century somehow could not keep away from horror. During a drunken party in Mexico in 1951, Burroughs undertook to play William Tell, using a pistol to shoot a glass off his wife's head. He put a bullet in her brain instead.

Evil is charismatic. A famous question: Why is Milton's Satan in *Paradise Lost* so much more attractive, so much more interesting, than God himself? The human mind romances the idea of evil. It likes the doomed defiance. Satan and evil have many faces, a flashy variety. Good has only one face. Evil can also be attractive because it has to do with conquest and domination and power. Evil has a perverse fascination that good somehow does not. Evil is entertaining. Good, a sweeter medium, has a way of boring people.

Evil is a word we use when we come to the limit of humane comprehension. But we sometimes suspect that it is the core of our true selves. In *Young Goodman Brown*, Nathaniel Hawthorne's Everyman goes to a satanic meeting in a dark wood, and the devil declares, "Evil is the nature of mankind. Welcome again, my children, to the communion of your race."

. . .

Three propositions:

1. God is all powerful.
2. God is all good.
3. Terrible things happen.

As the theologian and author Frederick Buechner has written, the dilemma has always been this: you can match any two of those propositions, but never match all three.

At the beginning of his *Summa theologiae,* Thomas Aquinas admitted that the existence of evil is the best argument against the existence of God.

Theologians have struggled for centuries with theodicy, the problem of a good God and the existence of evil. Almost all such exertions have been unconvincing. Augustine, speaking of the struggle to understand evil, at last wrote fatalistically, "Do not seek to know more than is appropriate." At the time of the Black Death, William Langland wrote in *Piers Plowman:* "If you want to know why God allowed the Devil to lead us astray . . . then your eyes ought to be in your arse."

The historian Jeffrey Burton Russell asks, "What kind of God is 42 this? Any decent religion must face the question squarely, and no answer is credible that cannot be given in the presence of dying children." Can one propose a God who is partly evil? Elie Wiesel, who was in Auschwitz as a child, suggests that perhaps God has "retracted himself" in the matter of evil. Wiesel has written, "God is in exile, but every individual, if he strives hard enough, can redeem mankind, and even God himself."

Perhaps evil is an immanence in the world, in the mind, just as 43 divinity is an immanence. But evil has performed powerful works. Observes Russell: "It is true that there is evil in each of us, but adding together even large numbers of individual evils does not explain an Auschwitz, let alone the destruction of the planet. Evil on this scale seems to be qualitatively as well as quantitatively different. It is no longer a personal but a transpersonal evil, arising from some kind of collective unconscious. It is also possible that it is beyond the transpersonal and is truly transcendent, an entity outside as well as inside the human mind, an entity that would exist even if there were no human race to imagine it." So here evil rounds back into its favored element, mystery.

Perhaps God has other things on his mind. Perhaps man is to God 44 as the animals of the earth are to man—picturesque, interesting and even nourishing. Man is, on the whole, a catastrophe to the animals. Maybe God is a catastrophe to man in the same way. Can it be that God visits evils upon the world not out of perversity or a desire to harm, but because our suffering is a byproduct of his needs? This could be one reason why almost all theodicies have about them a pathetic quality and seem sometimes undignified exertions of the mind.

. . .

An eerie scene at the beginning of the *Book of Job,* that splendid 45 treatise on the mysteries of evil, has God and Satan talking to each other like sardonic gentlemen gamblers who have met by chance at the racetrack at Saratoga. God seems to squint warily at Satan, and asks, in effect, So, Satan, what have you been doing with yourself? And Satan with a knowing swagger replies, in effect, I've been around the world, here and there, checking it out. Then God and Satan make a chillingly cynical bet on just how much pain Job can endure before he cracks and curses God.

Satan wanders. Evil is a seepage across borders, across great 46
distances. Herman Melville, in *Moby Dick*, wrote that a colt in rural
Vermont, if it smells a fresh buffalo robe (the colt having no knowledge
or experience of buffalo, which lived on the plains) will "start, snort,
and with bursting eyes paw the ground in phrenzies of affright. Here
thou beholdest even in a dumb brute the instinct of the knowledge of
the demonism of the world."

Evil and good have probably been more or less constant presences 47
in the human heart, their proportions staying roughly the same over
the centuries. And perhaps the chief dark categories have remained
constant and familiar. The first time that death appeared in the world,
it was murder. Cain slew Abel. "Two men," says Elie Wiesel, "and one
of them became a killer." The odds have presumably been fifty-fifty
ever since. The Old Testament is full of savageries that sound eerily
contemporary. (The British writer J.R. Ackerley once wrote to a friend,
"I am halfway through *Genesis*, and quite appalled by the disgraceful
behavior of all the characters involved, including God.")

Petrarch's rant against the papal court at Avignon in the 14th 48
century sounds like a hyperbolic inventory of life in certain neighborhoods of the late 20th century: "This is a sewer to which all the filths of
the universe come to be reunited. Here people despise God, they adore
money, they trample underfoot both human laws and divine law.
Everything here breathes falsehood: the air, the earth, the houses, and
above all, the bedrooms."

Western thought since the Renaissance has considered that the 49
course of mankind was ascendant, up out of the shadow of evil and
superstition and unreason. Thomas Jefferson, a brilliant creature of the
Enlightenment, once wrote, "Barbarism has . . . been receding before
the steady step of amelioration; and will in time, I trust, disappear from
the earth."

In the 20th century, Lucretius' shores of light vanished like the 50
coasts of Atlantis, carried under by terrible convulsions. The ascendant
civilizations (the Europeans, Americans, Japanese) accomplished horrors that amounted to a usurpation of the power of God over creation.
The world in this century went about a work of de-creation—destroying its own generations in World War I; attempting to extinguish the
Jews of Europe in the Holocaust, to destroy the Armenian people, the
Ukrainian kulaks and, much later, the Cambodians—all the reverberat-
ing genocides.

In any case, the 20th century shattered the lenses and paradigms, 51
the very mind, of reason. The universe went from Newton's model to
Einstein's, and beyond, into absurdities even more profound. An underlying assumption of proportion and continuity in the world per-
ished. The proportions between cause and effect were skewed. A

minuscule event (indeed, an atom) could blossom into vast oblitera-tions. Einstein said God does not play dice with the world. But if there was order, either scientific or moral, in God's universe, it became absurdly inaccessible.

If evil is a constant presence in the human soul, it is also true that 52 there are more souls now than ever, and by that logic both good and evil are rising on a Malthusian curve, or at any rate both good and evil may be said to be increasing in the world at the same rate as the population: 1.7% per annum.

. . .

The world is swinging on a hinge between two ages. The prospect 53 awakens, in the Western, secular mind, the idea that all future out-comes, good or evil, are a human responsibility. John Kennedy said in his Inaugural Address, "Here on earth, God's work must surely be our own." When there will no longer be any place to hide, it becomes important to identify the real evils and not go chasing after false evils. It is possible that people will even grow up on the subject of sex.

Religions over many centuries developed elaborate codifications 54 of sin and evil. The Catholic Church, for example, identified Sins that Cry to heaven for Vengeance, (oppression of the poor, widows and orphans, for example, or defrauding laborers of their wages), Sins Against the Holy Spirit, and so on, sins mortal and venial, virtues cardinal and sins deadly.

With the emergence of a new world will come a recodification of 55 evils. Obviously offenses against the earth are coming to be thought of as evils in ways we would not have suspected a few years ago. The developed world, at least, is forming a consensus that will regard violence to the planet to be evil in the way we used to think of unortho-dox sexual practices and partnerships as being outside the realm of accepted conduct.

A Frenchman named Jean Baudrillard recently wrote a book called 56 *The Transparency of Evil.* We live, says Baudrillard, in a postorgiastic age in which all liberations have been accomplished, all barriers torn down, all limits abolished. Baudrillard makes the (very French) case that evil, far from being undesirable, is necessary—essential to maintaining the vitality of civilization. That suggests a refinement of an old argument favored by Romantics and 19th century anarchists like Bakunin, who said, "The urge for destruction is also a creative urge." It is not an argument I would try out on Elie Wiesel or on the mother of a political prisoner disappeared by the Argentine authorities.

And yet . . . and yet . . . evil has such perversities, or good has such 57 resilience, that a powerful (if grotesque) case can be made that Adolf

Hitler was the founding father of the state of Israel. Without Hitler, no Holocaust, without Holocaust, no Israel.

. . .

Scientists working with artificial intelligence have a fantasy—   58
who knows if it is more than that?—that eventually all the contents of the human brain, a life, can be gradually emptied into a brilliant, nondecaying, stainless, deathless sort of robotic personoid. And the transfer of all the vast and intricately nuanced matter of the mind and soul has been accomplished, the memories of the cells etched onto microchips, the human body, having been replicated in a better container, will be allowed to wither and die.

Will evil be transferred along with good and installed in the   59
stainless personoid? Or can the scientists sift the soul through a kind of electronic cheesecloth and remove all the ancient evil traces, the reptilian brain, the lashing violence, the tribal hatred, the will to murder? Will the killer be strained out of the soul? Will the inheritance of Cain be left to wither and die with the human husk, the useless flesh?

If so, will grace and love, evil's enemies, wither too? The question   60
goes back to the Garden. Does the good become meaningless in a world without evil? Do the angels depart along with the devils? If the stainless canister knows nothing of evil, will Mozart sound the same to it as gunfire?

30

Language and Its Uses

Finally, no anthology of *Time* essays would be complete without several selections on one of the authors' favorite subjects: language. The following pieces examine the way we speak, the words we use, the way those words effect us. They give us a sense of how interested these writers have been, and continue to be, in the difficulties and delights of English.

From January 1980, Stefan Kanfer looks at " '80s-Babble: Untidy Treasure." From December that same year, in "Time to Reflect on Blah-Blah-Blah," Frank Trippett considers American gab. "Oops! How's That Again?," by Roger Rosenblatt, March 1981, analyzes our often hilarious tendency to misspeak. Frank Trippett's "Why So Much is Beyond Words," from July 1981, examines non-verbal communication. Trippett's "Watching Out for Loaded Words," May 1982, weighs language's emotional baggage. "Proverbs or Aphorisms?," by Stefan Kanfer, July 1983, compares two aspects of language and what they mean for their users. Otto Friedrich's "Of Words That Ravage, Pillage, Spoil," from January 1984, laments the spread of bureaucratic euphemism. Roger Rosenblatt, in "Poetry and Politics," from October 1986, looks at the relation between language and political behavior. "In Praise of the Humble Comma," by Pico Iyer, June 1988, speaks for the civilizing benefits of punctuation. And "Metaphors of the World, Unite!," by Lance Morrow, October 1989, considers the way language helps shape our sense of history.

'80s-Babble: Untidy Treasure

STEFAN KANFER

The rich have always liked to assume the costumes of the poor. 1
Take the American language. It is more than a million words wide, and
new terms are constantly added to its infinite variety. Yet as the decade
starts, the U.S. vocabulary seems to have shrunk to child size.

Those who thought that song lyrics had reached Rock bottom can 2
still hear the refrain of that disco hit: YMCA ... YMCA ... YMCA. The
Unicorn Hunters, a society of zealous word watchers based at Lake
Superior State College in Michigan, offer a list of current English
scourges. Among them: "ballpark figure," "preboarding—how can you
board a plane before you board it?" and "no problem." Even insult has
lost its point: "I couldn't care less" has degenerated to the meaningless
"I could care less." Greetings are equally vapid: telephone operators
now routinely use '80s-babble, chirping, "Have a nice day," the moral
equivalent of the smile button. *Kramer vs. Kramer* is advertised as a film
that is "absolutely today." Nouns continue to be overrun by the
jargonaut: the New York *Times* demands stronger sourcing, meetings
are preambled, situations are impacted. The New York *Post* recently
managed a dazzling double play with its offering: "Stunt man extraor-
dinaire Hal Needham will helm the film, which will also (hopefully)
include Roger Moore."

The air is thick with devalued buzz words, including "buzz 3
words." Behavioral science, always a leader in the euphemism derby,
has cut some gems and polished some others: psychologists persistently refer to unresponsive women as "pre-orgasmic," and Masters
and Johnson call foreplay a "stimulative approach opportunity," perhaps the most effective sexual turn-off since saltpeter. Therapists speak
of "actualizing," to mean the fulfillment of potential. "I hear you" has
descended from the aural to the banal; it means a total understanding
of the speaker's temperament. "Lifting" is the effort to derive the
utmost from every day; "Who are you screaming with?" a glancing
allusion to primal therapy, is now a query about any psychological aid
the subject is seeking.

According to Joel Homer, who chronicles such excrescences in his 4
forthcoming book, *Jargon*, these terms can fall into the category of

444

"nonverbal verbalizing . . . a speech system in which words are used more as images than conceptual symbols." Nonverbal verbalizing (itself an outstanding piece of jargon) flourishes best in its home, Washington, D.C. There, after the Three Mile Island accident gave more mileage to the term, "China Syndrome," Joseph Hendrie, then chairman of the Nuclear Regulatory Commission, concluded: "It would be prudent to consider expeditiously the provision of instrumentation that would provide an unambiguous indication of the level of fluid in the reactor vessel." Translation: we need more accurate measuring devices. A company vice president dismissed the incident as an exaggeration. What had happened, he said, was "a normal aberration." In the same spirit, federal antitrust lawyers refer to "conscious parallelism"—first cousin to price fixing.

In sport, the old sol of solecism, Howard Cosell, finds his work   5
done better by others. A San Francisco Giants star: "With today's victory we are definitely in the momentum-going bracket." Minnesota Twins Pitcher Jerry Koosman: "When the communications gap breaks down, it leads to not knowing the facts any more."

The gap breakdown can be seen in signs on office building doors: 6
EMERGENCY EXIT ONLY—NOT TO BE USED UNDER ANY CIRCUMSTANCES. It can be read in bank offerings of free gifts and in the Indiana advertisement: LAFAYETTE'S MOST UNIQUE RESTAURANT IS NOW EVEN MORE UNIQUE.

Throughout the nation the ize have it. An article in *Cue* magazine   7
informs readers how they can have their wrinkles "youthfulized." In Florida a cop, asked whether a perpetrator had become hostile when apprehended, tells a TV interviewer that the man "was already hostilized." And Treasury Secretary G. William Miller thought that Americans were not conserving gasoline because they were "not sufficiently incentivized."

NBC Commentator Edwin Newman (*A Civil Tongue*), who keeps   8
track of videosyncrasies, noted the ABC assurance that every night it would cover Iran "as long as the crisis remains critical" and that CBS urged viewers to "choose the candidate of your choice." Even computers have learned to commit verbal sins. In *The State of the Language*, Critic Hugh Kenner attacks such programmer tongues as FORTRAN, in which "vocabulary is 'a set of objects' [and] sentences are 'linear strings.' "

Such dark pronunciamentos draw the future in bleak and white.   9
We are, after all, only four years away from George Orwell's *1984*, with its ominous slogans and Newspeak: "Doubleplusungood refs unpersons rewrite fullwise upsub antefiling . . . WAR IS PEACE, FREEDOM IS SLAVERY, IGNORANCE IS STRENGTH." Yet that volume also offers an unmarked exit: *1984* imagines a time when "every concept that can ever be needed will be expressed by exactly *one* word, with its meaning rigidly defined and all its subsidiary meanings rubbed out and forgotten."

That seems precisely the opposite of what is occurring in Ameri- 10 can speech. Even severe grammarians note the constant refreshment of terms. In the past decade Americans have exhausted uptight and far out, situationwise and the bottom line, charisma and stonewalling, nano-nano and dy-no-mite, Koreagate and may the force be with you. Who knows whether current terms have a chance to last the decade—or even the year? Palimony, the term for sharing money after an unmarried couple have split, survives the Lee Marvin case; good buddy and 10-4 have become as much a part of the lingo as CB. Petrodollars and multinationals have set down roots; gasohol and meltdowns are not likely to flee from the headlines. But "humongous," the adolescent synonym for large, will never grow up; designer jeans may not last until next Christmas, and quadraphonic and shuttle diplomacy have already gone. Will such references to bosses as ayatullah and imam be as short-lived as Head Honcho and Big Enchilada?

These oscillations, like words themselves, are subject to interpre- 11 tation. Pessimists regard constant change as further evidence of national decline and fall. Neologisms and ungrammatical usage, they argue, are not, as defenders claim, "alternate modes of communicating" any more than kicking over the board is an alternate mode of playing backgammon. But their critique is hardly a signal for despair—for how else can we complain so richly except with that very speech?

In fact, since its beginning, our native tongue has been maligned 12 and mauled, invaded by foreigners and abused at home. No one has ever succeeded in making it uniform, and no one ever will. But then, as Henry Thoreau observed more than a century ago, "Where shall we look for standard English but to the words of a standard man?" As the '80s begin, Americans and their vernacular can be put down as fractious, infuriating, untidy, overbearing, cacophonous—but never as standard. The U.S. vocabulary may be dressed in blue jeans and work shirts, yet it cannot disguise one of the country's truest and most unassailable treasures: the American language.

Time to Reflect on Blah-Blah-Blah

Frank Trippett

Late in his career, Announcer Bill Stern made an endearing 1
confession about his vocal ways as the Christopher Columbus of television sportscasting. Said he: "I had no idea when to keep my big, fat,
flapping mouth shut." The insight dawned too late to be of much use
to Stern, but it might have been of value as a guide for his heirs.
Unfortunately, nobody in the broadcast booth was listening. The result
is the TV sports event as it is today: an entertainment genre in which an
athletic game must compete for attention with the convulsive concate-
nations of blah-blah-blah that passes for commentary.

Television sportscasters, in short, are still a long way from master- 2
ing the art of the zipped lip. It is this familiar fact that has legions of
sports fans eagerly looking forward to a special telecast of a football
game that NBC has promised for Saturday, Dec. 20. The teams and site
(Jets *vs.* Dolphins at Miami) are of little importance compared with the
radical innovation that will be the main attraction: the absence of the
usual game commentary. Thus the telecast will offer—and here Sports
Columnist Red Smith leads the cheers—"no banalities, no pseudo-
expert profundities phrased in coachly patois, no giggles, no inside
jokes, no second-guessing, no numbing prattle." Just one announcer
will be on hand, says NBC, to offer only the sort of essential information
(injuries, rulings) that a stadium announcer traditionally provides. The
prospect is engaging, even if it may be shocking to see a game presented
merely for the sake of the drama on the field.

This blabber-proof telecast looms as far too rare an occasion to 3
waste only in joy over a trial separation from the stream of half-
consciousness that usually accompanies athletic endeavors on the tube.
While sports fans will surely relish the moment, it should also be seized
for grander purposes, for awareness may just be dawning in the Age of
Communication that silence is indeed often golden. President-elect
Ronald Reagan has so far, often to the chagrin of the press, shown an
admirable reluctance to grab all of the many chances he gets to sound
off on just about anything. Given the possible alternatives, Yoko Ono's
fiat that John Lennon's passing be marked with ten minutes of silence
around the world was inspired. In truth, the day of the telecast experi-

ment would be a perfect time for the nation to reflect generally—and silently—on the whole disgruntling phenomenon of superfluous talk.

The American tendency to unchecked garrulity is most conspicu-   4
ous in the realm of TV sports, but it does not begin or end there by a long shout. The late-evening TV news, for example, is aclutter with immaterial chatter. "Hap-py talk, keep talkin' hap-py talk . . ." Rodgers and Hammerstein offered that lyrical advice to young lovers, but a great many TV news staffers have adopted it as an inviolable rule of tongue. Hap-py talk is not reprehensible, but should it be force-fed to an audience looking for the news? Surely not, no more than a sports fancier tuning in football should be obliged to endure Tom Brookshier and Pat Summerall happily going over their personal travel schedules.

Admittedly, there is not likely to be universal agreement on precisely what talk is superfluous when. The judgment is aesthetic, and tastes vary. Some Americans might regard all sermons, lectures and political speeches as superfluous. Such testiness, however, can be shrugged off as a symptom of hyperactive intelligence. The criteria for talk should be appropriateness and pertinency. The essential question is: Does it subtract from or enhance the moment into which it falls? The deeper reason that sports commentary is annoying is that it so often ruptures the flow of the main event. The effect is easier to see when one imagines it occurring in the middle of a true drama. *Othello*, say:

"Now here's the video tape again with still another angle on Iago as he   6
evilly fingers Desdemona's hanky. And look! Iago is curling the old lip just a
trifle. Nice curl too, eh, Chuck? This chap was learning lip curling when the
rest of that cast couldn't find the proscenium arch with both hands. Inciden-
tally, about that hanky —you know, the star himself bought that hanky for 79¢
at Lamston's just before opening when it turned out the prop man used the real
thing as a dustcloth. Now back to the action onstage . . ."

Existence today often means escaping from the latest Oscar award   7
acceptance speech only to be trapped within earshot of a disc jockey who considers it a felony to fall silent for a second. Some 5,000 radio and TV talk shows fill the air with an oceanic surf of gabble, a big fraction of it as disposable as a weather-caster's strained charm. It is easy to snap off and tune out, but it is not so simple to elude real-life blather. Try to get away from it all, and soon a stage-struck airline captain will be monologuing about terrain miles below and half-obscured by the cloud cover. Go to the dentist, and the procedure is all but ordained: thumbs fill the mouth, the drill starts to whine, and a voice begins to express all those unpalatable political opinions.

At the movies, it is usually the couple two rows back who turn out   8
to be practitioners of voice-over chic, tenderly broadcasting all the half-baked thoughts they ever half-understood about Fellini. Dial a phone number and the absent owner's talking machine coughs a set

piece of cuteness before granting a moment for you to interject a brief message. As for bridge players, the typical foursome hardly finishes the play of a hand before the air burbles with a redundant rehashing of it all.

Personality, roles and situations all work in the chemistry that   9 induces excessive chatter. And certain subjects pull the stopper on even temperate people. Food, for example, instigates a preposterous quantity of repetitious chat. Sex? It has already provoked such an excess of discussion—functional and gynecological—that it is fair to rule all future comment on the subject may be surplus.

Cabbies and barbers have long been assailed for marathon talking,   10 but it is unjust that they so often wind up at the top of the list of nuisances. Indeed, cabbies are often mute and sullen, and ever since barbers became stylists they have felt sufficiently superior to clients that their urge to talk has diminished.

To be nettled by untimely yakking does not imply the advocacy   11 of universal silence. A rigorous discipline, silence is practiced by certain monks and others who believe that it heightens the soul's capacity to approach God. For ordinary people, a bit of silence may occasionally seem golden, but what they mostly need is the conversation that keeps them close to others. Those who do not get enough talk tend to wither in spirit.

Says Linguistics Scholar Peter Farb in *Word Play:* "Something   12 happened in evolution to create Man the Talker." And a talker man remains, with speech his most exalting faculty. Talk is the tool, the toy, the comfort and joy of the human species. The pity is that talkers so often blurt so far beyond the line of what is needed and desired that they have to be listened to with a stiff upper lip.

Oops! How's That Again?

ROGER ROSENBLATT

"That is not what I meant at all. That is not it, at all."

—T.S. Eliot, *The Love Song of J. Alfred Prufrock*

At a royal luncheon in Glasgow last month Businessman Peter Balfour turned to the just-engaged Prince Charles and wished him long life and conjugal happiness with Lady Jane. The effect of the sentiment was compromised both by the fact that the Prince's betrothed is Lady Diana (Spencer) and that Lady Jane (Wellesley) is one of his former flames. "I feel a perfect fool," said Balfour, who was unnecessarily contrite. Slips of the tongue occur all the time. In Chicago recently, Governor James Thompson was introduced as "the mayor of Illinois," which was a step down from the time he was introduced as "the Governor of the United States." Not all such fluffs are so easy to take, however. During the primaries, Nancy Reagan telephoned her husband as her audience listened in, to say how delighted she was to be looking at all "the beautiful white people." And France's Prime Minister Raymond Barre, who has a reputation for putting his *pied* in his *bouche*, described last October's bombing of a Paris synagogue as "this odious attack that was aimed at Jews and that struck at innocent Frenchmen"— a crack that not only implied Jews were neither innocent nor French but also suggested that the attack would have been less odious had it been more limited.

One hesitates to call Barre sinister, but the fact is that verbal errors can have a devastating effect on those who hear them and on those who make them as well. Jimmy Carter never fully recovered from his reference to Polish lusts for the future in a mistranslated speech in 1977, nor was Chicago's Mayor Daley ever quite the same after assuring the public that "the policeman isn't there to create disorder; the policeman is there to preserve disorder." Dwight Eisenhower, John Kennedy, Spiro Agnew, Gerald Ford, all made terrible gaffes, with Ford perhaps making the most unusual ("Whenever I can I always watch the Detroit

Tigers on radio"). Yet this is no modern phenomenon. The term *faux pas* goes back at least as far as the 17th century, having originally referred to a woman's lapse from virtue. Not that women lapse more than men in this regard. Even Marie Antoinette's fatal remark about cake and the public, if true, was due to a poor translation.

In fact, mistranslation accounts for a great share of verbal errors. 3 The slogan "Come Alive with Pepsi" failed understandably in German when it was translated: "Come Alive out of the Grave with Pepsi." Elsewhere it was translated with more precision: "Pepsi Brings Your Ancestors Back from the Grave." In 1965, prior to a reception for Queen Elizabeth II outside Bonn, Germany's President Heinrich Lübke, attempting an English translation of *"Gleich geht es los"* (It will soon begin), told the Queen: "Equal goes it loose." The Queen took the news well, but no better than the President of India, who was greeted at an airport in 1962 by Lübke, who, intending to ask, "How are you?" instead said: "Who are you?" To which his guest answered responsibly: "I am the President of India."

The most prodigious collector of modern slips was Kermit Schafer, 4 whose "blooper" records of mistakes made on radio and television consisted largely of toilet jokes, but were nonetheless a great hit in the 1950s. Schafer was an avid self-promoter and something of a blooper himself, but he did have an ear for such things as the introduction by Radio Announcer Harry Von Zell of President "Hoobert Heever," as well as the interesting message: "This portion of *Woman on the Run* is brought to you by Phillips' Milk of Magnesia." Bloopers are the lowlife of verbal error, but spoonerisms are a different fettle of kitsch. In the early 1900s the Rev. William Archibald Spooner caused a stir at New College, Oxford, with his famous spoonerisms, most of which were either deliberate or apocryphal. But a real one—his giving out a hymn in chapel as "Kinquering Kongs Their Titles Take"—is said to have brought down the house of worship, and to have kicked off the genre. After that, spoonerisms got quite elaborate. Spooner once reportedly chided a student: "You have hissed all my mystery lectures. In fact, you have tasted the whole worm, and must leave by the first town drain."

Such missteps, while often howlingly funny to ignorami like us, 5 are deadly serious concerns to psychologists and linguists. Victoria Fromkin of the linguistics department at U.C.L.A. regards slips of the tongue as clues to how the brain stores and articulates language. She believes that thought is placed by the brain into a grammatical framework before it is expressed—this in spite of the fact that she works with college students. A grammatical framework was part of Walter Annenberg's trouble when, as the newly appointed U.S. Ambassador to Britain, he was asked by the Queen how he was settling in to his London residence. Annenberg admitted to "some discomfiture as a result of a need for elements of refurbishing." Either he was over-whelmed by the circumstance or he was losing his mind.

When you get to that sort of error, you are nearing a psychological　6
abyss. It was Freud who first removed the element of accident from language with his explanation of "slips," but lately others have ex-tended his theories. Psychiatrist Richard Yazmajian, for example, sug-gests that there are some incorrect words that exist in associative chains with the correct ones for which they are substituted, implying a kind of "dream pair" of elements in the speaker's psyche. The nun who poured tea for the Irish bishop and asked, "How many lords, my lump?" might therefore have been asking a profound theological question.

On another front, Psychoanalyst Ludwig Eidelberg made Freud's　7
work seem childishly simple when he suggested that a slip of the tongue involves the entire network of id, ego and superego. He offers the case of the young man who entered a restaurant with his girlfriend and ordered a room instead of a table. You probably think that you understand that error. But just listen to Eidelberg: "All the wishes connected with the word 'room' represented a countercathexis mobi-lized as a defense. The word 'table' had to be omitted, because it would have been used for infantile gratification of a repressed oral, aggressive and scopophilic wish connected with identification with the preoedipal mother." Clearly, this is no laughing matter.

Why then do we hoot at these mistakes? For one thing, it may be　8
that we simply find conventional discourse so predictable and boring that any deviation comes as a delightful relief. In his deeply unfunny *Essay on Laughter* the philosopher Henri Bergson theorized that the act of laughter is caused by any interruption of normal human fluidity or momentum (a pie in the face, a mask, a pun). Slips of the tongue, therefore, are like slips on banana peels; we crave their occurrence if only to break the monotonies. The monotonies run to substance. When that announcer introduced Hoobert Heever, he may also have been saying that the nation had had enough of Herbert Hoover.

Then too there is the element of pure meanness in such laughter,　9
both the meanness of enjoyment in watching an embarrassed misspeaker's eyes roll upward as if in prayer —his hue turn magenta, his hands like homing larks fluttering to his mouth—and the mean joy of discovering his hidden base motives and critical intent. At the 1980 Democratic National Convention, Jimmy Carter took a lot of heat for referring to Hubert Humphrey as Hubert Horatio Hornblower because it was instantly recognized that Carter thought Humphrey a windbag. David Hartman of *Good Morning America* left little doubt about his feelings for a sponsor when he announced: "We'll be right back after this word from General Fools." At a conference in Berlin in 1954,

France's Foreign Minister Georges Bidault was hailed as "that fine little French tiger, Georges Bidet," thus belittling the tiger by the tail. When we laugh at such stuff, it is the harsh and bitter laugh, the laugh at the disclosure of inner condemning truth.

Yet there is also a more kindly laugh that occurs when a blunderer does not reveal his worst inner thoughts but his most charitable or optimistic. Gerald Ford's famous error in the 1976 presidential debate, in which he said that Poland was not under Soviet domination, for instance. In a way, that turned out to contain a grain of truth, thanks to Lech Walesa and the strikes; in any case it was a nice thing to wish. As was U.N. Ambassador Warren Austin's suggestion in 1948 that Jews and Arabs resolve their differences "in a true Christian spirit." Similarly, Nebraska's former Senator Kenneth Wherry might have been thinking dreamily when, in an hour-long speech on a country in Southeast Asia, he referred throughout to "Indigo-China." One has to be in the mood for such a speech.

Of course, the most interesting laugh is the one elicited by the truly 11 bizarre mistake, because such a mistake seems to disclose a whole new world of logic and possibility, a deranged double for the life that is. What Lewis Carroll displayed through the looking-glass, verbal error also often displays by conjuring up ideas so supremely nutty that the laughter it evokes is sublime. The idea that Pepsi might actually bring one back from the grave encourages an entirely new view of experience. In such a view it is perfectly possible to lust after the Polish future, to watch the Tigers on the radio, to say "Equal goes it loose" with resounding clarity.

Still, beyond all this is another laugh entirely, that neither con- 12 demns, praises, ridicules nor conspires, but sees into the essential nature of a slip of the tongue and consequently sympathizes. After all, most human endeavor results in a slip of the something—the best-laid plans gone suddenly haywire by natural blunder: the chair, cake or painting that turns out not exactly as one imagined; the kiss or party that falls flat; the life that is not quite what one had in mind. Nothing is ever as dreamed.

So we laugh at each other, perfect fools all, flustered by the mistake 13 of our mortality.

Why So Much Is Beyond Words

FRANK TRIPPETT

"In the beginning," says the Gospel of St. John, "was the Word." 1
The mystical meanings that the Bible lays upon the word Word are not
embraced by everyone. Yet nobody can reasonably doubt that the
coming of the word, if not the Word, to humankind was the start of
something big in history. Human talk may have struck dyspeptic Nathaniel Hawthorne like "the croak and cackle of fowls," but the rise of
language, written and spoken, is all but universally rated as one of the
glories of the species. What is surprising is that in the common give and
take of daily living people still rely so little upon the verbal language
that distinguishes them from the beasts.

In fact, Homo sapiens, as a communicator, does not seem to have 2
come all that far from the time when grunts and gesticulations were the
main ways of getting messages across. Both individuals and groups still
send vital messages by gesture, by pantomime, by dramatics—by a
dizzy diversity of what scholars call nonverbal communication. The
reality is easy to overlook in an epoch that is bloated with pride in its
dazzling technical marvels of communication. Yet, in spite of human
garrulousness, perhaps as little as 20% of the communication among
people is verbal, according to experts; most, by far, even when talk is
going on, consists of nonverbal signals.

This is true of men, women, children, individually and in groups 3
of all sizes. Nations and the realm of politics lean heavily on indirect
gesture and charades to convey important messages. Take Secretary of
State Alexander Haig's talks in China: Was not his actual purpose to
send a signal to the Soviets? Societies signal prevalent values to their
members by what is applauded and what condemned; status symbol is
synonymous with status signal. "Language," said Samuel Johnson, "is
the dress of thought." But all over the world people act as though
language were mere costume—and usually a disguise. Everybody (evidently nobody can help it) tends to mimic that anonymous signaler
cited in *Proverbs:* "He winketh with his eyes, he speaketh with his feet,
he teacheth with his fingers."

This tendency to commune by semaphore has probably not in- 4
creased at all in centuries, but consciousness of it surely has. A spate of

454

books like this season's *Reading Faces* and last decade's popular *Body Language* have explored the individual's tendency to broadcast things (unconsciously and otherwise) through all manner of physical movement and facial gymnastics. Such matters, made widely familiar by pop sociology, anthropology and psychology, have become the stuff of common conversation. Michael Korda's *Power! How to Get It, How to Use It*, like other books of this ilk, is mainly a primer in how to manipulate others by a cold-blooded control of nonverbal signals that occur commonly in the workaday world: for example, how executives signal their style and presumptions of power by the clothes they choose and the way they arrange their office furniture.

At work or play, everybody emits wordless signals of infinite 5 variety. Overt, like a warm smile. Spontaneous, like a raised eyebrow. Involuntary, like leaning away from a salesperson to resist a deal. Says Julius Fast in *Body Language:* "We rub our noses for puzzlement. We clasp our arms to isolate ourselves or to protect ourselves. We shrug our shoulders for indifference." Baseball pitchers often dust back a batter with a close ball that is not intended to hit but only to signal a warning claim of dominance. The twitchings of young children too long in adult company are merely involuntary signals of short-fused patience. Any competent psychiatrist remains alert to the tics and quirky expressions by which a patient's hidden emotions make themselves known. People even signal by the odors they give off, as Janet Hopson documents in superfluous detail in *Scent Signals: The Silent Language of Sex*. Actually, it is impossible for an individual to avoid signaling other people; the person who mutely withdraws from human intercourse sends out an unmistakable signal in the form of utter silence.

Sociologist Dane Archer calls reading such signals "social intelli- 6 gence," but the phrase's greatest usefulness was probably in completing the title of his book *How to Expand Your Social Intelligence Quotient*. Urged Archer: "We must unshackle ourselves from the tendency to ignore silent behavior and to prefer words over everything else." The evidence all over is that while people meander the earth through thickets of verbiage (theirs and others), many, perhaps most, do pay more attention to wordless signals and are more likely to be influenced and governed by nonverbal messages.

Nothing but the daily news is necessary to show the reliance that 7 rulers and nations place upon nonverbal communication. Presidents soon learn that they can hardly do anything that is not taken to be a signal of some sort to somebody. So it is, too, with the governments under them. In March President Reagan, questioned about lifting the post-Afghanistan embargo on grain sales to the U.S.S.R., told reporters that he did not see how he could do it "without sending the wrong signal" —which is exactly what critics accused him of when he did kill the embargo the next month. Why did the Senate Foreign Relations Committee reject Ernest Lefever as the nation's top human rights official? Partly because of a fear that other countries might construe support of Lefever as a signal of national sympathy for his unenthusiastic attitude toward a strong American human rights policy. Why do some defense strategists support building the MX missile at a cost of about $40 billion? Not entirely because of its possible military efficacy, but also because of what a commitment to such a system might signal the Soviet Union about U.S. resolve.

The bloody history of the world ought to be the first item of 8 evidence in any case against relying on wordless signaling in international affairs. The opportunities for misunderstanding are immense and constant. Says Harvard Law Professor Roger Fisher, a specialist in international negotiations: "The chances of properly understanding signals in the midst of conflict is always very slight." For instance, during the Iran hostage negotiations, Secretary of State Cyrus Vance, intending to signal the belief that U.S.-Iran problems could be resolved, spoke of restoring "normal" diplomatic relations. Iran mistakenly took that to mean a return to things as they were under the despised Shah. Says Fisher: "Sending diplomatic signals is like sending smoke signals in a high wind."

As all but the very luckiest—or dullest—of people might testify, 9 individual signals have a way of misfiring just as easily, with results just as calamitous if not as earthshaking. The danger of misunderstanding increases dramatically when even the most elementary signals are used by people in different cultures. The happiest of overt American signals, the circled thumb and index finger, unless accompanied by a smile, amounts to an insult in France. The innocent American habit of propping a foot on a table or crossing a leg in figure-four style could cause hard feelings among Arabs, to whom the showing of a shoe sole is offensive.

People indulge in nonverbal communication not basically to be 10 clever or devious but because these ways of communicating are deeply embedded in the habits of the species and automatically transmitted by all cultures. So says Anthropologist Ray Birdwhistell, a pioneer in the study of kinesics, as body language is called. Other experts point out that signaling by movement occurred among lizards and birds, as well as other creatures, even before mammals emerged.

Unfortunately, no useful dictionary of gestures is really possible, 11 since every gesture and nonverbal expression depends for meaning on the variants of both the individual using it and the culture in which it takes place. Says Anthropologist Edward T. Hall, author of *The Silent*

Language and *Beyond Culture:* "Because of its complexity, efforts to isolate out 'bits' of nonverbal communication and generalize from them in isolation are doomed to failure. Book titles such as *How to Read a Person Like a Book* are thoroughly misleading, doubly so because they are designed to satisfy the public's need for highly specific answers to complex questions for which there are no simple answers."

Sooner or later, for any word lover, the human habit of wordless signaling leads to a simple question for which there is perhaps only a complex answer. The question is why has language, given its unique power to convey thought or feeling or almost anything else in the human realm, fallen so short as a practical social tool for man. The answer is that it has not. Instead, the human creature has fallen short as a user of language, employing it so duplicitously that even in ancient times the wise advised that people should be judged not by what they said but by what they did. That such advice holds good for today goes, alas, without saying. 12

Watching Out for Loaded Words

FRANK TRIPPETT

Via eye and ear, words beyond numbering zip into the mind and 1
flash a dizzy variety of meaning into the mysterious circuits of knowing. A great many of them bring along not only their meanings but some
extra freight—a load of judgment or bias that plays upon the emotions
instead of lighting up the understanding. These words deserve careful
handling—and minding. They are loaded.

Such words babble up in all corners of society, wherever anybody 2
is ax-grinding, arm-twisting, back-scratching, sweet-talking. Political
blather leans sharply to words (*peace, prosperity*) whose moving powers
outweigh exact meanings. Merchandising depends on adjectives (*new,
improved*) that must be continually recharged with notions that entice
people to buy. In casual conversation, emotional stuffing is lent to
words by inflection and gesture: the innocent phrase, "Thanks a lot," is
frequently a vehicle for heaping servings of irritation. Traffic in opin-
ion-heavy language is universal simply because most people, as C.S.
Lewis puts it, are "more anxious to express their approval and disapproval of things than to describe them."

The trouble with loaded words is that they tend to short-circuit 3
thought. While they may describe something, they simultaneously try
to seduce the mind into accepting a prefabricated opinion about the
something described. The effect of one laden term was incidentally
measured in a recent survey of public attitudes by the Federal Advisory
Commission on Intergovernmental Relations. The survey found that
many more Americans favor governmental help for the poor when the
programs are called "aid to the needy" than when they are labeled
"public welfare." And that does not mean merely that some citizens
prefer H_2O to water. In fact, the finding spotlights the direct influence
of the antipathy that has accumulated around the benign word *welfare.*

Every word hauls some basic cargo or else can be shrugged aside 4
as vacant sound. Indeed, almost any word can, in some use, take on that
extra baggage of bias or sentiment that makes for the truly manipulative
word. Even the pronoun *it* becomes one when employed to report, say,
that somebody has what *it* takes. So does the preposition *in* when used

to establish, perhaps, that zucchini quiche is *in* this year: used just so, *in* all but sweats with class bias. The emotion-heavy words that are easiest to spot are epithets and endearments: *blockhead, scumbum, heel, sweetheart, darling, great human being* and the like. All such terms are so full of prejudice and sentiment that S.I. Hayakawa, a semanticist before he became California's U.S. Senator, calls them "snarl-words and purr-words."

Not all artfully biased terms have been honored with formal 5
labels. Word loading, after all, is not a recognized scholarly discipline, merely a folk art. Propagandists and advertising copywriters may turn it into a polished low art, but it is usually practiced—and witnessed— without a great deal of deliberation. The typical person, as Hayakawa says in *Language in Thought and Action,* "takes words as much for granted as the air."

Actually, it does not take much special skill to add emotional 6
baggage to a word. Almost any noun can be infused with skepticism and doubt through the use of the word *so-called.* Thus a friend in disfavor can become a *so-called friend,* and similarly the nation's leaders can become *so-called leaders.* Many other words can be handily tilted by shortening, by prefixes and suffixes, by the reduction of formal to familiar forms. The word *politician,* which may carry enough downbeat connotation for most tastes, can be given additional unsavoriness by truncation: *pol.* By prefacing liberal and conservative with *ultra* or *arch,* both labels can be saddled with suggestions of inflexible fanaticism. To speak of a pacifist or peacemaker as a *peacenik* is, through a single syllable, to smear someone with the suspicion that he has alien loyalties. The antifeminist who wishes for his (or her) prejudice to go piggyback on his (or her) language will tend to speak not of feminists but of *fem-libbers.* People with only limited commitments to environmental preservation will tend similarly to allude not to environmentalists but to *eco-freaks.*

Words can be impregnated with feeling by oversimplification. 7
People who oppose all abortions distort the position of those favoring freedom of private choice by calling them *pro-abortion.* And many a progressive or idealist has experienced the perplexity of defending himself against one of the most peculiar of all disparaging terms, *do-gooder.* By usage in special contexts, the most improbable words can be infused with extraneous meaning. To speak of the "truly needy" as the Administration habitually does is gradually to plant the notion that the unmodified *needy* are falsely so. Movie Critic Vincent Canby has noticed that the word *film* has become imbued with a good deal of snootiness that is not to be found in the word *movie. Moderate* is highly susceptible to coloring in many different ways, always by the fervid

partisans of some cause: Adlai Stevenson, once accused of being too *moderate* on civil rights, wondered whether anyone wished him to be, instead, immoderate.

The use of emotional vocabularies is not invariably a dubious practice. In the first place, words do not always get loaded by sinister design or even deliberately. In the second, that sort of language is not exploited only for mischievous ends. The American verities feature words—*liberty, equality*—that, on top of their formal definitions, are verily packed with the sentiments that cement U.S. society. The affectionate banalities of friendship and neighborliness similarly facilitate the human ties that bind and support. The moving vocabularies of patriotism and friendship are also subject to misuse, of course, but such derelictions are usually easy to recognize as demagoguery or hypocrisy.   8

The abuse and careless use of language have been going on for a long time; witness the stern biblical warnings such as the one in *Matthew 12: 36:* "Every idle word that men shall speak, they shall give account thereof in the day of judgment." Yet the risks of biased words to the unwary must be greater today, in an epoch of propagandizing amplified by mass communications. "Never," Aldous Huxley said, "have misused words—those hideously efficient tools of all the tyrants, warmongers, persecutors and heresy hunters—been so widely and disastrously influential." In the two decades since that warning, the practice of bamboozlement has, if anything, increased. The appropriate response is not a hopeless effort to cleanse the world of seductive words. Simple awareness of how frequently and variously they are loaded reduces the chances that one will fall out of touch with so-called reality.   9

Proverbs or Aphorisms?

STEFAN KANFER

There are two classes of people in the world, observed Robert   1
Benchley, "those who constantly divide the people of the world into
two classes, and those who do not."

Half of those who divide quote Benchley and his fellow aphorists.   2
The other half prefer proverbs. And why not? The aphorism is a
personal observation inflated into a universal truth, a private posing as
a general. A proverb is anonymous human history compressed to the
size of a seed. "Whom the gods love die young" implies a greater
tragedy than anything from Euripides: old people weeping at the grave
site of their children. "Love is blind" echoes of gossip in the marketplace, giggling students and clucking counselors: an Elizabethan comedy flowering from three words.

"A proverb," said Cervantes, "is a short sentence based on long   3
experience," and to prove it he had Sancho and his *paisanos* fling those
sentences around like pesetas: "There's no sauce in the world like
hunger"; "Never look for birds of this year in the nests of the last";
"Patience, and shuffle the cards." His English contemporary was of two
minds about folklore, as he was about everything. Hamlet disdains it:
"The proverb is something musty." Yet the plays overflow with musty
somethings: "Men are April when they woo; December when they
wed"; "A little pot and soon hot"; "The fashion wears out more apparel
than the man"; and, more to the point, "Patch grief with proverbs."

Like Sancho and Shakespeare, those who praise proverbs favor   4
nature over artifice and peasantry over peerage. Benjamin Franklin
always preferred "a drop of reason to a flood of words" and filled *Poor
Richard's Almanac* with colonial one-liners: "Three may keep a secret, if
two of them are dead"; "The used key is always bright." Emerson
thought proverbs "the sanctuary of the intuitions." Tolstoy's knowledge of common tradition led him to an encyclopedia of wisdom.
Eastern European sayings have always assumed the clarity and force
of vodka: "Where the needle goes, the thread follows"; "The devil pours
honey into other men's wives"; "The Russian has three strong principles: *perhaps, somehow* and *never mind.*" In the epoch of the Romanoffs,
wisdom was the only thing that was shared equally. Cossacks who

conducted pogroms and victims in the shtetls flavored their remarks with the same sour salt. Russian: "The rich would have to eat money, but luckily the poor provide food." Yiddish: "If the rich could hire others to die for them, the poor could make a nice living."

No culture is without proverbs, but many are poor in aphorisms, a fact that leads Critic Hugh Kenner to hail the ancient phrases as something "worth saying again and again, descending father to son, mother to daughter, mouth to mouth." Gazing at *The Concise Oxford Dictionary of Proverbs*, he lauds the short and simple annals of the poor. But he holds *The Oxford Book of Aphorisms* at the proverbial arm's length: "What the aphorisms lack is the proverb's ability to generalize. They have the air of brittle special cases: How special indeed my life is! How exceptional!"

But that very air is the oxygen of the epigram. W.H. Auden, who collected and concocted them, readily admitted that "aphorisms are essentially an aristocratic genre. Implicit is a conviction that [the writer] is wiser than his readers." François de La Rochefoucauld was a duke; elbowed out of prominence in Louis XIV's court, he retreated to an estate to polish his words until nobility could see its face in the surface: "We all have strength enough to endure the misfortunes of others"; "In jealousy there is more self-love than love"; "Hypocrisy is the homage that vice pays to virtue"; "Lovers never get tired of each other, because they are always talking about themselves."

George Savile, first Marquis of Halifax, was alternately in and out of favor with the house of Stuart; his observations were worn smooth by disappointment: "Ambition is either on all fours or on tiptoes"; "The enquiry into a dream is another dream"; "Love is presently out of breath when it is to go uphill, from the children to the parents." By the time aphorisms became the property of the people, commoners had learned to speak like counts. The humbly born Sebastian Chamfort decided that "whoever is not a misanthrope at 40 can never have loved mankind." Nietzsche's phrases bore a strychnine smile: "The thought of suicide is a great consolation; with the help of it one has got through many a bad night"; "Wit closes the coffin on an emotion."

By the mid-19th century, the aphorism had become a favorite of the English. Oscar Wilde exposed the flip side of bromides: "Punctuality is the thief of time"—, "Old enough to know worse." But he could be as pontifical as the next prince: "A thing is not necessarily true because a man dies for it"; "One's real life is often the life that one does not lead." George Bernard Shaw saw the aphorism as the new home for political slogans: "All great truths begin as blasphemies." His contemporary G.K. Chesterton was the last master of the paradox: "Silence is the unbearable repartee"; "A figure of speech can often get into a crack too small for a definition"; "Tradition is the democracy of the dead."

That democracy remains in office; the custom of the sharpened 9
axiom continues. Elizabeth Bowen's "Memory is the editor of one's
sense of life" is a Shakespearean perception; Peter De Vries' "Gluttony
is an emotional escape, a sign that something is eating us" belongs with
the best of the Edwardians. Hannah Arendt's observation compresses
the century down to a sentence: "Power and violence are opposites;
where one rules absolutely, the other is absent."

Yet the aphorists do not enjoy the last frown. Even now, proverb 10
makers are at work. Traditions have to begin somewhere; today folk
sayings arise from economics: "There is no such thing as a free lunch";
from the comics: "Keep on truckin' "; and even from computers: "Garbage in, garbage out."

Which, then, has more application to modern life, the people's 11
phrases or the aristocrats'? Not aphorisms, says the proverb: "Fine
words butter no parsnips." Not proverbs, insists Alfred North
Whitehead's terse dictum: "Seek simplicity and distrust it." Still, both
categories are noted not only for their concision but their consolation.
Collectors of aphorisms may yet find support from the biblical proverb
"Knowledge increaseth strength." As for the partisans of folk sayings,
they can for once side with the fastidious William Wordsworth:

Wisdom is ofttimes nearer when we stoop
Than when we soar.

Of Words That Ravage, Pillage, Spoil

OTTO FRIEDRICH

When the Federal Government launched a program last fall to   1
gas chickens—more than 7 million so far—in an effort to contain an
influenza virus in Pennsylvania, it said it had "depopulated" the birds.
"We use that terrible word depopulation to avoid saying slaughter,"
explained a federal information officer, David Goodman.

Actually, it is not a terrible word but a rather distinguished one,   2
derived from the Latin *depopulare* and meaning, according to the *Oxford
English Dictionary*, "to lay waste, ravage, pillage, spoil." Shakespeare
used it in *Coriolanus* when he had the tribune Sicinius ask, "Where is
this viper/That would depopulate the city?" John Milton's *History of
England* referred to military forces "depopulating all places in their
way," and Shelley wrote in *Lines Written Among the Euganean Hills* of
"thine isles depopulate."

As with many words, though, the original meaning has faded, and   3
Webster's now defines depopulate only as "to reduce greatly the population of." Even that is probably too clear and specific. When Goodman
uses the word not as something done to an area but as something done
to the victims, then its only function is to be long and Latinate and
abstract. That makes it suitable as a euphemism for a blunter word, like
kill.

All governments deal in euphemisms, of course, since the purpose   4
of a euphemism is to make anything unpleasant seem less unpleasant.
And since killing is the most unpleasant of government functions, the
result is linguistic legerdemain. Killing reached its apotheosis in Nazi
Germany, and so did the language used to avoid saying so. Prisoners
sent to concentration camps in the east carried identity papers marked
"Rückkehr unerwünscht," meaning "return unwanted," meaning death.
Whole carloads of such prisoners were assigned to *"Sonderbehandlung,"*
meaning "special treatment," also meaning death. The totality of per-
secutions and killings was called *"die Endlösung,"* meaning "the final
solution," that too meaning death.

Though the Nazis have never been outdone in applying seem-   5
ingly harmless labels to the most hideous practices, most governments
sooner or later find euphemism an indispensable device. "Pacification"

464

has become a popular term for war ("War is peace," as the Ministry of Truth says in *Nineteen Eighty-Four*), but the Romans meant much the same thing by the term Pax Romana. "Where they make a desert, they call it peace," protested an English nobleman quoted in Tacitus. Viet Nam brought us new words for the old realities: soldiers "wasted" the enemy, some "fragged" their own officers, bombers provided "close air support." Even the CIA contributed a verbal novelty: "termination with extreme prejudice."

By changing the language that describes their actions, govern-   6
ments implicitly deny those actions. They invoke a kind of magic to guard their own authority. Language has always been a partly magical process, and the power to give names to things has always seemed a magical power. The *Book of Genesis* reports that when God created the lesser animals, every beast of the field and every fowl of the air, he "brought them unto Adam to see what he would call them." In China too, Confucius taught that the root of good government lies in the principle of *cheng ming*, or precise definition.

Ah, but what is precise definition? One nation's freedom fighter   7
is another nation's terrorist. Ronald Reagan is by no means the first President to put bright words on dark realities; Jimmy Carter, for example, called his aborted helicopter raid on Iran "an incomplete success." But Reagan seems to bring an exceptional dedication to the process. The term MX does not mean very much (the letters stand for "missile experimental"), but everybody knew the weapon under that name until Reagan began calling it the "peace keeper." After the Grenada invasion, which Reagan himself had first called an "invasion," he bristled at reporters for "your frequent use of the word invasion. This was a rescue mission." For such a small place, in fact, Grenada proved a richly fertile territory for linguistic flowering. The laurels go to Admiral Wesley L. McDonald, who, in trying to avoid admitting that the Navy had not known exactly what was happening on the island just before the U.S. landing, took a deep breath and declared, "We were not micromanaging Grenada intelligencewise until about that time frame."

Occasionally, of course, the military gets so carried away in its   8
passion to rename things that it cannot persuade anyone to use its most imaginative terms. Resisting any mention of retreat, it devised the word "exfiltration," but even its own spokesmen find that hard to say. A "combat emplacement evacuator" is a splendidly resonant euphemism for a shovel, but somehow it has never caught on. It was only public ridicule, however, that persuaded the Pentagon to abandon the term "sunshine units" as a measure of nuclear radiation.

Government does not involve only military affairs, to be sure.   9
Every aspect of economic policy attracts similar expressions of right thinking. When Reagan was convinced that taxes had to be increased,

after he had promised to cut them, he began referring not to taxes but to "revenue enhancements," a term apparently invented by Lawrence Kudlow, formerly of the Office of Management and Budget. The tendency seems to be spreading. A spokesman for Budget Director David Stockman won special recognition for declaring that the Administration was not considering a means test for Medicare but a "layering of benefits according to your income." The poor, in fact, are regularly euphemized into invisibility by being given new names such as "disadvantaged." One of the oddities of euphemisms, though, is that they tend to reacquire the unpleasant connotations of the words they supplant, like a facelift that begins to sag, and so they have to be periodically replaced. The world's poor nations have changed over the years from underdeveloped nations to developing nations to emerging nations.

Does the spread of such phrases—if they are indeed spreading— 10 mean that the Government is becoming increasingly deceptive, or that it has more to hide? That would be uncharitable, perhaps unfair. Consider it instead a perfectly understandable desire to think well of oneself and of one's work. Isn't everyone counseled to think positively, to look on the bright side, to observe the doughnut rather than the hole, to see that a half-empty glass is really half full? In a time of uncertainty, it is possible to give the Government the benefit of the doubt, just as any citizen customarily gives the same benefit to himself. After all, as the saying goes, nothing is certain except death and taxes. Or rather depopulation and revenue enhancement.

Poetry and Politics

ROGER ROSENBLATT

Land of the unwashed, goodbye!
Land of the masters, land of knaves!
You, in neat blue uniforms!
You who live like cringing slaves!
In my exile I may find
Peace beneath Caucasian skies,—
Far from slanderers and tsars,
Far from ever-spying eyes.

—Mikhail Lermontov

It seemed odd, on first hearing of it, that Nicholas Daniloff would   1
quote lines of poetry to mark his release from Soviet imprisonment.
Here was an incident that filled the news for a month, that brought the
world's two titans into open confrontation, that in the end, perhaps,
prodded them to agree on the presummit summit. Yet to cap off those
momentous political events, Daniloff, the center of the storm, reached
back into art for a poem by Mikhail Lermontov written almost 150 years
ago for another world and circumstance. Grant that it was more diplomatic of Daniloff to quote Lermontov's exasperation with Mother Russia than to express his own. Still, it is curious that one would articulate
feelings about so immediate and politically charged an event by using
a form associated with indirection and repose.

Not that poets themselves have ever avoided politics as subject   2
matter. Homer, Dante, Shakespeare, Milton, all found ways to hail or
rage against kings and governments through their work. Yeats, unpo-
litical as anyone could look in his fluffy neckties, wrote stinging political lines. As did Robert Lowell. As does Seamus Heaney. W.H. Auden's
September 1, 1939 is a beautiful muddle of a poem on Europe in the
shadow of war. Bertolt Brecht's *To Posterity*, about Germany under the
Nazis, is clear as a bell:

Ah, what an age it is
When to speak of trees is almost a crime
For it is a kind of silence against injustice.

For their part, political leaders have courted poets, supported   3
poets, quoted poets. Some have even been poets. Henry VIII, who liked
to write verse when he wasn't making life brutish or short for his wives.
Chairman Mao, who, when visited by the muse, commanded the largest
audience for poetry in history. Poet Léopold Senghor, former President
of Senegal. Poet José Sarney, current President of Brazil. If political
leaders happen not to be poets, they can always seek one's company, so
that he may write them into immortality or simply decorate a hard,
unlyrical business. John Kennedy had genuine affection for the work of
Robert Frost, but the poet's presence at Kennedy's Inaugural—the
poem flapping in the wintry wind—also served to give a magic power
to the occasion, like the blessing of the gods.

What clashes in the connection of poetry and politics is that on the   4
surface, the two forms of expression seem antipodal not only in tone
and structure but in the pictures of mind they convey. The poet is a
vague and hazy animal, the politician hunched forward like a cat. What
one would devour, the other would toy with in the air, angling the
world in his paws so as to know not the world itself but the light-play
on the world.

And yet, as the Daniloff incident suggests, these two sets of mind   5
have a way of coming together in the strangest places, which would
indicate that poetry and politics have basic things in common. One is
the need to create a sense of urgency. Poets and politicians are alike in
the frantic force of their opinions. When either speaks his mind, he is
like the Ancient Mariner; he seizes the public by the collar as if to say:
Accept my perspective and be converted.

Then, too, there are similar passions in poetry and politics. How-   6
ever dignified poetry or politics may appear, there is something sub-
limely irrational at their centers. Both appeal to the irrational as well,
to the zealot in you stirring in the ice of your calm and stately nature.
Zealots themselves, they seem to need to win something, to force a
climax almost sexual.

At the same time, both also depend on the continuity of living, on   7
the fact that no matter how heated the single moment, the realization
of that moment is of necessity incomplete. The art of politics seems to
dance between acting as if every issue were the end of the earth and
simultaneously acknowledging that tomorrow will hold up a dozen
fresh crucial issues. Poems imply this same incompleteness. Unlike
prose, the place that a poem aims and arrives at is less important to the
success of the poem than the ideas and images it uses to make the

journey. By those ideas and images the poet holds the reader to the process, by which he suggests that the poem pauses more than finishes and that the end is somewhere in the middle.

Poems also create their own state of mind, and politics does that 8 as well. Paul Valéry defined a poem as a "kind of machine for producing the poetic state of mind by means of words." The politician produces the political state of mind by means of words. Each does an act of hypnosis by persuading its audience that reality is the world that the poet or politician has constructed for them. In that, the two are equally imaginative. The world they create is an unreality. Yet that world must be grounded in reality, in facts—the real toads in imaginary gardens that Marianne Moore prescribed for poetry—or else the audience will not believe it.

Still, if poetry and politics are bedfellows in certain ways, the bed 9 is rarely comfortable. Poetry has none of the active power that politics has. It can protest or commemorate a war but cannot cause one. Assessing the poet's responsibility in the world, Allen Tate derided the romantic notion that if poets "behaved differently . . . the international political order itself would not have been in jeopardy and we should not perhaps be at international loggerheads today." Poets do not have that sort of influence, and undoubtedly would abuse it if they did.

The power poetry does have, however, is staying power. It out- 10 lives politics mainly because the language of poets outlives the language of politicians—so effectively that Daniloff could recite Lermontov to the world last week, and the world could appear to have been waiting for those words. That eternity of language, reaching as far back as forward, is what politicians fear most about poetry, when they do fear it, and it can make a terrible enemy. Politics touches some people at particular times. Poetry calls to all people at all times. By its existence it demands generosity and expansiveness. "When power narrows the areas of man's concern," said Kennedy, "poetry reminds him of the richness and diversity of his existence. When power corrupts, poetry cleanses." Last week Lermontov, dead 145 years, mocked all the prisons and praised all the skies.

In Praise of the Humble Comma

PICO IYER

The gods, they say, give breath, and they take it away. But the same could be said—could it not?—of the humble comma. Add it to the present clause, and, of a sudden, the mind is, quite literally, given pause to think; take it out if you wish or forget it and the mind is deprived of a resting place. Yet still the comma gets no respect. It seems just a slip of a thing, a pedant's tick, a blip on the edge of our consciousness, a kind of printer's smudge almost. Small, we claim, is beautiful (especially in the age of the microchip). Yet what is so often used, and so rarely recalled, as the comma—unless it be breath itself? 1

Punctuation, one is taught, has a point: to keep up law and order. Punctuation marks are the road signs placed along the highway of our communication—to control speeds, provide directions and prevent head-on collisions. A period has the unblinking finality of a red light; the comma is a flashing yellow light that asks us only to slow down; and the semicolon is a stop sign that tells us to ease gradually to a halt, before gradually starting up again. By establishing the relations between words, punctuation establishes the relations between the people using words. That may be one reason why schoolteachers exalt it and lovers defy it ("We love each other and belong to each other let's don't ever hurt each other Nicole let's don't ever hurt each other," wrote Gary Gilmore to his girlfriend). A comma, he must have known, "separates inseparables," in the clinching words of H.W. Fowler, King of English Usage. 2

Punctuation, then, is a civic prop, a pillar that holds society upright. (A run-on sentence, its phrases piling up without division, is as unsightly as a sink piled high with dirty dishes.) Small wonder, then, that punctuation was one of the first proprieties of the Victorian age, the age of the corset, that the modernists threw off: the sexual revolution might be said to have begun when Joyce's Molly Bloom spilled out all her private thoughts in 36 pages of unbridled, almost unperioded and officially censored prose; and another rebellion was surely marked when E.E. Cummings first felt free to commit "God" to the lower case. 3

Punctuation thus becomes the signature of cultures. The hot-blooded Spaniard seems to be revealed in the passion and urgency of 4 his doubled exclamation points and question marks ("*¡Caramba! ¿Quien sabe?*"), while the impassive Chinese traditionally added to his so-called inscrutability by omitting directions from his ideograms. The anarchy and commotion of the '60s were given voice in the exploding exclamation marks, riotous capital letters and Day-Glo italics of Tom Wolfe's spray-paint prose; and in Communist societies, where the State is absolute, the dignity—and divinity—of capital letters is reserved for Ministries, Sub-Committees and Secretariats.

Yet punctuation is something more than a culture's birthmark; it   5
scores the music in our minds, gets our thoughts moving to the rhythm of our hearts. Punctuation is the notation in the sheet music of our words, telling us when to rest, or when to raise our voices; it acknowledges that the meaning of our discourse, as of any symphonic composition, lies not in the units but in the pauses, the pacing and the phrasing. Punctuation is the way one bats one's eyes, lowers one's voice or blushes demurely. Punctuation adjusts the tone and color and volume till the feeling comes into perfect focus: not disgust exactly, but distaste; not lust, or like, but love.

Punctuation, in short, gives us the human voice, and all the   6
meanings that lie between the words. "You aren't young, are you?" loses its innocence when it loses the question mark. Every child knows the menace of a dropped apostrophe (the parent's "Don't do that" shifting into the more slowly enunciated "Do not do that"), and every believer, the ignominy of having his faith reduced to "faith." Add an exclamation point to "To be or not to be . . ." and the gloomy Dane has all the resolve he needs; add a comma, and the noble sobriety of "God save the Queen" becomes a cry of desperation bordering on double sacrilege.

Sometimes, of course, our markings may be simply a matter of   7
aesthetics. Popping in a comma can be like slipping on the necklace that gives an outfit quiet elegance, or like catching the sound of running water that complements, as it completes, the silence of a Japanese landscape. When V.S. Naipaul, in his latest novel, writes, "He was a middle-aged man, with glasses," the first comma can seem a little precious. Yet it gives the description a spin, as well as a subtlety, that it otherwise lacks, and it shows that the glasses are not part of the middle-agedness, but something else.

Thus all these tiny scratches give us breadth and heft and depth.   8
A world that has only periods is a world without inflections. It is a world without shade. It has a music without sharps and flats. It is a martial music. It has a jackboot rhythm. Words cannot bend and curve. A comma, by comparison, catches the gentle drift of the mind in thought, turning in on itself and back on itself, reversing, redoubling and returning along the course of its own sweet river music; while the semicolon

brings clauses and thoughts together with all the silent discretion of a hostess arranging guests around her dinner table.

Punctuation, then, is a matter of care. Care for words, yes, but also, and more important, for what the words imply. Only a lover notices the small things: the way the afternoon light catches the nape of a neck, or how a strand of hair slips out from behind an ear, or the way a finger curls around a cup. And no one scans a letter so closely as a lover, searching for its small print, straining to hear its nuances, its gasps, its sighs and hesitations, poring over the secret messages that lie in every cadence. The difference between "Jane (whom I adore)" and "Jane, whom I adore," and the difference between them both and "Jane— whom I adore—" marks all the distance between ecstasy and heartache. "No iron can pierce the heart with such force as a period put at just the right place," in Isaac Babel's lovely words; a comma can let us hear a voice break, or a heart. Punctuation, in fact, is a labor of love. Which brings us back, in a way, to gods.

Metaphors of the World, Unite!

LANCE MORROW

Forty-eight intellectuals from around the world recently assem- 1
bled to help celebrate the sesquicentennial of Boston University by
trying to find a metaphor for the age in which we live. It was an elegant
game, but also inadvertently right for an age of television and drugs, in
which the world is reduced to a sound bite or a capsule, a quick fix of
meaning.

"Postmodern Age" has always been an empty description, and 2
"Postindustrial Age" was a phrase about as interesting as a suburban
tract. They are not metaphors anyway, but little black flags of aftermath.
An age that is "post"-anything is, by definition, confused and dangerously overextended, like Wile E. Coyote after he has left the cartoon
plane of solid rock and freezes in thin air, then tries to tiptoe back along
a line of space before gravity notices and takes him down to a little *poof!*
in the canyon far below.

The metaphysics of the possibilities can flare and darken. The 3
Holocaust and other catastrophes of the 20th century invite the term
post-apocalyptic. But a world veering toward the 21st century sometimes has an edgy intuition that it is "preapocalyptic." Last summer
Francis Fukuyama, a State Department planner, resolved the matter
peacefully. He published an article proclaiming the "end of history," a
result of the worldwide triumph of Western liberal democracy. Hence
this is the posthistoric age, a fourth dimension in which the human
pageant terminates in a fuzz of meaningless well-being. Intellectuals
sometimes nurture a spectacular narcissism about the significance of
the age they grace.

Is there one brilliant, compact image that captures the era of 4
Gorbachev and the greenhouse effect, of global communications and
AIDS, of mass famine and corporate imperialisms, of space exploration
and the world's seas awash in plastic? The Age of Leisure and the Age
of the Refugee coexist with the Age of Clones and the Age of the Deal.
Time is fractured in the contemporaneous. We inhabit not one age but
many ages simultaneously, from the Bronze to the Space. Did the
Ayatullah Khomeini live in the same millennium as, say, Los Angeles?

The era's label should be at least binary, like Dickens' "the best of   5
times, the worst of times," again no metaphor. It is a fallacy to think
there is one theme. Like all ages, it is a time of angels and moping
dogs—after Ralph Waldo Emerson's lines: "It seems as if heaven had
sent its insane angels into our world as to an asylum, and here they will
break out in their native music and utter at intervals the words they
have heard in heaven; then the mad fit returns and they mope and
wallow like dogs."

In Boston, Historian Hugh Thomas (Lord Thomas of Swynnerton)   6
said the world now is a "tessellated pavement without cement." He was
quoting something Edmund Burke said about Charles Townshend, a
brilliant but erratic 18th century British statesman. Not bad, but somewhat mandarin. The audience had to remember, or look up, tessellation,
which is a mosaic of small pieces of marble, glass or tile. This age, thinks
Lord Thomas, is a mosaic of fragments, with nothing to hold them
together. Is it an age of brilliant incoherence? Yes. It is also an age of
incoherent stupidity.

One might put the mosaic in motion by thinking of this as the age   7
of the hand-held TV channel changer. The electronic worldmind (and
such a thing is coming into being, a global mass conformed by what
passes through its billion eyes into the collective brain) has a short
attention span and dreams brief dreams. When history vaporizes itself
this way—its events streaming off instantly into electrons fired into
space and then recombining mysteriously in human living rooms and
minds around the world—then people face a surreal pluralism of
realities. The small world that the astronauts showed us from space is
also, down here, a psychotically tessellated overload of images. The
planet reaches for the channel changer, a restless mind-altering instrument. Like drugs, it turns human consciousness into a landscape that
is passive, agitated and insatiable—a fatal configuration.

Historians can speak of the Enlightenment or the Baroque Era or   8
La Belle Epoque and not fear that they are describing developments in
only a fraction of the world. Now the metaphor must be global. There
is no figure of speech so powerful or acrobatic that it can cover such a
drama, the world that looks like the product of a shattered mind,
without some immense event (an invasion by aliens perhaps) that
overrides all else. Michael Harrington once called this the Accidental
Century. Intellectuals sometimes ignore the role of inadvertence. "The
fecundity of the unexpected," Proudhon said, "far exceeds the
statesman's prudence." If scientists ever perform the alchemy of cold
fusion, the age will have a name, and the future of the world will be
immeasurably altered.

Metaphors for the age tend to be emotional and subjective, as   9
poetry is. Perspective, passion and experience choose the words. Betty

Friedan, saturated with the history of feminism's Long March and where it began, speaks of amazing freedom, as if that were the song of the past 20 years. Others are haunted by the obliteration of artistic form, of moral values and all traditional stabilities. Some know that by now humankind has exhausted its capacity to surprise itself in the doing of evil.

Language takes its life from life, and gives it back to life as myth, as metaphor, something that has a counterlife of its own. In a world of blindingly accelerating change, language can no longer fashion its metaphors fast enough to stabilize people with a spiritual counterlife, and so self-knowledge may deteriorate to a moral blur, like the snow of electrons on a television screen. In some sense the world is plunging on without benefit of metaphor, a dangerous loss. The eyes do not have time to adjust to either the light or the dark.

Rhetorical Contents

PROCESS ANALYSIS

CAUSE AND EFFECT

Chronological Contents